ACCOMMODATING CULTURAL DIVERSITY

Accommodating Cultural Diversity

Edited by
STEPHEN TIERNEY
University of Edinburgh, UK

ASHGATE

© Stephen Tierney 2007

All rights reserved. No part of this publication may be reproduced, stored in a retrieval system or transmitted in any form or by any means, electronic, mechanical, photocopying, recording or otherwise without the prior permission of the publisher.

Stephen Tierney has asserted his right under the Copyright, Designs and Patents Act, 1988, to be identified as the editor of this work.

Published by
Ashgate Publishing Limited
Gower House
Croft Road
Aldershot
Hampshire GU11 3HR
England

Ashgate Publishing Company
Suite 420
101 Cherry Street
Burlington, VT 05401-4405
USA

Ashgate website: http://www.ashgate.com

British Library Cataloguing in Publication Data
Accommodating cultural diversity. - (Applied legal
   philosophy)
   1. Multiculturalism
   I. Tierney, Stephen
   305.8

Library of Congress Control Number: 2006940516

ISBN 13: 978-0-7546-2603-9

Printed and bound in Great Britain by MPG Books Ltd, Bodmin, Cornwall.

Contents

Foreword by The Honourable Justice Michel Bastarache		*vii*
List of Contributors		*ix*
1	Cultural Diversity: Normative Theory and Constitutional Practice *Stephen Tierney*	1

PART I   THE EVOLVING THEORY OF CULTURAL DIVERSITY

2	The Global Diffusion of Multiculturalism: Trends, Causes, Consequences *Will Kymlicka*	17
3	Towards a Hybrid Theory of Multinational Justice *Helder De Schutter*	35
4	Putting Kymlicka in Perspective: Canadian Diversity and Collective Rights *Dwight Newman*	59

PART II   INSTITUTIONAL ACCOMMODATION IN THEORY AND PRACTICE: THE CASE OF ABORIGINAL PEOPLES

5	Reasoning about the Identity of Aboriginal People *Avigail Eisenberg*	79
6	Self-Government in Canada: A Successful Model for the Decolonisation of Aboriginal Child Welfare? *Sonia Harris-Short*	99
7	Cultural Pluralism and the Return of Cultural Heritage *Kathryn Last*	123

PART III   DIVERSITY AND CONSTITUTIONAL INTERPRETATION

8	The Reasonable Person and the Discrimination Inquiry *Mayo Moran*	147

9	Quebec and the Amending Formula: Protection, Promotion and Federalism	
	Peter C. Oliver	167
10	Understanding the Rule of Law in Canada	
	Warren Newman	199
Index		*239*

Foreword

The Honourable Justice Michel Bastarache

The symposium organized by Stephen Tierney brought together a number of scholars from different countries and different disciplines to create a rich exchange of ideas on the theme of cultural diversity. This book is the result of that symposium.

For those who are mainly concerned with human rights from a legal perspective, this was a unique opportunity to learn more about the philosophical and sociological contexts that inform legal analysis. It was particularly interesting to see why there are so many conceptions of multiculturalism, for instance, and to discover why there has been an evolution in the way it is perceived as part of government policy. It was also a great forum to debate initiatives such as the *European Charter for Regional or Minority Languages* of 1992. One question that was examined is what aspect of identity gives rise to a fundamental right and whether the evolution of this concept, and its legitimacy, is now more in the hands of the judges or the legislators.

For those who are mainly conducting research in the humanities, this was also a unique experience because of the opportunity to question the role of judges in the age of human rights and their enlarged influence in defining social values and sometimes social institutions. Indeed, the role of the judge as mediator of national diversity is still a contentious one. It is even more contentious for those who question the fact that the law has become a product for exportation. While there is no legal authority to conceive a law for all nations, judges have played a central role in developing legal rules and finding applications throughout the world, particularly in the area of human rights. It has even been suggested that this trend is accelerated by a form of international judicial sociability.

The symposium also provided participants with an opportunity to look at the question of accommodation of cultural diversity in practice, by examining the case of aboriginal peoples. The very complex issues involving decolonization, recognition of cultural heritage and self-government were addressed. There is a very rich literature on these questions, but there is no doubt that things are evolving rapidly and that there is a need to bring together the resources of those working in different fields. We discovered we have a lot to learn about developing cooperation to this end.

This rich program could not have been realized without the leadership of a person of vision. We are indebted to Professor Tierney for this remarkable contribution to the study of cultural diversity.

The Honourable Justice Michel Bastarache
Ottawa, 2006

List of Contributors

Avigail Eisenberg, Faculty of Political Science, University of Victoria, British Columbia

Sonia Harris-Short, Department of Law, University of Birmingham

Will Kymlicka, Department of Philosophy, Queen's University, Kingston, Canada

Kathryn Last, School of Law, University of Aberdeen

Mayo Moran, Law School, University of Toronto

Dwight Newman, College of Law, University of Saskatchewan

Warren Newman, Department of Justice of Canada

Peter C. Oliver, School of Law, King's College, London

Helder De Schutter, Centre for Ethics, Social and Political Philosophy, University of Leuven

Stephen Tierney, School of Law, University of Edinburgh

Chapter 1

Cultural Diversity: Normative Theory and Constitutional Practice

Stephen Tierney

The management of cultural diversity within the state has become an increasingly prominent issue in recent times both for political actors and for scholars of law, philosophy, sociology and political science. There are certainly many reasons why multiculturalism has been the subject of such attention but of these perhaps the two most important are demographics and political mobilisation. On the one hand cultural diversity is an expanding social phenomenon in an age of migration, asylum, population transfer and the increasing diversification of identity patterns within traditionally homogeneous groups. These evolving demographic patterns have also been accompanied by a growing political assertiveness as cultural minorities, be these territorial sub-state nations, aboriginal groups, or migrant groups, demand in ever more vociferous terms political recognition and the constitutional accommodation of their cultural or societal particularity.

Although work on the issue of cultural diversity has also expanded enormously in recent years, it has tended to be separated fairly rigidly, as is so much work in the social sciences, among the disciplines of law, political science and political philosophy. This book intends to offer a different perspective by bringing together work from these different disciplines. Emerging as it does from a conference organised by the Centre for Canadian Studies and the School of Law at the University of Edinburgh in 2004, the book comprises ten essays including contributions from scholars of cultural diversity from a range of backgrounds which together offer a variety of perspectives, both describing how contemporary democracies manage diversity and offering normative prescriptions for how they might better do so. A very welcome participant at the conference was The Honourable Justice Michel Bastarache of the Supreme Court of Canada, himself a strong advocate of the accommodation of cultural diversity and language rights, and he has very generously contributed the Foreword to the book.

The book is divided into three thematic parts. Part I addresses the evolving theory of cultural diversity with three chapters concerning the development of normative theory in this area. Part II comprises a case study in the institutional accommodation of cultural diversity, focusing upon aboriginal peoples whose demands for full recognition have become a prominent and complex issue in a number of modern democracies. Finally, Part III of the book turns to what is very much a developing issue, namely the role of constitutional law and constitutional interpretation as a battleground for the playing out of cultural disputes concerning the political and constitutional status of sub-state cultural and national groups. In this part of the book one area of focus is the long-running dispute between Quebec and the rest of Canada concerning Quebec's claims to constitutional recognition of its sub-state national status within Canada. Given that the conference was concerned with Canadian issues this case study and a number of other references in the book are related to the Canadian experience as one of the most interesting arenas where multicultural and multinational issues are played out today. However, the book's reach is broader than this, raising theoretical issues of general application and drawing out lessons that have wide implications for other multicultural democracies.

Part I begins with a scene-setting chapter by Will Kymlicka who discusses the development of multiculturalism as a global phenomenon, offering suggestions as to why these debates have emerged now and what the prospects are for their future evolution. His account addresses the ways in which sub-state cultural groups have mobilised politically throughout the world, identifying both the differences that pertain from case to case as well as the commonalities shared by these diverse struggles for multiculturalism. The principal point of commonality in these struggles is a rejection of the traditional model of the unitary, homogeneous nation-state which has privileged the dominant national group through overt nation-building strategies and in consequence of which minority groups have either been assimilated or excluded from a full role in the life of the state. This model, however, is increasingly under challenge from different types of minority group, each of which brings diverse forms of claim: indigenous peoples; sub-state/minority nations; immigrant groups; and metics (by which Kymlicka means migrants who are not admitted as permanent residents, and future citizens, including illegal immigrants, asylum-seekers, students or 'guest-workers' who overstay their initial visa). Although these four groups have faced different problems historically and each seek to have their distinctive identities accommodated in different ways, Kymlicka argues that common to all of these struggles is the demand for a multicultural state which will recognise that the polity is not in fact composed of a single national group but that all groups should be recognised equally, which will respect the equal worth of their cultural traditions, and which will attempt to rectify past injustices resulting from assimilationist or exclusionist policies.

Kymlicka argues that, particularly in western democracies, considerable progress has been made in meeting the demands of each of these groups. Although this has had mixed results in the case of metics, success is particularly notable in the case of the first two types of group because there has been a dramatic move towards reconceptualising states which contain indigenous peoples or territorial national minorities as 'multinational' in character, with concomitant redistributions of political and economic power within the state. Kymlicka then considers why both the political mobilisation of minorities and the accommodation of their demands have occurred over the past three decades. Although specific political initiatives have been influential, Kymlicka also identifies certain structural factors that are common to all of those Western democracies that have engaged in the accommodation of diversity. Underlying dynamics which help explain why minority groups have become more assertive of their rights include demographic developments whereby these groups have not died out; an increase in rights-consciousness across the globe; and the spread of democracy. Additionally, two further factors help explain the willingness of states to accommodate multiculturalism: first, the improvement in global security, particularly since the end of the Cold War, which helped reduce strategic risks that were, in the post-war period, perceived to be involved in granting autonomy to national minorities; and secondly, the increased awareness that dominant and non-dominant groups share a liberal democratic consensus which in turn reduces the perception of risk within the dominant group that the recognition of cultural difference will lead to, and will indeed institutionally crystallise, a break-down in common political values across the state. With an eye to the prospects for the spread of multiculturalism to other parts of the world, Kymlicka suggests that the three principal factors which led to demands for change in the West are already in place elsewhere today; therefore, whether or not the accommodation of cultural diversity is to become a genuinely global phenomenon depends now very much upon whether the states which are newly involved in this process will respond positively to these demands.

Another lesson drawn out by Kymlicka from the Western experience of multiculturalism is that many of the worst fears about political instability and the breakdown of political authority are misplaced; as he argues, 'it's now clear that a multicultural state can be a successful state'. However, there is still a danger of backlash, largely he suggests due to misperceptions about the goals and consequences of multiculturalism. Many within the dominant elites had hoped multiculturalism was a passing problem, which once accommodated would cease to make demands of the state. But in fact, multicultural politics are clearly here to stay, and in fact will likely proliferate because patterns of accommodation actually encourage further demands by offering an institutional base from which these political movements can mobilise further. Challenges therefore remain because although people in Western democracies have generally accepted the idea of a multicultural state and the initial accommodation of difference, in other ways they resist the ongoing phenomenon of ethnic politics. Kymlicka concludes that the long-term success of multiculturalism will depend upon a change in this mind-set and an acceptance by dominant groups that ethnic politics are 'normal' democratic politics which are now a settled feature of political life.

It is appropriate that Will Kymlicka should contribute the opening chapter of the book given that his work more than that of any other philosopher in recent times has set the framework for normative debates about the political and constitutional accommodation of multiculturalism. A central thesis of Kymlicka's has been that multiculturalism and liberalism are not only compatible with, but are inextricably linked, to a true commitment to liberalism. Liberalism in fact requires the proper respect for and recognition of the cultural particularities that are so central to many people's lives. As is inevitable with any extensive and pioneering theory, Kymlicka's work has been subjected to critique from different directions. In this context the other two chapters in Part I of the book take issue with different aspects of Kymlicka's work.

Helder de Schutter's chapter focuses upon the multinational state and observes that there are two general approaches taken by normative liberal theorists to national pluralism within one state. On the one hand 'liberal nationalist' theorists such as Kymlicka argue that people who share a common national identity are entitled to a right of self-government or self-determination so that they can make collective decisions within their own national context; while a second group of cosmopolitan liberal theorists eschew such an approach and argue instead that national differences should be overcome or even overlooked, and that instead of offering intra-state autonomy to minority groups, the state should be fostered as one political community for all of its citizens.

De Schutter searches in his chapter for something of a third way between these positions. He accepts some of the ontological premises of the liberal nationalist position, but rejects its ultimate political conclusions as too essentialist. He argues that the liberal nationalist argument can be divided into two theses: one concerning the *value*, and the other the *unit*, of cultural membership. He is inclined to agree with the former thesis, which asserts that individuals are culturally embedded beings, who need a cultural context of choice in order for their cultural freedom to be maximised. However, he rejects the second thesis – and here his primary focus is upon Kymlicka – which contends that the cultural context of choice most relevant to individuals is the nation or, in Kymlicka's formulation, the 'societal culture' (Kymlicka 1995). De Schutter argues that this concentration on the nation or societal culture as the primary unit of attachment fails properly to take account either of mixed or hybrid identities that emerge either when two groups who were once separated but today share the same territory may in time develop a common loyalty and identity, and even a shared context of choice; or of individuals in a 'hybrid cultural situation', such as bicultural bilinguals who do not have a strong sense of belonging to one cultural group over another within the state.

De Schutter contends that it should be possible to respect and foster shared choice contexts whereby several national groups would enjoy cultural protection and recognition in the public sphere, but would co-govern the same societal context. This may be possible in certain contexts but a defender of Kymlicka's position might ask whether it would avoid the problem of domination by the majority nation which many of the remedies Kymlicka advocates are designed to obviate. Another interesting point in many of these debates is that societal cultures can themselves be open spaces whereby national identities therein are not necessarily thick or holistic, and that sub-state societal cultures are as likely to be open and multicultural as state societal cultures. Therefore, to advocate national recognition is not to offer a homogenised or illiberal account, since accounts such as Kymlicka's accept that national identities should be heterogeneous, open and liberal.

One aspect of Kymlicka's that clearly demonstrates his efforts to reconcile his theory with liberalism is his use of the distinctions between 'external protections' and 'internal restrictions' in evaluating normatively the devices that may be used to accommodate minority groups. For Kymlicka, external protections are 'the claim of a group against the larger society', and as such are generally compatible with liberalism, whereas internal restrictions are 'the claim of a group against its own members' and are generally and perhaps always incompatible with liberalism (Kymlicka 1995, 35). Dwight Newman's chapter critiques Kymlicka's use of this distinction. He argues that it is a particularly important part of Kymlicka's work because in many ways it underpins Kymlicka's theoretical structure by helping to demarcate which group-differentiated rights are permissible and which are not.

Newman questions the accuracy of the distinction in both empirical and normative terms. First he takes issue with Kymlicka's empirical claim that groups generally do not seek legal powers to impose internal restrictions. Newman uses examples from Canadian policy, particularly on religious school rights, language rights, and developing self-government agreements with aboriginal peoples, which he suggests demonstrate the regularity of such claims. He therefore argues that there are many situations which Kymlicka's theory does not account for and, as a result, there is a need for new distinctions in the area of group rights that better describe the actual claims of groups. Newman also challenges Kymlicka's normative belief that liberals should almost always reject such internal restrictions. He argues instead that internal restrictions can be morally viable and may even be to the benefit of all members of a group. In this respect Newman contends that Kymlicka's normative account fails to appreciate the justifiability of internal restrictions in certain circumstances because Kymlicka's theory is based upon a search for present equality and as such fails to take account of historical processes that may have led to the creation of 'historically-rooted rights' which are vested in the collective as well as the individual. On this basis he concludes that liberal theorists should develop theories of collective rights even if they potentially fall outside Kymlicka's distinction between 'external protections' and 'internal restrictions' because such group rights may be needed in order to make progress on diversity issues. These arguments demonstrate the complexity and normative difficulty for liberals in debating the extent to which restrictions on certain individual freedoms are permissible in order to enhance the freedoms of groups, and hence the freedom of individuals within these groups. These chapters illustrate the extent to which Will Kymlicka has set the agenda for contemporary normative theorising on the accommodation of cultural identities and how contemporary theorists like De Schutter and Newman are now taking the debate forward in light of evolving theoretical work and changing political circumstances and constitutional structures within and across states.

Part II of the book addresses aboriginal peoples as a case study in the institutional accommodation of cultural diversity. The three chapters in this part each focus upon the principle of self-determination as central to the aspirations of aboriginal peoples to be recognised as fully-functioning societies. In this sense they perhaps offer support to Kymlicka's argument that it is the nation or societal culture which provides the most crucial setting for minority cultures, not least by offering an institutional base from which to develop claims for improved recognition both within the host state and internationally.

Avigail Eisenberg addresses some of the potentially serious problems that arise in the public assessment of minority identity by institutions such as courts or legislatures, particularly where these institutions are dominated by a distinctive cultural, ethnic, linguistic or national majority. The problem she focuses upon is that although institutions frequently reason about identity, there is, she argues, usually nothing systematic about the way they do so in terms of applying a set of standards or criteria beyond their idea of common sense.

In this way she addresses the decision of the Supreme Court of Canada *R. v Van der Peet* in 1996 which did constitute an attempt to establish such a formal set of standards and criteria for reasoning through the identity claims of a minority group.

Here the court adopted a 'distinctive culture test' to decide whether an Aboriginal practice ought to be accommodated. This test requires that claimants prove first that the practice they wish to protect is endangered by state regulation, and secondly that the practice is an integral part of pre-contact indigenous culture, because only if it is will it be entitled to protection today. She observes that *Van der Peet* is by no means an isolated case, and in fact such attempts to assess the nature of minority identity and practice occur in many types of cases, not only those in relation to Aboriginal people. Given that this is the case she sets out to assess this trend, concentrating upon the possible benefits and the disadvantages of attempts to evaluate identity in public institutions.

In terms of the benefits that might accrue from this focus she presents several arguments as to why identity is emerging as a workable and perhaps even a promising focus for minorities in advancing their interests both within states and internationally, before addressing three challenges, presented particularly by critics of identity politics, to the general project of publicly assessing identity. These challenges arise also in the context of the dispute in *Van der Peet*, are: the problem of essentialism; the problem of ethnocentric bias; and the increase in identity politics which brings with it, according to certain critics, a tendency both for distracting us from more important issues and for generating more and more disputes.

Finally Eisenberg asks whether, on balance, the development of a standard set of criteria to be used in the public assessment of minority identity is more likely to improve or impoverish the protection of minority rights. She concludes that identity can be a useful device but that it must avoid attempts either to crystallise the meaning of group identities or to tie groups to practices that are anachronistic or stifling. Secondly, the criteria used in the assessment of identity should perhaps incorporate a broader purpose into the whole process, such as ensuring the continued survival and flourishing of the minority community. And thirdly, the project of protecting cultural identity is but one within the broader struggle by Aboriginal groups for self-determination and other wider claims. In this way reasoning about the identity of another group can help to generate institutional change and assist in efforts to resolve minority conflicts fairly.

By calling for a transparent set of criteria for assessing identity claims so that institutions will deal with these claims more fairly and systematically in a context that is more alive to threats of harm to individual or group claimants and to biases which exist in many institutional practices and methods by which minority claims are currently assessed, Eisenberg's theory in a sense echoes De Schutter's search for a third way that recognises the importance to individuals of their cultural identities but which also acknowledges that identities are multiple, over-lapping and diffused; hence an essentialist approach which excessively prioritises one site or articulation of identity will often represent an over-simplification of a complex cultural configuration and may lead to injustice for individuals by caricaturing, and hence failing to facilitate properly, their variegated patterns of identity and loyalty. Her approach also seems to elide in normative terms with Kymlicka's deep suspicion with internal restrictions (and hence perhaps to contrast somewhat with Newman's approach); it seems that for Eisenberg no less than Kymlicka, internal restrictions on the meaning and development of identity belie the complexity of identity patterns within and across cultural communities, risking the possibility that dominant voices within cultural groups will be permitted to marginalise certain individuals leading to more marginalised accounts of the meaning of particular identities.

Territorial self-determination also forms the central focus of Sonia Harris-Short's chapter as she addresses the issue of aboriginal self government in Canada in the context of the highly sensitive issue of child welfare. On the one hand she notes that there has been much suffering and inter-generational damage done to aboriginal communities in the past by the policies and practices of Canadian child welfare, and as such most commentators have identified the solution to be the implementation of First Nations self-government with full devolution of child welfare from provincial or federal governments. However, Harris-Short also argues that within certain native communities problems of domestic violence and sexual abuse exist, which make the issue more complex than simply one of the granting or denial of self-government over this issue. Therefore, a balance is needed and as such the aim of her chapter is to explore whether a clear and rational legal framework exists in the area of self-government over child welfare that will guarantee aboriginal autonomy while also protecting potentially vulnerable children living within aboriginal communities.

She observes that on the one hand Canadian constitutional and political developments have been moving towards recognition that family matters should fall within the jurisdiction of aboriginal governments, but that on the other the Canadian state also has a responsibility for child welfare across the state. She argues that the existing system goes too far towards permitting interference in aboriginal affairs with the Canadian Government continuing to impose non-native values on First Nations communities, and she contends that this is tantamount to cultural imperialism. Although the Canadian government has an understandable commitment to the core liberal values of Canada's constitution, the current system does not offer genuine self-determination to indigenous peoples.

However, although far more autonomy for aboriginal peoples is needed, the Canadian public do not seem prepared to accept this. Therefore, she argues that aboriginal communities may have to look beyond the Canadian State to international law for a solution. It is in the arena of international law that significant strides are being made. Although the right of indigenous peoples to self-determination has been generally encapsulated within the concept of 'internal' rather than 'external' self-determination, given that indigenous peoples are not entitled to, and generally don't want, full statehood under international law, Harris-Short notes that something of a third way may be developing; i.e. a new and distinctive collective right to self-determination for indigenous peoples which is wider than the internal right of self-determination that currently exists for national minorities, but which falls short of the full right of external self-determination and statehood which is an established international legal right of colonial peoples. Although the prospect of this new concept of aboriginal self-determination becoming a full, positive legal right is to say the least some way off, Harris-Short is encouraged by progress to date. Such a development would offer an important measure of decolonisation and autonomy for indigenous peoples, and it would also be more readily accepted by states than would a right to full, external self-determination since states would not be conceding a legal right of secession. Harris-Short also notes that such a development would not only confer rights but would also impose duties upon aboriginal peoples to accept the principles of international law in general, including international human rights standards and established rights concerning child welfare. Harris-Short does not envisage very much difficulty here since these values are already generally fully accepted by aboriginal peoples. In fact the importance of child welfare is recognised by the UN Draft Declaration on the Rights of Indigenous Peoples Article 33 which specifically refers to international human rights guarantees for vulnerable individuals living within self-determining communities. One final question raised by Harris-Short is whether there is a danger that international law, as the creation of states, may itself be seen as itself a western, ethnocentric, colonial regime which merely replaces the dominant role of the state in dictating solutions for aboriginal peoples. But despite this concern she argues that if international standards are drafted carefully and in a way that is sensitive to aboriginal cultures then they may be accepted by these communities as fully reflecting their own values and standards.

Kathryn Last also considers the contemporary condition of aboriginal peoples in the context of both municipal and international law in her focus upon claims by sub-state groups for the return of objects of cultural heritage. Hitherto this process has in fact taken place not through legal processes at all, since sub-state groups are invariably excluded from these, but as a result of negotiated repatriation settlements. In addressing these negotiated settlements she employs examples from Canada, the UK and the US, looking at both international and domestic law to highlight the problems faced by groups in making claims. She begins by looking at three preliminary issues, the definition of cultural heritage, the role of the repatriation process, and the distinction between restitution and repatriation. All of these it is argued illustrate the importance of the return of cultural heritage as well as the difficulties that arise in framing or applying substantive law in this area.

In terms of the definition of cultural heritage, the issues which are relevant to claims by groups are the role of cultural heritage in identity formation and control of the process of definition, both of which affect legal claims for return in terms of establishing a sufficient interest in an object and determining whether that object is covered by the relevant law. Control of the process of definition is particularly important for the heritage of sub-state cultures since it raises the question of whose definitional voice is, or should be, determinative in asserting the value of the object. The second preliminary issue, the role of the process of return, embraces different aspects: recognition of the relationship between the object and the group; and the symbolic function of reparation for and recognition of the group. In terms of the third preliminary issue it is important to distinguish between restitution and repatriation. The former is the return of an object to its owner based upon traditional property rights, where its character as an item of cultural heritage is generally irrelevant; repatriation, on the other hand, is return of an object to a particular territory which focuses avowedly upon the cultural value of the object. Much of the rest of the chapter addresses how sub-state groups are excluded from legal mechanisms for restitution of cultural heritage when the object is located in a state other than that within which the group is located. Here the rules of private international law are unhelpful because traditional rules of property law protect possessors of such objects. Claims for repatriation are also difficult to pursue for different reasons: the sub-state group may be dependent upon its host state to make a claim on its behalf; also the group may need a representative or institutional structure to make a claim, and the existence of such a structure may depend upon whether the group already possesses devolved autonomy. Finally Last notes that in certain states laws have been passed to facilitate the repatriation of cultural heritage, and she concludes by addressing briefly the legal regimes in the US, Canada and the UK, each of which take very different approaches to this issue.

Part III of the book examines how the constitution of the multicultural state has become a battleground in recent times for the playing out of cultural disputes. This has involved contentious disputes before constitutional courts but has also witnessed deeper levels of argumentation concerning the very tenor or spirit of a particular constitution and the ways in which it represents the cultural and national identity(ies) of the state's citizenry.

Mayo Moran's chapter addresses the equality guarantee contained in section 15 of Canada's *Charter of Rights and Freedoms* which is often lauded both in Canada and elsewhere for its strong substantive conception of equality in emphasising the inherent dignity of the individual. Moran notes that the early case law on the *Charter* justified this perception of section 15 as a strong embodiment of a substantive guarantee of equality in contrast to more formalistic readings of equality such as that of the Fourteenth Amendment to the American constitution. This issue is central to contemporary debates about culture and its constitutional accommodation because it raises the whole issue of neutrality. As has been observed, theorists like Kymlicka refute the idea of nation-states and dominant societies as being neutral in cultural terms; instead they argue all such societies operate as homogenising devices that serve to entrench, foster and promote their own cultural particularisms. Moran's chapter is a close, forensic analysis of one particular instance of how processes of constitutional interpretation can act in such a way as to impose, often unconsciously, the cultural preconceptions of certain dominant ways of thinking within a society. The concept of equality is her focus given its central importance in the management of difference. The idea of equality is fundamental to the normative self-confidence of liberal constitutionalism, since the idea of the equality of individuals before the law underpins the wider sense of legitimacy that contemporary western legalism draws upon in justifying the moral authority of its legal and constitutional systems. But in fact here we must step back and ask fundamental questions about constitutional interpretation. Given that many consider the concept of cultural neutrality to be a myth, it is significant that this idea of neutrality is called upon to underpin the notion of equality: if legal processes operate neutrally then they are capable of treating all people equally regardless of their cultural backgrounds. However, if neutrality within the democratic state is itself a chimera, then it seems we also need a more robust and critical approach to analysing claims to constitutional equality, since its meaning in practice is, like the notion of neutrality, also subject to the same cultural and other imbalances which pervade social structures.

Moran's thesis is that in recent times the Supreme Court of Canada has adopted a more conservative position in its application of the equality principle. Although the rhetoric employed by the Court remains strong, the focus of section 15 has shifted, and one particular device that is now used by the courts in determining whether the equality principle has been violated is the concept of 'the reasonable person'. Moran argues that this idea is now central to equality law because it is concerned with a particularly difficult but important issue, namely which decisions are and which are not discriminatory. For Moran it is especially odd that a court as progressive as the Supreme Court of Canada, in attempting to resolve equality issues, should turn for help to a concept that has always been a difficult and imprecise tool, and one which has in fact been criticised for leading to *inegalitarian* outcomes. The concept of the reasonable person seems to suggest that it is possible to ascribe neutral characteristics to a hypothetical actor or observer, when in fact, Moran argues, a basis of neutrality is very difficult to achieve in a situation where deep, structural inequalities prevail. Instead the court should have looked for a more contextualised stance from which to determine discrimination issues.

One important area in which the benchmark of the reasonable person has been employed is the determination of culpability such as in the criminal law defences of provocation and self-defence. These cases illustrate how problematic a standard it is to use given its high degree of indeterminacy. And in this context Moran asks a number of important questions concerning how we are to determine the precise nature of the subjective and objective characteristics of the reasonable person and indeed which characteristics of the reasonable person are fixed or objective and which are subjective and hence variable. Often the test collapses into notions of 'common sense' or 'ordinary' standards; but again these concepts are potentially very problematical in the discrimination context because discrimination itself often stems from common beliefs and attitudes, and therefore there is a danger that the reasonable person standard will actually legitimise discriminatory attitudes within the law itself. Accordingly, it is essential to separate the normative ideal of reasonableness from any association with what is ordinary or customary.

Moran then reviews recent cases before the Supreme Court of Canada in which the court has applied the reasonable person standard in section 15 discrimination analysis. She observes the problems that the court has faced in using this standard, problems which judges themselves at times are aware of. Despite efforts to use the principle to help establish an idealised judicial point of view, the over-riding problem remains that the reasonable person test can remain, even when applied by judges, a vehicle for the crystallisation of common prejudices within legal standards or a way of justifying the judge's position by accrediting it with a veil of objectivity. Therefore the identification of an objectifiably 'reasonable' position has the unfortunate consequence of effectively declaring the unsuccessful equality claimant to be unreasonable. In conclusion Moran advocates that the test should no longer be used. Instead the Court should express its own reasons for its judgments, taking responsibility for a decision not to accept a claim of discrimination rather than attempting to give its decision a cloak of objectivity by applying a purportedly reasonable person standard in justification for its own inevitably subjective opinion.

The final two chapters of the book address the debate about the cultural identity of the state in terms of the political and constitutional status of sub-state cultural and societal groups. They address in particular the dispute between Quebec and the rest of Canada concerning Quebec's claims to constitutional recognition of its sub-state national status within Canada that has become a dispute about the very nature of Canada as a multinational democracy. These chapters also demonstrate how the Supreme Court of Canada has become engaged in this debate, searching as it did in the *Quebec Secession Reference* for unwritten constitutional principles that would help to articulate the spirit of the Canadian constitution as an instrument capable of articulating and accommodating the state's complex patterns of diversity.

Peter Oliver's chapter focuses upon Quebec's status within the Canadian constitution, and in particular upon how proposals for the accommodation of Quebec as a distinct national community within Canada have been bound up for much of the last century with more general constitutional changes within Canada and in particular the process by which the Constitution of Canada is amended. As Oliver observes: 'No one denies that Quebec is different. Disagreement emerges in determining whether and how this difference should be reflected in the Constitution.' In his review Oliver sets out a complex matrix of the relevant factors which he argues are at the heart of this historical struggle, and this matrix is essential both to understanding Quebec's position vis-à-vis constitutional amendment, and to advancing suitable proposals for future change. Each side of the matrix has three variables. On one side Oliver lists three constitutional goals that might be enhanced by change: *protection*, *promotion* and *federalism*. The first represents Quebec's desire to protect what it has already achieved as an established North American society over three or four hundred years; 'promotion' refers to the need for new powers, in particular special constitutional powers for Quebec which will reflect its special role as 'source, guardian, guiding light, *etc.*' of French language and culture in Canada; and 'federalism' refers to the strong aspiration in Quebec to play a fuller role in federal institutions, with Oliver arguing that even when political elites in Quebec seek to remove the territory from Canada there is still a strong grass-roots commitment among the people to federal institutions. The other side of the matrix contains the three main policy positions that Quebec has taken with regard to the amending formula over the years: *unanimity*, *veto* and *opting out*, with Oliver explaining how these have each played roles in informing Quebec's negotiating position both prior to and since patriation of the constitution in 1982.

Today the amending formula of the constitution of Canada is contained in Part V of the Constitution Act, 1982. Although this requires the unanimous agreement of the provinces for a narrow range of important constitutional amendments, in general the Canadian constitution can be amended by seven out of ten provinces representing at least fifty percent of the population of all the provinces. These seven need not include Quebec, leaving Quebec with only a limited right to opt out of amendments with which it disagrees, since in many cases opt out is not possible. Quebec nationalists therefore have two main complaints: the first is that as the institutional embodiment of one of Canada's two national societies, Quebec should have the power to veto amendment proposals; and the second is that, failing this, it should at least have a right to opt out with compensation from all amendments with which it disagrees.

Oliver's chapter is taken up with a detailed consideration of the intersection of the different variables in his matrix, addressing Quebec's position in relation to the amending formula both pre-1982 and post-1982. He concludes that a constitutional veto for Quebec is objectively justified as providing most protection for Quebec's interests.

This is preferable to extending Quebec's opting out power, which although in some ways useful, is inadequate to include Quebec in federal decision-making processes where Quebec seeks a voice, not an exit. This veto power, however, should not be extended to all provinces symmetrically as it would lead to constitutional gridlock.

There are various complications here, however. One is that there is not the political will in English Canada to accommodate Quebec in such a special way; instead there is a commitment to provincial equality that at present seems very difficult to shift. Secondly, there is now a strong separatist movement in Quebec which no longer seeks reform of the confederation. However, Oliver does offer hope. If Quebec looks beyond its own provincial interests and rediscovers its historical role as representative of the French fact within Canada, and if this role can be articulated not just by leaders in Quebec but by counterparts in Ottawa and the other provinces, then there may eventually be a move away from rigid adherence to the idea of the constitutional equality of the provinces. Oliver considers progress here to be basically a matter of trust. Much of the existing goodwill disappeared between Quebec and the rest of Canada in the 1980s and 1990s. If this does not revive, then we can expect Quebec to develop a position like that of an independent state within a large political entity where unanimous consent to all decisions will be needed. The stakes are therefore high; and so English Canada needs to be prepared to abandon strict provincial equality in order both to recall Quebec's role as the leading protector and promoter of French-Canadian language and culture and to preserve the federation; while Quebec needs to move away from threats of secession in order to build this type of goodwill in English Canada and help rebuild there a binational vision of the country which seemed to prosper in English Canada in the 1950s and 1960s.

Despite further breakdown in goodwill around the Quebec referendum on sovereignty in 1995, since then some positive steps have been taken. The federal Parliament has guaranteed a veto for Quebec over constitutional changes by way of a statute, which although not having entrenched constitutional status, does guarantee a type of veto arrangement for each of Canada's regions, one of which is taken to be Quebec. On the other hand, Oliver advocates the radical step of possibly bypassing the Quebec National Assembly if the independent *Parti québécois* makes reciprocation impossible. He suggests that the present amendment formula could be altered to require a referendum with regional, *popular* vetoes for all amendments; in other words the veto would be vested ultimately in the hands of directly-determining provincial populations and not mediated through provincial legislatures. Quebec has already recognised the value of referendums in any process towards secession, and so this principle should be extended to the process of amendment of the existing constitution. Such a mechanism, argues Oliver, would finally satisfy Quebec's demands for *protection, promotion* and *federalism* while avoiding the risk that it could be hijacked by separatist elites in Quebec over the heads of the people of the province who may endorse it. Further tension has emerged since the publication, on 1 November 2005, of the Gomery Commission report into the activities of the federal government, which uncovered financial irregularities linked to government spending on a national unity campaign designed to combat the Quebec sovereignty movement following the 1995 referendum. This report has further heightened existing tensions between Ottawa and the Quebec sovereignist movement, demonstrating how fraught relations between Quebec and the rest of Canada continue to be, and hence how important it is that scholars like Oliver offer reflective analyses of the historical context of these difficulties and imaginative prescriptions for further attempts to unblock the existing impasse.

One response taken by the federal government in Canada to Quebec's 1995 referendum on sovereignty was to make a reference to the Supreme Court of Canada enquiring as to the legality of any proposed secession by Quebec. The opinion handed down by the Supreme Court was a highly sophisticated answer to the questions posed, and it is notable in particular for the way in which the court moved beyond the written terms of the constitution to identify what it took to be the 'fundamental and organizing principles',[1] which although unwritten nonetheless underpin the constitution of Canada: namely, federalism; democracy; constitutionalism and the rule of law; and respect for minorities. These principles were used to explain the multicultural nature of the state and the historical relationship between English and French Canada. Warren Newman considers how the use of unwritten principles by the Canadian courts had started to evolve before the *Secession Reference* and how they have continued to be used since. One major concern which emerges in Newman's chapter is that the use of unwritten principles to rival and perhaps even trump the written provisions of the constitution may challenge the principle of the rule of law, which according to Newman is embodied in fidelity to the written constitutional text. The rule of law is central to Newman's conception of the constitution, and he points to the preamble to the Charter and its express recognition of the rule of law as one of the founding principles of the Canadian state. As such he falls back upon English constitutionalism in which he locates the roots of Canadian constitutionalism by applying the theory of A.V. Dicey.

But the Canadian constitution differs fundamentally and crucially from the British constitution in that it is written, and as such the constitution accords supremacy to the written constitutional text. Indeed there is the express declaration in s.52 of the *Constitution Act, 1982* that the Constitution of Canada is the 'supreme law' of Canada; and within that to the supremacy of parliament, a principle brought to Canada within the framework of the *Constitution Act, 1867*. Following 1982, Parliament's authority is surpassed in terms of normative power only by the terms of the written constitution.

Therefore, Newman rejects the idea that the principle of the rule of law should be used by the courts to impose procedural and substantive requirements on Parliament unless when in exercising its legislative power it commits a breach of the constitution. Furthermore he rejects the idea that there are any unwritten principles that would exclude certain areas of subject matter from amendment in accordance with the amendment procedure contained in the constitution. Nonetheless the *Quebec Secession Reference* has created an area of doubt. The Supreme Court referred to constitutional principles as being 'not merely descriptive' but also 'invested with powerful normative force', and being 'binding upon both courts and governments'. For Newman this 'could not fail to encourage litigants to make new arguments based largely on principles rather than provisions'.

---

1 *Reference re Secession of Quebec* [1998] 2 S.C.R. 217, para. 32.

Since then in certain cases the courts have pulled back from this strong application of unwritten principles, but there have also been examples, especially the case of *Polewsky*, where they have been used seemingly to impose positive legislative requirements on a provincial legislature. Newman is critical of this, suggesting that it violates the principle of the separation of powers as well as that of parliamentary sovereignty. Therefore, his main thrust is to eschew a prescriptive role for unwritten constitutional principles in the judicial elaboration of fundamental law, certainly when such is used to assert norms superior to the *Constitution Acts* themselves. One reason is that this is unconstitutional; another is that it gives judges power for which they are not constitutionally accountable, nor to which they are by expertise suited: namely, engagement 'in prolix existential explorations into the meaning of law, politics and adjudication'.

Newman's account highlights the tensions between strict adherence to written constitutional text on the one hand and the search for legal solutions to developing problems in an increasingly diverse society on the other. A number of the preceding chapters argue that a firm adherence to constitutional formalism makes it more difficult to introduce a flexible and contextualised approach to constitutional meaning which allows constitutionalism to remain alive to the important social context within which democratic constitutions serve demographically complex, multinational and multicultural states like Canada, and are thereby able to defuse tensions which build up when minorities within constitutional democracies feel voiceless, neglected and unjustly treated. But Newman's account cautions against a different danger which should not be overlooked. He is fully supportive of the goals of cultural pluralism but highlights that this commitment should not require an 'anything goes' approach to constitutionalism. It seems that in the *Secession Reference* the Supreme Court of Canada was alive to this difficulty. The Court engaged fully with the written form of the constitution but also attempted to reach beyond the formal text in order to search for the historical and sociological roots of that document as well as for the political commitments which emerged from this historiography. It seems that it is by way of such a quest that a deeper understanding of the constitution as one that speaks to the precise and complex demography of the state can emerge, provided that a commitment to the rule of law is not sacrificed in the process. The chapters in this book have illustrated that the task of successful constitutionalism in complex, multicultural states is to do justice to the intricate social fabric of such a state, and that the successful fulfilment of this task may require constitutional actors to look beyond narrow linguistic constructions of constitutional texts in order to challenge dominant power patterns, to unpack in more contextualised ways the subjectivity of terms like equality and neutrality, and thereby to approach constitutionalism more imaginatively in the search for the better accommodation of the state's cultural and national diversity.

Reference

Kymlicka, W. (1995), *Multicultural Citizenship*, Oxford: Oxford University Press.

PART I
The Evolving Theory of Cultural Diversity

Chapter 2

The Global Diffusion of Multiculturalism: Trends, Causes, Consequences

Will Kymlicka[1]

Multiculturalism today is a global phenomenon. There are public debates and state policies regarding multiculturalism in every continent around the globe, although they take quite different forms in different countries. Indeed, it's not clear what, if anything, all of these different debates have in common.

Therefore, I will start by identifying what I take to be common features in struggles for multiculturalism around the world, and then note some of the many different forms these can take. I will then offer some reflections on why these debates have arisen now, and where they are likely to go in the future.

The World-wide Struggle for Multiculturalism

What all struggles of multiculturalism have in common, I believe, is that they reject earlier models of the unitary, homogenous nation-state. In order to understand the idea of a multicultural state, therefore, we need first to understand this older model of a homogenous nation-state, and why it has been rejected.

Until recently, most states around the world have aspired to be 'nation-states'. In this model, the state was seen as the possession of a dominant national group, which used the state to privilege its identity, language, history, culture, literature, myths, religion and so on, and which defined the state as the expression of its nationhood. (This dominant group was usually the majority group, but sometimes a minority was able to establish dominance – e.g., whites in South Africa under the apartheid regime, or *criollo* elites in some Latin American countries.) Anyone who did not belong to this dominant national group was subject to either assimilation or exclusion.[2]

---

[1] This chapter is based upon a paper presented at the International Conference on 'Leadership, Education and Multiculturalism in the Armed Forces', La Paz, Bolivia, 13 September 2004.

[2] This exclusion could take the form of exclusion from the halls of power within the state (e.g., through denial of the vote, or other forms of political disempowerment), or it could literally involve exclusion from the territory of the state, through racial restrictions on immigration, or through ethnic cleansing.

There is nothing 'natural' about such nation-states. Very few countries around the world are mono-national (Iceland, Portugal and the Koreas are the most frequently cited examples). In most countries, this sort of national homogeneity had to be actively constructed by the state through a range of 'nation-building' policies that encouraged the preferred national identity while suppressing any alternative identities. Public policies were used to promote and consolidate a common national language, national history and mythology, national heroes, national symbols, a national literature, a national education system, a national media, a national military, in some cases a national religion, and so on. Any groups that resisted these sorts of nationalising policies were subject not only to political disempowerment, but also typically to economic discrimination, and to various forms of 'demographic engineering' (e.g., pressuring members of the group to disperse, and/or promoting settlement by members of the dominant group into the homeland of indigenous/minority groups). These and other policies were aimed at constructing the ideal of a nation-state.

Virtually every Western democracy has pursued this ideal at one point or another, as have virtually all post-colonial states. As I discuss below, an increasing number of Western democracies have abandoned this goal in favour of a more 'multicultural' model of the state. But at one point or another, virtually every Western democracy has sought to define itself as a mono-national state. The only exception to this pattern in the West that I know of is Switzerland. Switzerland never attempted to try to construct a single national language on the territory of the state. It has always accepted that the French- and Italian-speaking minorities would exist as distinct linguistic groups into the indefinite future. But every other Western democracy – including some that are very diverse, and that now pride themselves on their diversity, like Canada – has at some point or other had the goal of inculcating a common national language and culture.

However, this nation-state model has increasingly been challenged and contested by all sorts of groups. There are many groups within the territory of the state that have their own language, their own history, their own culture, their own heroes, their own symbols. Such groups face either exclusion or assimilation by this process of nation-building. As a result, various groups, particularly indigenous peoples and other kinds of national groups, have contested this attempt to construct states through a form of homogeneous nation-building, and advocated instead for a more 'multicultural' model of the state.[3]

What would a multicultural state look like? The precise details vary from country to country, for reasons I discuss below. The sort of state reforms demanded by African-Americans in the US differs dramatically from the sort of reforms demanded by indigenous Maori in New Zealand or by Chinese immigrants in Canada. However, there are some general principles that I think are common to all of these different struggles for a multicultural state. First, a multicultural state involves the repudiation of the older idea that the state is a possession of a single national group. Instead, the

---

3   This struggle has not always been conducted in the name of 'multiculturalism', and some groups may indeed reject the term. For reasons discussed below, the struggle has often instead been conducted in the name of a 'multi*national* state', or various ideals of 'partnership', 'federalism', 'historic rights', or simply 'democracy'.

state must be seen as belonging equally to all citizens. Second, as a consequence, a multicultural state repudiates those nation-building policies that assimilate or exclude members of minority or non-dominant groups. Instead, it accepts that individuals should be able to access state institutions, and to act as full and equal citizens in political life, without having to hide or deny their ethnocultural identity. The state accepts an obligation to accord the history, language and culture of non-dominant groups the same recognition and accommodation that is accorded to the dominant group. Third, a multicultural state acknowledges the historic injustice that was done to minority/non-dominant groups by these older policies of assimilation and exclusion, and manifests a willingness to offer some sort of remedy or rectification for them.

These three inter-connected ideas – repudiating the idea of the state as belonging to the dominant group; replacing assimilationist and exclusionary nation-building policies with policies of recognition and accommodation; acknowledging historic injustice and offering amends for it – seem to me to be common to virtually all real-world struggles for 'multiculturalism'.

Different Forms of Multiculturalism

Of course, these points of commonality are very abstract, and as soon as we look at the details of specific countries, enormous differences emerge. The precise way in which minority groups wish to be recognised and accommodated, or to have their historic injustices amended, varies enormously from country to country, as well as between different minorities within a single country.

It would be impossible in this chapter to provide a comprehensive overall picture of the different forms that multiculturalism can take, but for the purposes of illustration, let me focus on three general trends. My discussion of these trends will be drawn primarily from the long-established Western democracies, which are the cases I know best.

Indigenous Peoples

The first trend concerns the treatment of indigenous peoples, such as the Indians and Inuit in Canada, the Aboriginal peoples of Australia, the Maori of New Zealand, the Sami of Scandinavia, the Inuit of Greenland, and Indian tribes in the United States. In the past, all of these countries had the same goal and expectation that indigenous peoples would eventually disappear as distinct communities, as a result of dying out, or inter-marriage, or assimilation. Various policies were adopted to speed up this process, such as stripping indigenous peoples of their lands, restricting the practice of their traditional culture, language and religion, and undermining their institutions of self-government.

However, there has been a dramatic reversal in these policies, starting in the early 1970s. Today, all of the countries I just mentioned accept, at least in principle, the idea that indigenous peoples will exist into the indefinite future as distinct societies within the larger country, and that they must have the land claims, cultural rights (including recognition of customary law) and self-government rights needed to sustain themselves as distinct societies.

We see this pattern in all of the Western democracies. Consider the constitutional affirmation of Aboriginal rights in the 1982 Canadian constitution, along with the land claims commission and the signing of new treaties; the revival of treaty rights through the Treaty of Waitangi in New Zealand; the recognition of land rights for Aboriginal Australians in the *Mabo* decision; the creation of Sami Parliaments in Scandinavia, the evolution of 'Home Rule' for the Inuit of Greenland; and the laws and court cases upholding self-determination rights for American Indian tribes. In all of these countries there is a gradual but real process of decolonisation taking place, as indigenous peoples regain their lands, customary law and self-government.

Substate/Minority Nationalisms

The second trend concerns the treatment of substate 'national' groups, such as the Québécois in Canada, the Scots and Welsh in Britain, the Catalans and Basques in Spain, the Flemish in Belgium, the German-speaking minority in South Tyrol in Italy, and Puerto Rico in the United States.[4] In all of these cases, we find a regionally-concentrated group that conceives of itself as a nation within a larger state, and mobilises behind nationalist political parties to achieve recognition of its nationhood, either in the form of an independent state or through territorial autonomy within the larger state. In the past, all of these countries have attempted to suppress these forms of substate nationalism. To have a regional group with a sense of distinct nationhood was seen as a threat to the state. Various efforts were made to erode this sense of distinct nationhood, often using the same tools that were used against indigenous peoples – e.g., restricting minority language rights, abolishing traditional forms of regional self-government, and encouraging members of the dominant group to settle in the minority group's traditional territory so that the minority becomes outnumbered even in its traditional territory.

However, there has been a dramatic reversal in the way Western countries deal with substate nationalisms. Today, all of the countries I have just mentioned have accepted the principle that these substate national identities will endure into the indefinite future, and that their sense of nationhood and nationalist aspirations must be accommodated in some way or other. This accommodation has typically taken the form of what we can call 'multination and multilingual federalism': that is, creating a federal or quasi-federal subunit in which the minority group forms a local majority, and so can exercise meaningful forms of self-government. Moreover, the group's language is typically recognised as an official state language, at least within their federal subunit, and perhaps throughout the country as a whole.[5]

---

4 We could also include the French- and Italian-speaking minorities in Switzerland, although some people dispute whether they manifest a 'national' consciousness.

5 It is important to distinguish such 'multination' federations from other federal systems where internal subunits are not designed to enable minority self-government, such as the continental United States, Germany, Australia, and Brazil. In these countries, none of the subunits was designed to enable a national minority to exercise self-government over its

At the beginning of the twentieth-century, only Switzerland and Canada had adopted this combination of territorial autonomy and official language status for substate national groups. Since then, however, virtually all Western democracies that contain sizeable substate nationalist movements have moved in this direction. The list includes the adoption of autonomy for the Swedish-speaking Aland Islands in Finland after the First World War, autonomy for South Tyrol and Puerto Rico after the Second World War, federal autonomy for Catalonia and the Basque Country in Spain in the 1970s, for Flanders in the 1980s, and most recently for Scotland and Wales in the 1990s.

This, then, is the second major trend: a shift from suppressing substate nationalisms to accommodating them through regional autonomy and official language rights. Amongst the Western democracies with a sizeable national minority, only France is an exception to this trend, in its refusal to grant autonomy to its main substate nationalist group in Corsica. However, legislation was recently adopted to accord autonomy to Corsica, and it was only a ruling of the Constitutional Court that prevented its implementation.

Immigrant Groups

A third trend concerns the treatment of immigrant groups. By immigrants, I mean groups formed by the decision of individuals and families to leave their original homeland and emigrate to another society, often leaving their friends and relatives behind. But it is essential to distinguish between two categories of immigrants – those who have the right to become citizens, and those who do not. I will use the term 'immigrant group' only for the former case, and will discuss the latter case, which I will call 'metics', below.

Immigrants, then, are people who arrive under an immigration policy that gives them the right to become citizens after a relatively short period of time – say, 3–5 years subject only to minimal conditions (e.g., learning the official language, and knowing something about the country's history and political institutions). This has been the traditional policy governing immigration in the four major 'countries of immigration' in the West – namely, United States, Canada, Australia and New Zealand.

In the past, these four countries had an assimilationist approach to immigration. Immigrants were encouraged and expected to assimilate to the pre-existing society, with the hope that over time they would become indistinguishable from native-born citizens in their speech, dress, recreation, and way of life generally. Any groups that were seen as incapable of this sort of cultural assimilation were prohibited from emigrating in the first place, or from becoming citizens. This was reflected in laws that excluded Africans and Asians from entering these countries of immigration for much of the twentieth-century, or from naturalising.

---

traditional territory, although that was certainly possible in the American case. Indeed, in the US, internal boundaries were drawn in such a way as to precisely prevent the possibility of a minority-dominated subunit. For more on the difference between multination federalism and other forms of federalism, see Kymlicka 2001, chapter 5.

However, since the late 1960s, we have seen a dramatic change in this approach. There have been two related changes: first, the adoption of race-neutral admissions criteria, so that immigrants to these countries are increasingly from non-European (and often non-Christian) societies; and second, the adoption of a more 'multicultural' conception of integration, one which expects that many immigrants will visibly and proudly express their ethnic identity, and which accepts an obligation on the part of public institutions (like the police, schools, media, museums, etc.) to accommodate these ethnic identities.

These two-fold changes have occurred, to varying degrees, in all of the traditional countries of immigration. All of them have shifted from discriminatory to race-neutral admissions and naturalisation policies. And all of them have shifted from an assimilationist to a more multicultural conception of integration. There are important differences in how official or formal this shift to multiculturalism has been. In Canada, Australia and New Zealand this shift was formally marked by the declaration of an official multicultural policy by the central government. But even in the United States, we see similar changes on the ground. The US does not have an official policy of multiculturalism at the federal level, but if we look at lower levels of government, such as states or cities, we often find a broad range of multiculturalism policies. If we look at state-level policies regarding the education curriculum, for example, or city-level policies regarding policing or hospitals, we'll often find that they are indistinguishable from the way provinces and cities in Canada or Australia deal with issues of immigrant ethnocultural diversity. As in Canada, they have their own diversity programs and/or equity officers. As Nathan Glazer puts it, 'we are all multiculturalists now' (Glazer 1997). Similarly, in Britain, while there is no nation-wide multiculturalism policy, the same basic ideas and principles are pursued through their race relations policy. All of these countries have accepted the same two-fold change: adopting race-neutral admissions and naturalisation policies, and imposing on public institutions a duty to accommodate immigrant ethnocultural diversity.

This trend is now quite widespread in the West. Amongst countries that legally admit immigrants as permanent residents and future citizens, the main exception to this trend is France, which clings to an assimilationist conception of French republican citizenship.

Metics

The fourth trend concerns those migrants who are not admitted as permanent residents and future citizens. This is actually a heterogeneous category, including people who enter a country illegally (e.g., North Africans in Italy), or as asylum-seekers (e.g., Kosovars in Switzerland), or as students or 'guest-workers' who have overstayed their initial visa (e.g., Turks in Germany). When they entered the country, these people were not conceived of as future citizens, or even as long-term residents, and indeed they would not have been allowed to enter in the first place if they were seen as permanent residents and future citizens. However, despite the official rules, they have settled more or less permanently. In principle, and to some extent in practice, many face the threat of deportation if they are detected by the authorities, or if they are convicted of a crime. But they nonetheless form sizeable communities in certain countries, engage in some form of employment, legal or illegal, and may marry and form a family. This is true, for example, of Mexicans in California, Turks in Germany, or North Africans in Italy or Spain. Borrowing a term from Ancient Greece, Walzer calls these groups 'metics' – that is, long-term residents who are nonetheless excluded from the polis (Walzer 1983). Since metics face enormous obstacles to integration – legal, political, economic, social, and psychological – they tend to exist in the margins of the larger society.

Generally speaking, the most basic claim of metics is to regularise their status as permanent residents, and to gain access to citizenship. They want, in effect, to be able to follow the immigrant path to integration into the mainstream society, even though they were not initially admitted as immigrants. In the past, Western democracies have responded to this demand for access to citizenship in different ways. Some countries – particularly the traditional immigrant countries – have grudgingly accepted these demands. Asylum-seekers whose refugee claims are accepted are granted permanent residence and access to citizenship, and not required to return to their country of origin even when the danger of persecution has passed. Guest-workers who overstay their visa are often able to gain permanent residence. Periodic amnesties are offered for illegal immigrants, so that over time they become similar to immigrants in their legal status and social opportunities.

But some countries – particularly those that do not think of themselves as immigrant countries – have resisted these demands. These countries often have no established process or infrastructure for integrating immigrants. Moreover, many of these metics have either broken the law to enter the country (illegal immigrants), or broken their promise to return to their country of origin (guest-workers), and so are not viewed as worthy of citizenship. Moreover, countries with no tradition of accepting newcomers are often more xenophobic, and prone to view all foreigners as potential security threats, or as potentially disloyal, or simply as unalterably 'alien'. In these countries, of which Germany, Austria and Switzerland are the best-known examples, the official policy has not been to try to integrate metics into the national community, but to get them to leave the country, either through expulsion or voluntary return.

In short, the hope was that if metics were denied citizenship, so that they only had a precarious legal status within the country, and if they were told repeatedly that their real home was in their country of origin, and that they were not wanted as members of the society, then they would eventually go home.

But it is increasingly recognised that this approach is not viable. Metics who have lived in a country for several years are unlikely to go home, even if they have only a precarious legal status. This is particularly true if the metics have married and had children in the country. At this point, it is their new country, not their country of origin, which has become their 'home'. Indeed, it may be the only home that the metics' children and grandchildren know. Once they have settled, founded a family, and started raising their children, nothing short of expulsion is likely to get metics to return to their country of origin.

So a policy based on the hope of voluntary return is unrealistic. Moreover, it endangers the larger society. For the likely result of such a policy is to create a permanently disenfranchised, alienated, and racially- or ethnically-defined underclass. Metics may develop an oppositional subculture in which the very idea of pursuing success in mainstream institutions is viewed with suspicion. The predictable consequences can involve some mixture of political alienation, criminality, and religious fundamentalism amongst the metics, particularly the second-generation, which in turn leads to increased racial tensions, even violence, throughout the society.

To avoid this, there is an increasing trend in Western democracies, even in non-immigrant countries, towards adopting amnesty programs for illegal immigrants, and granting citizenship to long-settled refugees and guest-workers and their children. In effect, long-settled metics are increasingly viewed as if they were legal immigrants, and are allowed and encouraged to follow the immigrant path to integration.

In all four of these contexts, then, we see shifts away from historic policies of assimilation or exclusion towards a more 'multicultural' approach that recognises and accommodates diversity. For our purposes, the first two trends regarding national minorities and indigenous peoples are perhaps the most important, and deserve special highlighting. These two trends help illustrate the extent to which Western democracies have moved away from older models of unitary, centralised nation-states, and repudiated older ideologies of 'one state, one nation, one language'. Today, virtually all Western states that contain indigenous peoples and substate national groups have become 'multination' states, recognising the existence of 'peoples' and 'nations' within the boundaries of the state. This recognition is manifested in a range of minority and indigenous rights that includes regional autonomy and official language status for national minorities, and customary law, land claims, and self-government for indigenous peoples.

Taken together, these trends represent a dramatic transformation in the relationship between states and ethnic groups. It's important to emphasise that these changes are not purely token or symbolic. On the contrary, they often involve a significant redistribution of economic resources and political power – something close to a genuine sharing of power – as well as giving non-dominant groups enhanced access to state institutions.

I suspect that in many cases, governments may have hoped and expected that token reforms would be sufficient. They may have hoped that it would be enough to put a few words of a minority language on the state currency, for example, or put an indigenous historical figure on a postage stamp, and this would satisfy aspirations for 'recognition'. However, whatever the original intention of government officials, non-dominant groups have used these multicultural reforms as a springboard for negotiating significantly enhanced access to public resources, powers and offices.

Causes of the Trend Towards Multiculturalism

These trends raise two obvious questions. First, why are these trends emerging now? Second, how well are they working? I will address the first question in this section, and then turn to the second at the end of the chapter.

Why have these trends emerged in the past thirty years? Most explanations that focus on a particular country tend to invoke factors that are specific to that country, such as particular personalities, the strategies of particular political parties, the nature of the electoral systems, and so on. These factors are undoubtedly important in explaining the details of any particular case. But once we recognise the pervasive nature of these trends, it seems clear that the main explanation must lie in factors that are common to all Western democracies, rather than factors specific to particular countries. There must be underlying structural factors that explain why virtually all Western democracies have moved in similar directions, despite their very different personalities, party structures and electoral systems.

I do not believe that we have a clear understanding of what these underlying factors are. However, let me suggest several factors that I believe have made the trend towards the greater accommodation of ethnocultural diversity possible, and perhaps even inevitable, in the West. We can divide these factors into two camps: (1) reasons why non-dominant groups have become more assertive of their rights; (2) reasons why states and dominant groups have been less resistant to these rights-claims. I will look at these two sets of factors in turn.

First, then, why have non-dominant groups become more vocal and assertive in claiming various multicultural rights and reforms? I would highlight three factors:

Demographics

The first factor is demographics. In the past, many governments had the hope or expectation that non-dominant ethnic groups would simply disappear, through dying out or assimilation or inter-marriage. It is now clear that this is not going to happen. Indigenous peoples are the fastest-growing segment of the population in the countries where they are found, with very high birth-rates. The percentage of immigrants in the population is growing steadily in most Western countries, and most commentators agree that even more immigrants will be needed in the future to offset declining birth rates and an aging population. And substate national groups in the West are also growing in absolute numbers, even if they are staying the same or marginally declining as a percentage of the population. No one anymore can have the dream or delusion that minorities will disappear. The numbers count, particularly in a democracy, and the numbers are shifting in the direction of non-dominant groups.

Rights-Consciousness

The second factor is the human rights revolution, and the resulting development of a 'rights consciousness'. Since 1948, we have an international order that is premised on the idea of the inherent equality of human beings, both as individuals and as peoples. The international order has decisively repudiated older ideas of a racial or ethnic hierarchy, according to which some peoples were superior to others, and thereby had the right to rule over them.

It is important to remember how radical these ideas of human equality are. Assumptions about a hierarchy of peoples were widely accepted throughout the West up until World War II, when Hitler's fanatical and murderous policies discredited them. Indeed, the whole system of European colonialism was premised on the assumption of a hierarchy of peoples, and this assumption was the explicit basis of both domestic policies and international law throughout the nineteenth century and first half of the twentieth century (including the racial restrictions on immigration I discussed earlier).

Today, however, we live in a world where the idea of human equality is unquestioned, at least officially. What matters here is not the change in international law per se, which has had little impact on most people's everyday lives. The real change has been in people's consciousness. Members of historically subordinated groups today demand equality, and demand it as a *right*. They believe they are entitled to equality, and entitled to it *now*, not in some indefinite or millenarian future.

This sort of rights-consciousness has become such a pervasive feature of modernity that we have trouble imagining that it did not always exist. But if we examine the historical records, we find that minorities in the past typically justified their claims, not by appeal to human rights or equality, but by appealing to the generosity of rulers in according 'privileges', often in return for past loyalty and services. Today, by contrast, groups have a powerful sense of entitlement to equality as a basic human right, not as a favour or charity, and are angrily impatient with what they perceive as lingering manifestations of older hierarchies.[6]

Of course, there is no consensus on what 'equality' means (and, conversely, no agreement on what sorts of actions or practices are evidence of 'hierarchy'). People who agree on the general principle of the equality of peoples may disagree about whether or when this requires official bilingualism, for example, or consociational power-sharing. But there can be no doubt that Western democracies historically privileged a particular national group over other groups who were subject to assimilation or exclusion. This historic hierarchy was reflected in a wide range of policies and institutions, from the schools and state symbols to policies regarding language, immigration, media, citizenship, the division of powers, and electoral systems. So long as leaders of non-dominant groups can identify (or conjure up) manifestations of these historic hierarchies, they will be able to draw upon the powerful rights-consciousness of their members.

Democracy

The third key factor, I believe, is democracy. Democracy is relevant for many reasons. At the simplest level, the consolidation of democracy limits the ability of elites to crush ethnic political movements. In many countries around the world, elites ban political movements of ethnic groups, or pay thugs or para-militaries to beat up or kill ethnic group leaders, or bribe police and judges to lock them up. The fear of this sort of repression often keeps non-dominant groups from voicing even the most moderate claims. Keeping quiet is the safest option for such groups in many countries.

In consolidated democracies, however, where democracy is the only game in town, there is no option but to allow ethnic groups to mobilise politically and advance their claims in public. As a result, members of ethnic groups are increasingly unafraid to speak out. They may not win the political debate, but they aren't afraid

---

6   The development of this rights-consciousness is related, in part, to growing levels of education amongst many minorities.

of being killed, jailed or fired for trying. It is this loss of fear, combined with rights-consciousness, which explains the remarkably vocal nature of ethnic politics in contemporary Western democracies.

Moreover, democracy involves the availability of multiple access points to decision-making. If a group is blocked at one level by an unsympathetic government, they can pursue their claims at another level. Even if an unsympathetic political party were to win power at the central level, and attempted to cut back on the rights of non-dominant groups, these groups could shift their focus to the regional level, or to the municipal level. And even if all of these levels were blocked, they could pursue their claims through the courts, or even through international pressure. This is what democracy is all about: multiple and shifting points of access to power.

These three factors help to explain the 'push' for policies of accommodation: increasing numbers; increasing rights-consciousness; and increasing access to multiple arenas of safe political mobilisation all help to explain the growing strength of ethnopolitical mobilisation by ethnic groups in the West. But they do not yet explain why dominant groups have been willing to accept these demands. After all, most Western states have a dominant national group that forms a clear numerical majority, and in a democracy 'majority rules'. So why have majority groups become more willing to respond to these demands, and to negotiate them? Why not use the power of the state to suppress these demands, with force if necessary, as was the case in the past?

I believe there are two factors that help to explain the growing tendency of dominant groups to accept (however grudgingly and reluctantly) these new models of accommodation. These two factors have helped reduce the perceived risks associated with multicultural reforms, and hence reduced the tendency of dominant groups to resist them.

Desecuritisation

The first factor is geo-political security. Where states feel insecure in geo-political terms, fearful of neighbouring enemies, they are unlikely to treat fairly their own minorities. More specifically, states will never voluntarily accord self-governing powers to minorities that they view as potential collaborators with neighbouring enemies. That is, they will not voluntarily accord rights and powers to groups that they view as a 'fifth-column' for a neighbouring enemy.

In the past, this has sometimes been an issue in the West. For example, prior to World War II, Italy feared that the German-speaking minority in South Tyrol was more loyal to Austria or Germany than to Italy, and would therefore support any attempt by Germany/Austria to invade and annex South Tyrol. Similar fears were expressed about the German minority in Belgium or Denmark. These countries worried that Germany might invade in the name of 'liberating' their co-ethnic Germans, and that the German minority would collaborate with such an invasion.

Today, however, this is essentially a non-issue throughout the established Western democracies with respect to national minorities and indigenous peoples.[7] It is difficult to think of a single Western democracy where the state fears that a national minority would collaborate with a neighbouring enemy and potential aggressor.[8] Part of the reason for this is that Western states do not have neighbouring enemies who might invade them. NATO has been spectacularly successful in removing the possibility of one Western country invading its neighbours. As a result, the question of whether national minorities and indigenous peoples would be loyal in the event of invasion by a neighbouring state has been removed from the table.

Of course, Western democracies do have more long-distance potential enemies – such as Soviet Communism in the past, Islamic fundamentalism today, and perhaps China in some future scenario. But in relation to these long-distance threats, there is no question that national minorities and indigenous peoples are on the same side as the state. If Quebec gains increased powers, or even independence, no one in the rest of Canada worries that Quebec will start collaborating with Al Qaeda or China to overthrow the Canadian state. Quebec nationalists may want to secede from Canada, but an independent Quebec would be an ally of Canada, not an enemy, and would cooperate together with Canada in NATO and other Western defence and security arrangements. Similarly, an independent Scotland would be an ally, not enemy of England; an independent Catalonia would be an ally of Spain, and so on.

This may seem obvious, but it's important to remember that in most parts of the world, minority groups are still seen as fifth column, likely to be working for a neighbouring enemy. This is particularly a concern where the minority is related to a neighbouring state by ethnicity or religion, or where a minority is found on both sides of an international boundary, so that the neighbouring state claims the right to intervene to protect 'its' minority.

Under these conditions, we are likely to witness what political scientists call the 'securitisation' of ethnic relations (for a more extensive discussion of the 'securitisation' of ethnic relations, see Kymlicka 2007, chapters 4, 6). Relations between states and minorities are seen, not as a matter of normal democratic politics to be negotiated and debated, but as a matter of state security, in which the state has to limit the normal democratic process in order to protect the state. Under conditions of securitisation, minority self-organisation may be legally limited (e.g., minority political parties banned), minority leaders may be subject to secret police surveillance, the raising of particular sorts of demands may be illegal (e.g., laws against promoting secession), and so on. Even if minority demands can be voiced, they will be flatly rejected by the larger society and the state. After all, how can groups that are disloyal have any legitimate claims against the state? So the

---

7 Since 9/11, there are security concerns in some Western states about their Muslim immigrants. But there is no comparable concern about their long-standing national minorities or indigenous peoples.

8 If we move beyond the established Western democracies, Cyprus is an obvious case: the Turkish-Cypriot minority is seen by the Greek-Cypriot-dominated state as likely to collaborate with aggression/intervention by Turkey.

securitisation of ethnic relations erodes both the democratic space to voice minority demands, and the likelihood that those demands will be accepted.

In most Western countries, however, ethnic politics have been almost entirely 'de-securitised'. Ethnic politics is just that – normal, day-to-day politics. Relations between the state and minority groups have been taken out of the 'security' box, and put in the 'democratic politics' box.

Liberal-democratic Consensus

A second factor that affects the willingness of states to accept multicultural reforms concerns the security, not of the state, but of individuals who live on the territory of a group claiming self-government. States are unlikely to accept self-government if they fear it will lead to islands of local tyranny within a broader democratic state. In particular, states will not voluntarily grant self-governing powers to non-dominant groups if they fear that members of the dominant group who live on the minority's territory will be dispossessed of their property, fired from their jobs, stripped of their citizenship, or even expelled or killed.

In the established Western democracies, this confidence arises from the existence of a deep consensus across ethnonational lines on basic values of liberal-democracy and human rights. As a result, it is taken for granted that any self-government powers that are granted to national minorities or indigenous peoples will be exercised in accordance with shared standards of democracy and human rights. Everyone accepts that these substate autonomies will operate within the constraints of liberal-democratic constitutionalism, which firmly upholds individual rights. In virtually every case of multination federalism in the West, substate governments are subject to the same constitutional constraints as the central government, and so have no legal capacity to restrict individual freedoms in the name of maintaining cultural authenticity, religious orthodoxy or racial purity.[9] In fact, these basic liberal freedoms and human rights are typically protected at multiple levels: regionally, nationally and internationally.

Not only is it legally impossible for national minorities in the West to establish illiberal regimes, but they have no wish to do so. On the contrary, all of the evidence suggests that members of national minorities are at least as strongly committed to liberal-democratic values as members of dominant groups, if not more so. Indeed, substate autonomies often adopt more progressive policies than those adopted at the central level. Policies on gender equality or gay rights, for example, are more progressive in Scotland than the rest of Britain; more progressive in Quebec than in other parts of Canada; and more progressive in Catalonia than other parts of Spain. Moreover,

---

9 The partial exception concerns Indian tribal governments in the US, which are partially exempted from some provisions of the US Bill of Rights, and this exemption has allowed some tribes to adopt policies that violate liberal norms. But it is worth emphasising that, while many tribal governments defend this partial exemption from the US Bill of Rights, they typically do not object to the idea that their self-government decisions should be subject to international human rights norms and international monitoring. See, on this, Kymlicka 2001, chap. 4.

support for cosmopolitan values is also typically higher in these substate regions than in other parts of the country, including support for foreign aid, or for strengthening the role of the European Court of Human Rights, or other international human rights instruments (for some of the evidence, see Kymlicka 2001, chaps 10–15; Cf. Keating 2002).

This removes one of the central fears that dominant groups have about self-government. In many parts of the world, there is the fear that once national minorities or indigenous peoples acquire self-governing power, they will use it to persecute, dispossess, expel or kill anyone who does not belong to the minority group. In the established Western democracies, however, this is a non-issue. There is no fear that self-governing groups will use their powers to establish islands of tyranny or theocracy. More specifically, there is no fear that members of the dominant group who happen to live on the territory of the self-governing minority will be subject to persecution or expulsion. The human rights of English residents of Scotland are firmly protected, not only by Scottish constitutional law, but also by European law, and this would be true even if Scotland seceded from Britain. The human rights of English-Canadian residents of Quebec, or of Castilian residents of Catalonia, are fully protected, no matter what political status Quebec or Catalonia ends up having.

Where there is a strong consensus across ethnic lines on liberal-democratic values, people feel confident that however issues of multiculturalism are settled, their own basic civil and political rights will be respected. No matter how the claims of ethnonational and indigenous groups are resolved – no matter what language rights, self-government rights, land rights, or multiculturalism policies are adopted – people can rest assured that they won't be stripped of their citizenship, or subject to ethnic cleansing, or jailed without a fair trial, or denied their rights to free speech, association and worship. Put simply, the consensus on liberal-democratic values ensures that debates over accommodating diversity are not a matter of life and death. As a result, dominant groups will not fight to the death to resist minority claims.[10]

This is the flip-side of the human rights revolution I mentioned earlier. On the one hand, the global diffusion of a human rights consciousness has inspired non-dominant groups to resist inherited ethnic and racial hierarchies; on the other hand, it has also given confidence to dominant groups that the resulting multicultural reforms will operate within a framework that firmly protects the basic individual rights and security of all citizens.

In my view, these are five key foundations of the Western trends towards accommodating diversity. Demographics, rights-consciousness and multiple access points for safe political mobilization help to explain why non-dominant groups have

---

10 This is an important issue even in contexts where the dominant group does not itself respect liberal-democratic values and human rights. Indeed, it can be especially important in such contexts. In countries where the dominant group has habitually mistreated minorities, there is likely to be a particularly strong fear that the minority will take revenge on local members of the dominant group once it acquires self-government. (Think about the fate of the Serbs in Kosovo.) In this context, it may be hypocritical for the dominant group to invoke 'human rights' as a grounds for rejecting federalism, but fear about the treatment of their co-ethnics living on the minority's self-governing territory is nonetheless a powerful factor.

become more assertive of multicultural claims; and the desecuritization of ethnic relations and a consensus on human rights help to reduce the risk to dominant groups of accepting these claims. When these five conditions are in place, I believe that the trend towards greater accommodation of ethnocultural diversity is likely to arise. If we consider the recent experience of the Western democracies, these trends have not depended on the presence or absence of particular personalities, or particular political parties, or particular electoral systems. We see enormous variation across the Western democracies in terms of leadership personalities, party platforms and electoral systems. Yet the basic trends regarding diversity are the same, and the explanation, I believe, rests in these five deep sociological facts about numbers, rights-consciousness, opportunity-structures, value-consensus, and geo-political security.[11]

If this is correct, it has implications for the likelihood that these forms of multiculturalism will be adopted around the world. These five factors are strongly present in most Western democracies, but are found very unevenly in the rest of the world. Where they are not present, the adoption and implementation of these policies is likely to remain quite difficult. To oversimplify, I would argue that the three factors that help to explain increased mobilisation by non-domination groups are increasingly found around the world, yet the two factors that help to assuage the fears of dominant groups are not as widely found. There are broad regions of the world where fears about geo-political security and individual security remain pervasive. If so, we are likely to witness a period of serious political turbulence as increasingly mobilised groups raise demands that the state views as high-risk.

Evaluating the Trends

So far, I have been focusing on describing and explaining the global trends towards multiculturalism. But are these trends a good thing? Are they working well? In one sense, it may too early to tell. Many of these changes have happened only in the past 30 years, in some cases only in the past 5–10 years. We do not yet know their long-term consequences.

What has become clear, however, is that the worst fears about multiculturalism have now been disproved. When these reforms were first debated and adopted, there were many people who predicted that they would lead to increasing political instability, the breakdown of political authority, and perhaps even violence. Ominous

---

11 A certain level of economic prosperity may be another precondition. But, if so, it is not because these policies of accommodation are themselves expensive. Federal or decentralised regimes can be just as efficient as unitary and centralised states, and even the costs of bilingualism are much lower than most people think. In any event, it is clear that the resistance of states to these policies usually has nothing to do with their expense: nation-building states have often rejected cultural rights that have no financial cost at all (e.g., allowing privately-funded minority schools). So if a certain level of economic prosperity is a precondition for the successful adoption of these models, it is not because the models themselves are expensive, but because one or more of the other conditions (e.g., democratic consolidation) may have economic prerequisites.

references to 'Balkanisation' were common, as if multiculturalism would lead us into the sorts of conflicts we saw in Kosovo and Bosnia.

In reality, the adoption of multiculturalism in the established Western democracies has not jeopardised the basic stability or functioning of the state. Consider the most basic functions of a liberal-democratic state: e.g., maintaining peace; following democratic procedures; respecting individual freedom; promoting economic growth and prosperity; and ensuring social justice. The adoption of multiculturalism has not jeopardised any of these values, and indeed I would argue it has significantly enhanced some of them. The adoption of multiculturalism has enhanced democracy by increasing political access for non-dominant groups; enhanced individual freedom by enabling cultural choices that had previously been forbidden or stigmatised; and enhanced justice by remedying the unjust effects of inherited racial and ethnic hierarchies (Kymlicka 2007).[12] In some countries, it has almost certainly enhanced peace as well, undercutting potential support for more revolutionary movements within non-dominant groups. And while it would be difficult to prove that multiculturalism in itself promotes economic growth and prosperity,[13] it would be even more implausible to argue that adopting multiculturalism has economically harmed these countries. On the contrary, the Western democracies that have adopted multiculturalism are amongst the most prosperous countries in the world, and the gap between them and the rest of the world has if anything grown over the thirty years of multicultural reforms.

So it's now clear that a multicultural state can be a successful state, upholding all of the basic functions of liberal-democratic governance. We have evidence from a wide range of cases, extending over many years, that the fears raised by critics have been consistently overstated.

This does not mean that the policies are now securely established, safe from backlash and reversal. On the contrary, multiculturalism remains intensely controversial in most Western countries, and the potential for a populist backlash is ever-present. This raises an interesting puzzle. If I'm right that the original fears about multiculturalism have largely been disproved, why are the policies still so controversial?

The answer, I think, relates to misperceptions about the goals and consequences of multiculturalism. Many people, particularly in the dominant group, had the hope and expectation that adopting multiculturalism policies would lead to a reduction in ethnic political mobilisation, and a return to 'normal' politics in which ethnicity is absent. People recognised that there was a particular 'ethnic problem' that needed to be addressed, but they hoped that adopting multiculturalism policies would resolve

---

12 Some people worry that multiculturalism has an ambiguous effect on social justice, reducing cultural injustices rooted in a status hierarchy, but distracting attention from issues of economic injustice rooted in the class hierarchy. This is often discussed as the 'recognition vs redistribution' trade-off. However, there is in fact no empirical evidence that the former erodes the latter. For detailed discussion, see Banting and Kymlicka 2006.

13 However, see the recent UN Human Development Report (2004), 'Cultural Liberty in Today's Diverse World' for the claim that multiculturalism is indeed conducive to economic development.

the problem, and ethnic mobilisation would then disappear. On this view, ethnic politics is 'abnormal' – a kind of pathology – and the success of multiculturalism policies is measured by how well they reduce it.

Insofar as members of the dominant group had this view, they have been sorely disappointed in multiculturalism. For it is clear that adopting multiculturalism rarely if ever leads to a reduction in ethnic political mobilisation. On the contrary, multiculturalism policies typically lead to an increase in ethnic politics. These policies enhance the capacity of non-dominant groups to mobilise, increase their access to the state, and implicitly legitimise their claims. In this sense, multiculturalism policies tend to institutionalise ethnic politics.

As it has become clear that ethnic politics will not diminish, there have been growing feelings of resentment and frustration on the part of many members of the dominant group. Minority groups have become perceived as ungrateful, selfish, and impossible to satisfy. Members of the dominant group start to think: 'Nothing we do will ever satisfy these groups, so why bother even trying to accommodate their claims? Whatever demands we accept today, they will just come back tomorrow and demand more.'

This is a paradox of multiculturalism as it is practiced in the established Western democracies. There is broad public acceptance of the idea of a multicultural state, but not broad acceptance of ethnic politics. Yet ethnic political mobilisation and a multicultural state are inseparable. The former sustains, and is sustained by, the latter. This suggests that the long-term success of multiculturalism requires changing people's views, not only about the nature of the state, but also about the nature of democratic politics. We need to understand that ethnic politics is 'normal' democratic politics. In multiethnic, multilingual and multinational states, ethnic political mobilisation should be expected as a normal and healthy part of everyday political life in a free and democratic society.

References

Banting, K. and Kymlicka, W. (eds) (2006), *Multiculturalism and the Welfare State*. Oxford: Oxford University Press.
Glazer, N. (1997), *We Are All Multiculturalists Now*, Cambridge, Massachusetts: Harvard University Press.
Keating, M. (2002), *Plurinational Democracies*, Oxford: Oxford University Press.
Kymlicka, W. (2001), *Politics in the Vernacular*, Oxford: Oxford University Press.
Kymlicka, W. (2007), Multicultural Odysseys: *Navigating the New International Politics of Diversity*. Oxford: Oxford University Press.
Walzer, M. (1983), *Spheres of Justice*, New York: Basic Books.

Chapter 3

Towards a Hybrid Theory of Multinational Justice

Helder De Schutter

How should we respond politically to the cultural diversity generated by the existence of more than one nation within a state? This is the question I will address in this chapter.

Two rough answers may in general be given to this question. The first argues that people who are united by a common national membership are entitled to self-government rights (or rights to self-determination).[1] These should enable national groups to politically and territorially secure their national boundaries so that they can collectively decide their own affairs in distinct units.

The second answer rejects the idea of granting self-government rights to national groups. This view argues that no political or territorial autonomy should be granted to sub-state groups. We should instead create or maintain one political community for all the individuals within the state, regardless of their cultural affiliation.

To examine this debate, I will critically engage with a nowadays widespread and prominent view that sets out to defend a version of the first answer to the question. This is the paradigm of *liberal nationalism*, developed by a recently formed group of political theorists, including Chaim Gans, Will Kymlicka, David Miller, Margaret Moore and Yael Tamir. Liberal nationalists are essentially committed to the belief that liberalism is compatible with a defence of the principle of nationality, which states that it is valuable for the boundaries of political units to coincide with national boundaries (see Miller 1995, 82).[2]

---

1   The literature does not clearly distinguish the difference between self-government and self-determination, though self-determination is more often used in the context of secession. Caney (1998, 152) distinguishes a strong from a weak version of self-determination: the strong version insists on secession, whereas the weaker 'requires only that a nation be given some form of self-government.' In this chapter I engage with the normative debates over the weak version, but to avoid misunderstandings, I will restrict my terminology to self-government rights only.

2   This way of phrasing the principle of nationality is partly derived from David Miller, who has defined it as follows: 'it is valuable for the boundaries of political units (paradigmatically, states) to coincide with national boundaries' (Miller 1995, 82). Here I omit the insertion '(paradigmatically, states)', since it is contested among liberal nationalists like Chaim Gans (2003, chapters 1 and 3) and Will Kymlicka (1995, 73, 186), with regard to both the assimilationist and the secessionist conclusions that could follow from it.

Liberal nationalists have brought a variety of arguments to the defence of this principle. Some have argued that the principle of nationality is worthwhile because it is conducive to social justice (Miller 1995). Others have stressed the importance of a common nationality and language for a genuine democracy (Kymlicka 2001a, 203–220; Moore 2001). Here I will concentrate on possibly the most crucial argument, which I will term the 'cultural membership argument'. This argument bases the case for national self-government rights on the value people attach to membership in their own national culture. More specifically, it is argued that, because national membership is a precondition for (the fulfilment of the liberal ideal of) individual autonomy or freedom, therefore national groups should be granted the right to self-government within distinct national units.

We can subdivide this argument into two theses: one about the *value* of cultural membership, the other about the *unit* of cultural membership. The first thesis states that individuals are culturally embedded beings, who are in need of a freedom-enabling cultural context of choice. Therefore, liberal nationalists argue, granting rights to enable groups to maintain their own cultural context is compatible with (or, in stronger versions, required by) the pursuit of the liberal goal of enabling individual freedom. Here the liberal nationalists stand opposed to those who would want to defend an instrumental or unembedded view that understands cultures (and languages) to be nothing more than private associations of individuals, analogous to sports clubs. This 'traditional liberal' answer typically pleads for a separation between culture and state along the lines set out for dealing with religious diversity.

The second thesis argues that the cultural context of choice that is relevant to individuals is the nation. Liberal nationalists claim that we should grant nations the right to maintain themselves as distinct societies, since the cultural membership that is argued to be valuable to individuals is national in nature. This thesis may be contrasted with a different understanding of the relevant unit of cultural membership, which stresses the inherent fluidity and hybridity of people's cultural frame of reference. This 'hybridity'-view argues that groups are not sharply delineated but fluid and that people have multiple and intermingling identities. Consequently, we should not treat cultures as distinct and autonomous but as fluid and intermingling entities.

Borrowing a famous metaphor from Ernest Gellner (1983, 139–140), we might characterise this second discussion as one between adherents of a mosaic *Modigliani*-way of perceiving our world, where stable boundaries mark off sharply delineated and transparent cultural and linguistic surfaces, versus those who understand cultures and cultural diversity to be structured more like in a *Kokoschka*-painting, with many complex relations between individual units in a very opaque landscape with fluid boundaries.

It seems to me that the liberal nationalist case stands on much firmer ground when arguing in favour of the freedom-enabling function of culture than when adhering to a Modigliani-view of the world. The world we inhabit is imbued with multiculturalism, multilingualism, and cultural opacity. It is always characterised by vague boundaries, cultural overlap, grey zones, diglossia, minorities within minorities, etc. So, the cultural landscape we are dealing with is often much more complex than a nationalist Modigliani-view suggests. Basing a normative theory on an empirical understanding of cultures as sharply delineated, monolingual and mononational entities is therefore misguided. This hybridity view further suggests that there is no reason to normatively assume that people's relevant context of choice is strictly uninational. People may be members of two national contexts of choice at once, or they may identify with contexts of choice larger (or smaller) than nations.

In this chapter, I would like to contribute to the development of such a hybrid theory of (multi)national justice. Interestingly, however, those views that equally want to defend, like I do, the importance of cultural hybridity tend to be very reluctant towards the idea of cultural recognition and protection (see, amongst others, Johnson 2000; Kukathas 2003; Laitin and Reich 2003 and Waldron 1995). They are opposed to the first answer to the question I started with above and often defend the second. I think this is an unfortunate fact, which is frequently instigated by a denial of the importance of cultural membership, or by a false belief in the possibility of remaining politically neutral to cultures (see also Kymlicka 2001a, 43 and Tamir 1993, 145–150 for a critique of this neutrality-belief).

I believe there is a more convincing way to draw normative conclusions from the awareness of cultural hybridity. In this chapter, I will develop an argument that, on the one hand, establishes the morally relevant importance of cultural membership and the correlating case for granting rights to national groups but, on the other hand, denies the desirability of concluding from this that granting territorial autonomy in distinct, mononational units is necessarily the best and only way to do justice to people's cultural embeddedness. The argument thus cuts through the distinction between a (mono)nationalist theory of cultural protection and a fluid hybridity theory allergic to the idea of group-differentiated measures.

Though the cultural membership argument seems to be shared by many, if not all, liberal nationalists (see Gans 2003; Kymlicka 1995; Margalit and Raz 1990; Miller 1995; Tamir 1993), here I will concentrate on one paradigmatic account of it, the one developed by Will Kymlicka, for whom the argument belongs to the heart of his theory.

To do this, in the first section of the chapter I will give a short summary of Kymlicka's account of this argument and its place in his larger theory of minority rights. I will subsequently analyse and evaluate the argument in two steps. A first step considers the value of cultural membership. I will argue that the merit of the freedom-argument of Will Kymlicka's theory of liberal nationalism is that it succeeds in establishing that people are constitutively embedded in cultural contexts of choice, as well as in showing why this fact justifies minority rights in the domains of language and culture. In a second step, I will focus on the concept of culture itself that forms the unit within which membership is found to be valuable by Kymlicka. Here I will argue that his theory neglects hybrid contexts of choice and unduly prioritises monolingual and mononational forms of cultural embeddedness. But in developing this criticism I do not intend to deny the issue of constitutive embeddedness nor the issue of the justice of granting minority rights to national groups. I will try to show this in the last part of the chapter, which deals explicitly with the compatibility of endorsing constitutive embeddedness and criticising monocultural contexts of choice.

There are two issues I will not discuss. The first is the case of immigrants. A discussion of immigration and the rights to which immigrants are entitled no doubt forms an essential part of a fully-fledged theory of multicultural justice, but including immigration in this debate would intensify the difficulty of the subject to an enormous extent. I therefore leave this issue for later discussion.[3] For a similar reason I will also not address the problems posed by the existence of illiberal nations. Consequently, the sorts of groups I will focus on are liberal national groups, such as the Catalans, the Flemish or the Québécois.

Kymlicka's Liberal Nationalism

Kymlicka starts with the observation that the idea of remaining politically neutral towards cultures is impossible:

> I think this common view is not only mistaken, but actually incoherent. The idea of responding to cultural differences with 'benign neglect' makes no sense. Government decisions on languages, internal boundaries, public holidays, and state symbols unavoidably involve recognizing, accommodating, and supporting the needs and identities of particular ethnic and national groups. (Kymlicka 1995, 108)

The implication of this is that we cannot but intervene in the cultural marketplace.

The just alternative to this idea of ethnocultural neutrality, Kymlicka argues, is a policy of granting minority rights. Kymlicka believes that self-government rights are the minority rights to which national groups are entitled.[4] The justification for this consists of two steps. The first is based on an ontological view of the subject, the second on an interpretation of the ideal of equality.

In the first step, Kymlicka emphasises the role played by cultural membership in promoting individual freedom or autonomy. If liberals are (and Kymlicka believes they should be) concerned with safeguarding and enabling individual freedom, he claims, they should be aware of its preconditions. Kymlicka argues that membership in a cultural community is a crucial precondition of individual freedom. To be autonomous beings, individuals need a cultural background that makes available various options. 'Put simply, freedom involves making choices amongst various options, and our societal culture not only provides these options, but also makes them meaningful to us' (Kymlicka 1995, 83). Our culture thus offers us a 'context of choice'.

Kymlicka understands the relevant context of choice for individuals to be a *societal culture*, which 'provides its members with meaningful ways of life across the full range of human activities, including social, educational, religious, recreational and economic life, encompassing both public and private spheres' (Kymlicka 1995,

---

3   See Patten (2001) for a similar way of proceeding.

4   Kymlicka's theory is larger than this account of it emphasises. It also provides a justification of minority rights for immigrants, which Kymlicka argues should take the form of 'polyethnic rights' to be distinguished from the further-reaching self-government rights for national groups, on which I focus here.

76). Societal cultures tend to be territorially concentrated and based on a shared language.

The liberalism Kymlicka endorses not only rests on the value of individual autonomy, but is also based on a commitment to equality of opportunity. Egalitarian liberals claim that morally arbitrary inequalities should be rectified. Following Dworkin's normative advice to be sensitive towards choice but insensitive towards endowments, Kymlicka maintains that, in addition to redressing social and natural inequalities, a just policy should also compensate those who suffer from (unchosen) *cultural* inequalities.

The conclusion of Kymlicka's argument is that, as the cultural inequality that arises when a national minority is not able to provide its members with their own context of choice cannot be avoided by remaining neutral with regard to cultures, group-differentiated rights are justified. The just remedy for cultural inequality is to grant the minority a right to its own culture. Self-government rights are then justified as a means of enabling national minorities to maintain their own societal culture.

Embedded Freedom

We can subdivide Kymlicka's freedom-argument into two theses: one about what it means to have a culture and one about the concept of culture itself. The first states that cultures provide individuals with contexts of choice that enable the liberal ideal of freedom. The second argues that the relevant contexts of choice are societal cultures. I postpone the analysis of the second thesis to the next paragraph and I will now set out to explain the first and defend it against some of its main opponents.

The freedom-argument Kymlicka and the liberal nationalists put forward contains a particular ontological view of the subject. It stresses the fact that humans are culturally embedded beings whose embeddedness is a constitutive feature of their identity. This is easiest to explain within the domain of language and the debates over linguistic justice, since in that field most of us are already committed to accept this view.

I think it is possible to relate many contemporary language policy approaches back to two different ways of understanding our embeddedness within a language, more specifically an instrumental versus a constitutive understanding. This is not a new distinction – I borrow it, in part, from Charles Taylor who has used it as a frame for the analysis of modern language theories (see Taylor 1995, chapters 5–7, 9). To put it very briefly: many early modern theories of language have focused on its function of communicating thought. Language was believed to be a collection of words that we can use as tools to name objects or thoughts. This representational point of view has received severe criticism, especially since Romanticism. People like Herder and Fichte have instead replaced instrumentalism with expressivism, i.e., the idea that language expresses or articulates things that we could not have without having language. Words are not tools that make available what we already have (ideas or feelings). Language brings a whole range of human feelings and ideas into existence. Language therefore constitutes our selves.

I believe this distinction can be employed for the analysis of contemporary debates over language policy. Take, for instance, the linguistic underpinnings of the critique of multiculturalism developed by Brian Barry. Barry thinks a just policy in a multicultural society should not grant special rights to minorities but simply implies a policy of political neutrality towards cultures: there should be a sharp separation of state and culture, in a way that is analogous to the separation between church and state. Yet, Barry concedes that remaining politically neutral vis-à-vis *language* is impossible: the state must provide its services in one or more particular languages; a-linguistic policies are simply inconceivable. But Barry hastens to add that 'it can be said of language as of no other cultural trait that it is a matter of convention' (Barry 2001, 107). Language belongs to the category of things of which we can just say: 'This is how we do things here' (Barry 2001, 107). In short, our language is not a constitutive aspect of our identity; it is just a 'local convention'.

Barry's understanding of the nature of our linguistic embeddedness is thus very instrumental. For him, language is essentially an arbitrary set of customs, a tool for communication. Consequently, when the goal of communication is impeded by the presence of linguistic diversity, then we are facing a genuine conflict. Therefore, 'democratic states that still have an open future [with regard to the development of distinct linguistic communities] have every reason for pursuing the course that leads to a linguistically homogeneous polity' (Barry 2001, 228). Barry also argues that it has to be recognised that compulsory instruction in Welsh in schools reduces the time students might devote to learning a major foreign language, that may be of greater practical use (Barry 2001, 106–107).

Barry's language policy approach of linguistic homogenisation is grounded in an underlying instrumental ontology of the nature of linguistic membership. This instrumental ontology primarily understands people's linguistic embeddedness as an external and arbitrary circumstance, like pictographic conventions in traffic signs. Language is nothing more than a practical agreement between beings whose linguisticality is merely accidental to their subjectivity. Language is thus one of the many devices that we have at hand but that do not constitute ourselves. Language is external, not intrinsic to our nature.

The discussion between instrumentalism and constitutivism may be clear now in the domain of language: you treat language as a mere instrument; or you understand it as having a more constitutive bearing on your identity. This distinction may also guide our understanding of non-linguistic cultural issues. But in that domain, a somewhat different distinction comes into play between a culturally-mediated versus an a-cultural view of choice. Following Dworkin and Kymlicka (Kymlicka 1995, 83; 2001a, 210), we can say that culture and language provide us not only with options but also with the spectacles through which we identify options as valuable. Language and culture can thus be seen as the media through which the individual preferences we have can be experienced as meaningful. Now, what is under dispute in the instrumental/constitutive discussion in the domain of language is not so much the idea that language is a pair of spectacles, a medium, even the instrumental side assumes that. The language policy debate focuses rather on the importance of *particular* languages, the question *which* spectacles we should give to people.

But this medium-view is not at all so clear from the start in the field of culture. And indeed, it turns out that Brian Barry is not willing to accept it. Barry seems to abstract from cultural media by ontologically and morally equating choices made on the basis of a cultural prescription with purely individual choices. Take, for instance, his view with regard to requests for exemptions from laws on the basis of cultural claims. According to Barry, the law that obliges every motorcyclist to wear a crash helmet does not discriminate against Sikhs who wear turbans for religious reasons, since the law does not forbid Sikhs to ride motorcycles; it only says that anyone who rides a motorcycle must wear a helmet. In this case, only the Sikhs' desire not to wear a helmet is relevant. The law does not restrict religious freedom; it only prohibits riding a motorcycle without a crash helmet. A Sikh's desire not to ride a motorcycle is in this sense comparable to a Muslim's wish to stop eating meat, given the prohibition of ritual slaughter. Both the Sikh's and the Muslim's preferences in these cases are instances of an 'expensive taste'. As Barry puts it,

> [W]e must insist on the crucial difference between a denial of equal opportunities to some group (for example, a law forbidding Sikhs to ride motorcycles) and a choice some people make out of that from a set of equal opportunities (for example, a choice not to ride a motorcycle) as a result of certain beliefs. (Barry 2001, 45)

I think this makes clear how Barry understands the relation between individuals and their cultural background. Cultural (and religious) beliefs are conceived by him as individual preferences because culture belongs to the private sphere. Wearing a turban is an individual choice resulting from an individual belief. The fact that culture is involved here is morally irrelevant. One might as well carry a hat. Carrying a hat can also be a choice as a result of a belief (for instance, that carrying hats is fashionable or that people carrying hats have benign personalities). In sum, cultures and religions are treated here as voluntary individual associations.

This underlying view of cultural membership in this paradigm is very different from Kymlicka's. But, interestingly, both Kymlicka and Barry converge on their egalitarian commitment: both support the rectification of unchosen disadvantages. Kymlicka, however, believes that belonging to a minority culture is disadvantageous in the same way as physical disability is, and that it has to be compensated for by the consolidation of the minority culture into a societal culture. This contrasts with Barry, who refuses to understand membership of a minority culture as an unchosen inequality. This is because he rejects the idea of constitutive cultural embeddedness.

Barry's cultural privatisation strategy thus holds a strict separation between the private and the public and relegates each instance of cultural affiliation or membership to the private sphere. As a result, he cannot differentiate the wish to wear a turban or a headscarf as a means of complying with a religious requirement from an individual preference for wearing hats because hats are beautiful. He admits that this view is more difficult to maintain with regard to languages, where he is inclined to accept the medium-view. But, then, he argues, languages can ultimately be understood as mere conventions, so that here again, the privatisation strategy is saved.

This is different from Kymlicka's liberal nationalist view. Instead of reducing culturally mediated choices to mere individual preferences, Kymlicka holds the medium-view and stresses the constitutivity of the embedding medium, the fact that my culture and language are not merely instrumental conventions to me.[5] His theory is based on an underlying embedded understanding of the value of cultural membership that conveys the idea that cultures are constitutive media or 'spectacles' through which we acquire freedom.

How should we evaluate this debate between these constitutive/mediating and instrumental/privatising views?[6] I believe that a theory of multinational justice should treat cultural membership as a constitutive and mediated issue and I would like to argue that the instrumental view is indefensible.

To start with, it should be stressed that the constitutive view seems to be much closer to how people experience their cultural membership. We tend to understand our language as something that is *not* external to us, something that we can*not* easily dispose of. We are linguistically embodied beings. An essential characteristic of an instrument is its replaceability: an instrument or a tool can be replaced the moment a better tool has been developed. Yet, many people feel deeply attached to their native tongues and would feel humiliated were they to be asked to simply leave their

---

5 At least, Kymlicka should argue that. Kymlicka's original defence of minority rights was somewhat ambiguous about this issue and he has been criticised for endorsing a too instrumental understanding of cultural embeddedness. In this respect, Margalit and Halbertal (1994) have argued that Kymlicka's understanding of culture as a precondition for individual freedom can only justify a right to culture, not a right to a particular culture. They argue that if a minority culture would be destroyed by the presence of a larger majority culture and if the members of the culture have the opportunity to assimilate (against their will), Kymlicka cannot object since their new culture can equally function as a context for individual choice. But this is not Kymlicka's intention and he has later corrected this ambiguity, arguing that identity-considerations provide a basis for specifying which culture will provide the relevant context for autonomy (Kymlicka 2001a, 55, n. 7).

6 Note that the distinction between instrumental and constitutive ideologies is not equivalent to the one between instrumental and intrinsic approaches, as invoked by Albert Musschenga (1998), and by Kymlicka (2001a: 62). In fact, the first distinction is about the ontological nature of cultural membership and the moral treatment of linguistic and cultural diversity, while the second concerns the moral *justification* for cultural policies. Musschenga attributes intrinsic value to languages and cultures, by claiming that they are morally valuable in themselves, apart from the value members attach to them. This intrinsic argument stands opposed to instrumental accounts, like Kymlicka's theory, which consider only the individual to be the bearer of rights. Musschenga criticises this instrumental point of view for the limited protection of languages and cultures it can justify: it can only protect cultures as far as they are valuable to individuals. The vast majority of existing political theories of multicultural justice, however, reject the idea of intrinsic value. In fact, both the instrumental and the constitutive ideologies discussed in this text seem to relate cultural policies back to an underlying view of cultural membership, and thereby already assume that cultures are there for the benefit of speakers. Typically, however, proponents of the intrinsic argument will side with the constitutive stance, in resolving the apparent problem that preserving cultures might be opposed to individual interests by claiming that individuals have intrinsic interests in their culture.

original language behind in order to linguistically assimilate, be it with 'just another convention'. If the instrumental picture were true, then it would be very hard to explain why multiculturalism is a complex problem in our contemporary world, and why many communities engage in conflicts over the justice of existing cultural and linguistic policies.

Barry's instrumental view of linguistic membership can also not account for the fact that many people are willing to forego wider opportunities in order to be able to live and grow up in their own linguistic environment – take, for instance, the case of parents who wish to educate their children in their original language when raising them in a majority language would open more opportunities.[7]

Above all, the instrumental or unmediated view neglects the fact that many people derive intrinsic value from membership in their cultural community and from being able to communicate, participate and live in their own cultural context. Whereas the instrumental view only looks at a-cultural ends (such as opportunity maximation, in Barry's case), the pursuit of which is taken to be the only legitimate justification for a just policy, we should realise that people also have cultural interests. Apart from communicative or opportunity-related interests, most people have an intrinsic interest in using their own language (see Réaume 2003, 283), and there is no reason to declare this interest illegitimate.

Now, of course, we can expect that people will differ with regard to their cultural embeddedness. A (small) number of people may experience their cultural membership as a mere conventional or external issue. They may claim that their cultural membership is not a constitutive characteristic of who they are. Why don't we take their view of cultural membership into consideration? Why should we base our theory of justice on the constitutive side? In short, why can't we just refrain from making cultural choices at all?

Two answers can be given in reply to these charges. The first is that we cannot avoid making a choice. Remaining politically neutral with regard to the issue of instrumentality versus constitutivity is impossible. Either we allow minorities to claim minority rights (say, the right to have educational systems in their mother-tongue) on the basis of their constitutive embeddedness, or we don't, arguing that the constitutive view is wrong, or unreasonable. No theory of justice can avoid taking at least some understandings of 'facts of the world' as given (see Levy 2000, 3–5). This seems to be one of those facts.

The only way to realistically defend the idea not to make a choice would be through designing a sort of 'anything goes' cultural policy, which accepts the fact that the state is inevitably culturally permeated but pretends that this is not problematic.

---

7   A useful way to illustrate this is by means of the thought experiment of the assimilation machine, developed by the Dutch philosopher Bart van Leeuwen (2003). Imagine that we have a machine at our disposal that performs surgeries on people that transform all their cultural and linguistic customs, values, constitutions and attachments from one to another language and culture. Even if we would limit the impact of the surgery to our linguistic nature (thereby leaving cultural issues unaffected), it is very likely that most people would not be willing to enter the machine, and, even more, that requiring immigrants to enter it would strike us as morally objectionable.

This seems to be the view of, amongst others, Johnson (2000) and Laitin and Reich (2003). This view wishes to take issues of linguistic and cultural membership out of the realm of normative reasoning. It sees the interest people have in their own culture as a legitimate interest, the pursuit and protection of which may be a legitimate aim for politics but should not be taken as an ideal of justice. This approach views the resolution of cultural issues and struggles as the proper subject of the democratic arena, in which every citizen has the right to mobilise support for (the recognition of) their particular cultural identities.

But this only seems possible by giving up the ideal of equality. Leaving all issues of culture and language to the democratic struggle in which proponents of majority cultures will confront cultural minority leaders offers no guarantee that the decision that will be taken at the end of the discussion will be just. Normative advice is particularly relevant where conflicts between majorities and minorities are at stake, since leaving minorities to the democratic arena makes them vulnerable to the risk of being outvoted.[8]

Secondly, given that the idea of cultural neutrality is an illusion and that an anything-goes policy is undesirable, we are left with the obligation to make a choice. And if we need to pick a standard case, it seems to me that choosing the constitutive side is the more just option. It is true that a small number of people are inclined to take an unmediated point of view to their cultural membership and are, consequently, willing to forego the advantages of staying or keeping their own language and culture. And there is every reason to argue that they should not be pressed, against their own will, to maintain their language and culture. But that is not how most people experience their membership. As Kymlicka puts it,

> For the purposes of determining people's claims of justice, material resources are something that people can be assumed to want, whatever their particular conception of the good. Although a small number of people may choose to forgo non-subsistence resources, this is seen as forgoing something to which they are entitled. Similarly, I believe that, in developing a theory of justice, we should treat access to one's culture as something that people can be expected to want, whatever their more particular conception of the good. Leaving one's culture, while possible, is best seen as renouncing something to which one is reasonably entitled. (Kymlicka 1995, 86)

To conclude, in this section I have argued that the ontological basis of Kymlicka's freedom-argument provides an accurate and successful background for the development of a just theory of cultural diversity. Such a theory will justify the idea of minority rights as a remedy for the injustice that arises when minorities are forced to live their life in the culture and language of majorities, who happen to possess the prerogatives of cultural power. Granting minority rights can thus be seen as a due recognition of people's constitutive embodiment.

---

8 In an 'anything goes' struggle between instrumentalists and constitutivists, the constitutive option may be expected to lose. The reason for this is that, interestingly, culturally unthreatened majorities are more likely to appeal to the instrumentalist view whereas minorities tend to base their claims on a constitutive understanding of their language and culture.

Hybridity

In the previous section I considered how Kymlicka's liberal nationalism understands the way in which we are embedded in culture. In this section, I analyse the concept of culture itself that underlies the freedom-argument, that is, the entity *wherein* we are embedded.[9]

Kymlicka starts from the assumption that we are embedded in nations, which he refers to as *societal cultures*. It is the *national* culture that provides the cultural spectacles that make our life choices and options meaningful to us. Protecting individual freedom thus implies protecting national groups, since national groups enable individual choice and support self-identity.

Kymlicka understands nations/societal cultures to be territorially concentrated, more or less constitutionally complete communities, sharing a distinct language and history. Justice entails giving each national group self-government rights in order to enable its members to maintain their own national context of choice. These national groups thus get linguistic, territorial and political autonomy. In the end, 'territorially bounded national communities will, and indeed should, continue to serve as the primary locus for the exercise of collective autonomy and self-government' (Kymlicka 2001b, 270). This allows him to conclude that, amid other things, we should (re)draw political boundaries in a multinational state in such a way as to make political and territorial boundaries overlap with cultural and linguistic ones (Kymlicka 1995, 71, 112–113; 2001a, 75, 110; 2001b).

It seems to me that this argument has several shortcomings. Before identifying these and going more deeply into them, I first describe three categories of cases in which the application of Kymlicka's theory would have undesirable consequences or where the normative conclusions of the theory are particularly unhelpful. The first and most evident situation where Kymlicka's argument runs into difficulties is in cases of territorial mixing. What if national communities are *not* territorially concentrated? What if redrawing boundaries is not an option as a result of the high level of cultural diversity within a territory? Take for instance those conflicts where two groups lay claim to the same land. This is illustrated by claims put forward by Aborigines that the government owns land that has unjustly been taken from them (see Kukathas 1997, 423), but also by what lies at the heart of, amongst many others, the conflicts in Jerusalem, Kosovo, and, to a less excessive extent, Brussels. Or take ethnodemographically heterogeneous and culturally intermixed situations where there is no mosaic of distinct and territorially-concentrated cultural blocs but rather a hybridity of cultural contacts, such as in, among many others, cities like Brussels or Bloemfontein (Prinsloo 1999), Latvian cities where both Russian and Latvian are spoken (Stepan 1998, 224), Romanian regions with intermingling Hungarian and Romanian groups (see Brubaker 2002), or many African countries, where cultural contacts have generated a vastly complex and intermingling cultural diversity.

Secondly, Kymlicka assumes that societal cultures are the cultures of territorially concentrated, monolingual members of mononational groups. He never considers the

---

9 In parts of this and the next section I rework ideas that I have outlined in De Schutter (2005).

idea that two groups who live on the same territory may in due time develop a sort of common loyalty and identity and even a (partly) shared context of choice. Kymlicka thus tends to homogenise national cultures through a rather dubious bottleneck. As a result he defines away multicultural societal cultures which derive their context of choice from more than one cultural background.[10]

A third case that makes Kymlicka's theory difficult to sustain is the fact of biculturality. Kymlicka's theory results in a certain neglect of those who find themselves in a hybrid cultural situation, such as bicultural bilinguals who do not consider themselves to be rooted predominantly in one group or another. Unlike the second case, here individuals derive their relevant cultural embeddedness not from one mixed cultural context of choice but from two different cultural contexts. There is no mention in Kymlicka of the mere possibility that people might experience membership in two societal cultures. Yet, if the right to culture is granted because of the value of cultures for individuals then it is difficult to see why we should confine the relevant subjects of self-government rights to monolingual and mononational cultures.

The overlapping identities that exist in many multinational states form another kind of biculturality. Kymlicka seems to believe that all members of a national group are united in the identical way they adhere to their context of choice. He attributes a shared cultural identity (membership of a distinct societal culture) to all the members of a certain group, and then bases his normative political conclusion on this identity.

But this may be an over-simplification. Several studies of the unit of national identity people refer to in multinational states point to the fact that many people identify with both the state as well as the sub-state as the context of their identity. Take for instance the Belgian state (but I believe that very similar remarks can be made in the case of Spain, see Moreno 2001, 112–126, and Canada, see Mendelsohn 2002). Kymlicka argues that in multinational states like Belgium and Canada, citizens share citizenship but not a national identity. For instance, he understands most people in Flanders to have Belgian citizenship but a Flemish national identity (Kymlicka 2001b, 256). In other words, their constitutive context of choice is not Belgium but Flanders, which then explains why Flanders is entitled to receive self-government rights in order to provide its members with their own context of choice. However, when probed for their national identity feelings, 42.2% of Flemish respondents in a 1999 survey answered that they self-identify as much with Flanders as with Belgium, whereas only 7% answered to be 'only Flemish' and 22.4% 'more Flemish than Belgian' (Meersseman, Billiet and Depickere 2002, 20–21). And in a research into the national identities of Belgian citizens (based on 1991 and 1995 data), the researchers conclude that, throughout the whole of Belgium, citizens experience a 'dual national identity', and that in Flanders, the strength of both national identities (Belgian *and* Flemish) are in balance (Maddens, Billiet and Beerten 1999). Thus, it is certainly highly questionable to understand people in Flanders to collectively refer to Flanders instead of Belgium as the unit of their national identity. Even more,

---

10 The importance of multicultural contexts of choice, and Kymlicka's neglect of them, have been highlighted by Joseph Carens (2000, chapter 3).

when pressed to make a choice between Flanders and Belgium as the relevant source of national identity, more people in Flanders opt for Belgium than for Flanders (Maddens, Billiet and Beerten 1999). In other words, there is much less intra-group homogeneity with regard to cultural issues than Kymlicka assumes. Kymlicka's view is problematic for more than this reason alone. It seems to result in a general inability to offer a normative grounding of multinational federations. Kymlicka can offer a reason why nations are entitled to minority rights, but he seems unable to argue, on cultural grounds, why a multinational state is preferable to granting each nation a state of its own (see Kymlicka 2001a, 93–94).

I believe the reason for the inability of Kymlicka's normative conclusions to accommodate these three cases can be located in his view of the unit of cultural embeddedness that lies at the core of this theory. It seems to me that his theory is grounded in an unrealistically homogeneous and monocultural concept of language and culture.

To see this, we should take a closer look at this concept. The unit within which Kymlicka thinks people are constitutively embedded is the nation, understood in a specific sense. Kymlicka is searching for a sort of outlook that might emphasise people's national embeddedness but that would at the same time prevent him from opening a communitarian box of Pandora. The solution he comes up with is the idea of a societal culture. We can understand a societal culture as the cultural structure (a term he later rejects, see Kymlicka 1989, 165 versus Kymlicka 1995, 83), which might be contrasted with the values or customs of a culture (Kymlicka 1989, 165–167).

> I call it a *societal* culture in order to emphasize that it involves a common language and social institutions, rather than common religious beliefs, family customs, or personal lifestyles. Societal cultures within a modern liberal democracy are inevitably pluralistic. (…) This diversity, however, is balanced and constrained by linguistic and institutional cohesion. (Kymlicka 2001a, 25)

Kymlicka's rejection of the ideal of ethnocultural neutrality does not amount to a rejection of the ideal of state neutrality with regard to diverse conceptions of the good. Consequently, he believes it is a natural state of affairs if the *character* of a culture changes as a result of choices made by its members, who have the freedom to choose their own way of life and, consequently, to question their beliefs (and those of the culture to which they belong). Therefore, Kymlicka's theory legitimates the protection of the cultural *context* of choice (i.e., the existence of culture or culture as a vehicle or structure), but strongly disapproves of publicly regulating the *content* or the character of culture (Kymlicka 1995, 35–44, 104–105).

So, far from postulating the homogeneity of the *character*, the *content* of culture, Kymlicka provides ample room for cultural pluralism and content-based cultural variety. But this liberal solution comes at a certain price. Since he understands cultures to be inherently pluralistic, the only way left open to save the idea of granting minorities the right to a separate culture is to draw a distinction between, on the one hand, the content, which is supposed to be pluralistic, and, on the other hand, the form of culture, the vehicle which contains the content, the existence of a culture itself, which is then supposed to be clear and transparent. That is why Kymlicka can say that societal cultures are 'inevitably pluralistic' while still attributing substance and cohesion to them.

It seems to me that this argument is vulnerable to two sorts of objections. The first concerns the neglect of units of embeddedness other than the nation, the second questions Kymlicka's characterization of the nation itself. The first objection states that, in choosing the concept of a societal culture as the empirical starting-point for a theory of multicultural justice, Kymlicka unduly restricts the form of culture within which people are constitutively embedded. Kymlicka takes for granted that we are embedded in monolingual, monocultural and territorially concentrated contexts of choice. But why should this be the case? Why does Kymlicka decide that the culture of the Belgian people who live in Flanders is Flemish and not Belgian? Why is it even not taken into consideration that people might experience the freedom-enabling dimension of culture in cultures larger than their immediate surroundings? People increasingly tend to identify with ever larger constellations: they do refer to the state alongside their embeddedness in sub-state regions; and we can imagine that the present globalisation of cultural contacts might generate a sense of cosmopolitan identity and citizenship.[11] So, there is no reason to believe that people can only take their necessary cultural context of choice from the nation.

Nor is there any reason to believe that people can only be embedded in one cultural context of choice at once. It is not clear why my sense of global cultural membership would overrule or preclude my national identity. It seems perfectly possible to assume both identities at once and we can imagine that both may provide cultural contexts of choice. This is also what people indicate when they report dual forms of national identity, referring both to their sub-state nation as well as to the larger 'multinational' federation. In short, contexts of choice may be larger (or smaller) than the nation and people may be members of more than one context at once.

The second but related objection zooms in on Kymlicka's rather idiosyncratic understanding of the nation as a societal culture. As mentioned above, Kymlicka

---

11 Kymlicka criticises cosmopolitans like Held for wishing to install forms of global citizenship in which individuals can participate directly in international organisations, to make them directly accountable to citizens. This might imply, for example, that in the EU more power should be devolved on to the Parliament, which is directly elected by citizens, instead of the Commission or the Council of Ministers, which operate through intergovernmental relations. Kymlicka replies to this that we should not hold international institutions directly but indirectly accountable to individual citizens, so that we can debate at the national level how we want our national governments to act in intergovernmental contexts. He does believe that transnational activism is a good thing, '[b]ut the only form in which genuine democracy occurs is within national boundaries' (Kymlicka 2001a, 325).

However, it is not clear why this should be the case, and part of the reason why Kymlicka privileges the level of the nation to such an extent seems to be his belief that the nation is the locus where individual freedom and democracy ought to be realised. But, given the fact that 'globalization is undoubtedly producing a new civil society' (Kymlicka 2001a, 326), why should we resist efforts to stimulate the creation of new forms of global or supranational citizenship? It seems to me that Kymlicka's argument here is unfounded.

bases his liberal conception of the nation on a distinction between the pluralism of character versus the transparency of the form of culture. Yet, I think it is important to cast doubt not only on the homogeneity of the *character* of culture (which is Kymlicka's point), but also on the homogeneity of culture as *vehicle*, which is the underlying assumption of Kymlicka's theory. The idea of a 'societal culture' reveals the idea that the culture in question is institutionally complete, distinct and territorially concentrated (see Kymlicka 1995, 76–77, 25; 2001a, 25, 269). As may be clear now, there is a tendency here to take as a starting-point a picture of the world as a transparent mosaic-like cultural and linguistic landscape, where clear and stable boundaries mark off monolingual and monocultural societal cultures.

But is this picture true? I don't think so. There are certainly many things that do not fit within it and this suggests that it is, more often than not, untrue. In general, the cultural landscape we inhabit is imbued with multiculturalism, multilingualism, and cultural hybridity and opacity. It is always characterised by vague or even contested boundaries, grey zones, minorities within minorities, bi- and multilingualism, etc. Neglecting this by taking a very homogeneous and monocultural perspective, both as an empirical starting-point and as a normative conclusion, is problematic. It will result in an inappropriate reduction of cultural reality. With Joseph Carens (2000, 65–66) we can therefore say that Kymlicka's concept of societal culture is 'much better suited to a *monocultural* conception of citizenship than to a multicultural one', and that he thereby evokes the 'old logic of the nation-state', which he claimed to have left behind (in contrast to liberals like Rawls or Dworkin whom Kymlicka criticises for working with a simplified nation-state assumption, see 1989, 177).

In endorsing this mosaic picture, Kymlicka runs the danger of falling into the trap of what Brubaker calls *groupism*; that is the 'social ontology that leads us to talk and write about ethnic groups and nations as real entities, as communities, as substantial, enduring, internally homogenous and externally bounded collectivities' (Brubaker 1998, 292). In this, the groupist picture is closely connected to a view of the social and cultural world in terms 'reminiscent of a Modigliani painting as a multichrome mosaic of monochrome ethnic or cultural blocs' (Brubaker 1998, 293). As Brubaker argues, this view is wrong and we should be wary of it when thinking about groups. Groupness and boundedness must be understood instead as '*variable*, as *emergent properties* of particular structural or conjectural settings; they cannot properly be taken as given or axiomatic' (Brubaker 1998, 298).

Kymlicka's understanding of nationality has 'groupist' tendencies insofar as he understands the structure or form of culture to be beyond dispute. Assuming such a consensus over the form of culture is a reduction of reality. The boundaries of the putative nation may be contested, and the cultural context of choice may be characterised by ethnic, cultural and linguistic intermingling, absence of territorial concentration, and mixed or multiple identity structures. Kymlicka's proposals make the most sense in a mosaic world consisting of internally homogeneous subunits, in which there is a minimum of mixing and intermingling (Hollinger 2001, 243), with members who have shared identity feelings with regard to a shared national choice context. It is, however, important to stress that our world is not a mosaic of monocultural units, and that this mosaic picture should therefore not be taken to be the standard case. A just approach to cultural diversity should not perceive whatever does not fit in the homogeneous Modigliani assumption to be mere noise, or unimportant irregularities. Maybe we shouldn't think of instances of cultural heterogeneity as details we should eliminate but rather as cracks in the old bastion of the nation-state assumption.

Constitutive Hybridity

Let us recapitulate. So far I have argued two things. First, the merit of the freedom-argument of Will Kymlicka's theory of liberal nationalism is that it succeeds in establishing that people are constitutively embedded in cultural contexts of choice, as well as in showing why this fact justifies political intervention in the domains of language and culture. Secondly, I have argued that the theory neglects hybrid contexts of choice and thereby unduly prioritises monolingual and mononational forms of cultural embeddedness. But in developing this criticism I do not intend to deny the issue of constitutive embeddedness nor the issue of the justice of regulation. Recognising the existence of cultural hybridity doesn't make minority rights unjustifiable.

In this section, I would like to consider the compatibility of legitimising the political recognition of cultures and emphasising hybridity. Interestingly, however, there is a certain tendency amongst those who, as I do, emphasise cultural hybridity and heterogeneity at the level of cultural and linguistic identities, to be reluctant towards the idea of cultural recognition and protection as a whole (see, amongst others, Johnson 2000, Kukathas 2003, Laitin and Reich 2003 and Waldron 1995).

I think this is an unfortunate fact. As Kymlicka has convincingly shown, granting minority rights to cultural groups is required by the liberal commitment to (embedded) freedom and equality. Indeed, it seems that rejecting the idea of minority rights is only possible if one is prepared to drop one of both ideals. Thus, the ideal of equality is deliberately pushed aside by Chandran Kukathas (2003), while Brian Barry (2001) defends a liberal egalitarianism that denies the idea of constitutive embeddedness.

I believe there is a way to combine regard for cultural protection with aversion for monocultural essentialism. To understand how this is possible, it is interesting to have a closer look at the alternative Kymlicka develops to the idea of remaining politically neutral to cultures. Kymlicka has convincingly shown that this idea is incoherent. In many areas, the state cannot avoid supporting this or that societal culture (Kymlicka 1995, 113). Not that this is a bad thing. Kymlicka does not see any reason to regret it; he is only concerned with how to ensure that the injustice this entails for national groups can be rectified (1995, 115). Therefore, after elucidating the hidden nation-state assumption inherent in any policy, he sets out to acknowledge and emphasise the value of national self-government and to grant it to majority and minority nations in an equal way. Self-government rights are intended to enable national groups to maintain their own societal culture, which, as mentioned earlier, comprises a comprehensive context of choice as well as a distinct language and territory.

> Self-government rights (…) are the most complete case of differentiated citizenship, since they divide the people into separate 'peoples', each with its own historic rights, territories,

and powers of self-government; and each, therefore with its own political community. (Kymlicka 1995, 182)

Similarly, in *Politics in the Vernacular*, he argues that federal politics should not only be 'monolingualised' but also 'nationalised' in the language and nation of the national group, which should lead to a politics in and through one's own nation (Kymlicka 2001a, 317–326). In general we can say that Kymlicka's alternative to the mistaken view of remaining politically neutral to cultures consists of granting each nation its own political and territorial sphere.

But this may be too quick. It is one thing to say that a strict separation between political and national communities is unworkable, but quite another to conclude that the relation between them has to be one-to-one. Kymlicka suggests that liberal nationalism is the only credible alternative to the mistaken belief in ethnocultural neutrality. But he thereby simplifies the issue: we can think of forms of policy in which a political community's cultural support is not limited to strictly one nation. The state cannot avoid taking culturally permeated decisions over the language of public schooling and public services, but it can allow for bilingual schools or different schools operating in different languages. We cannot 'replace the use of English in courts with no language' (Kymlicka 1995, 110), but we can recognise French alongside English in courts.

It seems possible to grant minority rights to national groups, while, at the same time, respecting culturally heterogeneous and hybrid situations, because self-government rights to a separate territorially-autonomous societal culture aren't the only means to protect cultural choice contexts. We might also consider publicly endorsing a *binational* societal culture. Such a policy would seek to stimulate participation over the boundaries of strictly monoculturally understood cultures but could nonetheless be based on the recognition of cultural particularities. It does not aim for a dubious separation between the private and the culturally neutral public, but upholds a pluralism in which two (or more) languages and cultures have a place. Bilingual and bicultural schools, police services, political parties, hospitals or clubs, are paradigm examples of how participation can go hand in hand with cultural recognition. Of course, some juxtaposition will be unavoidable, as it will be difficult for certain institutions (such as cultural centres for the benefit of a particular language) to operate in more than one language. But that is not a problem: the idea is not to eradicate all instances of monoculturalism but merely those instances of policies or institutions that intend to remove the cracks in the bastion of the nation-state assumption. What this pursuit of bi- or multinational societal cultures aims at is to allow for instances of hybridity to be afforded full scope instead of being polished away.

This argument is thus grounded in the idea of constitutive embeddedness, to which liberal nationalism is essentially committed. But Kymlicka believes that the unit *wherein* people are embedded is invariably a societal culture. Given the fact that an individual needs membership in his own societal culture (with stable linguistic and cultural boundaries, on a well-delineated territory), self-government rights are justifiable for national minorities. I think this understanding of the *unit* of embeddedness needs to be questioned, but doing so should not induce us to abandon the issue of embeddedness itself. Thus, to guide policies of cultural recognition in such a way as to make them respond to instances of cultural hybridity (both in the form of being embedded in things other than nations and in nations other than monocultural societal cultures), our normative theory should apply the normative argument in favour of minority rights – embeddedness is morally relevant and the pursuit of equality suggests equal embeddedness for all – to the more hybrid starting-point suggested by this criticism. When monolingual and monocultural members of national groups have a right to their own cultural context of choice, this should equally be the case for those who have hybrid choice contexts. If justice towards monocultural settings implies giving monocultural rights, then we should design an equivalent package of rights designed for those whose cultural belonging is structured in a more hybrid way.

To a certain extent, it might seem that the rights to which national groups are entitled, in the argument I am developing, will be less extensive than the rights Kymlicka grants them. Indeed it may be remarked that the rights for national groups are reduced here to what Kymlicka calls polyethnic rights. Kymlicka distinguishes polyethnic rights for immigrants from self-government rights for national groups. Whereas the second are intended to enable a nation to govern itself and maintain its own distinct societal culture, the first are offered to help ethnic groups to express their cultural particularity while becoming full and equal members of the societal culture of the majority, in other words to 'promote integration into the larger society, not self-government' (Kymlicka 1995, 31). After all, most immigrants 'choose to leave their own culture. They have uprooted themselves, and they know when they come that their success, and that of their children, depends on integrating into the institutions of English-speaking society' (Kymlicka 1995, 95–96).

But the analogy is not correct. In Kymlicka's view, polyethnic rights are intended to integrate without having to sacrifice cultural particularity. But the integration takes place into the larger nation of the host society. In the approach defended here the idea is not that national minorities have to integrate into a larger dominant society. Neither are their rights restricted to the mere possibility of expressing their own cultural particularities within a larger context defined by a majority. The basic idea is that in hybrid contexts or in cases where monocultural nationality is not the structuring feature of people's embedded freedom, it is undesirable as well as unnecessary to assign to each nation strict boundaries. The right to one's culture is indeed restricted but not to the level that Kymlicka deems appropriate for immigrants. The restriction is simply, in such cases, that the basic setting is not such that each culture occupies a distinct public sphere in distinct units, but that there may be multiple particularities that together make up the society and that are equally protected.

In general, this approach might generate a more appropriate way of dealing with the cases of which I claimed above that they were not satisfactorily dealt with in the liberal nationalist paradigm of Will Kymlicka. It suggests, first, an interesting way of dealing with cases of territorial mixing, since it will try not to perceive the world as a mosaic of homogeneous choice contexts but will stimulate ways of governing the same territorial or political unit together.

Equally, it is better able to deal with cases in which two previously separated choice contexts come together to develop a (partly) shared third one. The national pluralism the state upholds in this approach deliberately intends to enable and protect (the development of) such shared choice contexts with due consideration for the recognition of cultural particularities.

Thirdly, instances of biculturality are believed to be valuable. The endorsement the approach provides for bilingual schools or public services seems particularly helpful to those who are members of two nations at the same time. The approach also provides a way out of the deadlock Kymlicka seems to end up with in his attempt to normatively ground multinational federalism. What causes the deadlock is the monoculturalism of Kymlicka's theory. By grounding cultural protection in the value of monocultural choice contexts, he is only able to understand federalism as a mechanism for nations' self-government (see Kymlicka 2001a, 94). But what the hybrid perspective might add here is the idea that federalism might also (or rather) be understood as a fair solution to groups whose members have multiple identities. This understanding of federalism will be able to provide some federal glue, since, in this view, the federal level may be understood to provide a cultural context of choice of its own for many members, alongside the contexts of choice constituted by the nations that make up the multinational federation.[12]

In all three cases, the approach seems to be supported by Alfred Stepan's research findings that stress that if 'nationalist politicians, by the atmosphere they create (or social scientists and census-takers with their crude dichotomous categories) do not force polarization, many people may prefer to claim multiple and complementary identities' (Stepan 1998, 232).

Before bringing this discussion to a close, it should maybe be stressed that my argument does not entirely preclude giving a minority nation a distinct and monocultural context of its own. If there are regions where choice contexts are predominantly monoculturally structured, where territorial mixing is very low and where no rivalling nations are claiming the territory, there is no reason to refuse important levels of territorial autonomy. What I have tried to do instead is nothing more than to show that this monocultural solution is not the only one and that the liberal nationalist preoccupation with it, treating it as the standard case, is mistaken, unnecessary and undesirable. It is mistaken since it is inapplicable in a range of cases I have enumerated. It is unnecessary because protecting national groups on the basis of the value of cultural membership for individuals does not always have to result in monocultural regulation; in many cases, the

---

12 Though I cannot fully argue this here, I believe that this line of thinking might also be extended to issues of globalisation and global democracy. Kymlicka does not take into consideration that people might experience the freedom-enabling dimension of culture in cultural contexts larger than nations. But we can imagine that, in due time, a sense of cosmopolitan identity and citizenship might develop. The present approach is better able to grant some moral value to this form of identity (alongside the national and possibly other forms of identity), and might thus more easily support forms of global citizenship than Kymlicka's approach does (see note 11).

idea of protection in distinct self-governing units seems to be uncalled for by the nature of the freedom-argument. And it is undesirable since it suggests the idea that the only way to do justice to national choice contexts is by assigning each nation a territory, politics and society of its own. In a world that is increasingly characterised by, on the one hand, claims by national minorities, and, on the other, territorial mixing and multiple and overlapping identities, normatively defending a Modigliani-picture of the world in which people are expected to choose between mutually exclusive identities seems particularly unhelpful. On the contrary, I believe that political theorists should tackle the urgent task of exploring how our models of coping with demands by national groups can be developed in such a way that they contribute to the construction of postnational constellations, designed for such groups whose members disagree over the precise contours of their relevant cultural contexts of choice.

But, to repeat, saying all that does not mean that in predominantly homogeneous areas with a minimum of intermingling and mixed choice contexts, a constellation that gives territorial autonomy to national groups is necessarily wrong. In the end it thus turns out that we are left with two models for dealing with the existence of multiple national choice contexts within one state. The liberal nationalist solution starts from an empirical mosaic-like Modigliani world and defends it as a normative ideal. The more pluralist approach suggested here intends to respect and foster the construction of shared choice contexts, so that several national groups, while enjoying the right to receive cultural protection and recognition in the public sphere, can co-govern one and the same societal context.

This leaves of course the question which model is to be preferred in which specific case. It is impossible to answer this question a priori and by philosophical deduction. The 'just solution' will depend on the specific case at hand, and will necessarily involve a detailed study of numbers, geography, historical factors and public psychology. As a result, a full answer to this question cannot be developed here. But let me just stress this. I believe it is important to see that, in terms of cultural justice, the hybrid approach is not a second-best solution. The hybrid model succeeds in rectifying (through protecting cultural choice contexts) the unjust privileging of the majority language and culture that takes place in unprotected cultural regimes. More is not required in order for cultural justice to be fulfilled. In some situations, where there are no (major) disputes over land or nationhood, where group members are monolingual, where it is clear what the nation is and what its boundaries are, the liberal nationalist solution may perhaps be preferable. But, even then, whether it is preferable depends not on the cultural membership argument itself, but on other considerations or arguments, such as on reasons of efficiency, democracy or social justice. Taken on its own, the cultural membership argument only stipulates that protecting cultural choice contexts is morally required.[13] This means that cultural groups have the right to have their language and

---

13 It should be repeated that the argument developed in this chapter is limited in scope. I have only focused on one specific (though essential and widespread) argument in favour of granting nations cultural, political and territorial autonomy. This was the 'cultural membership argument' which grounds cultural protection in the value a national culture has for its members. I have not considered other lines of reasoning, such as the argument that a shared nationality

culture protected and to have institutions and a public sphere in which their language and culture is a structuring feature. The model of liberal nationalism is only one possible outcome of this argument, and, though it nowadays seems omnipresent in the literature, I have argued that it is often not the most appropriate one.

References

Barry, B. (2001), *Culture and Equality. An Egalitarian Critique of Multiculturalism*, Cambridge: Polity Press.
Brubaker, R. (1998), 'Myths and misconceptions in the study of nationalism', in Hall (ed.), *The State of the Nation. Ernest Gellner and the Theory of Nationalism*, Cambridge: Cambridge University Press, 272–306.
— (2002), 'Ethnicity without Groups', *Archives Européenes de Sociologie*, XLIII: 2, 163–189.
Caney, S. (1998), 'National Self-Determination and National Secession: Individualist and Communitarian Approaches', in Lehning, P. B. (ed.), *Theories of Secession*, London: Routledge, 152–183.
Canovan, M. (1996), *Nationhood and Political Theory*, Cheltenham: Edward Elgar.
Carens, J. (2000), *Culture, Citizenship and Community. A Contextual Exploration of Justice as Evenhandedness*, Oxford: Oxford University Press.
Derrida, J. (1996), *Le monolinguisme de l'autre*, Paris: Galilée.
De Schutter, H. (2005), 'Nations, Boundaries and Justice: on Will Kymlicka's Theory of Multinationalism', *Ethical Perspectives: Journal of the European Ethics Network*, 11:1, 17–41.
Gans, C. (2003), *The Limits of Nationalism*, Cambridge: Cambridge University Press.
Gellner, E. (1983), *Nations and Nationalism*, Oxford: Blackwell.
Hollinger, D. (2001), 'Not Universalists, Not Pluralists: The New Cosmopolitans Find Their Own Way', *Constellations*, 8:2, 236–248.
Johnson, J. (2000), 'Why respect culture?', *American Journal of Political Science*, 44:3, 405–418.
Kukathas, C. (1997), 'Survey Article: Multiculturalism as Fairness: Will Kymlicka's Multicultural Citizenship', *The Journal of Political Philosophy*, 5:4, 406–427.
— (2003), *The Liberal Archipelago. A Theory of Diversity and Freedom*, Oxford: Oxford University Press.
Kymlicka, W. (1989), *Liberalism, Community and Culture*, Oxford: Oxford University Press.
— (1995), *Multicultural Citizenship. A Liberal Theory of Minority Rights*, Oxford: Oxford University Press.
— (2001a), *Politics in the Vernacular. Nationalism, Multiculturalism and Citizenship*, Oxford: Oxford University Press.

---

is conducive to social justice, to active citizenship or to successful democratic deliberations. A more fully-fledged theory that would include these arguments might influence, either by strengthening or weakening, the conclusion I draw from the cultural membership argument.

— (2001b), 'Territorial Boundaries: A Liberal Egalitarian Perspective', in Miller, D. and Sohail, H. H. (eds), *Boundaries and Justice. Diverse Ethical Perspectives*, Princeton: Princeton University Press, 249–275.

Laitin, D.D. and Reich, R. (2003), 'A Liberal Democratic Approach to Language Justice', in W. Kymlicka and A. Patten (eds), *Language Rights and Political Theory*, Oxford: Oxford University Press, 80–104.

Leeuwen, van B. (2003), *Erkenning, identiteit en verschil. Multiculturalisme en leven met culturele diversiteit*, Leuven: Acco.

Levy, J. (2000), *The Multiculturalism of Fear*, Oxford: Oxford University Press.

Maddens, B., Billiet, J., and Beerten, R. (1999), 'De (sub)nationale identiteit en de houding tegenover vreemdelingen in Vlaanderen en Wallonië', in Deprez, K. and Vos, L. (eds), *Nationalisme in België. Identiteiten in beweging. 1780–2000*, Antwerpen: Houtekiet, 298–313.

Margalit, A. and Halbertal, M. (1994), 'Liberalism and the right to culture', *Social Research*, 61:3, 491–510.

Margalit, A. and Raz, J. (1990), 'National Self-Determination', *Journal of Philosophy*, 87:9, 439–461.

Meersseman, E., Billiet, J. and Depickere, A. (2002), 'De communautaire items. De opinie van de Vlamingen in 1999 over de staatsstructuur en hun (etno)territoriale identiteit', *ISPO-bulletin*, 49, 1–56.

Mendelsohn, M. (2002), 'Measuring National Identity and Patterns of Attachment: Quebec and Nationalist Mobilization', *Nationalism and Ethnic Politics*, 8:3, 72–94.

Miller, D. (1995), *On Nationality*, Oxford: Oxford University Press.

Moore, M. (2001) 'Normative Justification for Liberal Nationalism: Justice, Democracy and National Identity', *Nations and Nationalism*, 7:1, 1–20.

Moreno, L. (2001), *The Federalization of Spain*, London: Frank Cass.

Musschenga, A.W. (1998), 'Intrinsic Value as a Reason for the Preservation of Minority Cultures', *Ethical Theory and Moral Practice* 1, 202–225.

Patten, A. (2001), 'Political Theory and Language Policy', *Political Theory*, 29:5, 691–715.

Prinsloo, D. (1999), 'The Influence of Language Legislation on Language Shift in Traditional South African Cities', in Herberts, K. and Turi, J. G. (eds), *Multilingual Cities and Language Policies*, Vaasa: Abo Akademi University, 161–170.

Réaume, D. (2003), 'Beyond Personality: The Territorial and Personal Principles of Language Policy Reconsidered', in W. Kymlicka and A. Patten (eds), *Language Rights and Political Theory*, Oxford: Oxford University Press, 271–295.

Stepan, A. (1998), 'Modern multinational democracies: transcending a Gellnerian oxymoron', in Hall, J. A. (ed.), *The State of the Nation. Ernest Gellner and the Theory of Nationalism*, Cambridge: Cambridge University Press, 219–242.

Tamir, Y. (1993), *Liberal Nationalism*, Princeton: Princeton University Press.

Taylor, C. (1995), *Philosophical Arguments*, Cambridge/London: Harvard University Press.

Waldron, J. (1995), 'Minority Cultures and the Cosmopolitan Alternative', in W. Kymlicka (ed.), *The Rights of Minority Cultures*, Oxford: Oxford University Press, 93–122.

Chapter 4

Putting Kymlicka in Perspective: Canadian Diversity and Collective Rights

Dwight Newman[1]

Introduction

In this chapter, I seek to put Will Kymlicka's powerful theoretical account of appropriate responses to diversity in a different perspective and thereby contribute toward a better understanding of whether it provides lessons *from* Canada *for* Europe or elsewhere. The chapter skirts an important debate that arises on whether the lessons learned from Canada can be applied appropriately in other regions with different issues. Kymlicka himself has sensitively begun to explore some of these issues in his co-edited collection on the application of liberal multiculturalism to Eastern Europe (Kymlicka and Opalski 2001), and Jeff Spinner-Halev and Yael Tamir, amongst others, have raised such issues more broadly (Spinner-Halev 2001, 9–11, 14, 20; Tamir 1999, 77–82; cf. Acharya 2001, 108–109). The chapter also does not seek to challenge the wider range of Kymlicka's work, which also includes important empirical-type analyses and many other sorts of work usefully advancing the literature (e.g., Kymlicka, this volume). Rather, the chapter seeks to question whether aspects of Kymlicka's theoretical work on liberal multiculturalism even correctly describe, empirically or normatively, the issues arising in Canada. Nobody, of course, would contemplate denying the genuinely monumental achievement of Kymlicka's body of theoretical work in making the case that multiculturalism can be both consistent with and demanded by traditional liberal principles. But we can nonetheless challenge whether his theoretical approach is adequate and conclude that the debate on the issues in which Kymlicka is interested needs to go in a direction he has famously resisted.

To do so, I focus on one particular distinction of Kymlicka's, but one which is particularly well-known and particularly important. This is his distinction between 'external protections' and 'internal restrictions', which we will examine at greater length in the next section, but which essentially differentiates between a group's externally and internally directed claims. (This, of course, is a different matter from

---

[1] I thank Avigail Eisenberg, Timothy Endicott, Will Kymlicka, Chris McCrudden, Helder de Schutter, and John Whyte for their helpful comments on a previous draft of this chapter. This chapter draws on a portion of my D Phil thesis ('Community and Collective Rights'), which endeavours to develop a theoretical account of collective rights. I thank SSHRC for financial support of my project.

whether one distinguishes in some way between the claims of insiders and outsiders against the group, with which some have unfortunately confused the distinction.) Although Kymlicka's distinction may at first seem like one small part of a larger theory, it closely underpins other elements of Kymlicka's theoretical account. Kymlicka generally refers to what he perceives as a lack of utility in the concepts of collective rights or group rights (Kymlicka 1989, 138–139; Kymlicka 1995, 34–35; Kymlicka 1994, 18) and indicates that he prefers to discuss the issues in which he is interested as based on the category of group-differentiated rights; the 'external protections'-'internal restrictions' dichotomy is closely interlaced with this preference and actually partly determines what sorts of group-differentiated rights are permissible (Kymlicka 2001b, 27). He argues for certain kinds of group-differentiated rights, which are necessarily external protections, being rights held by one group relative to the larger society rather than rights of a group against its own members (Kymlicka 2001b, 27–28). In other words, this dichotomy has a correspondence with group-differentiated rights as Kymlicka's primary normative concept. Indeed, he rejects general talk of collective rights partly because such talk may seem to support claims to internal restrictions (Kymlicka 1995, 46–47). Thus, by questioning the 'external protections'-'internal restrictions' distinction, we do question more about the application of his stimulating theoretical framework to issues of diversity.

In this chapter, I will question both the empirical and normative accuracy of this distinction, particularly by using examples from Canadian policy on religious school rights, language rights, and evolving self-government agreements with First Nations peoples. I will argue towards developing collective rights potentially falling outside Kymlicka's distinction as the area we must further explore in order to progress on diversity issues.

Questioning Kymlicka's Distinction

According to Kymlicka's fundamental distinction, external protections are 'the claim of a group against the larger society', whereas internal restrictions are 'the claim of a group against its own members' (Kymlicka 1995, 35). Sometimes, these descriptions of the concepts lapse rapidly into more casual descriptions of internal restrictions as concerned with preserving the 'cultural purity' of the group against those seeking to revise elements of its traditions (Kymlicka 2001a, 60) or yet more pejorative descriptions of protections 'intended to protect the group from *external decisions*' as opposed to restrictions 'intended to protect the group from the destabilising impact of *internal dissent*' (Kymlicka 1995, 35). But this lapsing is without any explanation of why these particular intentions are necessary to the characterisation of a particular protection/restriction. Given that the pejorative categories cease to be jointly exhaustive (and may not be mutually exclusive), they become less helpful, meaning that the pejorative descriptions might be good politics but are problematic theorising and thus leading to a conclusion that we ought to take something close to the non-pejorative original statement as the key distinction. We can thus turn to analyse the claimed empirical and normative applications.

The distinction between external protections and internal restrictions derives fundamentally from Kymlicka's conception of legal rights held by groups as being justified by the group's role in providing a cultural context of choice that grounds the autonomy of members (Kymlicka 1989, 166ff.). His theory grounds protections for groups in a certain form of equalisation payment for members of groups that face obstacles in providing culturally-based freedom (at one point, referring explicitly to 'certain collective rights' as 'appropriate measures for the rectification of an inequality in circumstances which affects aboriginal people collectively': Kymlicka 1989, 194).

As a result, he accepts only cultural protections consistent with the advancement of such freedom. As he puts it at one point, 'the very reasons we have to support external protections are also reasons to oppose internal restrictions' (Kymlicka 1995, 44). Kymlicka initially drew the distinction between 'external protections' and 'internal restrictions' in *Liberalism, Community, and Culture* while discussing an example of what he termed 'theocratic American Indian bands' (Kymlicka 1989, 195–196). There, he was prepared to acknowledge the existence of 'difficult questions' about the acceptability of internal restrictions in what he insisted was the very rare case where a particular community 'really would disintegrate without restricting religious liberty' (Kymlicka 1989, 198). He also referred to the yet more unusual example of a willingness to allow temporary internal restrictions in the context of an Indonesian tribe whose children jumped off a cliff after viewing newly introduced television programmes so as to protect such children (Kymlicka 1989, 170).

However, his later works have arguably taken an even harder line. Indeed, he has now repeatedly asserted that internal restrictions are unjustified and that examples where they could be justified do not arise (Kymlicka 1995, 42–44; Kymlicka 1997, 58n.; Kymlicka 1998, 62; Kymlicka 2001b, 27–28). In one sense, then, one might read him as having sharpened the distinction. At the same time, Kymlicka has also arguably blurred the distinction in the other direction. Where he had initially implied that some internal restrictions could conceivably be acceptable, he has now implied that none are, and he also states that external protections 'become illegitimate if, rather than reducing a minority's vulnerability to the power of the larger society, they instead enable a minority to exercise economic or political dominance over some other group' (Kymlicka 2001b, 28), although this latter blurring of the distinction was perhaps always present based on the basic rationales he enunciated (in, for example, his discussion of apartheid: Kymlicka 1989, 245–252).

One challenge, however, might arise in relation to this interpretation of a relatively hard distinction. Kymlicka has recently written somewhat supportively of Quebec's language laws. We will return to this example, but we can note for the moment that even the aspect in which Quebec had banned the use of English on commercial signs in the quest for a 'visage linguistique' has now met some acceptance from Kymlicka. He has written (arguably somewhat surprisingly): 'These policies are sometimes described as illiberal. And perhaps they are. But here we reach a genuine dilemma. For such illiberal policies may be required if national minorities are to successfully integrate immigrants' (Kymlicka 2001a, 286). In the text, he went on to describe the importance of such successful integration to a transition in Quebec to a post-ethnic conception of nationalism (Kymlicka 2001a, 287–288). Kymlicka's writings, of course, are a subtle and sophisticated body of work, and he has here been ready to acknowledge the success of a policy that one would initially presume ran contrary to even his most fundamental normative distinction. In the same book, of course, he reiterates that normative distinction, rejecting the 'legitimacy of "internal restrictions"' (Kymlicka 2001a, 22, 60). He has, however, apparently indicated some willingness to make an exception in response to sufficiently pressing reasons, which for him include the importance of developing post-ethnic forms of nationalism.

This being said, Kymlicka has nonetheless overwhelmingly asserted the distinction as a general, bright-line rule. Let us endeavour to be clear as to the alleged meaning of the distinction. Kymlicka claims that the distinction has both empirically descriptive and normatively prescriptive dimensions. He maintains, first, that groups generally do not seek legal powers to impose internal restrictions. Although he refers to some counterexamples (such as claims within the British Muslim community to apply Islamic family law within their community), he says that '[m]ost of the demands for group-specific rights made by ethnic and national groups in Western democracies are for external protections' and that other sorts of claims have been rejected in any event (Kymlicka 1995, 42). Elsewhere, although acknowledging that illiberal minority nationalist movements exist and there are ongoing struggles within minority nationalist movements, he refers to what he calls 'the clear trend throughout most Western democracies' toward liberal conceptions of minority nationalism that would use external protections but not internal restrictions (Kymlicka 2001b, 28). So, the distinction is partly an empirical claim as to what sorts of claims groups make.

Kymlicka maintains, second, that this distinction maps onto the normative acceptability of group decisions. He maintains that 'liberals can and should endorse certain external protections, where they promote fairness between groups, but should reject internal restrictions which limit the right of group members to question and revise traditional authorities and practices' (Kymlicka 1995, 37; cf. Kymlicka 2001a, 22–23, 60). In this statement, he uses the more pejorative description of internal restrictions, so we might take it as either describing all internal restrictions as objectionable or as distinguishing between different kinds of restrictions, manifesting how the tendency to use the pejorative description can be rhetorically powerful but unfortunately less clear.

We may thus endeavour to bring additional clarity to the distinction to get at what Kymlicka might reasonably have meant by it, or at least what provides a reasonable interpretation. Obviously, he cannot have meant literally that every internally directed decision is problematic. That a group exercising some powers of governance establishes reasonable traffic rules, say, surely does not cross the line into the unacceptable imposition of internal restrictions, or the distinction would be untenable from the outset. And some of Kymlicka's language might give rise to a stronger interpretation. For instance, at one point, he describes the concern about internal restrictions as arising 'where the basic civil and political liberties of group members are being restricted' (Kymlicka 1995, 36). This could give rise to an interpretation where 'internal restrictions' include only those restrictions actually infringing individual rights.

However, there are two problems with this approach. First, it does not fit fully consistently with Kymlicka's text, as several pages after that seemingly helpful description, he goes on to refer to all internal taxes (which presumably do not automatically infringe individual rights) as being internal restrictions in his sense (Kymlicka 1995, 42). Out of charity, we might of course read out that particular statement for the sake of making out a stronger position. But a second problem arises in that the approach we are now considering would arguably entail a certain circularity. A major objective of the distinction is to try to delineate circumstances in which individual rights, all-things-considered, differ from those we might have envisioned without Kymlicka's insights. After all, external protections similarly reshape individual rights. However, internal restrictions cannot be defined in terms of that which they are meant to help delineate.

This conclusion leaves us in some possible uncertainty as to the meaning of the distinction. It has to be a distinction that actually illuminates rather than merely repeats. Can we interpret it so as to attend to the language of external protections or internal restrictions as flowing from a 'claim' as against the larger society or against group members (Kymlicka 1995, 35)? On this phrasing, we might then get the sense of a protection or restriction going beyond those that would reasonably exist without the particular justifications giving rise to these claims. In other words, we might interpret internal restrictions and external protections specifically as only those group claims going beyond what would be permitted in the absence of justifications developed specifically for internal restrictions or external protections. This reading may still seem to have an air of circularity to it, but we can perhaps see a non-circular conception behind it, this being that both concern limits on rights, not all-things-considered but as-considered-without-analysis-of-groups. Reading Kymlicka in this way, he thus claims that there is a fundamental normative schism between external protections that limit ordinary liberal rights as they would be analysed without reference to these considerations and internal restrictions that limit ordinary liberal rights as they would be analysed without reference to these considerations. This interpretation, in some ways, renders the distinction into a distinction speaking to political theory, not a political theory distinction applicable to political reality. That said, we might of course go ahead and apply it as if it were offered as an actual claim concerning reality and see how it fares.

Some theorists, of course, have questioned the very precision of the distinction between internal restrictions and external protections. As we have noted, Kymlicka himself admits, for instance, that measures designed as external protections often have internal implications, if nothing else, at least in requiring taxation where these protections have a monetary cost (Kymlicka 1995, 42). Ayelet Shachar has highlighted other challenges on the precision of the distinction, highlighting the issues raised by Kymlicka's reference in the course of his first enunciation of his distinction (Kymlicka 1989, 197) to *Santa Clara Pueblo v Martinez*, 436 US 49 (1978). In the case, the United States Supreme Court ultimately upheld the Pueblos' autonomy over membership rules as against challenges that these membership rules were discriminatory on the basis of sex. Shachar expresses concerns that internal discrimination is rendered into an external protection and thus protected under Kymlicka's distinction (Shachar 2001, 18–20), ultimately drawing the conclusion that 'the external aspects of multicultural accommodation are not so easily distinguished from the policy's internal impact' (Shachar 2001, 30).

The distinction is, however, subject to a yet more problematic critique. The distinction actually cannot deal meaningfully with many of the cases Kymlicka himself touches upon as examples, cases that deal precisely with who is and is not a member, and thus with *what is external or internal*. Cases like *Santa Clara Pueblo v Martinez* are thus significant in ways beyond what Shachar identified. Kymlicka's distinction presupposes a previously defined boundary between external and internal, when it is often this very boundary that is the subject to which we would need to try to apply the rule. That is, we cannot know in advance if the practice of the Pueblos concerning membership is an internal restriction or external practice, because asking such a question presumes that we know whether those affected are internal or external to the Pueblos, when that is what the membership practice seeks to answer. The breaking down of the distinction is itself problematic, and these critiques raise important concerns to which we might expect answers. But they are just the beginning of the distinction's problems.

Questioning Kymlicka's Empirical Claim

Kymlicka, of course, does not maintain that his distinction applies empirically in every case. As we have already noted, rich as his theorising is, he appropriately qualifies it as describing the claims only of 'most' groups (Kymlicka 1995, 42; Kymlicka 2001a, 23n.). We could, of course, take this as a statistical claim, to which an appropriate response might be an amassing of quantitative data concerning how many groups claim which kinds of rights. But this would not seem the most helpful interpretation (nor one true to the more likely nature of the claim), and there is an alternative way of approaching the claim. In this section, we will see that the distinction's helpfulness as an empirical generalisation is limited because there are *qualitatively important* exceptions. If the distinction does not cope with approaches taken on central issues within discussion of diversity, then it is not the empirical tool it is claimed to be. In particular, given the genesis of Kymlicka's theory in Canada, I will point to three qualitatively important areas in Canadian responses to diversity that seem to diverge from his distinction, these being in the areas of religious school rights, language rights, and Aboriginal self-government rights. To the extent that these qualitatively important areas manifest divergence from Kymlicka's empirical claim, they demonstrate a genuine problem with the empirical accuracy of the distinction.

We can begin with an area that illustrates a sort of internal implication to which we saw Kymlicka refer. Religious school rights are established in the constitutional arrangements under which a number of Canadian provinces entered into the Confederation, typically providing for the right of the Catholic or Protestant minority in a given district to establish a separate school board. These religious school rights often give rise to some forms of internal restrictions, often including taxation of individuals by the relevant religious group in ways other than they might choose to be taxed. This point is neatly illustrated by a case of the Saskatchewan Court of Appeal,

Buhs v Board of Education of Humboldt Rural School Division No. 47 (2002), 217 Sask. R. 222, 2002 SKCA 41 (cf. Newman 2004a, 47–48). The appellants in the case had sought to be separate school supporters, but the public school division appealed to the Board of Revision to claim that the appellants were not members of the minority religious faith as required in order to be supporters of the Englefeld Protestant Separate School Board. Justice Lane, writing for the Court, and dealing with some complex points concerning legislative interpretation, ultimately held that the legislative framework left a taxpayer's claimed religion subject to challenge. A taxpayer is required to support the school system actually according with his or her religious faith. In the Canadian polity, certain religious groups having the right to establish school boards thus also have a right to internally restrict members by subjecting them to taxation and by preventing them from redirecting this taxation. Individuals are subject to taxation by their religious group for purposes of religious schooling. This point, notably, is not a singular conclusion of Saskatchewan's Court of Appeal but is rather a generalisation applicable to much education legislation across Canada.

Although taxation for the provision of schooling systems might not seem like the most dramatic internal restriction, and could arguably be characterised as a merely incidental exception to any general norm against internal restrictions, it is at least arguable that the example says something more. It is an example of a situation in which internal restrictions on rights as they would otherwise exist (and as Kymlicka presumably would agree, given his reluctance to permit protections of religion: Newman 2003) are accepted in actual Canadian political practice, thus beginning to undermine Kymlicka's empirical claim. This example ought to alert us at once to the reality that the categories must be more complex and that internal restrictions arguably cannot be categorically condemned.

Language policy is another area in the Canadian approach to pluralism where we see qualitatively important policies that do cross from external protections into internal restrictions. Notably, the collective aspiration of the Québecois for *la survivance* (cf. Taylor 1994) has led to Quebec language policy that does involve restrictions on members of the very community this policy seeks to protect and perpetuate. Under Bill 101, also known as the *Quebec Charter of the French Language*, language policy developed that went so far as to limit access to English-language schooling and to prohibit non-French-language commercial signage. This latter aspect in particular led to the Supreme Court of Canada striking down the law as unconstitutional in *Ford v Quebec*, where the Court reasoned that a less restrictive law requiring French as the dominant language of signage would have met the law's objectives (*Ford v Quebec (Attorney General)* [1988] 2 SCR 712 at 780). The Quebec government responded by using the 'notwithstanding clause', the provision in the Canadian constitution allowing a temporary democratic override of judicial interpretations of certain constitutional clauses, so as to maintain the law (SQ 1988, c. 54). Upon the impending expiration of the override and in a politically pressured situation after the United Nations Human Rights Committee ruled against the legislation, a later government essentially accepted the Supreme Court's reasoning and amended the legislation to involve only a requirement of French predominance in signage (SQ 1993, c. 40). More recently, the courts have essentially accepted the continuing constitutionality of these amended provisions. Following a 1999 trial decision declaring inoperative the signage provisions in the absence of evidence to show that they remained justified limitations on constitutional rights (*R c WFH Enterprises ltée* [1999] JQ no. 4586 (CQ pén.)), the question arose as to whether the portions of the Supreme Court reasoning allowing for the less strict law could be taken as having continuing currency in the absence of proof to such effect. The higher courts accepted that they did, thereby tacitly accepting the modified legislation as constitutional (*R c WFH Enterprises ltée* [2000] JQ no. 1165 (Que. SC), *R c WFH Enterprises ltée* [2001] JQ no. 5021 (Que. CA), leave to appeal to SCC refused [2001] SCCA No. 625).

This legislation includes some substantial internal restrictions. First, and less constitutionally contentious (although recently subjected to analysis and some reading down in a series of cases including *Solski (Tutor of) v Quebec* 2005 SCC 14), ss. 72–73 of the legislation limit children attending publicly-funded schools to French-language schooling unless their parents had English-language schooling. The law thus restricts francophone parents from sending their children to English-language schools for such purposes as the economic benefits attained by learning English. Second, and in the most contentious provision, s. 58 of the legislation restricts expression by limiting the medium of expression in certain contexts of commercial signage to a particular language, thus restricting individuals from expressing themselves in the manner they would choose. These restrictions would seem to be internal restrictions of the sort Kymlicka's theory would try to rule out. Someone might try to claim that these restrictions do not restrict ordinary liberal rights, such as by claiming that there is no right to send a child to school in any language chosen. Indeed, I will argue in the next section for the normative acceptability of these restrictions in the appropriate circumstances. But that is precisely the point: the circumstances of a group's collective life affect our response to these restrictions. Away from such circumstances, nobody would defend restrictions on the language of expression in commercial signage; they are clearly restrictive of ordinary rights as they would exist in a world without groups. Away from the circumstances of collective life at hand, nobody would suppose that a group of parents could not at least propose whatever language they wished for their children's education. For example, if enough parents in Vancouver wanted their children to be educated in Japanese immersion programmes in public schools so as to gain advantages in developing future trading relationships with Japan, they would normally be free to propose this. The Quebec legislation rules out *ab initio* a request for education in a particular language that might offer certain individual economic benefits. Again, the legislation's provisions surely amount to internal restrictions.

Although they have produced immense controversy, these internal restrictions have ultimately been accepted (and, as I will argue below, for good reason) as a delicate compromise and a democratic protection of the French language in Québec. They are a qualitatively important instance of a minority group using internal restrictions to protect its language and culture in a collective effort at *la survivance* and, I claim, an instance of *la survivance* giving a minority group reasons to impose internal restrictions not accommodated in Kymlicka's theory.

Some will object to the last sentence, claiming that the francophone community is not the relevant 'minority group' and that any attention to a minority ought to be to the anglophone and allophone minority within Quebec. This is essentially a manifestation of the phenomenon commonly labelled a 'Russian doll problem': as we peel off layers, the majority and minority groups keep changing. We obviously cannot solve this complex problem here, but what we can note for present purposes is simply that because this 'Russian doll problem' poses particular challenges for Kymlicka, his argument faces problems on both the main argument and on this objection to the main argument. Kymlicka's choice to distinguish between external protections versus a majority and internal restrictions within a minority, aside from the other presuppositions it makes, presupposes an identification of the majority and the minority. It makes strong assumptions here, beyond what we would need in a theory that did not depend on the same distinctions between internal and external.

Some might also object to the claims against Kymlicka here, noting (as we did above) that Kymlicka has explicitly noted possible justifications for Quebec's sign law (Kymlicka 2001a, 286–289). However, as we also noted above, he did not discuss the Quebec sign law in terms of its giving rise to amendments to the 'internal restrictions'-'external protections' dichotomy but simply as an *ad hoc* policy suited to particular circumstances in which it helped Quebec to move toward a post-ethnic conception of nationalism. In one sense, then, he admits limits to the application of his distinction, himself eroding the empirical claim initially at stake. In another, he reiterates the distinction, implying that the internally restrictive aspects of the law make it 'illiberal' (Kymlicka 2001a, 286) but accepting the occasional use of an illiberal policy for the sake of a greater good. An alternative interpretation, and one we will strengthen later in the normative discussion, is that the presence of an internally restrictive aspect is not automatically the basis on which we must initially accept or reject a policy. For the moment, however, we can already see the empirical usefulness of the distinction continuing to decay.

Let us turn now to a third example of an area posing qualitatively important challenges to Kymlicka's distinction, that of self-government agreements for indigenous peoples being reached with Canada's Aboriginal First Nations. Although the Supreme Court of Canada remains due to pronounce more definitively on the matter, the Canadian federal government has explicitly recognised that an inherent right of Aboriginal self-government exists and is protected by s. 35 of the *Constitution Act, 1982*, although its document does endeavour to prescribe certain features of self-government (Canada Department of Indian Affairs and Northern Development, 1995). The Canadian government has subsequently entered into negotiations of self-government agreements, and I will turn to some important clauses from self-government agreements momentarily which will further challenge Kymlicka's distinction.

Someone might argue that Kymlicka's account can explain claims for self-government. After all, self-government is an issue he explicitly addresses (Kymlicka 1995, 38–40). Kymlicka is, of course, right to alert us to the fact that a group claiming what it calls 'collective rights' might be claiming group-differentiated rights (Kymlicka 2001a, 70). And the monumental achievement of Kymlicka's writings right from *Liberalism, Community and Culture* is his persuasive argument that some such group-differentiated rights can be accepted and advocated within an entirely liberal framework.

However, self-government is sometimes considered a species of internal self-determination, which in the international legal arena is the pre-eminent right giving rise to extended discussions on collective rights differing from traditional liberal rights (e.g., Crawford 1988). And just as any nation's self-government would seem to presuppose the possibility that it might limit individual rights in certain contexts, so too it would seem that Aboriginal First Nations exercising their right of self-government might do so. Other nation-building projects have involved internal restrictions. In saying that, of course, we do not say that nations or First Nations ought to be able to infringe individual rights in every way imaginable. Some restrictions have been, and are, inappropriate, but the point is that their inappropriateness does not derive directly from their nature as internal restrictions. Other principles can govern which right trumps which, and individual rights will often be vitally important. Any broad assumption that there cannot be internal restrictions is overly sweeping. Such a requirement would rob self-government of a substantial part of its meaning and render Aboriginal self-government into a poor second cousin of self-government more broadly.

The self-government agreements being negotiated with Canada's Aboriginal First Nations arguably recognise the possibility of self-government leading to restrictions on the rights of members, as we see in very different ways from the two most prominent examples in recent extensive self-government agreements. The *Nisga'a Final Agreement*, concluded in May 1999, thus took pains to require that the Nisga'a government respect the Canadian *Charter*, though with intriguing additional language: 'The *Canadian Charter of Rights and Freedoms* applies to Nisga'a Government in respect of all matters within its authority, bearing in mind the free and democratic nature of Nisga'a Government as set out in this Agreement' (Nisga'a Final Agreement, ch. 2, art. 9). Though there might conceivably be other meanings intended by the language as well, the latter clause must arguably be taken as textually suggesting an expectation that many Nisga'a government actions would qualify for justification under s. 1 of the *Canadian Charter of Rights and Freedoms* as limits on rights 'necessary in a free and democratic society'.

The more recent *Tlicho Self-Government Agreement* concluded in August 2003 (and which received royal assent on 15 February 2005) contains yet more intriguing provisions. Although the Tlicho government is explicitly subject to the Canadian *Charter* on matters within its authority (Tlicho Agreement, art. 2.15.1), the *Agreement* also provides for a Tlicho Constitution, subject to a requirement, amongst others, that it provide 'protections for Tlicho citizens and for other persons to whom Tlicho laws apply, by way of rights and freedoms *no less than* those set out in the *Canadian Charter of Rights and Freedoms*' (Tlicho Agreement, art. 7.1.2). The drafting is of course beyond opaque. The language clearly contemplates variation, or it would refer simply to 'the rights set out in the *Charter*' rather than rights 'no less than' those in the *Charter*. Yet any variation implies the possibility that some rights will indeed be given a more limited extent, since a different interpretation on some rights will end up implicitly constraining others. This latter point arises particularly when we read the terminology together with the accompanying provisions on the Tlicho government's powers, such as that to enact laws in relation to 'protection of spiritual and cultural beliefs and practices of Tlicho Citizens and protection and promotion of the Tlicho language and of the culture of the Tlicho First Nation' (Tlicho Agreement, art. 7.4.4). The Agreement arguably implies a Tlicho power to protect the Tlicho 'distinct society', even where this may require limits on certain rights not normally permitted by the Canadian *Charter* and liberal jurisprudence.

Such variations are, of course, contemplated in the *Charter* itself. Notably, s. 25 of the *Charter* itself mandates that '[t]he guarantee in this Charter of certain rights and freedoms shall not be construed so as to abrogate or derogate from any aboriginal, treaty or other rights or freedoms that pertain to the aboriginal peoples of Canada...'. The legally correct interpretation of s. 25 is, of course, debated, with some taking it as a general interpretive prism (Pentley 1988), others suggesting it may provide some interpretive shield for Aboriginal governments even though these authors claim the section did not contemplate the idea (Hogg and Turpel 1995, 214–216), and yet others identifying a wide range of possible protections it might provide for Aboriginal self-government (Arbour 2003). There have thus far been few mentions of the section in case law (Arbour 2003, 15ff.), likely because there have not thus far been many challenges posed to decisions of Aboriginal governments. At the very least, however, s. 25 must be read as having some protective effect for Aboriginal practices such that they can diverge from elements of the rest of the *Charter* in some ways, thus allowing First Nations communities to protect some of their practices even where doing so might involve variations on the usual set of Canadian citizenship rights.

Although reading an 'external protections'-'internal restrictions' rule into the interpretation of Aboriginal self-government provisions might not be inherently impossible, such a reading would be neither the most natural interpretation nor the one corresponding structurally to the concept of self-government. Even though Kymlicka himself has anticipated, and indeed enriched, some of the debates on whether the *Charter* should apply to Aboriginal First Nations, and argued for the possibility of different mechanisms for enforcement of individual rights in the self-government context (e.g., Kymlicka 2001a, 86–88), the provisions actually included in self-government agreements seem to go farther than his claims. These self-government agreements arguably accept a very real possibility of some internal restrictions being legitimate means of pursuing collective purposes connected with maintaining First Nations communities. Again, rights to impose internal restrictions are more widely claimed than Kymlicka would have had us believe and, indeed, are actually accepted within the delicate compromises of Canadian federation.

Even within his intended limits, qualitatively important examples go beyond the empirical claims of Kymlicka's theory. We can thus question whether Kymlicka's key distinction is as empirically accurate as claimed, and we can perceive the need to develop new distinctions in the area of group rights that better describe the actual claims of groups – as well as the actual policy and legislation of states such as Canada in their responses to diversity.

Questioning Kymlicka's Normative Claim

I wish now to challenge whether Kymlicka's distinction is as normatively useful as it is intended to be. Although the larger work from which this chapter is drawn will develop a broader challenge and different normative distinctions, we can actually be clear from the outset that Kymlicka's distinction is problematic from a normative point of view. As we can see from a brief form of the argument to come, Kymlicka's approach regrettably cannot accommodate even appropriate solutions to standard coordination problems concerned with public goods.

Let us return to the example of a cultural-linguistic community with political power over matters such as the educational system to which its members are subject. Suppose that this community seeks to ensure the preservation of its culture by preserving its language. To do so, it enacts legislation, which we shall call Bill ABC, requiring its members to attend educational institutions in the community's language. It does so, in particular, because some individuals otherwise have an incentive at the individual level to attend school in a dominant language of the broader region so as to attain individual economic benefits. On one interpretation, Bill ABC thus harms individual members who are now denied a choice about their education. On another, however, by enacting Bill ABC, the community simply protects the public good individual members would otherwise have had distorting incentives to work against. That is, the legislation corrects the incentive individuals would otherwise have to focus only on their individual non-membership interests and actually benefits members by protecting a flourishing of the community that contributes to the flourishing of their individual lives. Indeed, we could envision the legislation going even farther on the same basis, even restricting public signage in the dominant language that threatens to supplant the linguistic-cultural community. What might have initially seemed to some to have no possible basis except as an act of tyranny now begins to seem like a plausible policy to protect a collective interest that actually benefits members (cf. Buchanan 1994, 10; Levy 2000, 115ff.).

This example, admittedly, is both abstracted and idealised. We have, to a degree, implicitly assumed a homogeneous community in which protection of that community's culture is of benefit to everyone within that community. In the real world, of course, any such situation is inherently more complex because communities are non-homogeneous. The promotion of a public good will be neutral or even harmful, on balance, for some members. There will be some individuals for whom cultural membership is less valuable than the individual interests they might pursue outside the legislative framework. That point in itself, of course, does not say much. The same could be said of any public good problem. So long as the community still serves such members in other ways on balance and in a broad sense, however, we would not automatically say that the community does them an injustice (unless this particular step simply goes too far as against a particularly weighty individual interest, considering it in light of the competing individual aims and collective interests). As long as we do not believe the promotion of every public good is inherently unjustifiable, the point gives us no grounds for rejecting the normative point from the idealised example that Kymlicka's theory fails in a standard public goods problem, which of course may or may not mean it fails to give the right answer on particular facts but which does diminish the degree to which it is compelling at the level of normative theory.

Helder de Schutter's work (e.g., De Schutter, this volume) points toward another objection that might arise. Why, one might ask, are those who seek to know more than one language depicted as 'free riders'? Why, that is, are they not free to develop a distinctive 'bilingual identity' (which could equally be a cross-cultural identity, without reference to language) if this is what is actually valuable to their flourishing? Such questions, however, are a variant on the same point we have already discussed. Obviously, if the interests of individuals ultimately do not justify the preservation of some particular cultural–linguistic framework, which might be because it is of no value to anyone or because it is actually of disvalue to some who flourish better in a different framework, and where this fact undermines an argument for promoting the public good, then there is no public good argument. But those who make the point bear a heavy onus to demonstrate that the preservation of a culture, of value to members of a community over time, can never be more weighty than the potential interest of some in a bilingual existence where their bilingual existence threatens to undermine the ongoing survival of a minority culture in the face of homogenising forces. In the absence of a very compelling argument along those lines, it remains the case that Kymlicka's argument elides a standard public goods problem in a manner undermining the normative force of Kymlicka's distinction.

Kymlicka's distinction is thus not the morally relevant distinction it purports to be. As we see in the example of Bill ABC, an internal restriction may actually be to the benefit of most – or even all – members. An internal restriction can contribute to individuals' lives by promoting the flourishing of a community that in turn contributes to their lives. The initial restriction of their pursuit of other individual non-membership interests may be necessary to the fulfilment of more important or weighty interests as members. The morally relevant distinction is thus not on Kymlicka's line but between compliance and non-compliance with other moral requirements. I will develop elsewhere in the larger work from which this chapter is drawn such requirements as I call the 'service principle', a requirement that the community serve its members in a broad sense, and argue that these better describe the morally relevant distinctions (cf. Newman 2004a). We can, of course, understand why Kymlicka's distinction originally had an intuitive appeal. It expresses a concern to which we are no doubt alive, that some individuals should not become persecuted minorities suffering perpetually under their community's restrictions. But we can develop such a concern as an adjunct to what it means to require, say, that a community serve its members. In defining the normative principles, however, a strict distinction between 'external protections' and 'internal restrictions' surely does not figure as prominently as Kymlicka claims. We have not yet ruled out its being an appropriate factor to consider in decisions about the application of the service principle, but it does not have the moral determinacy Kymlicka claimed for it.

Indeed, there are other reasons to object to Kymlicka's distinction as well, though I will refer only briefly to one of these reasons. Kymlicka's distinction has the potential to distract us from other arguments for the rights at issue, and such distraction in turn would have the potential to distort the rights. To make this tangible, consider the wording of instruments on Aboriginal self-government. The preamble to the *Tlicho Self-Government Agreement* explains that it was negotiated 'in order to define and provide certainty in respect of the rights of the Tlicho relating to land, resources, and self-government' (Tlicho Agreement, pmbl.) In an analogous phrase, s. 35 of Canada's *Constitution Act, 1982* states: 'The existing aboriginal and treaty rights of the aboriginal peoples of Canada are hereby recognised and affirmed.' In the modern self-government discussions, the premise is a previously existing right of self-government claimed on a largely historically-rooted basis. Kymlicka's account is generally of legal rights we can give to individuals and groups who need them now for protection against present inequalities in the opportunities afforded by cultural contexts, thereby implicitly neglecting any historical dimension to the claims. His main argument, in this sense, is based on present equality and does not take account of historical processes that could actually have given rise to historically-rooted rights. Even Jeremy Waldron, who has used arguments of present justice to argue for limits on Aboriginal rights, has admitted that these arguments must be counterbalanced with historically-rooted rights, which also have weight (e.g., Waldron 2002). Kymlicka might not reject these historical considerations, but he certainly does not fully develop them. His primary normative distinction is one based on arguments related to present autonomy and present equality. In this way, Kymlicka implicitly neglects deeper underpinnings of modern treaty and constitutional rights, again raising questions as to the normative force of his approach relative to a fuller account of collective rights that might leave room for historically-rooted claims.

Kymlicka's distinction is thus less normatively applicable than originally claimed and even has some potential to work normative harm. Given the empirical and normative problems apparent, there is thus arguably a manifest need to work toward theorising collective rights in a manner going beyond Kymlicka's framework.

Respect for Collective Rights

Rather than taking group-differentiated rights and those defined by Kymlicka's distinction as the operative categories, we can work toward the development of other theories that explain the moral appropriateness of group rights. In this section, I will very briefly defend the appropriateness of doing so against two influential attacks and gesture toward the related sets of issues that make questions about collective rights both appropriate and interesting.

First, Kymlicka himself has put one influential objection to study of collective rights as an operative concept, stating that that collective rights constitute a 'large and heterogeneous' category and that such rights 'have little in common, and it is important not to lump the idea of group-differentiated citizenship with the myriad of other issues that arise under the heading of "collective rights"' (Kymlicka 1995, 35; Kymlicka 1994, 18). But such a claim ignores one important factor. Opponents of collective moral rights question their conceptual coherence and thus reject any right falling within the category (e.g., Narveson 1991, 345; Hartney 1991, 312). Kymlicka's decision not to deal with collective rights is simply not equipped to deal with such objections, as Kymlicka has made a partly strategic decision to take a different tack. Kymlicka's so-called objection is actually an explanation of why he argues for certain kinds of rights without using the concept of collective rights. So it expresses strategy: he wants to make his argument on other grounds. If we take the statement as more, as a challenge to the concept of collective rights, then my claim is that his challenge is mistaken. At the very least, it prejudges without real justification the issue of whether we can develop a theory of collective rights that shows their common foundation, when some of the opposition itself implies that common issues are at stake. In answering such opponents through a theory of collective rights, we would see the common issues at stake.

Second, Jeff Spinner-Halev has recently asserted that arguments for entitlements or rights for different groups must proceed from different bases, meaning that the rights of different groups do not fit within one simple, powerful theory (Spinner-Halev 2000). Other considerations like historical agreements and basic considerations of justice will often be very important and may be the most important aspects in particular situations. But my claim is that respecting collective rights is a coherent, unifying strand that can explain much about such questions and that collective rights have a common structure allowing for a generalised argument.

Although space limitations preclude a full development of this point here, we can attain some sense of the common issues at stake in collective rights contexts by contemplating the collective claims arising in a variety of circumstances. Sometime in the not-too-remote past, people identifying as members of some cultural, ethnic, or religious group had their land and rights brutally stripped away, and many were harmed or killed. We cannot identify the lawful heirs of the precise individuals who suffered. Today, people who identify as members of this same cultural, ethnic, or religious group claim some compensation, ongoing protection, or benefit. We feel some intuitive sympathy with their claim. Why? A constitutional text contains a clause granting the citizens of some state 'freedom of association'. Union activists say this clause should be read so as to give unions some powers not otherwise possessed by their members. Religious activists similarly claim that this clause protects some entitlement on their part to engage in communal acts of worship. We say that judges should be prepared to listen to these arguments. Why? A province with distinctive linguistic and cultural features holds a referendum in which a majority of its population voted to secede from the larger state of which it had been a part. The government officials of this province claim that it is entitled to secede, notwithstanding that some people within it object that they voted against secession and that some of their interests will be adversely affected. In at least some circumstances, we will still agree with the government officials. Why? These circumstances raise common issues about whether groups hold rights and on what basis, and, if so, what principles determine which groups hold which rights. Although Kymlicka's theory is in some ways meant to discourage the endeavour at the outset, any evaluation of these claims depends ultimately on elaborating a more developed theory of collective moral rights that faces up to the generalised criticisms levelled at these rights (cf. Newman 2004a). If such rights are heterogenous, they are no more so than individual rights, and much ink has nonetheless been spilled on attempts to analyse the justifications of individual rights. Collective rights deserve no less.

Canada as Precedent for Collective Rights

The conclusions to which I am building are that any lessons from Canada are different from those that might initially be suggested. Contrary to the lessons from Canada's approach to pluralism as described by Kymlicka's leading body of theoretical work on liberal multiculturalism, Canada does manifest a complex web of both individual and collective rights, the latter not corresponding exclusively to the group-differentiated concept and not being appropriately explicated solely in terms of the 'external protections' – 'internal restrictions' dichotomy.

Canada's constitutional and legislative frameworks embody a number of collectively-based protections for religious groups, cultural groups, linguistic groups, indigenous peoples, and others. Although in some instances the claims of these groups may fit the 'external protections' category, they do not necessarily do so in key, qualitatively important contexts. And there are important normative reasons for saying that they should not always do so. Kymlicka's dichotomy, as we have seen, is neither empirically nor normatively exhaustive.

Rather, Canadian groups have rights, as we have seen, that may include some abilities to restrict their individual members. Canada provides a precedent for very real examples of collective rights that are not necessarily captured by Kymlicka's distinction. As a result, these collective rights give rise to serious challenges related to potential conflicts between collective and individual rights. Kymlicka's distinction would admittedly avoid these challenges but potentially at the cost of missing many of the key questions. We need to work toward a theorising of collective rights that recognises Kymlicka's enormous contribution but that develops in new directions recognising the real possibility of collective rights (cf. Newman 2004a).

References

Acharya, A. (2001), 'Equality, Difference and Group Rights: The Case of India', unpublished PhD thesis, University of Toronto.

Arbour, J.M. (2003), 'The Protection of Aboriginal Rights Within a Human Rights Regime: In Search of an Analytical Framework for Section 25 of the Canadian Charter of Rights and Freedoms', *Supreme Court Law Review*, 21 (2d series), 3–71.

Buchanan, A. (1994), 'Liberalism and Group Rights', in J.L. Coleman and A. Buchanan (eds) *In Harm's Way: Essays in Honor of Joel Feinberg*, Cambridge: Cambridge University Press.

Canada Department of Indian Affairs and Northern Development (1995), *Aboriginal Self-Government: A Federal Policy Guide*, Ottawa: Minister of Public Works and Government Services.

Crawford, J. (ed.) (1988), *The Rights of Peoples*, Oxford: Clarendon Press.

Hartney, M. (1991), 'Some Confusions Concerning Collective Rights', *Canadian Journal of Law and Jurisprudence*, 4, 293–327.

Hogg, P.W. and Turpel, M.E. (1995), 'Implementing Aboriginal Self-Government: Constitutional and Jurisdictional Issues', *University of British Columbia Law Review*, 74, 187–224.

Kymlicka, W. (1989), *Liberalism, Community and Culture*, Oxford: Clarendon Press.

— (1994), 'Individual and Community Rights', in J. Baker (ed.), *Group Rights*, Toronto: University of Toronto Press.

— (1995), *Multicultural Citizenship*, Oxford: Oxford University Press.

— (1997), *States, Nations, and Cultures*, Assen: Van Gorcum.

— (1998), *Finding Our Way: Rethinking Ethnocultural Relations in Canada*, Oxford: Oxford University Press.

— (2001a), *Politics in the Vernacular*, Oxford: Oxford University Press.

— (2001b) 'Western Political Theory and Ethnic Relations in Eastern Europe' in W. Kymlicka and M. Opalski (eds), *Can Liberal Pluralism be Exported? Western Political Theory and Ethnic Relations in Eastern Europe*, Oxford: Oxford University Press.

Kymlicka, W. and Opalski, M. (eds) (2001), *Can Liberal Pluralism be Exported? Western Political Theory and Ethnic Relations in Eastern Europe*, Oxford: Oxford University Press).

Levy, J. (2000), *The Multiculturalism of Fear*, Oxford: Oxford University Press.

Narveson, J. (1991), 'Collective Rights?', *Canadian Journal of Law and Jurisprudence*, 4, 329–345.

Newman, D.G. (2003), 'Liberal Multiculturalism and Will Kymlicka's Uneasy Relation with Religious Pluralism', *Bijdgragen International Journal of Philosophy and Theology*, 64, 265–285.

— (2004a), 'Collective Interests and Collective Rights', 49 *American Journal of Jurisprudence*, 127–163).

— (2004b), 'The Jurisprudence of the Saskatchewan Court of Appeal, 2002', *Saskatchewan Law Review*, 67, 13–58.

Pentley, W. (1988), 'The Interpretive Prism of Section 25', *University of British Columbia Law Review*, 22, 21–59.

Shachar, A. (2001), *Multicultural Jurisdictions: Cultural Differences and Women's Rights*, Cambridge: Cambridge University Press.

Spinner-Halev, J. (2000), 'Land, Culture and Justice: A Framework for Group Rights and Recognition', *Journal of Political Philosophy*, 8, 319–342.

— (2001), 'The Universal Pretensions of Cultural Rights Arguments', *Critical Review of International Social & Political Philosophy*, 4, 2–24.

Tamir, Y. (1999), 'Theoretical Difficulties in the Study of Nationalism', in R. Beiner (ed.), *Theorizing Nationalism*, Albany: SUNY Press.

Taylor, C. (1994), 'The Politics of Recognition', in A. Guttman (ed.), *Multiculturalism: Examining the Politics of Recognition*, Princeton: Princeton University Press.

Waldron, J. (2002), 'Redressing Historic Injustice', *University of Toronto Law Journal*, 52, 135–160.

PART II
Institutional Accommodation in Theory and Practice: The Case of Aboriginal Peoples

PART II

Chapter 5

Reasoning about the Identity of Aboriginal People

Avigail Eisenberg

The public assessment of minority identity by institutions such as courts or legislatures is often unavoidable. This is because some assessment of minority identity is usually an inevitable part of the process of deciding whether a minority practice or set of rules ought to be prohibited by or protected from public regulation. This process of assessment, or reasoning about identity, arises all the time in relation to questions now well familiar within liberal public discourse about the limits of minority accommodation. For instance, reasoning through the answer to the question of whether Sikh boys in Quebec or Vancouver should be prohibited from wearing ceremonial daggers known as kirpans strapped to their bodies when they attend public school implicates an understanding of the role of the kirpan in Sikhism. The question of whether fundamentalist Mormons should be prohibited from practising polygamy is answered, in part, by understanding the role of polygamy in Mormon religious belief. The question of whether public signs should be bilingual in Breton, Quebec, Wales or California implicates understanding the importance of minority languages to these national minorities. And the question of whether Aboriginal peoples should be exempt from international and national regulations regarding whaling, fishing, hunting and many other disputed practices implicates knowledge about the importance of these practices to the ways of life of Aboriginal communities. While these questions don't encompass all that is entailed by minority rights, they nonetheless lead directly to a set of complex issues at the heart of how well or poorly minorities are treated. If these kinds of questions are addressed in terms of how they are often raised, then public institutions cannot avoid assessing the nature and importance of disputed practices to the identities of groups or individuals who make them. Sometimes the only alternative to publicly and explicitly assessing minority identities is for public institutions to leave such assessments to the private discretion of the agents within those institutions, e.g., to figure out why the kirpan, polygamy, street signs in French or hunting out of season is important to the group in the first place.

At the same time as reasoning about identity is part of the process of answering some conventional questions about minority rights and public policy, the assessment of identity, particularly when it occurs within institutions dominated by a distinctive cultural, ethnic, linguistic or national majority, is fraught with potentially serious problems. One concern that critics of 'identity politics' frequently raise is that any public assessment of identity is bound to be ethnocentric and favour the majority's values in interpreting what is important to minorities. Such assessments, some argue, are inherently subjective,[1] and whether they are accurate in some sense or not, a second problem is that they will end up essentialising groups by selecting for recognition what is central to the group's identity as stipulated by one subset of the group at one time in history. Thirdly, focusing on identity in politics is said to distract attention from more important social problems – like poverty, environmental degradation, and sexual inequality – and also has the potential to ignite large social conflicts. These are important concerns and ones that are well-rehearsed within the scholarship on identity politics. (For liberal critics, see Barry 2001; Weinstock 2006; for post-modern critics, see Brown 1995, especially chapter 5, and Butler 1990. Also see generally, Brubaker and Cooper 2001, as well as Creppell 2003, especially chapter 1.) But, if the assessment of identity is simply a conventional part of understanding the importance, or even the meaning, of a disputed practice to a minority group, how, in light of these problems, should public institutions respond to claims that directly implicate the identities of groups and individuals while avoiding considerations of identity?

This gives rise to the problem on which I focus here. Although institutions 'reason about identity' all the time, there is usually nothing systematic about the way they do so. In the course of deciding whether disputed practices ought to be accommodated or prohibited, public institutions usually examine how practices arise, they want to know whether a practice is contentious within the group, how the practice functions to sustain the group, how central it is to a group's sense of itself or way of life, its role in the group's history, and what consequences follow from protecting or prohibiting it. But, as commonplace and necessary as these assessments sometimes are, they usually occur without any appeal to standard criteria. Rarely do courts display an awareness of how the standards used to reason about one group's identity compare to the standards used to reason about the identity of another group. Sometimes, public institutions will avoid these issues by leaving it to the discretion of their agents – e.g., lawyers, judges, commissioners, legislators, etc. – to answer identity-based questions. In addition to relying on personal discretion, courts rely on lawyers to bring forth whatever relevant evidence advances their cases, or they rely on the briefs of interveners to point out implications of a conflict that might otherwise be ignored. These kinds of inputs sometimes cover a broad range of concerns and draw upon evidence from several sources – the group itself, anthropologists, theologians, historians, archeologists – about the group's identity and the role of a disputed practice or set of rules in that identity. Legislatures, commissions of inquiry, and tribunals often consider similar kinds of information and sort through this kind of evidence in an attempt to understand how best to shape regulations. But in very few contexts are the agents within these institutions applying a set of standards or

---

1   Barsh and Henderson use the anthropological distinction between 'emic' – i.e. that which is a matter of subjective meaning – and 'etic' – i.e. a phenomenon which can be reliably and consistently measured by outsiders – to characterise the majority's decision in *Van der Peet*. According to Barsh and Henderson, "the extent to which an idea, symbol or practice is central to the culture identity of a particular society is inescapably subjective to that society – or, in the jargon of anthropologists, 'emic'" (1997, 1000).

criteria beyond their commonsense for how to understand and use this evidence in the assessment of identity claims.

Therefore, it's interesting to see what happens when a public institution tries to establish a formal set of standards and criteria for reasoning through the identity claims of a minority group. This is precisely what the Supreme Court of Canada attempted to do in the case of *R. v Van der Peet* ([1996] 2 SCR 507). *Van der Peet* is one of a series of Aboriginal rights cases[2] decided by the Supreme Court of Canada (SCC) in which a legal test, called the 'distinctive culture test' (which I describe below) was used to establish a standard set of criteria for deciding whether an Aboriginal practice ought to be accommodated based on whether the practice is an integral part of a distinctive Aboriginal culture.

The first thing about *Van der Peet* worth noting is that it involves a dispute about the rights of Aboriginal people. This dimension sets it apart from other minority rights cases in which group identity is an issue. Aboriginal people in Canada and elsewhere in the world are involved in on-going struggles with the state about their status as a distinct people with rights that are inherent and that were not extinguished by the settler communities which colonised their territories. This feature makes Aboriginal claims different from the claims of ethnic or religious minorities because, unlike Aboriginal peoples, these other kinds of minorities want accommodation for their practices but do not dispute the state's sovereignty. This difference between Aboriginal and other minority disputes heightens the problems that arise when public, mainstream institutions assess the identity of a group. Cases like *Van der Peet* are likely to reveal more vividly than other minority rights cases the political objections to the assessment of minority identity by public institutions.

This chapter begins by examining how and why identity is arising in legal disputes about minority rights, including the Aboriginal rights cases in Canada. The second section considers some of the benefits to this focus and to further developing a conceptual vocabulary that institutions can use in relation to cases that involve identity. The third section turns to three challenges to the general project of publicly assessing identity and the ways in which these challenges apply to the dispute in Canada involving *Van der Peet*. The final section looks at whether, on balance, the development of a standard set of criteria to be used in the public assessment of minority identity is more likely to improve or impoverish the protection of minority rights.

Identity and Public Institutions

In the last 15 years, political and legal institutions at the local, state and global levels have steadily expanded their use of the term identity, especially in documents that offer minority rights protection. The context today in the international arena and within many western states for groups to make claims for the protection of their identity is possibly more congenial than ever before because of the growing number of institutions, protocols, declarations and conventions which establish standards

---

2   See *Mitchell v MNR* [2001] 1SCR 911 and *R v Powley* [2003] 2 SCR 207.

specifically meant to protect identity. A commitment to protect identity has been explicitly written into the *Charter of Fundamental Rights of the European Union*,[3] *The Draft Declaration on the Rights of Indigenous Peoples*,[4] and *ILO Convention No. 169* (1989),[5] the *UN Convention on the Rights of the Child*,[6] as well as the *Declaration on the Rights of Persons Belonging to National or Ethnic, Religious and Linguistic Minorities* (1992),[7] to name but a few. These documents, all of which explicitly mention the need to protect the identities of adults and children, have been developed in part to fill the gap left by older protections, like Article 27 of the *International Covenant on Civil and Political Rights*.[8] This new set of minority protections recognises groups, rather than just individual members of groups, as the bearers of identity, and frames violations of cultural, religious, indigenous and other group-based rights in terms of positive state obligations to protect group identity, rather than merely in the negative terms of not denying groups their rights.

Not only is the term identity cropping up more frequently in legal and political documents, existing political and legal institutions seem to be more open to arguments in which the identity of a group – i.e., its way of life, system of beliefs or self-understanding – is part of legal and political reasoning (see Webber 2006). Courts in the United States, for example, have had to devise methods of analysing so-called cultural defences, where cultural identity and beliefs are proposed as mitigating factors to assessing the gravity of a crime for the purposes of sentencing (see Renteln 2004). In this context, Canada's Supreme Court developed its 'distinctive culture test,' in the 1990s as a means to assess Aboriginal claims to fish, hunt and trade in particular places and ways. Even where laws do not explicitly offer protection for so-called 'group identity', cultural, religious, linguistic, national groups and indigenous peoples often advance identity claims for the protection of their communities by

---

3   The Preamble discusses commitment to common values while respecting 'the diversity of the cultures and traditions of the peoples of Europe as well as the national identities of the Member States...'.

4   UN DocE/CN.4/Sub:2/1994/2/Add.1 (1994): which discusses the protection of 'collective and individual rights to maintain and develop their distinctive identities and characteristics...'.

5   General aims of the convention are stated as: 'Recognising the aspirations of these peoples to exercise control over their own institutions, ways of life and economic development and to maintain and develop their identities, languages, and religions, within the framework of the States in which they live.' In addition, Article 2(b) requires governments to promote 'the full realization of the social, economic and culture rights of these peoples with respect for their social and cultural identity, their customs and traditions and their institutions'.

6   Article 8.2 states: 'Where a child is illegally deprived of some or all of the elements of his or her identity, States Parties shall provide appropriate assistance and protection, with a view to re-establishing speedily his or her identity.'

7   Article 1 states: 'States shall protect the existence and the national or ethnic, cultural, religious and linguistic identity of minorities within their respective territories and shall encourage conditions for the promotion of that identity.'

8   Article 27 reads that: 'In those States in which ethnic, religious or linguistic minorities exist, persons belong to such minorities shall not be denied the right, in community with the other members of their group, to enjoy their own culture, to profess and practise their own religion, or to use their own language.'

seeking intervener status before the courts or by presenting evidence to commissions, tribunals and regulatory bodies that explain the ways in which a contested regulation or dispute affects their identity. The World Trade Organisation, for instance, has come under pressure from member states to modify its criteria for assessing food-related disputes to include considerations of identity, not just food safety, in light of controversies surrounding genetically-modified foods, artificial growth hormones in animals and raw milk cheeses (Brom 2004). In Germany, Denmark, and Spain, religious and cultural identity are cited as relevant factors to be weighed when setting European standards about animal cruelty and slaughter, intellectual property, and genomics research. In Mexico, the protection of the identities of indigenous peoples who rely on wild corn strains has been proposed as a reason to halt the dissemination of genetically modified corn strains (see Stabinsky 2002; on similar controversies about wild rice strains, see Carlson 2002).

So numerous are the cases and documents where protections are presented in terms of their role in the identity of groups that international institutions have developed a set of criteria, though not as formal as Canada's distinctive culture test, for assessing these claims. These criteria include, for instance, the requirement to protect practices that are essential to the cultural survival of groups, including economic activities, and to require that states consult groups whose central practices are affected by regulations (Scheinin 2000).

Why has identity arisen as a central feature of so many minority rights documents and cases? One reason might be due to the rise of multicultural politics, which draws attention to the salience of cultural, religious, linguistic and other aspects of identity. In the best known philosophical accounts of multiculturalism, minority rights and the accommodation of minority practices are justified because of their role in protecting crucial features of individual identity. Will Kymlicka's argument for minority rights, for example, is premised on the importance of individual autonomy which requires that individuals lead their lives 'from the inside' and thus according to their sense of themselves. The importance of this capacity derives precisely from the observation that individuals are deeply (though not irrevocably) tied to communities and that these attachments constitute their identity. Although 'no end is immune from ... potential revision,' (Kymlicka 1995, 91) '[t]ies to one's culture,' he argues following Rawls, 'are normally too strong to give up' (1995, 87) and "considerations of identity provide powerful reasons for tying people's autonomy-interest to their culture" (1997, 87, footnote 6). Thus the mark of liberalism, Kymlicka maintains, is the capacity of individuals to reflect on their identity.[9]

The rise of multiculturalism, including the rationale for minority rights that links the protection of identity-constituting communities with individual well-being may be acting as an incentive for groups to frame and advance their interests in terms of identity. This isn't necessarily a good thing. One could argue, along with theorists as diverse as Jeremy Waldron (2000) and Wendy Brown (1995), that minority groups

---

9 Kymlicka's insistence on the individual's capacity to revise her attachments is highlighted in his criticisms of Rawls's position, taken in 'Justice Political, not Metaphysical,' that some religious commitments are neither revisable nor autonomously affirmed. See Kymlicka 1995, 158–163.

currently have an incentive to frame their grievances in terms of a threat or injury to some aspect of their identity. If legal and political institutions are sympathetic to identity claims, as seems to be evident from the increasing use of the term in law and politics, groups will present their interests in terms of their identity. In this sense, groups (and especially their advocates) use their identities strategically and advance identity arguments that they believe will convince the court or the public of their case. (Concerns about the strategic use of identity claims have also been explored by Johnson 2000 and Brubaker and Cooper 2001). This concern, however, counts less as a reason to avoid identity than an invitation to ask why this strategy exists and what sort of normative possibilities it opens or forecloses. The fact is that strategy is used, one way or another, in advancing claims before public institutions. In this respect, rights are also a strategy used within a political and legal discourse to advance particular interests. As in the case of identity, the political question that informs normative assessments of rights is whether rights are a good strategy and how they shape the interests of groups or individuals who use them.

R. v Van der Peet and Some Other Cases

In the case of *R. v Van der Peet* identity proved to be a poor strategy to advance the rights and interests of the Sto:lo First Nation. At issue in *R. v Van der Peet* is whether Dorothy Van der Peet, a member of the Sto:lo Nation, is exempt from regulations that restrict individual fishers from selling salmon without a licence. Van der Peet argued that her right to trade in salmon is derived from her membership in the Sto:lo nation whose cultural identity is intimately tied to salmon fishing, and thereby protected by Canada's Constitution.[10] The majority found against Van der Peet and argued that trade in salmon (as opposed to fishing and consuming salmon) did not count as a protected Aboriginal right in this case. For a practice to receive constitutional protection it must pass a 'distinctive culture test'. The test requires first that claimants show that their practice is jeopardised by state regulations, and then, that the practice is *integral* to the *pre-contact* indigenous culture of their community. In other words, to be protected, practices must be central not incidental to the culture, and only those practices which existed before Aboriginal-European contact (i.e. 'pre-contact') count as ones eligible for constitutional protection.[11] In *Van der Peet*, the court found that

---

10 Section 35 of Canada's Constitution Act, 1982 reads, '(1)The existing aboriginal and treaty rights of the aboriginal peoples of Canada are hereby recognised and affirmed; (2) In this Act, 'aboriginal peoples of Canada' includes the Indian, Inuit and Métis peoples of Canada; (3) For greater certainty, in subsection (1) 'treaty rights' includes rights that now exist by way of land claims agreements or may be so acquired; (4) Notwithstanding any other provision of this Act, the aboriginal and treaty rights referred to in subsection (1) are guaranteed equally to male and female persons.'

11 If this can be shown, then the practice must be balanced with the legal system with which it conflicts – in this case Canadian common law. The Court's job is to render Aboriginal perspectives 'cognizable to the non-Aboriginal legal system' through a reconciliation process that places equal weight on each perspective (*Van der Peet* at 551). Borrows (1997-8, 45–52) provides an excellent analytic overview of the test.

trade in salmon was not a protected constitutional right because it did not pre-date contact with Europeans. Trade in salmon was 'incidental and occasional' at best and no established 'market system' existed until well into the 19th Century. Sto:lo trade in salmon, the court concluded, was not central to the pre-contact Sto:lo identity and therefore could not count as a protected aboriginal right.

As I've suggested above, the argument in *Van der Peet* arises at a time when the venues and opportunities for framing minority rights arguments in terms of identity are expanding in local, national and international arenas. In the last 20 years especially, several important international cases involving the rights of indigenous peoples have been decided explicitly in relation to the assessment of Aboriginal identity. Usually these cases are associated with an older provision of international law found in Article 27 of the United Nation's 1966 International Covenant on Civil and Political Rights which, as noted above, protects the cultural, religious and linguistic rights of minorities. These cases led the UN Human Rights Committee to assess evidence about whether disputed practices are central to a group's identity and the extent to which central practices are jeopardised by state regulation. Most of the Aboriginal cases decided in this context are similar to *Van der Peet* in that they also involve disputes between Aboriginal peoples and settler states about land claims and property use. Like *Van der Peet*, these cases have required that the Committee determine how central a disputed or threatened practice is to various indigenous communities, including, for instance, the Sami in Finland (*Länsman v Finland* No 511/1992), the Lubicon in Canada (*Ominayak v Canada* No 167/1984) and the Hopu in Tahiti (*Hopu v France* No 549/193).[12] Also, like *Van der Peet*, the threat to Aboriginal practices in each case is posed by state-sanctioned land development and resource extraction. Yet, a formal legal test is not developed or used in these cases. Instead, a set of less formal criteria for assessing identity claims is taking shape within them. These criteria include the requirement to protect practices which are essential to the cultural survival of groups and the state's duty to consult groups whose central practices are affected by regulation (Scheinin 2000).

In sum, *Van der Peet* is by no means an isolated case, and cases that involve the assessment of minority identity are not especially rare either in relation to Aboriginal people or in relation to other minorities. The questions which then arise are what to make of this trend and whether the drawbacks of assessing identity outweigh the positive benefits of doing so. I turn first to some possible benefits of assessing identity in public institutions.

Is Identity Workable in Relation to Minority Claims?

For at least three reasons it would be a mistake to dismiss identity as incoherent or too elusive to be useful within the context of contemporary democratic politics. One reason is because, for better or worse, institutions are already engaged in assessing the identities of groups and setting standards and thresholds for the protection of

---

12 *Hopu* was not decided on the basis of Article 27 because France has made a reservation to Article 27. Instead, the Committee relied on articles that recognise the rights to family such as 17(1) and 23(1). For commentaries on these cases, see Scheinin 2000 and Macklem 2004.

their identities. They have engaged in this activity partly because minority groups have tried to use institutional means to defend their identities and partly because developments (including group pressure) in international law and organisations have led to the proliferation of laws and institutions in which the assessment of identity might take place. Regardless of how incoherent identity might be as a concept in ideal and abstract political theory, it is quickly becoming a concrete and well-used term in law and politics with particular criteria and norms attached to it. For this reason alone, the particular criteria and norms attached to the concept should be an issue for normative dialogue and debate. Since at least the 1960s, institutional practices within western states and at a global level have contained a set of understandings and best practices in relation to how identity ought to be understood, assessed and protected. Very little political research has examined what this notion of identity amounts to or what it means for the protection of minorities. But that it exists, and that it is given meaning by legal and political institutions, is beyond a doubt.

A second reason not to dismiss identity is because, whether intentionally or not, many existing approaches to the protection of minorities rest on prior and implicit understandings of what the protection of group or individual identity requires. In the context of specific disputes, a group's identity forms the basis upon which minority rights for cultural protection or linguistic accommodation are interpreted. This is because the connection that exists between a contested practice or activity and a group's identity is the only basis upon which to fully understand what is at stake for a group in a particular dispute. A decision about whether a minority has a right to 'X' requires, at some point, understanding what counts as a threat to the group, which in turn requires understanding what is central and integral to that group's identity such that a right to 'X' is necessary. This connection is made implicitly all the time in cases that involve minority groups whose practices and identities have historically shaped public institutions and regulations, such as recognised language groups and some religious and ethnic groups.

But, minorities, and especially minorities that have been historically excluded from public discourse and debate and therefore those whose practices are relatively unfamiliar to the majority, often have to defend their practices and values by first presenting convincing arguments that their practices are indeed important to their community's identity (see Vallance 2006). In some cases, the burden placed on minorities is not only to defend the claim that a given practice is central to their identity and therefore merits legal accommodation, but often also to prove that a given practice is *their* practice – that is, that it is a practice which is related to their identity. The very presence of this burden offers some indication of the bias which inform majority institutions with respect to what counts as important or unimportant to the identities of groups. These biases might or might not be defensible. But regardless, they first need to be understood as bias. One way to disclose biases is to focus directly on the relation between institutional practices and the identities of groups that are affected by these practices.

Third, raising the general salience of identity is not altogether a bad thing from the perspective of the social groups which seek the means to empower and mobilise their members in response to disadvantage or oppression. Group claims become framed in terms of identity partly because identity offers a powerful set of terms by which groups are able to mobilise their own members (see Gutmann 2005; Moore 2006 and Young 1989). Identity motivates social groups because groups often view the harm that is done to them by state regulations or mainstream practices as a harm done to their way of life or their understanding of how they should conduct their life. In this sense, identity provides a powerful set of terms with which groups can empower themselves and an understanding of their collective experience and interests in relation to the broader societies in which they are a minority.[13] In other words, identity is a good way for groups to motivate and mobilise their members.[14]

In sum, for three reasons identity is emerging as a workable and perhaps even a promising set of terms for minorities to use in advancing their interests both within states and internationally. First, identity is becoming a well-used term within politics and law with particular and concrete criteria and norms attached to it. Yet, these criteria are by no means fully worked out or the subject of wide agreement. In short, the time is now and the scope is broad for meaningful normative dialogue and debate about the criteria that ought to guide institutional assessments of identity. Second, understanding the identity of a group is often an unavoidable aspect of settling disputes that involve minorities. In most cases, forming some understanding of what counts as a threat to group identity is just part of the process of figuring out what is at stake for the different actors in a dispute. The choice is rarely between framing disputes in terms of identity or not. Usually the choice is between assessing the identity of a group based on publicly vetted and transparent criteria or leaving it up to decision-makers to use their own discretion and bias. Third, identity politics can be empowering and motivating for groups. Identity involves a set of values and relational experiences that speak to the core of an individual's sense of self and a group's self understanding. This makes identity dangerous stuff. But for groups that are fragile and fragmented due to historical oppression and disadvantage, identity can provide the means of empowerment and mobilization and the conceptual terms to explain the kinds of relational harms that groups experience.

The Drawbacks of Publicly Assessing Identity

Despite the promise that identity might hold for the advancement of minority rights, the critics of identity politics have raised serious challenges to using identity to frame and resolve conflicts that involve minorities. Here I examine three general categories

---

13 Iris Young makes a similar claim in arguing for the representation of disadvantaged social groups. See Young (1989) 261. However, Young has also written that she does not view group identity as a beneficial means to organise social groups because of the potential for identity to essentialise groups and unfairly include or exclude particular individuals from groups. See, in particular, Young 1997.

14 Some critics of identity politics make the similar observation, that identity provides a powerful – some might say explosive – means to motivate and mobilise groups because identity is so core to the values that we seem to care about. While Dryzek (2005), Weinstock (2001 and 2006) and Waldron (2000) point to this as a reason why identity is dangerous to democratic discourse, Moore (2006) and Gutmann (2005) argue that this is what makes identity important and even useful to democratic politics.

of concerns: 1) the problem of essentialism; 2) the problem of ethnocentric bias; and 3) the distracting and inflationary tendencies of identity politics. None, I find, pose the sort of obstacles that some of their proponents claim they do.

Essentialism

The challenge of essentialism is probably the most common objection to identity politics in the political theory scholarship especially amongst scholars who focus on gender, ethnicity and race. Usually the objection begins with the observation that because culture is constantly being made and remade through human interactions, it should not be reified by public institutions (see McRanor 2006 and Scott 2003). In a case like *Van der Peet*, when the court identifies one practice as 'central and integral' to a community and deems another practice to be peripheral or contingent, it ends up freezing a culture artificially to particular practices (Borrows 1997–8). Therefore, to place the recognition of identity at the centre of decision-making and dispute resolution is sure to disrupt the ebb and flow of cultural change and the interdependence and integrated nature of cultural practices. It is to isolate cultural identity from the means by which cultural practices are reshaped (Narayan 1997).[15]

This objection makes a good deal of sense in the abstract. But how this reification of identity occurs in the context of more concrete political relations amongst peoples suggests that often the choice is not between freezing a culture or allowing members to freely negotiate their own terms of change, but rather between different ways of establishing terms upon which cultural change can be negotiated. Cases like *Van der Peet* can be understood as centrally concerned with the terms on which cultural change ought to occur; in part, this is what makes them problematic though not quite as confining as some of the critics have suggested. How and when practices arise, who views them as central to a group's identity, how long they have been central, and what is the nature of internal debates about the practices, are central questions in cases that focus on identity. In contrast, these kinds of questions are likely to be precluded by approaches that ignore identity and, instead, aim merely to determine whether a law restricting particular practices was passed in a procedurally correct manner or whether it contradicts other legally recognised rights. An approach that focuses on the identity of a group is likely to raise questions about cultural history and cultural change in a manner that is more direct and translucent than other approaches.

Those worried about essentialism will not find this response comforting largely because the force of the challenge that essentialism raises is not that the *wrong*

---

15 A different kind of essentialism, individual essentialism, is concerned with the ways in which individuals within minorities are made more vulnerable by attempts of mainstream institutions to protect minorities. Often the practices that are important to minority groups have implications for the status of women and others who are vulnerable within the group. Therefore, protecting minorities or central minority practices may serve to increase the vulnerability of minorities within minorities. Ayelet Shachar has coined the useful phrase, 'the paradox of multicultural vulnerability' to express this problem. See Shachar 2001. I don't deal with this objection here.

practices will be protected by courts or legislatures,[16] but that *any* practice which is protected is eventually the wrong practice because of the ever-changing nature of identity. Yet, it is difficult to understand how to avoid this sort of essentialism in a practical political context whether identity claims are accommodated or not. This is because, in the cases that arise where a fragile minority is seeking protection for a practice because it is central to its identity, the alternatives to protecting the group's claim tend to reify other values or practices.

For instance, the accommodation of minorities often exists in a zero-sum relation to nationalist ideologies, which emphasise the need for unity and uniformity. This is particularly true in cases that involve national minorities and indigenous peoples. What is often presented in Canada, in mainstream scholarship and public policy, as the alternative to recognising exemptions for Aboriginal practices in Canadian law are approaches that favour the assimilation of Aboriginal peoples into mainstream Canadian society in which no group is granted such exemptions (see, e.g., Flanagan 2000).

A second alternative is to favour mechanisms that are supposedly identity neutral but end up also emasculating minority values in favour of the majority's identity. When the identity of the national majority is not directly invoked, other 'identity-neutral' solutions, like 'leaving it to the market', or reifying a 'one law for all' approach, will accomplish similar aims. For instance, in the case of *Länsman v Finland*, one alternative to protecting Sami reindeer husbandry in Finland from quarry-building was to favour regional development schemes that offered no exemptions to any group, which treated all group interests as appropriately vetted through competitive market forces, and therefore which were dependent on the sovereign values of the market. Generally speaking, the alternative to protecting minority practices is to favour what is often a substantive and essentialised notion of the state as homogeneous in character with laws and values that apply to every citizen in the same way and that protect a similar basket of opportunities for everyone (see Kymlicka 2005, 22, footnote 29). As I suggest above, approaches that focus on identity may be more likely to draw attention to the ways in which decision-making impacts the identities of all groups involved in a dispute, including groups whose identities are protected by majoritarian, market-based rules and approaches that seem to be 'identity-neutral'.

A third alternative is for minorities to resolve identity-related disputes themselves through decision-making processes internal to their communities. But, it cannot escape the challenge of essentialism because recognising a community's right

---

16 There is no doubt that, in assessing identity, the wrong practices might gain protection. The controversy over *Van der Peet* provides a good illustration of one way in which this happens. The distinctive culture test ties eligible rights-bearing practices to pre-contact times and, in this sense, has been described as 'freezing rights' to practices that, while of ancient origin, may be only incidental to how contemporary Aboriginal peoples survive as distinctive communities (see Borrows 1997–8). But this is not, as I argue below, the essentialism objection. Rather, this is more accurately understood as a problem that arises because the Canadian state refuses to acknowledge the inherent right to self-determination of Aboriginal people whose settlement pre-dates Europeans and refuses to question the legitimacy of the sovereign power of the state to make (and change) law for Aboriginal people.

to decide often entails reifying the identity and values of the group as expressed through decision-making procedures that dominate the community at a given time. When a court decides that the fairest way to resolve disputes within an Aboriginal community is to leave to that community the task of working out solutions according to the community's traditions and customs, it is, in effect, giving authoritative status to particular rules at a particular time within the community.[17] From the vantage of the essentialism problem, there is little difference in practice between a court respecting the processes internal to minority groups and imposing a substantive decision in favour of one set of values over another.

Ethnocentricity

A second concern with approaching minority rights cases in a manner that focuses on identity is that any public assessment of a minority identity is bound to be ethnocentric because it sanctions the majority's interpretation of the minority's cultural identity. Some authors suggest that what is central or peripheral to a culture is entirely subjective (see Barsh and Henderson 1997, 1000). Culture is inseparable from each human interaction and from the power that informs these interactions. What is 'cultural' is, itself, of 'culture' (see Scott 2003). 'Insofar as culture is articulated and employed within relations of power [as it inevitably is], it is an effect of that power' (McRanor 2006).

The grounds for understanding disputed practices in relation to the groups that practise them is certainly limited if the role, meaning and centrality of a practice within a culture is entirely subjective. But many commentators are unwilling to rely on this argument. In relation to the *Van der Peet* case, for instance, John Borrows raises the problem that the distinctive culture test is ethnocentric, but not because the role of any practice is entirely subjective,[18] but rather owing to the fact that the test fails a much more basic requirement, namely the requirement that the court consider Aboriginal laws and perspectives in relation to the meaning of the rights at stake. '[N]owhere in these cases does the Chief Justice use the laws of the people charged, or the laws of any other Aboriginal people, to arrive at the standards through which he will define these rights. As such, the Court does not use "intersocietal" law in developing its test for Aboriginal rights' (Borrows 1997–8, 61). Instead of relying on Aboriginal perspectives, judges rely on their own discretion – their bias and stereotypes (Borrows 1997–8, 56–57) – in understanding which practices and values are central and integral to the culture of an Aboriginal community. This discretion extends to deciding, in strikingly arbitrary ways, what counts as culture and what historical framework ought to be imposed in determining what counts as Aboriginal culture. As Borrows explains the court's perspective, 'Aboriginal is retrospective. It is about what was, "once upon a time," central to the survival of a community, not

---

17 This problem is discussed in relation to rules within religious communities towards women and dissenters by Shachar 1998, 290. It is discussed in relation to Aboriginal communities in Eisenberg 2003, 46–50.

18 Although Borrows mentions this argument in quoting one of the dissenting opinions in *Van der Peet* written by Justice McLachlin. See Borrows 1997–8, 56.

necessarily about what is central, significant and distinctive to the survival of these communities today. [The Chief Justice's] test invites stories about the past' (Borrows 1997–8, 43).

Patrick Macklem (2001) argues, in a similar vein, that culture is notoriously elastic and can invite too much discretion by the courts. Legal inquiry of the sort that the distinctive culture test sanctions, turns Aboriginal identities into sets of practices and traditions which are protected by public institutions only by, ironically, allowing judges to disrupt the negotiation of these practices amongst people whose identity they inform.[19] According to Macklem, this poses a dilemma for judges; on one hand, the purpose of legal inquiry is to protect the identity of a vulnerable minority, yet, on the other hand, the nature of legal inquiry allows (one might say requires) judges to enter into negotiations about Aboriginal identity.

Macklem acknowledges that judges cannot always avoid this dilemma. Although both Borrows and Macklem recognise that cases like *Van der Peet* are centrally about self-determination, not cultural interpretation, both also recognise that sometimes legal institutions must assess the importance of particular practices to the identity of groups. Conflicts between a practice – like selling salmon – and a law that regulates that practice, could conceivably arise in a variety of contexts including national and international contexts where Aboriginal communities are self-governing. Where self-determination for Aboriginal people is recognised, Canadian courts and Aboriginal institutions will sometimes be required to interpret and understand the cultural identity of the other group in order to settle disputes that arise between them. As Macklem states, 'the judiciary presumably would be charged with the responsibilities of policing the boundaries of Aboriginal jurisdiction' (2001, 168) and questions of identity are likely to inform some of these cases. The coexistence of different peoples gives rise to intersocietal disputes and therefore requires intersocietal laws.[20] Some of these disputes will involve questions of identity. And therefore the question of how to address these disputes arises one way or another.

Even in cases like *Van der Peet,* where stereotypes of Aboriginal cultures are pervasive amongst the mainstream group with the power to render judgment, the bias that informs this decision is not accurately explained in terms of cultural subjectivism or failed cultural interpretation. In fact, opting for this kind of explanation obscures what leads the court to formulate its judgment. The central aspect of the distinct cultural test, namely the requirement that only practices developed *pre-contact* are eligible for exemption from Canadian laws, reflects a careful attempt to define the terms of protecting Aboriginal culture in a manner that does not threaten Canadian sovereignty over Aboriginal people. Through the pre-contact requirement, the test

---

19 See Macklem 2001, 168; Borrows 1997–8, 52. Moreover, as Barsh and Henderson argue, the distinction between practices that are core to a culture and those which are peripheral ignores the fact that what is peripheral is often connected to and supportive of what is central. See Barsh and Henderson 1997, 1000.

20 Borrows emphasises the intersocietal nature of disputes like that at issue in *Van der Peet* and argues that a far better approach would be one in which the court relied on the common law's recognition of Aboriginal ancestral laws and customs and thereby anchored their judgments on the 'time-honoured methodology of common law' while, at the same time, encouraging the development of Aboriginal law.

explicitly establishes as a standard for Aboriginal rights, the presence of European settlers (Borrows 2002, 72) and the norms of European culture precisely because without explicitly doing so, these standards would not exist as the background against which to judge Aboriginal claims. Aboriginal practices that were developed solely as a result of contact with European cultural practices, and which respond to the need for survival in light of the development of settler society, are not eligible for protection even though no credible interpretation of what is integral or important to a culture would leave these practices out.[21] Rather than being the result of subjectivism, the pre-contact rule is a means by which the court limits the logic of cultural protection. Without such a limit, the implications for Canadian law of the requirement to protect practices that are central and integral to the distinctive culture of a group are potentially far-reaching and dramatic.[22]

Most commentators, including Macklem and Borrows, object in the first instance to the distinctive culture test because it serves to cement the imperialistic relations between the Canadian state and Aboriginal people. The problem with culture in relation to public institutions then, is not that it is opaque and subjective, but rather, as Macklem puts it, it is elastic, and as Borrows argues, it can apply either, generally, to any practice that sustains a community's survival, or narrowly, to specific practices that are distinctive to a group at a particular time in a particular place. Without criteria in place to control the elasticity of the concept of culture when it is used in political and legal decision-making, institutions will render decisions that interpret minority cultures narrowly, especially where broad interpretations are likely to have a large impact on law or policy decisions. The question that follows, then, is not whether courts ought to be allowed to render decisions that set some of the terms by which cultural identity is negotiated, but rather who sets these terms and what criteria should they use?

The Inflationary Tendencies of Identity Politics

The elasticity of culture is connected to the final problem examined here which is often raised by critics of identity politics, namely that, under the banner of 'cultural protection', groups will advance all sorts of 'lavish' claims and present these claims in a manner that raises the stakes in democratic discourse so that compromise amongst different groups becomes impossible (see Johnson 2000 and Weinstock 2006). However, when we examine the direction that most legal cases and political activity have taken, this third objection is more ironic than anything else. Political practice suggests that the opportunities within law and politics for groups to frame their claims in terms of identity is more likely to raise the opposite problem to lavish claims, namely that identity unreasonably restricts and narrows the kinds of interests

---

21 As Borrows rightly notes, post-contact practices are central to the physical and cultural survival of Aboriginal communities (1997–8, 49).

22 The potential for cultural protections to have a dramatic and far-reaching impact on the law of nation-states is implicitly acknowledged by the United Nations Human Rights Committee in a general comment on Article 27, which stipulates that nothing in Article 27 may be interpreted so as to confer on a minority the right to self-determination.

that groups can advance. Aboriginal people have complained that identity narrowly restricts the sort of claims that they can make, that it fails to capture their relevant interests in a particular dispute, and that it acts as a distraction from what is really at stake in many of these cases. One of the central worries is that opportunities to argue for the protection of discrete identity-related practices are replacing venues to argue for broader claims to self-determination and self-government (see Borrows 1997–8, 47–48). So, whereas the critics worry that identity claims will open the flood gates for all sorts of group-based interests whether they are about identity or not, the concern expressed by Aboriginal peoples, who are often in the position of making such claims, is that identity arguments unfairly restrict and narrow the sort of claims that they can make because venues to argue for self-determination are increasingly unavailable.[23]

None of these developments addresses the concern that groups will act unreasonably in advancing their identity claims. Of course, groups might act unreasonably regardless of whether or not they have access to identity framing, identity discourse or identity-based rights. But are the critics correct to suggest that identity is more likely to incite social conflict because it touches the centre of our sense of self? Overall the evidence is mixed and seems largely dependent on context. In relatively stable societies, courts often hear evidence about the different ways in which a minority's traditions are followed and the various ways in which practices can be disaggregated. Disputes about sensitive issues related to religious identity and practices, for instance, are often publicly discussed and the subjects of compromise. This is partly because religious practices are complex phenomena, so one part of a practice might be regulated without jeopardising the whole tradition or undermining the value system of which it is a part. This is not to suggest that institutional decisions aren't sometimes resented or the subject of protest by minority groups. But there is little reason to believe that decisions that directly focus on 'identity' *per se* have incited more resentment amongst minorities than have decisions which ignore identity but nonetheless have an impact on the minority's identity.

In sum, essentialism, ethnocentricity, and the inflationary and distracting tendencies of identity politics raise important challenges in relation to the public assessment of identity claims. But these challenges are just that – challenges – and not insurmountable obstacles to the development of fair criteria that can be used by institutions like courts and legislatures to assess the identity claims of groups. The challenge of essentialism arises regardless of whether mainstream institutions explicitly assess group identity, whether they explicitly avoid such assessments and opt for 'neutral' solutions like letting 'the market decide', or whether they leave it to minority groups to settle disputes internally through mechanisms like self-government. The challenge of essentialism makes no sense as a reason to avoid defining or shaping culture or religious identities in all cases and ways. Rather, the challenge suggests the need to develop terms for the assessment and protection

---

23 International institutions have gone to substantial lengths to recognise this problem and address it in part by insisting on a strict divide between instruments used to establish cultural rights and those used to establish the right to self-determination. See Human Rights Committee, General Comment 23, Article 27: UN Doc. HRI/GEN/1/Rev.1 at 38 (1994).

of identity that are anchored to and justified in terms of important purposes, like protecting individuals from harm. These terms also have to allow for the development and negotiation of group identity within broad parameters.

Second, the challenge of ethnocentricism includes the need to ensure that public institutions have access to a full range of interpretations and perspectives about what groups consider important to their identity. Possibly no better source of such information exists than the laws and regulations by which groups govern themselves or have done so in the past. Beyond this, I have argued that the main problem in the case of *Van der Peet* has little to do with the ethnocentric biases of the courts. Moreover, to understand culture as thoroughly subjective only serves to obscure the fact that often bias informs the decisions of mainstream courts in order to protect the power of the mainstream group. This is especially true in cases that involve Aboriginal peoples. Bias, of the sort reflected in the pre-contact rule in *Van der Peet*, is imposed by the court not because it fails to understand what Sto:lo culture needs in order to survive but because of the far-reaching ramifications of protecting the cultural survival and flourishing of a group like the Sto:lo.

Third and finally, when institutions, and especially courts, focus on sorting out identity claims they will likely interpret cases narrowly and in ways that are limited to assessing whether a particular practice or tradition can be accommodated within an unchanged legal order.[24] Thus framing claims in terms of identity is unlikely to challenge in any fundamental way the legal or political order of the mainstream society. The challenge in this respect is to ensure that identity does not become the primary or only way to advance claims and that identity does not occlude other dimensions of disputes like self-determination.

This third challenge is, in some ways, the most significant problem to be faced in cases like *Van der Peet* where an approach which focuses on identity easily serves as a convenient way for the courts to avoid the larger issue of self-determination. The court was able to take a case that involved the questionable sovereignty of the Canadian state over Aboriginal people and turn it into a case about whether trading salmon is integral to Sto:lo cultural identity and whether or how it can be accommodated within existing Canadian law.[25] Generally stated, the challenge is how can approaches predicated on considering identity in a political and legal context avoid obscuring what motivates conflicts that involve national minorities? Often these conflicts turn on the denial of self-determination, regardless of whether or not cultural difference exists between groups. Therefore, approaches that focus on accommodating identity-related differences may be just another way of seeking to legitimise colonial rule (see Green 2000). On this basis, the protection of identity proved to be a poor strategy in the case of *R. v Van der Peet*.

Yet, at the same time, identity claims have proved to be a powerful means to mobilise and empower groups, including Aboriginal peoples. In addition, many existing approaches to the protection of minority rights rest on prior and implicit understandings of what the protection of group identity requires. To understand the way in which a dispute relates to the identity of a group is sometimes an unavoidable

---

24 This criticism is discussed in relation to *Van der Peet* by Borrows 1997–8, 46–47.
25 Thanks to Hamar Foster for pointing this out.

aspect of settling disputes involving minority rights, including intersocietal disputes. Public institutions need to establish fair and transparent criteria for the public assessment of identity. These criteria must include setting some terms by which groups can negotiate their identities. These terms, I have argued, must be informed by important purposes, like protecting against harm, and must include consideration of the perspectives of the minority group and of the broader society. The terms must avoid unfairly freezing group identity or wedding groups to practices that are anachronistic or stifling. In addition, the criteria used in the assessment of identity must address the problem of culture's elasticity, possibly by tethering the protection of cultural identity to a broader purpose of ensuring the continued survival and flourishing of the minority community. And finally, the project of protecting cultural identity cannot be used to divert attention from other claims like self-determination. To the contrary, reasoning about the identity of marginalized groups, in law and politics, should stimulate the development of new institutions and drive the need for considering different sorts of institutional responses and preconditions to resolving minority conflicts fairly.

References

Barry, B. (2001), *Culture and Equality*, Cambridge, Mass: Harvard University Press.

Barsh, R. and Henderson, J.Y. (1997), 'The Supreme Court's Van der Peet trilogy: naive imperialism and ropes of sand', *McGill Law Review*, 42:4, 993–1009.

Borrows, J. (2002), *Recovering Canada: The Resurgence of Indigenous Law*, Toronto: University of Toronto Press.

— (1997–8), 'Frozen rights in Canada: constitutional interpretation and the trickster', *American Indian Law Review*, 22, 37–64.

Brom, F.W.A. (2004), 'WTO, public reason and food public reasoning in the "trade conflict" on GM-food', *Ethical Theory and Moral Practice*, 7, 417–431.

Brown, W. (1995), *States of Injury*, Princeton NJ: Princeton University Press.

Brubaker, R. and Cooper, F. (2001), 'Beyond Identity', *Theory and Society*, 29, 1–47.

Butler, J. (1990), *Gender Trouble*, London: Routledge.

Carlson, B. (2002), 'The Bio-piracy of wild rice: genome mapping of a sacred food', *GeneWatch*, 15:4 <http://www.gene-watch.org/genewatch/articles/15-4wildrice.html>.

Creppell, I. (2003), *Toleration and Identity: Foundations in Early Modern Thought*, London: Routledge.

Dryzek, J. (2005), 'Deliberative democracy in divided societies', *Political Theory*, 33:2, 218–242.

Eisenberg, A. (2003), 'Diversity and equality: three approaches to cultural and sexual difference', *Journal of Political Philosophy*, 11:1, 41–64.

Flanagan, T. (2000), *First Nations? Second Thoughts*, Montreal and Kingston: McGill-Queens University Press.

Green, J. (2000), 'The difference debate: reducing rights to cultural flavours', *Canadian Journal of Political Science*, 33:1, 133–144.

Gutmann, A. (2005) *Identity in Democracy*, Princeton: Princeton University Press.

Johnson, J. (2000), 'Why respect culture?', *American Journal of Political Science*, 44:3, 405–418.

Kymlicka, W. (2005), 'The moral foundations and geopolitical functions of international norms of minority rights: a European case study', paper presented at the IVR World Congress, Granada, Spain, May 26.

— (1997), 'Do we need a liberal theory of minority rights?: Reply to Carens, Young, Parekh and Forst', *Constellations*, 4:1, 72–87.

— (1995), *Multicultural Citizenship*, Oxford: Oxford University Press.

Macklem, P. (2004), 'Indigenous peoples and human rights: international developments, domestic consequences.' Unpublished manuscript.

— (2001), *Indigenous difference and the constitution of Canada*, Toronto: University of Toronto Press.

McRanor, S. (2006), 'The imperative of "culture" for liberal political theory and Canadian state practice', in A. Eisenberg (ed.), *Diversity and Equality: The changing framework of freedom in Canada*, Vancouver: UBC Press, 54–77

Moore, M. (2006) 'Identity claims and identity politics: a limited defense', in Primoratz, I. and Pavkovic, A. (eds), *Identity, self-determination and secession*, London: Ashgate, 23–48.

Narayan, U. (1997), '"Westernization", respect for cultures, and third-world feminists', in U. Narayan (ed.), *Dislocating cultures: identities, traditions, and third world feminism*, London: Routledge, 3–39.

Renteln, A. D. (2004), *The Cultural Defense*, New York: Oxford University Press.

Scheinin, M. (2000), 'The right to enjoy a distinct culture: indigenous and competing uses of land', in T. S. Orlin, A. Rosas and M. Scheinin (eds), *The Jurisprudence of Human Rights Law: A Comparative Interpretive Approach*, Turke: Institute for Human Rights Abo Akademi University, 159–222.

Scott, D. (2003), 'Culture in political theory', *Political Theory*, 31:1, 92–115.

Shachar, A. (2001), *Multicultural Jurisdictions*, Cambridge: Cambridge University Press.

— (1998), 'Group Identity and Women's Rights in Family Law: The Perils of Multicultural Accommodation', *The Journal of Political Philosophy*, 6:3, 285–305.

Stabinsky, D. (2002), 'Transgenic maize in Mexico: two updates', *GeneWatch*, 15:4 (July) <http://www.gene-watch.org/genewatch/articles/15-4maize.html>.

Vallance, N. (2006), 'The use of 'culture' by the Supreme Court of Canada,' in A. Eisenberg (ed.), *Diversity and Equality: The changing framework of freedom in Canada*, Vancouver: UBC Press, 97–113

Waldron, J. (2000), 'Cultural identity and civic responsibility', in Kymlicka, W. and Norman, W. (eds), *Citizenship in Diverse Societies*, Oxford: Oxford University Press, 155–176.

Webber, J. (2006), 'The Irreducibly Religious Content of Freedom of Religion', in A. Eisenberg (ed.), *Diversity and Equality: The changing framework of freedom in Canada*, Vancouver: UBC Press, 178–200.

Weinstock, D. (2006), 'Is 'Identity' a Danger to Democracy', in I. Primoratz and A. Pavkovic (eds), *Identity, self-determination and secession*, London: Ashgate, 3–22.

— (2001), 'Les 'identités' sont-elles dangereuses pour la démocratie,' in J. Maclure, and A. Gagnon (eds), *Repères en mutation: Identité et citoyenneté dans le Québec contemporain*, Montréal: Éditions Québec-Amérique, 227–250.

Young, I.M. (1997), 'Difference as a Resource for Democratic Communication', in J. Bohman and W. Rehg (eds), *Deliberative Democracy: Essays on reason and politics*, Cambridge, MA: MIT Press, 383–406.

— (1989), 'Polity and group difference', *Ethics*, 99:2, 250–274.

Chapter 6

Self-Government in Canada: A Successful Model for the Decolonisation of Aboriginal Child Welfare?

Sonia Harris-Short[1]

Introduction

On 26th June 1984, Richard Cardinal, a seventeen year old Métis child, was found hanging in the garden of his latest foster home.[2] Richard's short life had been spent in the care of Alberta Social Services. Between the ages of 4 and 17 Richard experienced twenty-eight different placements in Alberta – 16 of those were foster homes, 12 were group homes or a form of secure facility. Four years was the longest Richard spent in any one home. By the age of 13 he was experiencing psychological problems manifested by bed wetting, getting into trouble with the law and failing at school. At the age of 16 he was arrested for shoplifting and placed on probation. By this stage in his life he had already attempted suicide twice. Richard spent the last two years of his life in various youth homes and shelters before his final placement where, after one failed attempt at suicide, he finally hung himself from a tree in the back garden. The judicial inquiry into Richard's death revealed 'serious inadequacies in the provincial child welfare system.' His suicide provides a shocking example of the non-native system failing a native child.

The suffering and inter-generational damage which has been caused to aboriginal communities by the past policies and practices of the Canadian child welfare system is widely recognised (see e.g. Royal Commission on Aboriginal Peoples (RCAP), vol. 3, 1996, pp. 34–36). The almost unanimous condemnation of that system in its application to aboriginal children and families, particularly among the academic community, is striking (see e.g. Monture, 1989; White and Jacobs, 1992; Kline, 1992; Kline, 1995). Perhaps even more striking, however, is that not only are these voices united in criticism, they are also united in the solution. It is consistently asserted in the academic literature that the decolonisation of aboriginal child welfare in Canada can only be achieved through the implementation of First Nations self-government, integral to which is autonomous control of their own child welfare system, free from the ethnocentric laws, standards and scrutiny of the Provincial or Federal governments (White and Jacobs, 1992; Kline, 1992, pp. 423–425; Monture, 1989, pp.

---

1 Thanks to John Borrows and Colin Warbrick for their helpful and detailed comments on an earlier draft of this chapter. I would also like to thank the British Academy for their financial support for this project.

2 The account of Richard's story is taken from 'Richard Cardinal – Cry from the Diary of a Metis Child', Canadian Film Board, 1986.

6–7; Lynch, 2001, p. 505). There is also a surprising level of support for aboriginal self-government over child welfare at the governmental level, with control over child welfare often identified as a clear example of the kind of power which would be 'core' or central to a self-governing First Nations community. Indeed, in recent years important steps have been taken towards the implementation of at least some measure of 'self-government' over aboriginal child welfare at the community level. For example, on 17th May 1997 the Nisga'a Tribal Council and the British Columbia Ministry for Children and Families announced that the Nisga'a Nation located in the Nass Valley, Northern British Columbia, were to begin the process of retaking control over their community's child welfare with the ultimate aim of introducing Nisga'a legislation providing the mandate for a fully autonomous Nisga'a controlled child welfare agency.[3] Many First Nations communities across Canada have taken similar tentative steps. In British Columbia, for example, there are now 21 aboriginal controlled child welfare agencies, 19 of which exercise delegated provincial powers and deliver a range of child protection, guardianship and family support services.[4]

It is a fundamental premise of this chapter that the Canadian First Nations hold an inherent and existing right to 'sovereign' jurisdiction over their people, their culture and their lands, including child welfare. It is clearly hoped by many aboriginal communities currently involved in self-government negotiations that the recognition and implementation of their inherent aboriginal and treaty rights will provide the much needed answers to their continuing social, political and economic problems (RCAP, vol. 2, 1996, p. 140). Building from an appreciation of the debilitating effects of colonialism, it is stressed that if the 'culture of dependency' (Boldt, 1993, pp. 170–174) and general despondency which has developed within some First Nations communities is to be successfully addressed, the paternalistic relationship between the First Nations people and the Canadian State must end. By restoring authority and control over their own lives to First Nations people through self-government, it is anticipated that aboriginal people will be able to re-establish their sense of identity and self-worth as functioning political communities, thereby facilitating self-sufficiency, economic growth and cultural rejuvenation (RCAP, vol. 2, 1996, p. 140). In turn the rebuilding of healthy, prosperous communities, supported by the revival of community values and traditions, will, it is hoped, have a dramatic effect on the current levels of violence and abuse within the communities.

However, whilst there are certainly strong grounds for optimism, solutions to the colonization of aboriginal people are unlikely to be that simple. The complexity of the damage caused by colonialism means that it cannot be undone by what Monture-Angus describes as simple 'linear' solutions (1999, pp. 10–11) – in essence, self-government may not be the panacea it is often held out to be (see e.g. Borrows,

---

3 British Columbia, Ministry for Children and Families Area Office, *News Release* 97:042 'Nisga'a Tribal Council to Assume Responsibility for Child and Family Services' (13 May, 1997). The Nisga'a Lisims Government now provides an almost full range of child and family services (guardianship and family support services) to the Nisga'a people but have yet to enact their own child welfare legislation.

4 For the latest developments see the list of delegated agencies at http://www.mcf.gov.bc.ca/about_us/aboriginal/pdf/aboriginal_delegated.pdf.

2002, pp. 138–158). As communities gradually assume control of key areas such as child welfare, the consequences of enduring centuries of colonial rule have begun to manifest themselves. Although it is important to recognize that the recent social and political problems experienced by aboriginal communities are by no means unique to Canadian First Nations, the legacy of colonialism has intensified these difficulties for aboriginal communities as they have moved towards the implementation of a self-governing regime.

On 6th March 1988, Lester Desjarlais, a member of the Sandy Bay reserve community in Manitoba shot himself at the home of his latest foster parents.[5] He was 15 years old. Throughout his childhood Lester suffered horrific abuse at the hands of his family and community. For the six years preceding his death he had been in the care of Dakota Ojibway Child and Family Services, a native controlled child welfare agency operating under provincial mandate. At the Inquiry into his death Justice Giesbrecht was absolutely damning of Dakota Ojibway. In his words:

> It was negligence and incompetence pure and simple ... The agency that was supposed to be protecting the boy was compounding his agony ... The inmates were running the asylum (Office of the Chief Medical Examiner, 1992, pp. 22–23).

The Desjarlais Inquiry paints a portrait of a child welfare agency that was headed by unqualified, incompetent staff (pp. 183–209); was abandoned by the provincial government at the earliest opportunity (pp. 88–89, 181–182, 221–222, 247 and 259–274); was rendered useless by political interference and manipulation by powerful families on the reserve (pp. 29–41, 56–57, 71–80, 120–146, 162–169 and 210–232); was placing almost blind trust in 'lost', distorted or simply inappropriate traditions (pp. 21, 23–25, 90–94, 134 and 216); and was hopelessly struggling to serve a deeply dysfunctional community with intractable socio-economic problems including an apparent collapse of any kind of community norms or standards – something that was manifested in the total denial, even amongst the agency's own staff, of the rampant violence and sexual abuse occurring on the reserve (pp. 14, 57–61, 96–106 and 233–274).

The death of Lester Desjarlais stands as a shocking testament to the fact that community control over child welfare is not some magic solution. We need, of course, to be cautious in drawing wide, generalized conclusions from this one particular case. It must be remembered that similarly shocking examples of negligence and incompetence caused by a myriad of factors such as under-funding, inappropriate training, overworked staff and inadequate systems of accountability can be found in non-native child welfare systems all over the world. Despite the best efforts of governments children will continue to be abused and some children will die. Aboriginal controlled agencies should not be condemned on the basis of higher, more exacting, perhaps even impossible standards. Nevertheless, the Desjarlais Inquiry reveals a depth and intensity of problems within Sandy Bay that raises very serious questions about the capacity of that particular community to exercise responsible government and protect its most vulnerable members. And those problems are not

---

5 The following account of Lester's story is taken from the Inquiry into his death (Office of the Chief Medical Examiner, 1992).

unique to Sandy Bay. The voices of many aboriginal women regarding the extent of intra-familial violence and abuse within their communities, as well as their clear concern at the inadequate response of their political leadership to that phenomenon, provides strong support for Justice Giesbrecht's conclusion that the serious problems he had identified were common to many aboriginal communities across Canada (see e.g. Nahanee, 1996, pp. 360–366; McGillivray and Comaskey, 1999; Manitoba Justice Inquiry (MJI), 1991, pp. 475–507; RCAP, vol. 4, 1996, pp. 62–68; RCAP, vol. 3, pp. 54–86).

In light of these problems there are clear grounds for concern that insufficient attention has so far been paid within the self-government debate to the implications of self-government for potentially vulnerable children living within self-governing communities. With this central concern in mind, the aim of this chapter is thus to explore whether or not there exists a clear and rational legal framework for the implementation of self-government over child welfare that respects, on the one hand, the cultural and political 'sovereignty' of aboriginal peoples, whilst, on the other hand, respecting the rights and interests of potentially vulnerable children living within those communities. It will be argued that whilst the Canadian Government has clearly been alive to this issue, its purported solutions, rooted as they are in Canada's existing legal and constitutional provisions, perpetuate the continuing imposition of non-native values on First Nations communities and therefore undermine the central tenets of self-determination as a process of decolonisation. The current approach of the Canadian Government is therefore rejected as amounting to inappropriate cultural imperialism. The chapter thus moves on to consider whether a more principled and just solution may lie in the realm of international law.

The Canadian Constitutional Model for Delivering Self-determination

Despite recent attempts to reform the provincial child welfare system, it is clear that trying to work within the existing system is always going to have its problems and its limitations – it is not decolonization.[6] Essentially, the solutions to these problems will have to come from within the communities and that can only be achieved by truly empowering those communities and recognizing that they have the ultimate responsibility for their own children. It means self-government.

The Inherent Right to Self-government

Arguments in favour of affording legal recognition to the First Nations' inherent right to self-government are generally founded on the existence of aboriginal communities as organized socio-political entities holding inherent sovereign powers of government over their own people prior to the arrival of the Europeans. The inherent nature of the purported right is of vital importance. As an inherent right, its existence is not contingent upon a grant, or some other act of recognition, by the

---

6 Substantial reforms are currently being introduced in Manitoba and British Columbia. For more information see http://www.aji-cwi.mb.ca and www.mcf.gov.bc.ca/about_us/aboriginal/index. For a critical discussion of these reforms see MacDonald, 2005.

Canadian Government. It simply finds its source from within the collective lives, laws and traditions of aboriginal communities and the fact of their prior occupation and sovereignty over Canadian soil (RCAP, vol. 2, 1996, p. 110). Under the common law it is argued that neither the initial unilateral assertion of British sovereignty over Canadian territory nor subsequent acts of infringement by the Crown have operated to extinguish the inherent 'aboriginal right' to an autonomous form of government – such a right being an essential or 'integral' part of the lives of aboriginal peoples. Such unextinguished common law aboriginal rights now of course enjoy constitutional status and protection under s.35 of the Constitution Act 1982 (*R v Sparrow* [1990] 1 R.C.S. 1075).

The Canadian Supreme Court has yet to uphold the inherent right of aboriginal peoples to self-government, with the Court clearly preferring to leave such a politically difficult and sensitive matter to tripartite negotiations between the Federal and Provincial Governments and the First Nations communities. In fact, recent decisions of the Canadian Supreme Court have not been encouraging. In *R v Pamajewon* [1996] O.A.C. 241, having conceptualized the aboriginal right in question, not as a broad and inclusive right to self-government, but as 'the right to participate in and to regulate high stakes gambling activities on the reserve', the Supreme Court held that as high stakes gambling did not constitute 'an integral part of the distinctive culture' of the Ojibwa, the right fell outside the scope of s.35. In the subsequent case of *Delgamuukw v British Columbia* [1997] 3 R.C.S. 1010, the Supreme Court simply refused to address the question of self-government, concluding after years of litigation that errors of fact made by the judge at trial prevented them from determining the claim. The issue was remitted to trial. The case law on the more specific question of whether aboriginal self-government over child welfare constitutes an 'aboriginal right' under s.35 is also disappointing. In 2000, the parents of an Innu child served notice on the Attorney General of Quebec of their intention to challenge the constitutionality of the Youth Protection Act P.34.1 on the grounds that it infringed the inherent right of the Innu Nation to self-government over all matters concerning the protection of Innu youth (*Re Adolescent* [2001] 4 C.N.L.R. 1). The claim was, however, dismissed on technical grounds, the court holding on the basis of the Supreme Court's decision in *Delgamuukw*, that, having 'provided no particulars as to the nature of the Aboriginal right at issue, other than to mention that the Innu had a policy of settling disputes concerning youth protection within the Nation, the community or the extended family', the claim had been pleaded in insufficient detail and at an excessive level of generality. The question has recently arisen again in the Saskatchewan Queen's Bench (Family Law Division) in *In the matter of the Child and Family Services Act and in the Matter of R.T., M.T., M.A.T., A.L. and K.A.* (2004) SKQB 503 (*Re R.T.*). The case concerned the placement of five aboriginal children all of whom had been in foster care for substantial periods of time. The Saskatchewan Department of Community Resources and Employment (DCRE) had adopted a policy whereby First Nations children could not be placed for adoption without the consent of the child's band and/or the relevant First Nations child welfare agency. Because the children could not be placed with members of the extended family or the Sturgeon Lake Band, the band refused to give their consent thereby preventing the children from being placed for adoption pursuant to a 'permanent order.' The aboriginal child welfare agency and the band defended DCRE's policy on the basis that the aboriginal community had a constitutionally protected right under s.35 to 'speak for the children.' Although a strange way in which to conceptualise the right (motivated no doubt by the requirement in *Delgamuukw* to identify the exact nature of the activity in question with precision), it amounted in essence to a self-government claim over the placement and adoption of aboriginal children:

> In this case, the NASC Agency/band argue that aboriginal "notions of community and kinship" are an integral part of aboriginal society. First Nations families and communities share responsibility for the upbringing, training, education and well-being of their children. They submit that the aboriginal right of self-government includes the legal right and moral obligation to speak for persons who are under a legal disability, such as children. As this "right" has never been extinguished, *The Child and Family Services Act* cannot impair it by placing aboriginal children for adoption without the band's consent. (para. 58)

Ryan-Froslie J. gave only the briefest consideration to the argument, holding that there was insufficient evidence in this case to support the band's position:

> The only evidence called by the NASC Agency/band was that of Dr. Katz who testified that "kinship" is an aboriginal "value" and that "community" plays an important role in the raising of aboriginal children. There was no evidence of what happens to aboriginal children when no "kinship" or "community" resources are available to care for them. His evidence falls far short of establishing the right asserted by the NASC Agency/band. Moreover, the "right" asserted appears to be of a general nature and not a defining feature of the culture in question. Even if such a right did exist, there is no evidence that its existence was "pre-contact." (para. 60)

Given the importance of this issue for aboriginal communities, the brevity of the discussion is disappointing. However, both cases clearly illustrate the difficulties facing aboriginal communities in satisfying the stringent conditions imposed by the Supreme Court for establishing an aboriginal right under s.35, particularly with respect to the importance of the way in which the aboriginal right is conceptualised and the evidence required to establish the 'distinctive culture' and 'pre-contact' tests.

Developments outside the courts have been more promising. The strong and consistent view amongst commentators is that the First Nations hold an existing, inherent right to self-government, which is recognised and protected under s.35 of the Canadian Constitution (see e.g. Borrows, 1992; Borrows, 1994; Asch and Macklem, 1991; and Hogg and Turpel, 1995). Significantly, this view was unequivocally endorsed by the Royal Commission on Aboriginal Peoples in 1996 with the Royal Commission arguing that 'family matters, including marriage, divorce, adoption and child custody; and social services and welfare, including child welfare' will fall within the core, non-negotiable jurisdiction of aboriginal governments (Royal Commission on Aboriginal Peoples, vol. 2, 1996, pp. 166–168, 186–213 and 240–244). Moreover, the 'inherent right policy' with respect to self-government has also been the official policy of the Canadian Federal Government since 1995. The Federal Policy Guide provides:

The Government of Canada recognizes the inherent right of self-government as an existing Aboriginal right within section 35 of the Constitution Act, 1982... The Government of Canada's recognition of the inherent right is based on the view that the Aboriginal peoples of Canada have a right to govern themselves in relation to matters that are internal to their communities, integral to their unique cultures, identities, traditions, languages and institutions, and with respect to their special relationship to their land and resources (DIAND, 1995, p. 5).

The Federal Government also identifies child welfare as falling within the core jurisdiction of aboriginal governments. The Federal Government's crucial acceptance of the inherent right of the First Nations to self-government has meant that, in practice, despite the recent disappointing decisions on aboriginal rights in the Canadian Supreme Court, self-government is, for many First Nations communities, no longer a vague and distant dream – it is a present reality.[7] The Federal and Provincial governments of Canada are currently engaged in self-government negotiations with 437 aboriginal communities.[8]

Important Limitations on the 'inherent right' to Self-Government – Securing 'non-native' Standards

Arguments in favour of the inherent 'sovereign' right of the First Nations to self-government clearly pose a direct challenge to the assumption of 'sovereign' power over aboriginal peoples by the Canadian State by which they purport to justify their right to unilaterally extinguish and, post-1982, infringe protected aboriginal rights – a right which has hitherto simply been assumed by the Canadian courts without any clear legitimate basis. However, by insisting that self-government proceed through political negotiation and agreement, rather than by litigation or the unilateral exercise of the right protected under s.35 of the Constitution, the Federal Government is able to avoid jurisprudentially difficult questions about the basis of their own assertion of sovereignty (DIAND, 1995, p. 25). By proceeding in this way the Federal Government is also able to circumscribe the right to self-government in accordance with its own priorities and interests, including retaining the power to demand from aboriginal communities that certain standards, conditions and requirements will be met, even within core areas of aboriginal jurisdiction such as child welfare. It is undoubtedly an important consideration for the Canadian Government that whilst aboriginal peoples remain part of the Canadian State, it is the Canadian Government who remains ultimately responsible for securing the fundamental rights and interests of First Nations children, as for all other children living within its constitutional boundaries – a point made clear by Ryan-Froslie J in her analysis of the Government's obligations to aboriginal children under section 15 of the Canadian Charter in *Re R.T.* (2004 SKQB 503, at [75]–[93]).

---

7 For the current status of ongoing treaty negotiations see the web-site of the Department of Indian and Northern Affairs at www.ainc-inac.gc.ca/pr/agr/index_e.html#Self-Government%20Agreements

8 UN Doc. E/CN.4/2005/88/Add.3.

In the course of the self-government negotiations, the Federal Government has employed a variety of methods to address concerns about the rights and interests of vulnerable individuals living within self-governing communities. One such method has been to make the recognition of certain basic standards of good democratic government a precondition of recognizing First Nations self-government. The Federal Government's 1995 policy statement makes it clear that before the Federal Government will enter into an agreement with a First Nations community, they must first have developed adequate systems of accountability to be enshrined within their constitutions (DIAND, 1995, pp. 12–14). That policy is reflected in the various Yukon self-government agreements and the Nisga'a Final Agreement, all of which include detailed provisions as to the substantive content of their respective constitutions (for the purposes of the following analysis the Yukon–Vuntut Gwitchin Self-Government Agreement will be used).

Another important mechanism which has been used by the Federal Government to try and secure certain standards are met is to insist that when a First Nations Government is exercising jurisdiction, it is exercised in accordance with Federal or Provincial standards. The Nisga'a Agreement, for example, states that whilst the Nisga'a have jurisdiction over the delivery of child welfare services, including legislative powers, a precondition of exercising the jurisdiction is that they establish standards that are comparable to provincial standards:

> 11.89. Nisga'a Lisims Government may make laws in respect of child and family services on Nisga'a Lands, provided that those laws include standards comparable to provincial standards intended to ensure the safety and well-being of children and families.

A similar precondition is placed on Nisga'a jurisdiction over adoption. Whilst the Agreement establishes that Nisga'a Government will be able to make laws in respect of the adoption of Nisga'a children, it is prescribed that those laws must meet the provincial standard of making the best interests of the child the paramount consideration.[9] A similar underlying concern with providing for comparable standards of service delivery is evident in the Yukon self-government agreements, albeit the language in the individual agreements is considerably more open than that found in the Nisga'a Agreement. For example, as regards the delivery of *devolved* programs and services, although the Yukon Umbrella Agreement and the Vuntut Gwitchin Final Agreement state that financial transfer agreements are to be entered into with the intention of specifying 'the obligations of all parties, including minimum program delivery standards' (Umbrella Final Agreement, para. 24.6.1.2. and Vuntut Gwitchin Final Agreement, para. 24.6.1.2), the Final Agreement and the Vuntut Gwitchin Self-Government Agreement make it clear that the formulation of basic common standards are to be the subject of *negotiation* rather than unilateral imposition (Vuntut Gwitchin Final Agreement, para. 24.6.1.2 and Vuntut Gwitchin

---

9   The Agreement provides: '11.96 Nisga'a Lisims Government may make laws in respect of the adoption of Nisga'a children, provided that those laws: (i) expressly provide that the best interests of the child be the paramount consideration in determining whether an adoption will take place; and (ii) require Nisga'a Lisims Govt. to provide BC and Canada with records of all adoptions occurring under Nisga'a laws.'

Self-Government Agreement, para. 17.3.5). Moreover, the law-making powers of individual Yukon First Nations, which under the Vuntut Gwitchin Self-Government Agreement are stated to include, 'provision of social and welfare services to Citizens' (para. 13.2.4.) and 'guardianship, custody, care and placement of Vuntut Gwitchin children' (para. 13.2.7), would appear to be subject to no express limitations or restrictions.

A third mechanism employed by the Federal Government has been to retain paramount authority over certain specific areas of jurisdiction. As the 1995 Policy statement provides:

> The government takes the position that negotiated rules of priority may provide for the paramountcy of Aboriginal laws, but may not deviate from the basic principle that those federal and provincial laws of overriding national or provincial importance will prevail over conflicting Aboriginal laws (DIAND, 1995, p. 11).

It could be argued that as laws pertaining to the 'protection of the health and safety of all Canadians' constitute matters falling within the 'national interest', this provides the constitutional basis for the Federal Government to retain overriding jurisdictional authority in an area such as child welfare. This is not, however, the approach that has been taken to child welfare in the Nisga'a Agreement, where Nisga'a law, to the extent of any inconsistency or conflict with federal or provincial law, is expressly protected as paramount (para. 11.91). Less clear is the Vuntut Gwitchin Self-Government Agreement which simply provides that Canada and the Vuntut Gwitchin First Nation shall enter into negotiations to conclude an agreement providing for those areas in which Vuntut Gwitchin legislation shall prevail over federal laws 'of general application.' It would appear no such agreement has yet been concluded but the qualification that the law must be of 'general application' would seem to preclude the Federal Government passing overriding legislation in the specific field of aboriginal or, more specifically, Vuntut Gwitchin child welfare.

More worrying is the lack of constitutional status given to the Yukon Self-Government Agreements under s. 35 which renders them vulnerable to 'unilateral repudiation by a legislature exercising its legislative sovereignty' – albeit subject to a duty of consultation as specified in the Yukon Umbrella Final Agreement (see Dickson, 2004, pp. 421, 430, 431 and 450–451). Even in the case of the Nisga'a Agreement, which is given constitutional protection under s.35, the Federal Government is able to infringe, perhaps even extinguish, constitutionally protected aboriginal and treaty rights, provided the prescribed justificatory standard set down by the Supreme Court in *Sparrow* is met: (i) the Government must show that there is a valid legislative objective for the interference – such objective being 'compelling and substantial'; and (ii) it must show that its actions are consistent with the special trust relationship between the aboriginal peoples and the Crown (*R v Sparrow* [1990] 1 R.C.S. pp. 1113–1114). This justificatory standard was given expansive interpretation in the subsequent case of *Gladstone* [1996] 2 R.C.S. 723 with Lamer CJ holding:

> Because ... distinctive aboriginal societies exist within, and are a part of, a broader social, political and economic community, over which the Crown is sovereign, there are circumstances in which, in order to pursue objectives of compelling and substantial

importance to that community as a whole (taking into account the fact that aboriginal societies are a part of the community), some limitation of those rights will be justified. Aboriginal rights are a necessary part of the reconciliation between aboriginal societies with the broader political community of which they are a part; limits placed on those rights are, where the objectives furthered by those limits *are of sufficient importance to the broader community* as a whole, equally a necessary part of that reconciliation. (pp. 774–75, emphasis added)

These broader considerations, developed by Lamer CJ in *Delgamuukw*, represent a significant departure from the stringent test envisaged in *Sparrow* and make it perfectly plausible to argue that infringements of aboriginal law-making powers could be justified, in accordance with the Federal Government's fiduciary obligations and the broad principles articulated in *Gladstone* & *Delgamuukw*, to 'protect the aboriginal peoples from themselves', the 'broader public interest' or 'for the good of the community as a whole.'

It is therefore questionable whether real autonomy is being secured for aboriginal self-governing communities when the Canadian government is still so clearly defining the 'rules of the game.' By subjecting aboriginal law-making authority to existing non-native standards and by reserving to itself substantial overriding control, the Federal Government has successfully narrowed the constitutional space in which aboriginal difference can emerge. With the existing tenets of the Canadian State remaining completely unchallenged, it is certainly questionable whether self-government in Canada has made any significant inroads into the colonial power structures of non-native society. It hardly amounts to successful decolonisation. There is, moreover, a fourth and final weapon of control in the armoury of the Federal Government and that is its 'non-negotiable' requirement that all aboriginal governments be bound by the Canadian Charter of Rights and Freedoms. The federal policy guide provides:

> The government is committed to the principle that the Canadian Charter should bind all governments in Canada, so that Aboriginal peoples and non-aboriginal Canadians alike may continue to enjoy equally the rights and freedoms guaranteed by the Charter. Self-government agreements, including treaties, will therefore have to provide that the Canadian Charter applies to aboriginal governments and institutions in relation to all matters within their respective jurisdictions and authorities. (DIAND, 1995, p. 4).

The Royal Commission took exactly the same view arguing, 'all people in Canada are entitled to enjoy the protection of the Charter's general provisions in their relations with governments in Canada no matter where in Canada the people are located or which governments are involved' (RCAP, 1996, vol. 2, p. 230). As the Charter purportedly represents the embodiment of Canadian society's most fundamental norms and values, its uniform application across all Canadian governments has clearly acquired vital symbolic significance for the Federal Government. It has also acquired great symbolic importance for those concerned about vulnerable individuals living within aboriginal communities. Indeed, the mandatory application of the Charter to all aboriginal governments has attracted strong support from some aboriginal women, most notably NWAC, who argue that the subordination of the individual to the group has no legitimate foundation within contemporary aboriginal cultures and the Charter therefore constitutes an appropriate and vital source of protection for individual women and children against public, and perhaps even private, abuses of power (see, e.g. Nahanee (1996), pp. 367–377). For aboriginal children, as confirmed in *Re R.T.* in addition to the general guarantees of good democratic government enshrined within the Charter, 'the right to life, liberty and security of the person' guaranteed under section 7, provides specific protection against potentially abusive child welfare policies and practices (2004 SKQB 503, [65]–[69]).

The application of the Charter to self-governing aboriginal communities has, however, proved extremely contentious. It has attracted strong opposition from a range of aboriginal leaders, including leading aboriginal scholars, who argue that the norms, values and individual rights embodied in the Charter are fundamentally inconsistent with the values, socio-economic organization and basic cultural norms of traditional aboriginal communities (see esp. Turpel, 1989–1990; Turpel, 1992; Boldt and Long, 1992; Monture-Angus, 1999, pp. 135–150). To put it in its starkest terms, Mary Ellen Turpel has argued that on one side stands the Charter with its 'Western' liberal tradition of 'individualism, competition and self-interest', on the other stands the aboriginal philosophy of 'spiritual unity, consistency, co-operation and self-denial'(1992, p. 243). While such an extreme and oppositional dichotomy between the two cultures may well be over-stated, it is clear that in the view of many aboriginal and non-aboriginal commentators, the application of the Charter to aboriginal communities, given its clear cultural bias, poses a 'serious threat' to their identity and survival as distinct cultural communities - that it is, in other words, just another tool of assimilation in the hands of a colonial government (Boldt and Long, 1992, p. 247).

The Charter has clearly been a divisive issue within many aboriginal communities. It raises complex questions about trying to define and articulate the essential values of a living culture and how marginalized and disempowered groups are to secure a meaningful role within that process. Monture-Angus is, for example, critical of NWAC whose approach, she argues, is not based 'in a cultural understanding of Aboriginal reality' and who are unable, in her view, to give a voice to aboriginal 'tradition'. She thus argues that whilst NWAC is able to give a voice to those who have experienced the effects of 'urbanization' and 'disenfranchisement', it does not and should not purport to represent the position of all aboriginal women (1999, pp. 148–149). It is important to emphasize, however, that there is nothing unusual or problematic about the existence of dissent and debate between the different factions of a mature political community. The question of the application of the Charter to aboriginal governments is, essentially, an issue for each individual community to resolve as an exercise of its right to self-determination. Should a community choose to adopt the Charter as an appropriate reflection of the normative basis of its society, it is clearly free to do so. What is, however, inappropriate is for the Federal Government to impose the Charter on aboriginal self-governing communities. As Monture-Angus argues:

> [O]ne must conclude that an unconsented to application of the Charter to Indian governments acting in both their traditional capacity and in a traditional way (where gender

respect is an absolute requirement) would be an unlawful and unallowable intrusion on the sovereignty of Indian nations. Such an incursion must be seen as a direct threat and a re-entrenchment of colonial patterns of oppression, which many people see as the source of the majority of our present difficulties (1999, p.150).

The process of colonization in Canada has clearly shown the internal destruction which can be caused to the very fabric of a society by the *imposition* of the culturally rooted norms, mores and practices of another socio-political community, when, given the particular worldview and socio-economic organization of the former, such traditions and practices simply do not make sense. There is, however, a second important problem with this approach. Imposed 'solutions' lacking cultural grounding and a required sense of community acceptance and/or ownership are not only an inappropriate perpetuation of colonialism, they are also ultimately likely to fail. It is therefore deeply unfortunate that this continuing imposition of another's 'worldview' represents the current approach to the implementation of aboriginal self-government in Canada.

To summarise thus far, it is contended that the implementation of self-government in Canada through the modern treaty process has failed to secure the successful decolonization of aboriginal children and families. Whilst the concern of the Canadian Government to maintain its constitutional integrity based on core liberal values and the protection of its individual citizens is understandable, the current approach fails to secure real self-determination to indigenous peoples. It is clear that if self-determination is to be secured for aboriginal peoples, the Canadian Government must be willing to return to aboriginal communities much greater power and authority over their internal affairs than has so far been the case. However, the defensive approach of the Canadian government to the current treaty negotiations and the recent retreat of the Supreme Court on the question of aboriginal rights under s.35, suggests that only slow and limited progress on fundamental questions such as internal aboriginal 'sovereignty' is likely to be made at the domestic level. Given the unreceptive nature of the domestic audience, the answer for aboriginal communities might therefore have to be found by looking beyond the constitutional boundaries and 'Western' mindset of the Canadian State, to international law. It perhaps needs to be faced that at the domestic level there is a certain point beyond which neither the Federal Government, nor the Supreme Court, is ever likely to go. Key to understanding the policy of the Federal Government on self-government and the decisions of the Supreme Court in *Sparrow*, *Gladstone* and *Delgamuukw* is the unquestionable assertion of Crown sovereignty over aboriginal peoples. Whilst that assertion of sovereignty remains unchallenged, aboriginal peoples will always be subject to the overriding control of the Canadian State. However, despite the jurisprudential problems with justifying Crown sovereignty over aboriginal peoples, as evidenced by the obvious tension in the jurisprudence of the Supreme Court on this question, it is highly questionable whether the Supreme Court will ever take the momentous step of bringing the very legitimacy of the Canadian State and, indeed, its own legitimacy into doubt – even more so, the political organs of the Canadian State. The current position of the Federal Government may therefore represent the 'high' point of Canadian policy and jurisprudence on aboriginal rights unless it is subjected to some form of external authority or pressure. International law may provide that source of pressure. The final section of this chapter will thus explore whether the normative standards enshrined within international law may provide a more appropriate framework for reconciling the rights and interests of the Canadian State, indigenous peoples as a group and, perhaps most importantly, the basic rights and interests of indigenous children.

International Law as a Model for Delivering Self-determination

From the perspective of indigenous peoples, it must be recognised that, as with domestic law, there is a certain danger for aboriginal peoples in engaging with international law. It is important to recognize that international law played a pivotal role in legitimating and 'normalizing' the colonization and subjugation of indigenous peoples to the will of the European States and in securing the exclusion of indigenous peoples from the international arena (Anaya, 2004, pp. 15–48; Corntassel and Primeau, 1995, 343). However, where the right to self-determination is being pursued against the State and the rights and interests of the latter are thus at stake, it is important that indigenous peoples have access to a forum where the actions of the State are subject to some form of external scrutiny and control – where the State is not, in other words, the ultimate arbiter of power.

The Right to Self-determination under International Law

The right of indigenous peoples to self-determination under international law remains a fiercely contested issue. On a positive note, there is an emerging body of state practice, strongly supported in particular by the UN Human Rights Committee (HRC), that indigenous peoples are entitled to recognition of their 'people-hood' under international law.[10] Such acceptance is of *potentially* enormous significance for indigenous peoples. In the classic decolonization process of the 1960s and 1970s, once the population of a colonized territory had been recognised as a 'peoples' alongside States, the right to self-determination followed. However, the basis upon which the status of indigenous peoples as a 'peoples' has been recognised, and the implications of that recognition for the right to self-determination, remains unclear. The HRC does not, for example, explain whether they are affording recognition to the 'people-hood' of indigenous peoples on the basis that they are a colonial peoples falling within the existing categories of 'peoples' under international law, or whether, in their view, indigenous peoples should now be regarded as constituting a third and distinct category of 'peoples' with a yet undefined right to self-determination. Similarly, whilst the movement in state practice as to the status of indigenous peoples as a 'peoples' is encouraging, it remains to be determined whether movement on that

---

10 See, for example, UN Doc. CCPR/C/79/Add.105, *Concluding observations of the Human Rights Committee: Canada*, at [7] and [8]; U.N. Doc. CCPR/C/SR. 1856, *Summary record of the 1856th meeting: Australia 29/07/2000*, at [67] and U.N. Doc. CCPR/C/79/Add.112, *Concluding Observations of the Human Rights Committee Norway 01/11/99*, at [17].

issue has only been forthcoming at a price – that price being the scope and meaning of the right to self-determination as applied to their particular situation.

It can be argued that indigenous peoples, as a 'peoples' under international law, have a right to self-determination in accordance with customary international law or on the basis of treaty rights as provided for in common Article 1 of the International Covenant on Civil and Political Rights and the International Covenant on Economic, Social and Cultural Rights. Common Article 1 provides:

> All peoples have the right of self-determination. By virtue of that right they freely determine their political status and freely pursue their economic, social and cultural development.

The right of aboriginal peoples to self-determination is repeated in identical terms in Article 3 of the UN Declaration on the Rights of Indigenous Peoples, 2006 (UN Declaration).[11] Although the unqualified right to self-determination as expressed in the Declaration remains fiercely disputed,[12] the HRC has confirmed that the collective right to self-determination is indeed a right pertaining to aboriginal peoples under Article 1 of the Covenants – something which has been evident in the practice of the HRC for some time.[13] The correct interpretation of this right is, however, controversial. In principle, if the right to self-determination is a right pertaining to 'all peoples' without discrimination or distinction, it should be unfettered in its application to aboriginal peoples, save only that it will be constrained in the manner of its exercise by the general principles of international law, including the right of States to respect for their territorial integrity (see Debeljak, 2000, pp. 170–181 and 194; Islam, 1997, pp. 157–158). This of course raises particularly complex and difficult questions in the context of indigenous peoples living within 'settled colonies.' It is however important to note that the right to territorial integrity is not absolute – there is a well-founded argument that it may be displaced where the right to self-determination in its internal dimensions is being denied.[14]

State practice does, however, remain cautious, with the attitudes of the various participants to the HRC Working Group on the drafting of the UN Declaration being particularly telling. The majority of states appeared to reconcile themselves to the fact that if indigenous peoples are a 'peoples' under international law they will be

---

11 The Declaration was adopted by the UN Human Rights Council (Resolution 2006/2) on 29 June 2006. However, the Declaration remains extremely controversial and the Third Committee of the General Assembly recently decided to adjourn a decision on the adoption of the Declaration, albeit with a view to seeking consensus on its adoption by the General Assembly before the end of the current sixty-first session. See UN Doc. GA/SHC/3878.

12 It is the apparently unqualified right to self-determination in Article 3 which would appear to have prevented or at least delayed the adoption of the Declaration by the General Assembly. *Ibid.*

13 See U.N. Doc. CCPR/C/79/Add.105, *Concluding observations of the Human Rights Committee: Canada 07/04/99*, at [8]. See also Anaya, 2004, pp. 112–113 and 229–230.Cf Quane, 1998, pp. 558–562 and 571.

14 See *Declaration on Principles of International Law Concerning Friendly Relations and Co-operation among States in Accordance with the Charter of the United Nations* (G.A. Res. 2625 (XXV) Oct. 24, 1970) and *Supreme Court of Canada: Reference Re Secession of Quebec* 37 I.L.M. 1340 (1998) at [109]–[139].

entitled to the right to self-determination. Indeed, at the HRC Working Group, Costa Rica, Cuba, Denmark, Ecuador, Finland, Norway, Peru, Guatemala and Mexico all aligned themselves with indigenous peoples and expressed support for the inclusion of an unqualified right to self-determination as enshrined in Article 3.[15] This position was argued with some force by Cuba:

> [T]he right of self-determination was well developed in the 1970 Declaration on Principles of International Law concerning Friendly Relations and Cooperation among States in Accordance with the Charter of the United Nations. Cuba considered the concerns of some States with respect to self-determination as unfounded, given that it is clearly expressed in this declaration that nothing in it shall be construed as authorizing or encouraging any action which would dismember or impair, totally or in part, the territorial integrity or political unity of sovereign and independent States. He affirmed that the Cuban delegation could not form part of an eventual consensus that would seek to modify or reduce in an arbitrary manner a principle of international law.[16]

The majority of states, however, whilst willing to adopt the language of 'people-hood' and self-determination made it absolutely clear that self-determination as applied to indigenous peoples would mean something very different from self-determination as applied to the decolonization claims of the population of an overseas colonized territory. In particular, the majority of states remained absolutely resolute in their conviction that the right of indigenous peoples to self-determination could not violate or jeopardize the territorial and sovereign integrity of the state.[17]

In order to protect themselves against possible territorial and constitutional disintegration, states participating in the debates on self-determination at the HRC Working Group thus embarked upon the process of transforming and re-defining the scope and meaning of the right to self-determination as applied to the case of indigenous peoples. Most importantly, the right of indigenous peoples to self-determination was re-conceptualised as an internal right only.[18] Outside the context of indigenous peoples, internal self-determination has attracted intense debate. However, despite the emphasis now placed on internal self-determination, the external right to self-determination has not ceased to exist or ceased to be of relevance – the two aspects of the right remain inextricably linked. It is simply the case that whilst a peoples' external right to self-determination is recognised and respected through

---

15 UN Doc. E/CN.4/2003/92, at [20].

16 UN Doc. E/CN.4/2001/85, at [70]. See also UN Doc. E/CN.4/1998/106, at [44](b) and (c); UN Doc. E/CN.4./2000/84, at [67] (Pakistan); UN Doc. E/CN.4/2001/85, at [92] (Denmark); UN Doc. E/CN.4/2003/92, at [11] (Guatemala).

17 UN Doc. E/CN.4/1996/84, at [45]–[46] and UN Doc. E/CN.4/1997/102, at [42]. See also: UN Doc. E/CN.4/1998/106, at [44](f); UN Doc. E/CN.4/2000/84, at [53] (Brazil), [54] (Columbia), [56] (Ecuador), [61] (Russian Federation), [73] (Guatemala), [74] (Mexico), [78] (New Zealand), [80] (Venezuela), [81] (Norway); UN Doc. E/CN.4/2001/85, at [64] (Mexico), [82] (Norway), [83] (Spain); UN Doc. E/CN.4/2001/85, at [109] (New Zealand).

18 See, for example, UN Doc. E/CN.4/2000/84, at [50] and UN Doc. E/CN.4/2001/85, at [85] (Canada); UN Doc. E/CN.4/2000/84, at [70] and UN Doc. E/CN.4/2001/85, at [76] (Finland); UN Doc. E/CN.4/2000/84, at [81] (Norway); and UN Doc. E/CN.4/2000/84, at [49] and UN Doc. E/CN.4/2003/92, at [92] (USA).

their international personality as a sovereign state, international concern has naturally turned to focus on the internal dimensions of the right. The idea that indigenous peoples as a 'peoples' have no external right to self-determination but only a discrete *collective* right to autonomous self-government within the state, thereby divorcing the internal aspects of the right from its external dimensions, is, however, a novel concept under international law. What is emerging at the international level with respect to indigenous peoples is something of a 'third way' – a new and distinct *collective* right to self-determination that offers indigenous peoples something more than that to which all individuals, minorities and sub-state groups are entitled pursuant to the right of the whole peoples of the state to internal self-determination, yet something less than the jus cogens right of 'colonial peoples' to both external and internal self-determination as currently enshrined and understood in international law. It is a sui generis concept for a distinct category of 'peoples'.

The key question which therefore remains is what this internal right to self-determination will mean in practice if accepted by the international community as the correct interpretation of Article 3 of the UN Declaration. On the one hand, if the internal right to self-determination remains true to its origins as a means of liberating peoples from 'alien subjugation, domination and exploitation' and respects the peoples' 'right to freely determine their political status and freely pursue their economic, social and cultural development' (*Declaration on the granting of independence to colonial countries and peoples* (GA Resolution 1514 (XV) paras. 1 and 2), the internal right to self-determination has the potential to deliver innovative models of shared sovereignty and an effective re-structuring of governmental relations within the State. A more conservative interpretation of the internal right could, however, mean, at best, self-government or 'self-management' in accordance with the domestic policies of states.

The extensive discussions on this issue at the HRC Working Group failed to produce any clear consensus as to the substantive meaning to be attributed to this new internal right to self-determination. In fact, the views of the participating states as to what the right would mean in practice were generally expressed in very vague and abstract terms. This is therefore a question on which a great deal more work clearly needs to be done. Article 4 of the UN Declaration, which was envisaged by states as effectively qualifying the right to self-determination as contained in the immediately preceding paragraph,[19] generally attracted little opposition in the Working Group and provides some guidance as to the intended substance of the right:

> Indigenous peoples, in exercising their right to self-determination, have the right to autonomy or self-government in matters relating to their internal and local affairs, as well as ways and means for financing their autonomous functions.

As well as attracting quite strong support amongst states, there is much within this that would satisfy indigenous peoples, with indigenous representatives indicating to the HRC Working Group that they were happy that 'article [4] expresses their inherent right to self-determination.'[20] Indeed, the position taken by some states is

---

19 UN Doc. E/CN.4/2006/79, at [20].
20 UN Doc. E/CN.4/1996/84, at [88].

encouraging – suggesting a strong substantive content to the internal right to self-determination and providing support, in varying degrees, for the establishment of some form of separate autonomous, perhaps even sovereign, political and economic system, including very importantly a measure of control over indigenous traditional territories and their natural resources. Thus, if international law remains true to the basic premises of the right to self-determination even this more limited internal right promises to deliver an important measure of decolonization and autonomy to indigenous peoples.

The Implications of an Internal Right to Self-determination

From the perspective of the Canadian Government, an internal right to self-determination, as discussed above, has the strong attraction that it would not mean territorial and constitutional disintegration. What it would require is a different constitutional vision where the accommodation of aboriginal peoples' cultural diversity is truly respected. However, at the same time, the basic protection of the fundamental rights of all its individual citizens, including First Nations children, would be secured. Under international law, self-determination does not constitute an either/or choice between the collective and the individual. In light of the importance afforded to the protection of the individual under international human rights law, international law has developed to successfully accommodate the complex and interrelated needs of both the individual and the group – whether the group in question is the State or some smaller sub-State entity. Although international law has always respected the sovereign rights of the State, no political community can now claim to enjoy absolute sovereignty over its internal affairs. Sovereignty is a relative concept. It follows that emerging self-determining communities will be no different – they will be subject to the same internationally recognised standards and restraints as any other political community. The duty to protect the basic fundamental rights and interests of aboriginal children will properly rest in the first instance with aboriginal governments (see generally Slattery, 1992). Similarly, in aboriginal governments, as in all political communities, those who exercise public power should, in the first instance, be held directly accountable to their community according to their own internally recognised standards and through their own culturally grounded mechanisms of control. Again, however, as with any other political community there should also exist some form of independent external scrutiny to serve as an important check on the power of the governing elite. In today's increasingly global society where the discourse of international human rights has become firmly entrenched within the discourse of even the most powerful states, international human rights law can provide those standards.

Adequate Protection for the Rights of Individuals?

International law currently provides two potential mechanisms for the protection of vulnerable individuals. The first source of protection derives from the growing body of state practice supporting the contention that the exercise of self-determination will be subject to a number of conditions aimed at securing compliance with core international human rights standards. For example, following the break-up of the former Yugoslavia, the Badinter Committee required the newly emerging states to provide sufficient guarantees concerning the protection of minorities and certain core human rights before the applicant State would be secured international recognition (see, e.g. McCorquodale, 1994, p. 877; Cassese, 1995, pp. 138 and 266–268; and Franck, 1993, pp. 24–25). This emerging relationship, even interdependence, between the external exercise of the right to self-determination and core human rights standards is further supported by the growing body of jurisprudence in which the concept of self-determination is being interpreted in its internal dimensions to guarantee to citizens of a self-determining entity the right to a representative 'democratic' form of government and respect for their fundamental human rights (see, e.g. Cassese, 1995, pp. 53–54, 284, 298 and 337; Thornberry, 1993, pp. 134–137; Rosas, 1993, p. 239; and Kamenka, 1988, pp. 133 and 139). It is perhaps significant that whilst the UN Declaration on the Rights of Indigenous Peoples does recognise the right to self-determination, that right in its internal dimensions is expressly qualified by core human rights guarantees. Thus Article 34 provides:

> Indigenous peoples have the right to promote, develop and maintain their institutional structures and their distinctive customs, spirituality, traditions, procedures, practices and, in the cases where they exist, juridical systems or customs, *in accordance with international human rights standards*. [Emphasis added]

These internal limitations on the scope of self-determination should go some way to help assuage concerns about the potential exclusion of dis-empowered groups, such as women and children, from the process of self-determination – a concern which is perhaps born out by the otherwise rather cursory consideration given to the rights and interests of indigenous individuals in the UN Declaration.[21]

The second source of potential protection for vulnerable individuals living within self-determining communities lies in the external controls found in the existing body of international human rights law.[22] It is important to bear in mind that the right of indigenous peoples to a form of internal self-determination is a right which will be exercised against the Canadian State within the territorial boundaries of Canada and within the overriding framework of international human rights law. This has important implications for the manner in which self-determination can be exercised, for not only is Canada under a legal obligation to respect the collective right of indigenous peoples to self-determination, it also remains responsible for ensuring that the individual human rights of all its citizens, including the fundamental rights

---

21 The Declaration draws a clear distinction between the collective rights of indigenous peoples as 'peoples' and the rights of indigenous people as individuals. The majority of provisions in the Declaration are primarily concerned with indigenous peoples' collective rights. However, in the latter stages of the drafting of the Declaration, there was a clear attempt by states to secure greater protection of individual rights, with some success. See, e.g., Articles 1, 7, 22, 34, 44 and 46.

22 For an excellent analysis of how the rights of vulnerable individuals can be reconciled with the right to self-determination within a human rights framework see McCorquodale, (1994), esp. pp. 874–878 and 883–885.

of aboriginal individuals who live within its territorial boundaries, are adequately protected (McCorquodale, 1994, pp. 874–75). This web of rights-based claims and duties means that the collective right of indigenous peoples, like many other fundamental human rights, will not be absolute (McCorquodale, 1994, pp. 875–76). Where the right of a particular peoples to self-determination comes into conflict with other rights recognised and protected under international law, including of course individual human rights, some kind of reconciliation or balance must be found. In seeking to strike an acceptable balance between conflicting rights, international law usually affords considerable discretion to the State (McCorquodale, 1994, pp. 875, 878 and 885). The State would, for example, have considerable freedom to regulate or restrict the right of a religious minority to carry out a certain practice in accordance with its traditions and beliefs if that restriction was deemed necessary to protect the competing individual right of a child not to be subjected to inhuman or degrading treatment. However, when the conflict of rights involves the right of a 'peoples' to self determination, it logically demands a different and more complex relationship between the State, the group and the individual.

The right to self-determination, because of the very nature and content of the right in question, should limit the usual discretion of the State to balance the competing rights and interests of aboriginal peoples (held both as collectives and as individuals) in accordance with its own core values and priorities. The core effect of the right to self-determination is to vest principal responsibility over all matters internal to the self-determining community, including responsibility for protecting the various rights and interests of its members, in the aboriginal community itself – not the State. It therefore follows that provided the self-determining community is acting in accordance with international standards, that is, it is effectively protecting the recognised rights and interests of its individual citizens or, alternatively, drawing an acceptable balance between competing claims, the Canadian State will have no basis on which to intervene. If it does, it will be violating the right of the indigenous group to self-determination. The role of the Canadian State with respect to self-governing indigenous communities is therefore very limited. Only if the community fails to comply with international human rights standards, thereby rendering Canada in breach of its international obligations, will the Canadian Federal Government have a legitimate basis for intervention. To give a short example of how this may work in practice, an aboriginal child welfare agency may decide to place a child who has been abused by her mother with an extended family member on the reserve. The agency takes the view that, despite the fact the child may have some continuing contact with her mother, it is better both for the development of the child's identity and for the future of the aboriginal community as a whole that the child remain with its family on the reserve. The Canadian government may disagree with how that balancing of the various interests has been carried out. It may have given greater weight to the right of the child to be protected from abuse than the weight afforded by the aboriginal community to the child's right to cultural identity, and it may well have disregarded the interests of the aboriginal community altogether. However, provided the community's balancing of interests is in accordance with the child's internationally recognised rights (see, in particular, Articles 8.1,[23] 19.1,[24] 20.3[25] and 30[26] of the UN Convention on the Rights of the Child) there will be no breach of the child's rights under international human rights law, no international obligation on the Canadian State to act and therefore no basis for the State to intervene.

Conclusion

To seek to mediate the issue of aboriginal self-determination through the framework of international law has a number of important advantages, perhaps the most important of which is that it frees the debate from the debilitating colonial constraints of Canadian constitutional law and politics. This does not, however, necessarily guarantee effective decolonisation for the aboriginal peoples of Canada. If indigenous peoples are to engage with the international legal system to push forward a more liberating vision of self-determination, they will have to accept that they will nevertheless be subjected to the existing body of international human rights law, the base line of protection. This in itself may seem relatively unproblematic with aboriginal communities being asked, in effect, to do no more than any other self-governing political community operating within the international community: to regulate its behaviour in accordance with recognised international standards. However, the extent to which this can be reconciled with the overriding objective of securing the effective decolonisation of Canada's aboriginal peoples will depend on one crucial factor: the 'cultural legitimacy' of the existing body of international human rights law and its ability to accommodate the ethos, norms and cultural practices of many diverse aboriginal groups. In other words, is to subject indigenous peoples to the will of the international community, simply to replace one western ethnocentric colonial regime with another?

An exhaustive analysis of the 'cultural legitimacy' of international human rights law is beyond the scope of this chapter. The UN is, however, a forum in which the reality of cultural diversity has to be faced and accommodated if it is to have any

---

23 'States Parties undertake to respect the right of the child to preserve his or her identity, including nationality, name and family relations as recognised by law without unlawful interference.'

24 'States Parties shall take all appropriate legislative, administrative, social and educational measures to protect the child from all forms of physical or mental violence, injury, or abuse, neglect or negligent treatment, maltreatment or exploitation, including sexual abuse, while in the care of parent(s), legal guardian(s) or any other person who has the care of the child.'

25 'Such care [alternative public care provided by the State] could include, inter alia, foster placement, *kafalah* of Islamic law, adoption or if necessary placement in suitable institutions for the care of children. When considering solutions due regard shall be paid to the desirability of continuity in a child's upbringing and to the child's ethnic, religious, cultural and linguistic background.'

26 'In those States in which ethnic, religious or linguistic minorities or persons of indigenous origin exist, a child belonging to such a minority or who is indigenous shall not be denied the right, in community with other members of his or her group, to enjoy his or her own culture, to profess and practice his or her own religion, or to use his or her own language.'

claim to legitimacy or practical effectiveness. Through its normative standards the UN has to speak in a way that has meaning for many diverse groups, including indigenous peoples. The highly abstract nature of international human rights law allows considerable scope for the development of a culturally sensitive interpretative framework whereby individual norms can be situated within and mediated through an individual community's own particular cultural framework (Tilley, 2000, pp. 514 and 520; Brems, 1997, p. 158). If international standards can be drafted, interpreted and implemented in such a way that they can respond effectively to cultural difference, aboriginal communities will be able to claim those standards as 'their own' – that is as an accepted and integral part of their own cultures - rather than rejecting them as a foreign, inappropriate and irrelevant imposition. In the particular context of child welfare, it is promising that the UNCRC represents the high point of UN efforts, to date, to find that kind of cross-cultural legitimacy. At the very least the UNCRC may provide a more culturally appropriate *starting point* for a genuine cross-cultural dialogue between self-governing indigenous communities, the Canadian State and the international community over how best to secure the effective protection of the basic fundamental rights of aboriginal children. It is therefore within the international arena that Canada's indigenous peoples may finally find the space and freedom they need for developing culturally grounded mechanisms of protection and accountability – space and freedom which is currently not possible when working within the suffocating constraints of the 'legal and political imagination' of the Canadian State.

References

Anaya, J. (2004), *Indigenous Peoples in International Law*, 2nd Edition, New York: Oxford University Press.

An-Na'im, A. (1995), 'Conclusion', in A. An-Na'im (ed.), *Human Rights in Cross-Cultural Perspectives – A Quest for Consensus*, Philadelphia: University of Pennsylvania Press.

Asch, M. and Macklem, P. (1991), 'Aboriginal Rights and Canadian Sovereignty: An Essay on R v Sparrow', *Alberta Law Review*, 29:2, 498.

Barsh, R. (1996), 'Indigenous Peoples and the UN Commission on Human Rights: A Case of the Immovable Object and the Irresistible Force', *Human Rights Quarterly*, 18:4, 782.

Boldt, M. (1993), *Surviving as Indians. The Challenge of Self-Government*, Toronto: University of Toronto Press.

Boldt, M. and Long, A. (1992), 'Tribal Philosophies and the Canadian Charter of Rights and Freedoms', in Banfield, J. (ed.), *Readings in Law and Society*, Concord: Captus Press.

Borrows, J. (1992), 'A Genealogy of Law: Inherent Sovereignty and First Nations Self-Government', *Osgoode Hall Law Journal*, 30:2, 291.

— (1994), 'Constitutional Law From a First Nation Perspective: Self-Government and the Royal Proclamation', *University of British Columbia Law Review*, 28:1, 1.

— (2002), *Recovering Canada: The Resurgence of Indigenous Law*, Toronto: University of Toronto Press.

Brems, E. (1997), 'Enemies or Allies? Feminism and Cultural Relativism as Dissident Voices in Human Rights Discourse', *Human Rights Quarterly*, 19:1, 136.

Canada: Council for Yukon Indians, Yukon Territory, Canada Department of Indian and Northern Affairs (1993), *Umbrella Final Agreement*, Ottawa: Ministry of Indian Affairs and Northern Development.

Canada: Department of Indian Affairs and Northern Development (DIAND) (1995), *Federal Policy Guide for Aboriginal Self-Government. The Government of Canada's Approach to Implementation of the Inherent Right and the Negotiation of Aboriginal Self-Government*, Ottawa: Department of Indian Affairs and Northern Development.

Cassese, A. (1995), *Self-determination of peoples – A legal reappraisal*, Cambridge: Cambridge University Press.

Corntassel, J. and Primeau, T. (1995), 'Indigenous "Sovereignty" and International Law: Revised Strategies for Pursuing "Self-Determination"', *Human Rights Quarterly*, 17:2, 343.

Debeljak, J. (2000), 'Barriers to the Recognition of Indigenous Peoples' Human Rights at the United Nations', *Monash University Law Review*, 26:1, 159.

Dickson, T. (2004), 'Self-Government by Side Agreement?', *McGill Law Journal*, 49, 419.

Franck, T. (1993), 'Postmodern tribalism and the right to secession', in Brolmann, C., Lefeber, R. and Zieck, M. (eds), *Peoples and Minorities in International Law*, Dordrecht: Martinus Nijhoff.

Hogg, P. and Turpel, M.E. (1995), 'Implementing Aboriginal Self-Government: Constitutional and Jurisdictional Issues', *Canadian Bar Review*, 74, 187.

Holder, C. and Corntassel, J. (2002), 'Indigenous Peoples and Multicultural Citizenship: Bridging Collective and Individual Rights', *Human Rights Quarterly*, 24:1, 126.

Islam, M. (1997), 'Indigenous Self-Determination in the Final Draft Declaration of the UN Working Group', *Macquarie Law Review*, 1, 139.

Kamenka E. (1988), 'Human Rights, Peoples Rights', in Crawford (ed.), *The Rights of Peoples*, Oxford: Clarendon Press, 127.

Kline, M. (1992), 'Child Welfare Law, "Best Interests of the Child" Ideology and First Nations', *Osgoode Hall Law Journal*, 30:1-2, 375.

— (1995), 'Complicating the Ideology of Motherhood: Child Welfare Law and First Nations Women', in Fineman and Karpin (eds), *Mothers in Law: Feminist Theory and the Legal Regulation of Motherhood*, New York: Columbia University Press, 118.

Lynch, P. (2001), 'Keeping them Home: The Best Interests of Indigenous Children and Communities in Canada and Australia', *Sydney Law Review*, 23, 501.

MacDonald, F. (2005), 'Progress or Regress: A Critical Examination of the Canadian Government's Shift to "Autonomous" First Nations Child Welfare', Conference Paper, University of Edinburgh Centre of Canadian Studies, Annual Conference, First Nations First Thoughts, 5–6 May 2005. Papers available at <http://www.cst.ed.ac.uk/2005conference/archiveA-M.html>.

Manitoba Justice Inquiry (1991), *Report of the Aboriginal Justice Inquiry of Manitoba: The Justice System and Aboriginal People*, vol. 1, Winnipeg: Manitoba.

McCorquodale, R. (1994), 'Self-Determination: A Human Rights Approach', *International and Comparative Law Quarterly*, 43, 857.

McGillivray, A. and Comaskey, B. (1999), *Black Eyes all of the Time: Intimate Violence, Aboriginal Women and the Justice System*, Toronto: University of Toronto Press.

Monture, P. (1989), 'A Vicious Circle: Child Welfare and the First Nations', *Canadian Journal of Women and the Law*, 3, 1.

Monture-Angus, P. (1999), *Journeying Forward. Dreaming of First Nations Independence*, Halifax, N.S: Fernwood Publishing.

Nahanee, T. (1996), 'Dancing with a Gorilla: Aboriginal Women, Justice and the Charter', in Royal Commission on Aboriginal Peoples Round Table Discussion on Justice Issues, Ottawa: Minister of Supply and Services, Canada, 359.

Office of the Chief Medical Examiner (1992), *The Fatalities Act – Respecting the Death of Lester Norman Desjarlais*, Brandon: Ministry of Social Services and Housing.

Quane, H. (1998), 'The United Nations and the Evolving Right to Self-Determination', *International and Comparative Law Quarterly*, 47, 537.

Rosas, A. (1993), 'Internal Self-Determination', in Tomuschat, C. (ed.), *Modern Law of Self-Determination*, Dordrecht: Martinus Nijhoff.

Slattery, B. (1992), 'First Nations and the Constitution: A Question of Trust', *Canadian Bar Review*, 71, 261.

Stavenhagen, R. (2005), Report of the Special Rapporteur on the situation of human rights and fundamental freedoms of indigenous people, Rodolfo Stavenhagen. Mission to Canada, UN Doc. E/CN.4/2005/88/Add.3 (2 December 2004).

Thornberry, P. (1993), 'The Democratic or Internal Aspect of Self-Determination with Some Remarks on Federalism', in Tomuschat (ed.) *Modern Law of Self-Determination*, Dordrecht: Martinus Nijhoff, 101.

Thornberry, P. (2002), *Indigenous Peoples and Human Rights*, New York: Juris Publishing, Manchester: Manchester University Press.

Tilley, J. (2000), 'Cultural Relativism', *Human Rights Quarterly*, 22:2, 501.

Turpel, M.E. (1989–1990), 'Aboriginal Peoples and the Canadian Charter: Interpretative Monopolies, Cultural Differences', *Canadian Human Rights Yearbook*, 6, 3.

Turpel, M.E. (1992), 'Aboriginal Peoples and the Canadian Charter of Rights and Freedoms: Contradictions and Challenges', in J. Banfield (ed.) *Readings in Law and Society*, Concord: Captus Press.

White, L. and Jacobs, E. (1992), 'Liberating Our Children Liberating Our Nations', Report of the Aboriginal Committee, Community Panel Child Protection Legislation Review in British Columbia, British Columbia: Queen's Printer.

Wright, S. (2001), *International Human Rights, Decolonisation and Globalisation. Becoming Human*, London: Routledge.

Chapter 7

Cultural Pluralism and the Return of Cultural Heritage

Kathryn Last

There are many examples of claims by nation states for the return of objects of cultural heritage, such as the Ethiopian claim for the return of the Maqdala Treasures and the Greek claim for the return of the Parthenon sculptures (House of Commons 2000, para. 128, 148–52). However, for the purposes of this chapter I intend to highlight some of the issues raised by claims for the return of objects of cultural heritage to sub-state groups.[1] I will be considering the claims for the return of cultural heritage to sub-state groups, rather than nation states, because of the particular issues such claims raise both within composite political units and internationally. The sub-state groups with which this chapter is concerned range from indigenous groups[2] to sub-state national societies (as defined by Tierney 2004).

Examples of successful claims for the return of cultural heritage by indigenous groups include the return of the Ghost Dance Shirt to the Lakota Sioux by Glasgow Museum and the return of the potlatch collection to the Kwakiutl peoples of British Columbia from the Canadian Museum of Civilization and the Royal Ontario Museum (Statt, Solowan and Bell 2003). In the context of sub-state national societies, a prime example is the return of the Stone of Destiny to Scotland from Westminster Abbey (Palmer 2001, 514).[3] Interestingly, all of these returns took place not as a result of legal action but as a result of negotiated repatriation settlements, and this chapter will illustrate how sub-state groups are often excluded from legal processes such that negotiated settlements are the only avenue when seeking the return of their cultural heritage. I will be drawing on examples from Canada, the UK and the US, looking at both international and domestic law to highlight the problems faced by groups in making claims.

---

 1 One difficulty that this presents is that 'the definition of a group is not an easy task for there are no specific boundaries' (Osman 1999, 980).
 2 For a definition of indigenous peoples see Gupta (1999, footnote 3).
 3 There have also been some unsuccessful claims, for example, in 2002, a member of the Welsh Assembly, Alison Halford, called for the return of the Gold Cape of Mold, a Bronze Age artefact from Wales held in the British Museum (BBC News 24 January 2002). In addition, there have been claims for the return of objects to regions within a state such as the return of the Lindisfarne Gospels to the North East of England (Palmer 2001, 500). Although the Stone of Destiny was returned to Scotland in 1996, there has been continuing controversy about the Stone being in Edinburgh rather than in Scone (*Glasgow Herald* 5 May 2003).

Before turning to the substantive legal issues, I will look at three preliminary issues, the definition of cultural heritage, the role of the repatriation process and the distinction between restitution and repatriation. This will demonstrate the importance of the return of cultural heritage and will highlight some of the issues that must be considered when assessing the substantive law.

The Definition of Cultural Heritage

The first preliminary issue that deserves mention is the definition of 'cultural heritage'. There is not space in this chapter to address all aspects of this issue,[4] however, I would like to highlight a couple of points pertinent to claims by groups: the role of cultural heritage in identity formation and control of the process of definition, both of which have implications for legal claims for return in terms of establishing a sufficient interest in an object and whether that object is covered by the relevant law.

Cultural Heritage and Identity

It is important when considering the concept of cultural heritage to recognise its importance in the formation of cultural identity.[5] Lewis (1981, 5) recognises 'the contribution made by a nation's heritage in promoting cultural identity'. Heritage, according to Wagner (2001, 22), can be seen as 'a dynamic and defining part of the construction of an identity'. This can be seen in the preamble to the UNESCO Declaration Concerning the Intentional Destruction of Cultural Heritage 2003, in the statement that 'cultural heritage is an important component of ... cultural identity'.[6] This role is reflected in the numerous legal definitions of cultural heritage that refer to items of 'national' importance and the widespread restrictions on the international movement of cultural heritage.[7]

The role that heritage plays in cultural identity is relevant to groups other than simply nation states. Although Wagner (2001, 17) notes how 'as a modern endeavour, the question of identity found its answer in the idea of the nation', identities and consequently heritage tend to have a more local or national focus. Indeed, Weber (2001, 6) argues that, 'the local sphere may be the level at which the individual needs for a sense of identity and belonging find expression'. Thus, as Lowenthal (1993,

---

4   For a fuller discussion of the issue see Blake (2000).

5   According to Stétié (1981, 8), it is 'something that, for a particular people, is a living thing which enables a people to achieve confidence in itself and is, thus, able to imagine its future.'

6   Similarly, the UNESCO Preliminary Draft Convention on the Protection of the Diversity of Cultural Contents and Artistic Expressions (2004, preamble) states that cultural goods (which are often viewed as constituting heritage) 'convey identities'.

7   An example of this is the Canadian Cultural Property Export and Import Act 1985 which refers to an object being of significance 'by reason of its close association with Canadian history or national life' and 'of such a degree of national importance that its loss to Canada would significantly diminish the national heritage'. RSC 1985, c. C-15, section 11(1)

3) notes in the context of Great Britain, 'Heritage normally connotes English, or Scottish, sometimes British'. Thus, cultural heritage can play an important role for the identity of sub-state groups as well as nations.[8]

However, if, as Wagner suggests, the relationship between cultural heritage and identity is symbiotic, the definition of cultural heritage is potentially very wide. Some writers have argued that return is appropriate for only a limited sub-category of objects. For example, John Merryman (1998, 140) argues that only those objects of religious or ceremonial importance possess qualities that justify their return. He distinguishes objects that are essential to the welfare of a group, for which return may be appropriate, from objects used as symbols of national ideals or as the embodiment of national history or culture for which return is not justified according to his reasoning. He argues that only for this limited category of objects does the relationship between object and culture depend upon propinquity. As a consequence, he regards the cultural value of relics of earlier cultures, such as the ancient Egyptians, as independent of propinquity and his logic dictates that these should not be repatriated. In contrast, Osman (1999, 981) argues that 'the Egyptians of today are sufficiently related to the ancient Egyptians to possess rights in ancient Egyptian antiquities'.

However, the items that Merryman excludes may form the core of the cultural heritage of a group because of their relationship to its culture and identity. Thus his criteria for whether an object should be returned (1998, 141) – that the culture that gave the object its cultural significance is alive and that the object be actively employed for the religious or ceremonial purposes for which it was made – are unduly exclusive. Merryman's argument also runs counter to the ideas underpinning the UNESCO Resolution on *Repatriation of African Art*, which in resolution 5(b) urges nations to acknowledge 'the right to request repatriation of dispossessed artefacts during times of war, colonization, and occupation', which is not limited to particular types of artefact. I would submit that it is not only those objects actively employed for religious or ceremonial purposes that we should be concerned with.[9] Merryman's approach would exclude, for example, the Stone of Destiny.[10] This broader approach is supported by Stétié (1981, 9) who argues for the return of any object 'which is considered to be sufficiently important for a given cultural tradition, to the extent that, without that object, the cultural tradition in question cannot be explained, above all, to those who have inherited it'. Similarly, Harding (1999, 344) argues that:

> If the intrinsic value of cultural heritage is intimately connected to the value of cultural experience and the value of cultural experience exists in something like its dialogic relationship to the individuals who comprise the culture, then this tells us something about

---

8   Daes (1995, iii) refers to the 'identity of a people' in defining heritage.

9   Merryman is actually discussing the retention of objects rather than their repatriation but he admits that analysis on one issue is applicable to the other.

10 This was the stone used for the coronation of Scotland's kings. It was taken to England and was kept in Westminster Abbey until 1996 when it was returned after a lengthy campaign. It is unlikely to be employed for its original purpose, yet its importance to Scotland is undoubted.

the appropriate treatment of cultural heritage. If an object, custom, story or ritual has a living context it should remain in or be returned to that context.

Controlling the Definitional Process

The control of the process of definition is particularly important when one considers the heritage of sub-state cultures. It raises the question of whose definitional voice is, or should be, determinative when there is a discrepancy between the value attached to objects by those who currently possess them and their claimants.

For example, under the UNESCO Convention on the Means of Prohibiting and Preventing the Illicit Import, Export and Transfer of Ownership of Cultural Property 1970, it is State Parties that are responsible for defining the objects to which the Convention will apply. This gives scope for national approaches that reflect the values attributed to objects in that particular state. However, in multinational states where one culture is dominant, there is a risk that the heritage of minority cultures will be excluded. Recommendation 1 of the 1993 Mataatua Declaration on Cultural and Intellectual Property Rights of Indigenous Peoples states that indigenous peoples should 'define for themselves their own ... cultural property', yet it is notable that there is no equivalent international recommendation for other sub-state groups.

Even if the heritage of minority cultures is included in state definitions, its inclusion may be premised upon different values. This was evident in the controversy over the Bighorn Medicine Wheel, where the US Forest Service was concerned only with its archaeological value rather than its continuing use as a sacred site (Chapman 1999). Definition is often a political as well as a legal issue. One of the inherent problems with legal definitions of cultural heritage is that they reflect the culturally specific values of those framing the legislation, given that categories of material culture are socially constructed (Mclaughlin 1996, 770). An example of this is the US Native American Graves Protection and Repatriation Act 1990, which distinguishes secular and religious objects yet this distinction does not exist in some native cultures (Chapman 1999, 6).

In this context it is notable that the Canadian government (1992, 1) has recognised this issue, stating:

> A fundamental concern to Aboriginal groups [is] that the existing heritage protection system is not sensitive to Aboriginal cultural values. Instead they felt, it is geared more towards protecting sites and objects as archaeological resources – *resources for the scientific study of past cultures* – rather than as the heritage legacy of living cultures.

Therefore, when considering claims for the return of heritage it must be recognised that the definition of heritage is not objective.

The Role of the Process of Return

Turning now to the second preliminary issue, the role of the process of return, this encompasses three aspects: recognition of the relationship between the object and the group, the symbolic function of reparation and recognition of the group.

The Object/Group Relationship

Recognition of the relationship between the object and the group can often be one of the most controversial aspects of return. In the context of claims by nation states, it has been argued that

> It is not self-evident that something made in a place belongs there, or that something produced by artists of an earlier time ought to remain in or be returned to the territory occupied by their cultural descendants, or that the present government of a nation should have the power over artifacts historically associated with its people or territory. (Boyd 1990, 922).

Thus, one could question whether sub-state groups should 'have an exclusive right to determine whether and how objects associated with their cultures should be treated' (Boyd 1990, 922), particularly where they form part of a multicultural nation. It might be argued that a consequence of cultural pluralism is that those groups do not have a right to possession of objects for which their culture has the most direct association, particularly if those objects are viewed as the heritage of the whole state. However, I would defend the position that objects of cultural heritage are important to sub-state groups and that their return plays an important role in this respect because 'possession of a people's material culture ... implicates both power and control over the underlying culture' (Mclaughlin 1996, 771). The return of objects of cultural heritage, particularly within the state can counter allegations of cultural dominance by the majority culture.

Reparation

The return of cultural heritage also performs a symbolic function: reparation for past wrongs. For example, the UNESCO Resolution on *Repatriation of African Art* states that, 'the repatriation of African art has a strong symbolic character that will set the precedent for the global response to the aftermath of colonization.' Similarly, Webster (1995, 141) notes that the claim by the Kwagu'l for repatriation of the potlach collection was 'to rectify a terrible injustice that is part of our history'. When asking for the return of the Ghost Dance Shirt, which had been removed from the body of a warrior killed at the battle of Wounded Knee, Marcella LeBeau, secretary of the Wounded Knee Survivors Association maintained that the return of the shirt would 'bring closure and healing to a sad, horrible event in the history of our people'.

Group Recognition

Finally, a consequence of the process of return is that it forces the party returning the object indirectly to recognise the party to whom it has been returned. The perception of the Haida is that since repatriation efforts began they are now seen as a living, healthy nation.[11] This has led one commentator to argue that, 'there is a danger that Native American groups will mistakenly view the reacquisition of material culture

---

11 <http://repatriation.ca/history.htm>.

as a means of achieving federal recognition and the privileges and economic benefits linked thereto' (Hershkovitz 1995). This is particularly important where claims for return form part of broader claims for self-government (Bell and Paterson 1999, 184), because the ownership of cultural heritage is often perceived as being linked to issues of sovereignty and economic independence. This has led Thomas Boyd (1990, 923) to argue that: 'While perhaps not an independent sovereign under law, Native American tribes may argue that they are independent nations in a cultural sense ... in support of their claims for the return of Native American religious and cultural objects.' As a consequence, there is a risk that the process can be used to deny the legitimacy of the leaders of a group. In the negotiations for the return of the wampum belts to the Onondaga Nation, negotiation was conducted only with designated representatives of the Onondaga nation, not with the Grand Council of the Haudenosaunee,[12] because state authorities resisted a transaction that gave even implicit legitimacy to the Grand Council (Sullivan 1992, 289).

Restitution or Repatriation?

It is important to distinguish at this point between restitution and repatriation.[13] Restitution is the return of an object to its owner, based on an analysis of property rights.[14] The nature of the object as an item of cultural heritage is generally irrelevant in such considerations.

Repatriation, in contrast, is a return to a territory and is premised upon the culturally specific value of the object. Even though Kowalski (2001b, 163) argues that repatriation is 'a return to *patria*, which means fatherland understood as a state', it also applies to objects returned to sub-state groups and is often applied where the claim is perceived as being moral rather than legal. Isar (1981, 21) gives the example of: 'objects which have left their countries of origin as a result of colonial situations or an imbalance of power between nations and where, quite obviously, no one would claim for their return on legal grounds of any kind. This claim is quite different. It is a moral claim.'

As we will see, many claims by sub-state groups are claims for repatriation, phrased in terms of moral obligation, rather than claims for restitution based on an assertion of property rights because of the difficulties that attend such actions. However, even claims for repatriation face legal obstacles and are generally only pursued against institutions rather than individuals.

---

12 A group of traditional Iroquois leaders regarding itself as the rightful governing body of all six Iroquois Nations.

13 Merryman (1990, 521) criticises the use of the term repatriation as a form of 'romantic nationalism', however, this is due to his avowedly internationalist stance.

14 For a discussion of the concept of restitution see Kowalski (2001a) and Gerstenblith (2001).

Restitution: Problems of Private International Law

The issue to which I will now turn is how sub-state groups can be excluded from legal mechanisms for restitution of their cultural heritage when the object is located in a state other than that within which the group is located. The rules of private international law present a number of problems for claimants, but the particular difficulties will depend on the circumstances surrounding the object's removal.

Seemingly the most straightforward scenario is a claim arising from the theft of an object, yet the heterogeneity of claims is vast. Probably the easiest claim to resolve, and one that is rarely litigated, is a title dispute between the original owner of an object of cultural heritage and the person who stole it. The legal position is generally straightforward because a thief does not acquire title to the property. For example, in England and Wales, section 4 of the Sale of Goods Act 1980 provides that the limitation period does not apply to an action against the thief of the object.

In addition to theft, claims have also arisen as a consequence of transfers of title that are disputed.[15] Within this category, the most complex claims are those involving transfers of title based on *prima facie* valid contracts. These claims raise different issues to cases of outright theft and, as Palmer (2000, 4) notes, 'claims based on surviving title are probably more difficult to pursue where the deprivation was not, at the time of its occurrence, locally unlawful'.[16]

Limitation of Actions

One must consider the possibility that an original owner's right of action, or even their title, has been extinguished through lapse of time if the dispute concerns property that is now in the hands of a third party, however it was removed. The lengths of these limitation periods and the date at which they start to run vary widely, however, claims by sub-state groups often relate to objects that have been appropriated some time ago. As Tolhurst (1998, 16) notes, 'in many cases evidence touching upon how possession was lost in the first place is no longer available and ... technical rules about limitations and bona fide purchase would rule out any favourable court proceeding.' Actions for restitution will often be time-barred because many of these limitation periods are relatively short. This is highlighted by the refusal by the government of New Zealand to return the carved meeting house of Mataatua to the people of Ngati Awa because of the passing of the limitation period (Mead 1995, 74).

---

15 Although it is sometimes difficult to distinguish such cases from claims of theft. Probably the most famous example of this is the request by Greece for restitution of the Parthenon sculptures based on the claim that they were not acquired legally by Lord Elgin (Greenfield 1996, 56).

16 These disputes can concern a number of different, and often complex, scenarios, as illustrated by the case of Frédéric Gentili di Giuseppe whose collection of paintings was sold by auction in 1941 because his estate had debts and his family had fled France. The heirs of Gentili di Giuseppe sued the Musée du Louvre, which had possessed the paintings since they were returned to France after the war, and the Paris Court of Appeal ruled that the auction was a nullity (Palmer 2000, 15). However, many such claims are not resolved through legal action, such as the return of *L'Olivette* by Van Gogh to Gerta Silberberg (BBC News 4 June 1999).

In England, the limitation period is 6 years from the date of purchase by a bona fide purchaser, whereas in Scotland, the period is 20 years from the theft. In contrast, in the US, many states have rules that favour the original owner and enable actions to recover the object after a considerable period of time. The decision in *Autocephalus Greek-Orthodox Church of Cyprus v Goldberg & Feldman Fine Arts, Inc.* (1990) concerned Byzantine mosaics removed from the Kanakaria Church in Northern Cyprus and purchased by Goldberg in the 'free port' area of Geneva airport. The court held that the action was not out of time because, under Indiana law, which it judged to be the correct jurisdiction, the period did not start to run until Cyprus discovered that the Mosaics were in Goldberg's possession.[17]

A similar effect is achieved in states that have a demand and refusal rule. This can be seen in *Kunstsammlungen zu Weimar v Elicofon* (1981), where a German art gallery sued an American art collector for the return of paintings that had disappeared after the Second World War. The Second Circuit held that a cause of action against a bona fide purchaser did not accrue until the purchaser refused to comply with a demand for the return of the paintings.

Article 3(3) of the UNIDROIT Convention on Stolen or Illegally Exported Cultural Objects 1995 provides a 50-year limitation period, but by virtue of article 10, the convention is not retrospective in its effect and few states have ratified.

Forum

Civil law and common law jurisdictions take very different approaches to the issue of acquisition of title by a bona fide purchaser. Most civilian systems allow a purchaser of stolen property to acquire title if they are in good faith, whereas common law systems often rely on the maxim *nemo dat quod non habet* to maintain the rights of the original owner. As a consequence, a common scenario will involve jurisdictional issues where the object has been moved among different states to take advantage of these differences. The *lex situs* rule means that the appropriate jurisdiction for determining the validity of transfers of property is the country in which the transfer took place. A strict application of this rule is evident in the decision in *Winkworth v Christie Manson & Woods Ltd* (1980) where a collection of netsuke were stolen in England, purchased in Italy then returned to England for sale. The original owner was unable to secure the return of his property because Italian law was applicable and the purchaser had acquired good title to the objects.[18]

However, the issue of forum is subject to varying interpretations by different states. In *Autocephalous Greek-Orthodox Church of Cyprus v Goldberg* (1989) Goldberg argued that Swiss legal forum had jurisdiction under the *lex situs* rule.[19]

---

17 For a full discussion of the case see Farrell (1992). A similar result regarding limitation can be seen in *O'Keefe v Snyder* (1980).

18 Winkworth had tried to argue that English law, which would have given him a right to return of the collection on the principle of *nemo dat quod non habet*, should apply because of the close relationship with England but the court rejected this argument.

19 Switzerland has generous rules regarding the acquisition of title by purchasers and it has been suggested that the reason for the transaction occurring in Switzerland was to benefit

However, the Indiana court held that Indiana law applied because of the residence of the defendants, the origin of the purchase money and the current location of the object. Thus it may be unclear which legal system's rules will apply to any claim for return.

Group-specific Problems

The issues of the limitation of actions and forum present problems for all claims for restitution of cultural heritage. However, there are also a number of issues that present particular problems for claims by sub-state groups: legal personality and property rights. Both are related to the restitution paradigm of private international law, which is concerned only with restitution not repatriation.

Claims for restitution are usually made by an individual 'owner' or by a state that has proprietary rights in the object. However, the claimant must be recognised as a juristic entity in the courts of the forum. The recognition of sub-state groups can face similar problems to unrecognised nation states, as in the case of *Federal Republic of Germany v Elicofon* (1973) where the court held that an agency of the East German government could not assert a claim to works of art in an American court because East Germany was not recognised at the time.

Some jurisdictions are flexible in interpreting the requirements of standing, and a good example of this is the case of *Bumper Development Corp v Commissioner of Police of the Metropolis* (1991) where the English Court of Appeal held that an Indian temple, from which a statue had been stolen, was entitled to sue for recovery of the statue in England because it was accorded legal personality in Indian law. However, with many indigenous groups, ascertaining the appropriate community authority to represent that group may be difficult. 'It may not necessarily be the band council or other political body. For example, in the case of sacred property it could be the elders or religious societies within the community' (Bell and Paterson 1999, 208).

The second issue for sub-state groups making claims for restitution is the need to establish a property right. Again, this can pose difficulties even for states. A number of states have umbrella statutes, which vest ownership of archaeological material discovered within its territory in the state (Callahan 1993, 1325). Yet even in such situations, restitution is not assured. The question is whether other jurisdictions will recognise the state's ownership. The case of *US v Schultz* (2003) is an example of a successful claim by a state. It concerned the effect of Egyptian Law 117, The Law on the Protection of Antiquities, pursuant to which the Egyptian government claimed ownership of all antiquities discovered after 1983. The question for the court was whether the antiquities were 'stolen' under the US National Stolen Property Act. Schultz argued that Egyptian Law 117 did not vest ownership in the Egyptian government but was merely an attempt to prevent export. The United States Court of Appeals, Second Circuit, held that Egyptian Law 117 was 'clear and unambiguous, and that the antiquities that were the subject of the conspiracy ... were owned by the Egyptian government' (402).[20]

---

from this.

20 The decision was based upon that in *United States v McClain* (1979), which is discussed in Gerstenblith (2001, 214).

In contrast, in the case of *Attorney General of New Zealand v Ortiz* (1984), New Zealand brought an action in respect of a series of five Maori carved panels, which were removed from New Zealand without an export licence. Under New Zealand's Historic Articles Act 1962, this gave rise to forfeiture of the property and the Attorney General's claim was therefore based on a right of ownership. The English House of Lords held that since seizure of the property had not taken place, the Crown was not its owner. The interesting point about *Ortiz* is that the claim had been brought by the state because it was considered too difficult for the Maori group from whom the panels had been taken to establish their claim to ownership.[21]

Furthermore, claims for the return of illicitly excavated antiquities often founder on the issue of establishing the territory from which they were excavated. This issue arose in the case of *Republic of Lebanon v Sotheby's* (1990), which concerned the Sevso treasure claimed by Lebanon, Yugoslavia and Hungary (Kaye 1996, 29). In such circumstances there may be difficulty in establishing that the item was removed from the territory of the sub-state group rather than elsewhere in the state or even in another state.

Establishing original property rights can be particularly difficult in the case of communal property. For example, totem poles are considered collective property by some indigenous groups because of their relationship to the land, history, spirituality, culture, and ceremonies (Bell and Paterson 1999, 185). The difficulty relates to the fact that many legal systems focus on Western assumptions of property and individualism and often fail to recognise communal property.

This problem is exacerbated where the object has been transferred by a member of the group rather than stolen; bringing it within the category of appropriation that is prima facie lawful. It may be difficult to establish that a purchaser has not acquired good title to the object when the group's argument is based on tribal custom and law that the original transferring party did not have the authority or right to transfer title to the object in the first place (Boyd 1990, 912). For example, 'To traditional Iroquois people ... no individual could ever own a wampum belt because the belts are the property and heritage of all the people' (Sullivan 1992, 286). Thus a transfer of such property by an individual raises particular problems. The object may have been sold by someone appointed as its caretaker, who did not have authority to sell (Woodford 2002). This was the situation with the wampum belts of the Onondaga Nation,[22] which were sold by the tribe's designated wampum-keeper to a US Government official in 1891 (Sullivan 1992, 286). As Boyd (1990, 912) points out, 'A significant amount of personal property, particularly sacred objects, may have been owned or possessed by the tribe as a whole and consequently cannot be transferred in any other manner but collectively.' Although Hurtado (1993, 67) has argued that US courts would not recognise the validity of a sale by an individual Native American of property that belonged to a Native American tribe or nation as a whole, the invalidity

---

21 Failing in their claim of title to the carving, the Crown had only a claim for violation of its export law, which was unenforceable as foreign penal law.

22 This was acting as wampum-keeper for all of the six nations comprising the Iroquois Confederacy: the Mohawk, the Oneida, the Onondaga, the Cayuga, the Seneca and the Tuscarora Nations.

of such sales may not be recognised by the courts of the forum, particularly if the sale has taken place in a jurisdiction that allows bona fide purchasers to acquire title.

Bell and Paterson (1999, 180) argue that in Canada:

> Aboriginal perspectives on the rights of individuals to transfer such property will be considered along with common-law principles of property and contract law to establish the tests for legitimate acquisition and transfer of title. In situations where an individual has removed, sold, or donated collective property without consent of the appropriate community authority, the combination of Aboriginal perspectives with principles of property law may operate to invalidate title that assumes the object is capable of individual ownership.

However, this approach may not be taken in other jurisdictions. In addition, for some indigenous groups proof of ownership can sometimes be established only through oral testimony. Bell and Paterson (1999, 176) note that in Canada, 'judges are reluctant to give weight to oral histories that consist of out-of-court statements passed through successive generations of Aboriginal peoples.' In this respect, the decision in *Delgamuukw v British Columbia* (1998) regarding the admissibility of oral evidence will assist those attempting to make a claim.[23] But again this approach may not be taken in other jurisdictions.

A Solution in Public International Law?

The difficulties in bringing an action for restitution resulted in the UNESCO Convention on the Means of Prohibiting and Preventing the Illicit Import, Export and Transfer of Ownership of Cultural Property 1970. Article 7(b) requires State Parties to take appropriate steps to return cultural property stolen from a museum or secular public monument in another State Party to the Convention, provided that such property is documented as appertaining to the inventory of that institution.

However, this being an instrument of international law, its concern is with states, and sub-state groups face problems accessing the system. The return of cultural property under the UNESCO Convention is dependent upon the State from which it was removed making a claim. A sub-state group cannot utilise the Convention unless the State is prepared to act on its behalf. This is therefore a microcosm of a much bigger issue, that of efforts of sub-state groups to develop an international presence, what has come to be known as paradiplomacy.

Furthermore, the UNESCO Convention applies only to those objects designated by the state and stolen from a museum or public monument. I mentioned earlier the risk that the state may not include the cultural objects of minority cultures in this regime and many items that are the subject of repatriation claims by groups have not been removed from museums or public monuments. Thus the usefulness of the UNESCO Convention for claims by sub-state groups is limited.

---

23 'In *Delgamuukw* the Chief Justice reiterated that the unique nature of Aboriginal rights demands that courts must not reject evidence of oral history outright but must identify specific features of the evidence in question that justify treating it with suspicion' (Paterson 1999, 206).

Repatriation

Because of the difficulties that attend a claim for restitution, many sub-state groups must instead frame their claim for the return of items of cultural heritage as requests for repatriation. In general, claims for repatriation are increasingly arising as a consequence of the withdrawal of colonial powers.[24] As Kowalski (2001b, 139) notes, 'composite political structures have shown a tendency to accumulate in their capitals the most valuable works of art and books, even though these constituted a very sensitive part of the cultural heritage of the nations inhabiting the subordinated territories.' Upon independence of these subordinated territories, claims arise for the return of items of cultural significance to the independent state.[25]

Yet it is not just independent states that wish to make such claims. Kowalski's observation is equally pertinent to sub-state groups. Restitution claims are unlikely to be successful because of the circumstances surrounding the removal of the object. Claims are often complicated by the facts surrounding their removal and subsequent acquisition by their current possessor.[26] As Mastalir (1993, 1049) notes, 'restitution may be the norm for objects looted during armed conflicts ... [but] objects removed by economic or colonial conquest are treated differently. The products of ... 'Elginism' ... have often remained in the acquisitive nation.'

Due to the numerous difficulties associated with legal claims for the return of items of cultural heritage, groups are seeking alternatives modes of dispute resolution.[27] This is reflected in the fact that there is a general absence of litigated claims and in most countries the majority of claims are the subject of private negotiations (Paterson 1999, 207). As mentioned earlier, these claims for repatriation are often viewed as moral rather than legal claims but legal rights continue to play a role, albeit as part of the negotiation process, defining the parameters of potential agreements (Bell and Paterson 1999, 169).

Claims for repatriation can be less attractive to sub-state groups because, unlike an order for restitution of property, conditions are often imposed in the agreement

---

24 Such as the request by the Nigerian Parliament for the repatriation of artefacts removed during British colonial rule (BBC News 24 January 2002).

25 For example, Egypt's call for the return of the Rosetta Stone (BBC News 21 July 2003). The UK has returned some items, such as the Turkish marble sculptures found on a shipwreck off the coast of Kent (BBC News 15 July 1998). However, the more typical approach of the UK government is represented by its attitude to the claim for return of the Parthenon Sculptures (*Times* 22 June 1998; *Guardian* 13 December 1999; BBC News 5 February 2000; BBC News 22 June 2001; BBC News 15 January 2002).

26 An example of this is the fragment of a soapstone sculpture of a bird taken from the Great Zimbabwe ruins that has recently been returned to Zimbabwe. In 1907, a German Missionary sold it to the Ethnological Museum in Berlin. It was then taken to Leningrad by Russian forces at the end of the Second World War and was returned to Germany after the end of the Cold War. A German Museum handed it over to President Robert Mugabe in 2003 (BBC News 14 May 2003).

27 Such an approach is justified because 'unlike the purchase of other property, cultural property is a unique category, requiring different consideration from normal recovery laws' (Kastenberg 1995, 39).

for return and there is often a presumption of return to an alternative museum rather than to the group itself for continuing use. A classic example is the Ghost Dance Shirt returned to the Lakota Sioux by Glasgow Museum. Glasgow Museum imposed a number of conditions regarding care in the agreement to return the shirt.[28] These included an obligation to preserve the Ghost Dance Shirt in perpetuity and to ensure that it is displayed at all times in an appropriate place accessible to members of the public. The agreement also contained an obligation to loan the shirt for public display in Glasgow.

In this context, the return of the ceremonial head-dress to the Blood tribe of Canada by Aberdeen's Marischal Museum is unusual. The University agreed that the head-dress should be returned to its traditional role and no conditions were imposed. Furthermore, the University agreed not to ask for a replica or to publish photographs of the head-dress as that would run counter to the acceptance of the spiritual importance of the head-dress (Associated Press 7 July 2003).

If a group is required to house an item in a museum this may negate the effect of its return to the group and its value within that group and thus its nature as cultural heritage. This is particularly problematic where the group wants possession of an artefact that they perhaps intend to destroy. Different concepts of stewardship can impede claims for repatriation because those representing the museum often give priority to the conservation and security of the object and to its continuing accessibility for scientific purposes. Indeed Lewis (1981, 6) has argued that, 'unless there is adequate technical support to maintain them in good condition, the return of certain items must be seriously questioned.' Yet this reflects a culturally specific view of the value of these items. With the Zuni war gods, 'physical preservation of the objects is diametrically opposed to their cultural function' (Mastalir 1993, 1046).

The first stage in making a claim for repatriation is to establish the relationship between the object and the group, often referred to as 'cultural affiliation'.[29] Although there is not a requirement to prove continuing title, the question of this relationship is fundamental to any claim for repatriation because the basis of such claims is the

---

28 (1) To preserve in perpetuity the Ghost Dance Shirt; (2) ensure that the Ghost Dance Shirt is displayed at all reasonable times in an appropriate place where the shirt and details of its historical and cultural significance is accessible to members of the public; (3) acknowledge, in any public display of the Ghost Dance Shirt, the role of the people of Glasgow in its history and preservation; (4) agree to loan the Ghost Dance Shirt, which would be accompanied by representative(s) of the Wounded Knee Survivors Association, for public display in Glasgow for such periods as may be agreed between Glasgow City Council and the Association.

29 This is to be distinguished from approaches that rely on a territorial link. The problem with focusing on territory is in establishing the appropriate territory, often referred to as the 'country of origin'. The issues raised by such terminology are highlighted by Lewis (1981, 6): 'does the phrase signify the country of manufacture; the nationality of the maker; the last country to hold the object before its removal; or … the site of its discovery?' Even if the site of discovery is adopted as the criterion, if we take the example of the Lydian hoard claimed by Turkey from the Metropolitan Museum of Fine Art, since the fall of Lydia, Asia Minor has been occupied by the Assyrian, Bronze Age Greek Roman, Byzantine and Turkish civilizations: *Republic of Turkey v Metropolitan Museum of Fine Art* (1990).

cultural significance of the object. As Tolhurst (1998, 20) notes, 'the arguments for the indigenous side are not only based upon notions of property but also on the fact that the claimant's actual personhood is partly dependent on this property.' As a consequence 'most demands for repatriation are based on the argument that the treasures are vital to the spiritual health of native communities' (Webster 1995, 140). This has led Mead (1995, 71) to argue that there is 'unanimous agreement that important items of their cultures should be returned to them ... [as] part of a process of reassembling the dislocated portions of a culture.'

The issue of cultural affiliation can be seen in the criteria established by the Glasgow City Council Repatriation Working Group. This was established in 1998 to consider the Ghost Dance Shirt claimed by the Lakota Sioux.[30] The criteria developed by the working group include: (1) the right of those making the request to represent the community to which the artefact originally belonged, (2) the continuity between the community which created the object and the current community on whose behalf the request is being made and (3) the cultural and religious significance of the object to the community. The group concluded that the shirt should be returned even though there was no legal obligation to return it (BBC News 2 August 1999).[31]

However, some approaches to repatriation have been criticised because 'the determination of what is "culturally significant" has sometimes been unilaterally made by the museum or institution in possession of the relevant object, with very little input from Indigenous Peoples themselves' (Gii-dahl-guud-sliiaay 1995, 183). A further problem with relying on arguments about cultural significance is that claims for repatriation are sometimes met with the argument that the object now forms part of the culture of another society. For example, Vittorio Sgarbi, an official from the Italian Culture Ministry claimed that the Obelisk of Axum removed from Ethiopia had become Italian through a process of 'naturalisation' (BBC News 20 July 2001). Similarly, the Director of the British Museum has claimed that the Parthenon sculptures are part of the heritage of mankind rather than simply the cultural heritage of Greece (BBC News, 15 January 2002).[32] Tolhurst (1998, 21) argues that such claims lack authority when they concern indigenous artefacts: 'a ceremonial mask could be in the British Museum for 1000 years, yet it could hardly be termed part of England's cultural heritage in the sense that a distinct aspect of cultural heritage which originated in England owes its existence to this artefact.' Yet he concedes that, although

> The argument that the item has been in the country so long it now forms part of its cultural heritage ... is unlikely to apply to many artefacts of indigenous peoples ... [it] is more likely to arise where the indigenous artefact has been attached to some other object or incorporated in to some other object. (Tolhurst 1998, 25)

---

30 The shirt had been purchased by Kelvingrove Museum, thirteen months after the massacre at Wounded Knee, from the Lakota interpreter for Buffalo Bill Cody's travelling Wild West Show.

31 Although the Lord Provost of Glasgow had argued against its return claiming the shirt to have greater cultural value in Glasgow that South Dakota (*Telegraph* 20 November 1998).

32 Similarly, the Leading Article in *The Times* (22 June 1998) claimed that the sculptures are 'uniquely the common property of Western Civilisation'.

The example that he gives is the Koh-i-Noor diamond, which is attached to one of the Crowns in the British Crown Jewels.[33]

Claims for repatriation also raise the issue of who is the claimant. The group still needs a representative or institutional structure in order to make a claim and for title to the object to be transferred to them. It is here that constitutional status associated with self-government plays a role. If power is devolved, the associated institutional structure enables claims to be made.[34]

In addition, there is a reluctance to return items where there is no legal duty to do so because many museums are inhibited by the fear of a flood of claims that would denude their collections. This approach is reflected in the Declaration on the Importance and Value of Universal Museums (2003), which refers to the 'threat to the integrity of universal collections posed by demands for the restitution of objects to their countries of origin'. Furthermore, there are concerns about potential liability to claimants who may come forward in the future and perhaps have a legal case for return.

Legislative Repatriation

In some states there has been legislation enacted to facilitate the repatriation of cultural heritage. The three states that I will look at, the USA, Canada and the UK, have very different approaches to this issue. I intend to give only a brief overview of the most important aspects of each jurisdiction for the repatriation of cultural heritage to sub-state groups to illustrate the differing approaches and the problems that attend domestic claims.

USA

In the USA, specific legislation relating to the repatriation of the cultural heritage of Native Americans has been enacted in the Native American Graves Protection and Repatriation Act 1990 (NAGPRA). However, it suffers from a number of problems associated with the definition of the objects to which it applies and the groups that can access its provisions.

---

33 The diamond is claimed by Pakistan, Iran, India and Afghanistan (BBC News 26 April 2000; BBC News 7 November 2000).

34 For example, until the devolution of powers to Scotland, there was no body that could make a claim on behalf of the people of Scotland for the return of items of cultural heritage. It will be interesting to see how the plans for Regional Assemblies in England will affect this issue, because there are a number of examples of claims for the return of items to particular regions, such as the Lindisfarne Gospels (*Telegraph* 3 July 1997).

NAGPRA applies to three categories of object: cultural items,[35] sacred objects[36] and cultural patrimony,[37] which are defined in section 2. However, the statutory definitions embody a western concept of religion and culture, distinguishing sacred objects and objects of cultural patrimony. As Mclaughlin (1996, 774) notes, 'the Act does not accommodate the practical consideration that groups must confer sacredness upon objects, an active cultural process.' The Act also adopts a static concept of culture based on traditional use. Furthermore, some objects may be described both as sacred objects and objects of cultural patrimony.[38]

The Native American Graves Protection and Repatriation Act Regulations 1995[39] recognise the possibility of an object occupying more than one legal category, however, it is the museum holding the object that will make the initial determination on the character of the object, rather than the group. This is important because the category determines the obligations upon the museum with respect to repatriation.

In order to make a claim under NAGPRA, the group must be 'culturally affiliated' to the objects. This is defined in section 2(2) of NAGPRA as 'a relationship of shared group identity which can be reasonably traced historically or prehistorically between a present day Indian Tribe or native Hawaiian organization and an identifiable earlier group'. Yet again it is the museum that makes the initial determination of cultural affiliation.

The Act does not provide guidance on the situation where multiple claimants, all with roughly equal cultural affiliation, have differing views on who should speak for an object. An example of this is the claim in 1990 from the Hopi Tribe for return of a shield held by the Heard Museum in Phoenix. The trustees of the Museum found it difficult to identify which Hopi individual, group or village might be the most appropriate claimant. This was because traditional Hopi religious leaders do not recognize the Hopi Tribe as their government, yet the Tribe was the entity making the request on their behalf (Sullivan 1992, 290). As a result, the museum decided to keep the shield in a form of trust until a consensus emerged from among the claimants.[40]

The issue of recognition of groups is also important because under section 2(7) of NAGPRA, objects will be repatriated only to federally recognised tribes. An example of the difficulties that this poses is the situation of the Gabrielino/Tongva and the Juaneno/Acjachemem, who were stated to be culturally affiliated to a collection of

---

35 In addition to human remains, cultural items include both associated and unassociated funerary objects.

36 These are defined as ceremonial objects that are needed for the practice of traditional religions by present-day adherents.

37 This is an object having ongoing historical, traditional, or cultural importance, which cannot be alienated by an individual.

38 For example, the Zuni war gods.

39 60 Fed Reg 62134.

40 Similarly, the Museum of New Mexico 'found that determining legitimate tribal leadership is a difficult process' (Livesay 1992, 297).

objects. Neither is recognised by the federal government and they are thus unable to claim the repatriation of their cultural objects in their own name.[41]

Canada

In Canada, there has been some scepticism regarding the extent to which legislation can aid the repatriation process (Bell and Paterson 1999, 168). However, Alberta has enacted specific legislation, the First Nations Ceremonial Objects Repatriation Act 2000,[42] which allows for the return of sacred objects for ceremonial purposes to First Nations. Many of the details of the procedure are set out in the Blackfoot First Nations Sacred Ceremonial Objects Repatriation Regulation 2004.[43] This defines terms in the Act, such as 'First Nation'.[44] The Act applies only to objects used for sacred ceremonial traditions that are vital to the practice of those traditions. Under section 4 of the Regulation, claims can only be made where an individual has agreed to put the object back into use as a sacred ceremonial object. It therefore covers fewer objects than NAGPRA. In section 3, the Regulation deals specifically with the issue of who can represent the group. The body that applies for repatriation must be an incorporated society acting as a representative of the First Nation. The Minister, who must agree to the repatriation unless he deems repatriation inappropriate, will determine applications for repatriation. Legal title to the repatriated item is issued to the First Nation who will hold it on behalf of all the people of that First Nation. As with NAGPRA, claims under the First Nations Ceremonial Objects Repatriation Act 2000 relate to items held by public institutions.[45]

An alternative approach that has been used in Canada is that of dealing with repatriation as part of treaty negotiations. The Nisga'a Final Agreement of 1998, signed between the Nisga'a First Nation of British Columbia and the governments of British Columbia and Canada, is the first example of a Canadian treaty that deals specifically with the repatriation of cultural property. The Museum of Civilization and the Royal British Columbia Museum will each return a portion of their Nisga'a collections to the Nisga'a First Nation (Paterson 1999, 207). Those items that remain with the museums are to be shared between the museum and the Nisga'a Nation and their care is subject to an agreement by the museums to respect Nisga'a laws and practices.

Furthermore, the 1992 Task Force Report, produced by the Canadian Museums Association and the Assembly of First Nations, provides guidance to museums on repatriation and makes recommendations regarding the return of objects.

---

41 In the circumstances, the Luiseno Intertribal NAGPRA Coalition claimed the collection for these tribes (Putnam 2000).
42 RSA 2000, c.F-14.
43 Alta. Reg. 96/2004.
44 This is defined in section 1 as the Blood Tribe, the Siksika Nation and the Piikani Nation.
45 The Provincial Museum of Alberta, the Glenbow-Alberta Institute or the Crown.

UK

In the UK there is no legislation providing for the repatriation of objects of cultural heritage to sub-state groups. Many items of importance for sub-state groups within the UK reside in the British Museum or other institutions in London. For example, the Lewis chessmen, discovered on the Isle of Lewis are currently in the British Museum despite repeated calls for their return to Scotland.[46] However, in the absence of specific provision, and the devolution settlements were silent on this issue, legal claims must be framed as actions for restitution and will face the difficulties highlighted above of establishing legal personality and property rights.

Furthermore, the recent decision in *Attorney General v Trustees of the British Museum* (2005) highlights the impediments to repatriation where museums and galleries in the UK are concerned. Section 3(4) of the British Museum Act 1963 restricts the ability of the British Museum to deaccession objects. The case concerned four Old Master drawings acquired by the museum between 1946 and 1949, which had been stolen by the Gestapo in 1939. Despite recognising the moral claim of the heirs of the original owner, the English High Court held that the Museum could not return the paintings in the absence of a successful claim for restitution. A number of other museums and galleries in Britain are subject to similar restrictions on deaccessioning in their statutes and this is a serious obstacle to claims for repatriation.[47]

Conclusion

In conclusion, I hope that I have demonstrated that a number of difficulties attend claims by sub-state groups for the return of their cultural heritage, whether through claims for restitution or repatriation. Even where specific legislation has been enacted, as in the US, the conceptual framework underpinning the legislation often fails to recognise the particular issues facing sub-state groups. Many of these difficulties stem from issues surrounding the recognition of these groups and their constitutional status.

References

Bell, C.E. and Paterson R.K. (1999), 'Aboriginal Rights to Cultural Property in Canada', *International Journal of Cultural Property*, 8:1, 167–211.

Blake, J. (2000), 'On Defining the Cultural Heritage', *International and Comparative Law Quarterly*, 49, 61–85.

Boyd, T.H. (1990), 'Disputes Regarding the Possession of Native American Religious and Cultural Objects and Human Remains: A Discussion of the Applicable Law and Proposed Legislation', *Missouri Law Review*, 55, 883–936.

---

46 The Lewis chessmen were displayed at the Uig Community Centre on Lewis on a loan from the British Museum (BBC News 6 April 2000).

47 See for example the Museums and Galleries Act 1992.

Callahan, C. (1993), 'Warp and Weft: Weaving a Blanket of Protection for Cultural Resources on Private Property', *Environmental Law*, 23, 1323–1351.

Canadian Cultural Property Export and Import Act (1985), RSC 1985, c.C-15.

Canadian Government (1992), *The Proposed Heritage Legislation and Aboriginal Heritage Stewardship*.

Chapman, F. (1999), 'The Bighorn Medicine Wheel 1988–1999', *CRM*, 3, 5–10.

Daes, E.I. (1995), *Protection of the Heritage of Indigenous People*, New York: United Nations Publications.

Farrell, P. (1992), 'Foreign Relations – Unrecognized Foreign States – Title to Church Mosaics Unimpaired by Confiscatory Decrees of Unrecognized State, Autocephalous Greek-Orthodox Church of Cyprus v Goldberg and Feldman Fine Arts, Inc.', *Suffolk Transnational Law Journal*, 15, 790–800.

Gerstenblith, P. (2001), 'The Public Interest in the Restitution of Cultural Objects', *Connecticut Journal of International Law*, 16, 197–246.

Gii-dahl-guud-sliiaay (1995), 'Cultural Perpetuation: Repatriation of First Nations Cultural Heritage', *University of British Columbia Law Review* 'Special Issue – Material Culture in Flux: Law and Policy of Repatriation of Cultural Property', 183–201.

Greenfield, J. (1996), *The Return of Cultural Treasures,* 2nd Edition, Cambridge: Cambridge University Press.

Gupta, R. (1999), 'Indigenous Peoples and the International Environmental Community: Accommodating Claims Through a Cooperative Legal Process', *New York University Law Review*, 74, 1741–1784.

Harding, S. (1999), 'Value, Obligation and Cultural Heritage', *Arizona State Law Journal*, 31, 291–354.

Hershkovitz, M. (1995), 'Tribes struggles to reclaim sacred artifacts', *Columbia Spectator*, 119:1, 6.

Hurtado, D.J. (1993), 'Native American Graves Protection and Repatriation Act: Does it Subject Museums to an Unconstitutional "Taking"?', *Hofstra Property Law Journal*, 6, 1–83.

Isar Y.R. (1981), *Lost Heritage: The Question of the Return of Cultural Property: Report on the Symposium Held in London 1981*, Commonwealth Arts Association and the Africa Centre.

Kastenberg, J.E. (1995), 'Assessing the Evolution and Available Actions for Recovery in Cultural Property Cases', *DePaul-LCA Journal of Art and Entertainment Law*, 6, 39–60.

Kaye, L.M. (1996), 'The Future of the Past: Recovering Cultural Property', *Cardozo Journal of International and Comparative Law*, 4, 23–41.

Kowalski W. (2001a), 'Restitution of Works of Art Pursuant to Private and Public International Law', *Recueil des Cours*, 288, 9–244.

— (2001b), 'Repatriation of Cultural Property Following a Cession of Territory or Dissolution of Multinational States', *Art, Antiquity and Law*, 6:2, 139–166.

Lewis, G. (1981), 'Lost Heritage – Some Historical and Professional Considerations', in *Lost Heritage: The Question of the Return of Cultural Property: Report on the Symposium Held in London 1981*, Commonwealth Arts Association and the Africa Centre.

Livesay, T.A. (1992), 'The Impact of the Federal Repatriation Act on State Operated Museums', *Arizona State Law Journal*, 24, 293–301.

Lowenthal, D. (1993), 'Landscape as Heritage: National Scenes and Global Changes', in J.M. Fladmark (ed.), *Heritage: Conservation, Interpretation and Enterprise*, London: Donhead Publishing.

Mastalir, R.W. (1993), 'A Proposal for Protecting the "Cultural" and "Property" Aspects of Cultural Property Under International Law', *Fordham International Law Journal*, 16, 1033–1093.

Mclaughlin, R.H. (1996), 'The Native American Graves Protection and Repatriation Act: Unresolved Issues Between Material Culture and Legal Definitions', *University of Chicago Law School Roundtable*, 3, 767–790.

Mead, H.M. (1995), 'The Mataatua Declaration and the Case of the Carved Meeting House Mataatua', *University of British Columbia Law Review*, 'Special Issue – Material Culture in Flux: Law and Policy of Repatriation of Cultural Property', 69–75.

Merryman J. (1990) '"Protection" of the Cultural "Heritage"?', *American Journal of Comparative Law*, 38 (Supplement), 513–522.

— (1998), 'The Retention of Cultural Property', reproduced in J. Merryman (2000), *Thinking About the Elgin Marbles*, The Hague: Kluwer Law International, 122–156.

Osman, D.N. (1999), 'Occupiers' Title to Cultural Property: Nineteenth Century Removal Egyptian Artifacts', *Columbia Journal of Transnational Law*, 37, 969–1002.

Palmer, N. (2000), *Museums and the Holocaust*, Leicester: Institute of Art and Law.

— (2001), 'Repatriation and Deaccessioning of Cultural Property: Reflections on the Resolution of Art Disputes', *Current Legal Problems*, 54, 477–532.

Paterson, R.K. (1999), 'Cultural Issues in Canadian Law: A Summary of Recent Developments', *Media and Arts Law Review*, 4:3, 205–208.

Putnam, J. (2000), 'Repatriation Report Raises Concerns', *On-line 49er*, 7:102, 5 April 2000 <http://www.csulb.edu/~d49er/spring00/news/v7n102-report.html>.

Select Committee on Culture, Media and Sport, Seventh Report. (2000) *Cultural Property: Return and Illicit Trade*, London: HMSO.

Statt, G., Solowan, M. and Bell, C. (2003), 'Protection and Repatriation of First National Cultural Heritage: A National Survey of Recent Issues and Initiatives', <http://www.law.ualberta.ca/research/aboriginalculturalheritage/>.

Stétié, M.S. (1981), 'The View of UNESCO's Intergovernmental Committee', in *Lost Heritage: The Question of the Return of Cultural Property: Report on the Symposium Held in London 1981*, Commonwealth Arts Association and the Africa Centre.

Sullivan, M. (1992), 'A Museum Perspective on Repatriation: Issues and Opportunities', *Arizona State Law Journal*, 24, 283–291.

Tierney, S. (2004), *Constitutional Law and National Pluralism*, Oxford: Oxford University Press.

Tolhurst, G.J. (1998), 'A Comment on the Return of Indigenous Artefacts', *Art, Antiquity and Law*, 3:1, 15–26.

Wagner, P. (2001), 'From Monuments to Human Rights: Redefining "Heritage" In the Work of the Council of Europe', in *Forward Planning: the Function of Cultural Heritage in a Changing Europe*, Council of Europe, <http://www.coe.int/T/E/Cultural_co-operation/Heritage/Heritage_and_Society/3Planning.asp#TopofPage>.

Weber, R. (2001), 'Introduction: Role of Heritage in a Changing Europe', in *Forward Planning: the Function of Cultural Heritage in a Changing Europe*, Council of Europe, <http://www.coe.int/T/E/Cultural_co-operation/Heritage/Heritage_and_Society/3Planning.asp#TopofPage>.

Webster, G.C. (1995), 'The Potlach Collection Repatriation', *University of British Columbia Law Review*, 'Special Issue – Material Culture in Flux: Law and Policy of Repatriation of Cultural Property', 137–141.

Woodford, R. (9 December 2002), 'Repatriation Conference Helps Clans Learn About Bringing Their Past Home', *The Juneau Empire*, <http://www.sealaskaheritage.org/news/articles/nagpra_seminar.htm>.

PART III
Diversity and Constitutional Interpretation

Chapter 8

The Reasonable Person and the Discrimination Inquiry

Mayo Moran

The equality guarantee of Canada's *Charter of Rights and Freedoms* is often pointed to by courts and commentators as among the most significant features of Canada's rights-protecting regime. Unlike its American counterpart, the Fourteenth Amendment, Section 15 of the *Charter* is routinely described as embracing a more robust substantive conception of equality. The entrenchment of this distinctive form of equality was partly the result of the energies of equality-seeking groups that played a significant role in drafting the language of s.15. Their efforts to ensure that the Canadian *Charter* enshrined a more substantive understanding of equality continued through strategic litigation in many of the formative equality cases litigated under s.15. And the Canadian law of equality has come to serve as an important model of equality for other newly constitutionalised regimes. To no small degree, this is because it embraces a more robust impact-sensitive conception of equality centered on the inherent dignity of the individual.

For much of its early history, the jurisprudence of s.15 has stood as a powerful alternative to the more formalistic understanding of equality exemplified by the equal protection jurisprudence under the Fourteenth Amendment. Courts and commentators from many jurisdictions have stressed the distinctiveness of the Canadian approach to equality and have lauded the promise that this model holds in an increasingly diverse and multi-cultural world. Recently however, the Supreme Court of Canada appears to be more cautious about its commitment to this robust and potentially transformative conception of equality. So while the rhetoric of substantive equality has if anything become more emphatic, it is increasingly accompanied by a less generous approach to s.15.[1] One way that this has manifested itself is by shifting the focus of the s.15 analysis from the complainant to the government. This in turn has made it much more challenging to establish a violation of s.15 and has consequently dramatically reduced the role of s.1 in the analysis. Though this has occurred in a variety of ways, one particularly important part of this shift was accomplished when the Supreme Court of Canada incorporated the reasonable person into the analysis of constitutional equality. Indeed, the reasonable person has come to play a vital role for it is now the central conceptual device in the most fraught aspect of the equality analysis – the determination of when an impugned distinction amounts to discrimination.

---

1   I discuss this phenomenon more generally in Moran (2006).

To observers of the reasonable person in many of his[2] other manifestations, this new role as a tool for evaluating claims of discrimination is an extremely surprising innovation, particularly for a progressive well-informed court like the Supreme Court of Canada. After all, in many of his other appearances, the reasonable person has created at least as many problems as he has resolved. Most significantly perhaps he has been persuasively critiqued on the ground of his distinctly *inegalitarian* impact. In fact, in areas of law where the reasonable person has long been a staple feature, egalitarian critics have suggested that the only way to ensure that he does not undermine the equality of legal norms is to introduce specifically egalitarian values and constraints, many of which are drawn from constitutional equality-protecting regimes.

Thus, across areas as diverse as criminal law, private law and administrative law, the reasonable person has increasingly been a cause for concern among those attentive to the egalitarian implications of the law. Indeed, the Supreme Court itself was well aware of the controversies already swirling around the reasonable person when it introduced him into s.15. So it is surprising the Court did not examine those controversies more closely when it imported the reasonable person into the equality guarantee. Had they done so, they would most certainly have been alerted to the complexity of the relation between the reasonable person's 'empirical' qualities and the fixed normative component of the standard. Indeed, the debates surrounding the reasonable person illustrate the special difficulty of attributing any 'neutral' characteristics in a context characterised by profound and structural inequalities. It thus proves extremely difficult to determine which personal characteristics or subjective qualities should be incorporated into the reasonable person and which should not. And the literature also highlights deeper difficulties with reliance on a fictional agent as a standard. Interrogating the reasonable person more closely thus reveals the underlying conceptual confusion that this appealing fiction too often obscures. All of this suggests that closer examination of the broader debate may have prompted the Supreme Court of Canada to find another way to articulate the relevant point of view for judging claims of discrimination.

In order to consider these issues, it is helpful to briefly examine the critiques of the reasonable person in his other appearances. Since this reveals the extent to which the reasonable person standard is particularly vulnerable on equality grounds, we must next consider how he came to play such a vital role in Canada's equality jurisprudence. In particular, what do the controversies surrounding the reasonable person tell us about the continued viability of the kind of inclusive and substantive conception of constitutional equality that is the Supreme Court of Canada's stated ambition? Asking this ultimately also raises some larger concerns about the Supreme Court of Canada's new turn in equality jurisprudence.

Biography and Pathology: A Brief Survey of the Reasonable Person

The reasonable person has long been employed as a standard in private, criminal and administrative law. Among his many tasks, the delineation of culpability is perhaps

---

2   I use the masculine advisedly.

the reasonable person's most prominent role. Thus, the reasonable person forms the centerpiece of the standard of care in negligence and is at the heart of many of the criminal law defences including provocation and self-defence. But the reasonable person also serves rather different purposes in other contexts. So for instance the reasonable person has come to play a particularly prominent and controversial role in the American law of sexual harassment. But the very frequency of the reasonable person's appearances suggests that the task of determining what unifies his many roles is by no means easy.

Courts seem to reach for the reasonable person when an inquiry demands both some sensitivity to the particular qualities or attributes of the involved individuals as well as a more objective or fixed dimension. But if this is true of the reasonable person, it is equally true that the test is characterised by a lack of clarity about the exact nature of the subjective and objective characteristics of the reasonable person. Most puzzling of all perhaps, but also most crucial, is the question of how the objective and subjective characteristics of the reasonable person relate to each other. How does one determine which qualities of the reasonable person are fixed or objective and which are subjective and hence vary with the implicated individuals? These difficulties are exacerbated by the fact that the reasonable person appears in a wide array of doctrinal roles and accomplishes quite different things across those roles. So while the reasonable person undoubtedly possesses a certain 'common sense' appeal, it has proven extremely difficult to systematise his significance.

However, looking at the reasonable person across his many appearances does alert us to how often he is simply a stand in for the common or ordinary man. In this sense, the famous 'man on the Clapham omnibus' is but one illustration of a far more persistent association between the reasonable person and the ordinary man. Thus, both in the law of negligence and in the criminal context, the objective content of the reasonable person is closely linked to standards of ordinariness or normalcy. Though this is quite explicit in private law, where the reasonable person is insistently described as a standard of ordinariness and *not* a standard of moral fault, similar patterns are also evident in the criminal law context. But as commentators across fields of inquiry have illustrated, this linkage poses a profound equality worry.[3] For if the reasonable person characteristically holds common or ordinary beliefs and attitudes, then precisely because discrimination is constituted by widely shared beliefs about the lesser humanity of certain others, the reasonable person standard will actually tend to build discrimination into the legal standard itself.

This effect of the reasonable person is apparent in many areas of the law and is most acute where the egalitarian content of the legal norm is either in dispute or in flux. To capture a sense of these equality effects of the reasonable person, it is therefore useful to briefly survey how they manifest themselves in some key doctrinal areas. This in turn ought to enable us to examine the significance of these effects for the introduction of the reasonable person into the discrimination inquiry.

---

3   I discuss these critiques of the reasonable person in detail in *Rethinking the Reasonable Person*, 144-157, 164-197, 202-231. In the criminal law context, see Donovan and Wildman (1981); Horder (1998); Yeo (1993); Leader-Elliott (1996); and Bandalli (1995).

Let us begin by a brief examination of the use of the reasonable person in the criminal law defences.

In many ways, the egalitarian critiques of the reasonable person are most developed in the criminal law context. This is hardly surprising of course for the criminal process has unique significance for both the accused and the complainant. In addition, given the prevalence of male violence against women, feminist advocates have devoted considerable energy to critiquing the effect of the criminal law and in particular the reasonable person on women. More recently, critical race theorists, queer theorists and others concerned with the impact of the criminal process on those who are marginalised or disadvantaged have also focused attention on the impact of legal standards including the reasonable person. Though the critiques vary in their details, the overall message concerning the reasonable person is tolerably clear: without some kind of modification, the reasonable person will simply privilege the beliefs and attitudes of the common or ordinary man. When it is employed as a standard for assessing culpability, it will therefore give rise to serious egalitarian difficulties for women and many other marginalised individuals who do not find themselves well-depicted by the common man. A few brief examples serve to illustrate the nature of these difficulties.

In the law of self-defence, the reasonable person has long been the standard for assessing the reasonableness of the use of deadly force. To the extent that the actions of the accused mirror those of the reasonable person, those actions are considered justified by the criminal law. But for most of the history of the law of self-defence, the common law's reliance on the reasonable person (or more accurately, reasonable man) effectively precluded women who killed their abusive partners from successfully pleading self-defence. Because women rarely possess the physical size and strength of men, women who killed abusive partners did not typically do so in the face of the kind of imminent threat that characterised standard male-on-male self-defence claims. And when courts applied the reasonable man standard, they implicitly read the assumptions of their imagined standard case – two parties relatively equal in size and strength – into their understanding of the contours of self-defence. The consequence of treating this 'bar room brawl' scenario as the paradigm case for self-defence was the entrenchment of the imminence requirement, which in turn effectively precluded women who killed their abusive partners from claiming self-defence.[4]

Another area where the reasonable person standard has become increasingly controversial for egalitarian and other reasons is the law of provocation. In common law jurisdictions, provocation constitutes a partial excuse to homicide, typically resulting in a conviction for manslaughter not murder. Here the reasonable person (or in some jurisdictions the ordinary person[5]) serves as the standard for judging

---

4   On this topic see the Supreme Court of Canada in *R v Lavallee* [1990] 1 SCR 852. I discuss all of these situations and their equality effects in *Rethinking the Reasonable Person* (204-205).

5   In the provocation context, some jurisdictions (such as Canada and Australia) have moved from the reasonable person standard to the ordinary person standard in face of the obvious difficulty that the reasonable person would not kill another in anger. Other

the reasonableness of the reaction to provocation and hence the availability of the defence. However, significant problems have also begun to surface concerning the impact of the reasonable person standard on the availability of the provocation defence. The worry was first and most forcefully articulated by Jeremy Horder in his excellent book entitled *Provocation and Responsibility*. Horder examined the English case law on provocation and noted (as other studies have subsequently confirmed) that the defence primarily benefits men who attempt to use violence to secure female acceptance, particularly to enforce sexual fidelity.[6] This suggested, in Horder's view, a profound gender bias in the law of provocation, a bias embodied by the reasonable person. Further evidence of this gender bias in the provocation context is found in the treatment of female accused. While provocation is often successfully invoked by men who kill in response to their female partner's infidelity, women who kill their male partners in response to long term physical abuse rarely experience similar success.[7]

Similar concerns about the equality effects of the standard in provocation have also been raised in the context of what is referred to as the Homosexual Advance (or Panic) Defence (HAD). Critics have noted with concern the willingness of courts to excuse resort to lethal violence in situations where one man initiates a sexual advance towards another.[8] The consequence is that many critics, including Horder himself, have argued that the discrimination that results from the biases inherent in provocation are so severe that the defence should be abolished. And the reasonable or ordinary person that is at the heart of the defence is also at the heart of these critiques.

But it is worth noting something else about the above illustrations of the egalitarian difficulties with the reasonable person – all are drawn from criminal law where the role of the standard relates to the determination of culpability. This is undoubtedly an important use of the reasonable person and there are certainly lessons to be drawn from the extensive debates in that area. However it is also instructive to look in more detail at the operation of the reasonable person in another context – the American law of sexual harassment. This example is particularly useful, I would suggest, because in addition to the relatively similar role occupied by the reasonable person,

---

jurisdictions such as England retain the reasonable person standard. In the provocation context at least however there is virtually no difference between the two formulations. They exhibit similar problems some of which are general and some of which are specific to provocation: see Moran, *Rethinking the Reasonable Person* (207-220).

6   See Horder (1998), 192-194. In the American context, see Estrich (1994). In the Canadian context, see 'Reforming Criminal Code Defences' (1998) Department of Justice Canada. In that study it was found that out of the 115 murder cases where a defence of provocation was raised, 62 involved domestic homicides and of those 55 involved men killing women. See also *New South Wales Law Reform Commission Discussion Paper: Provocation, Diminished Responsibility and Infanticide* (Sydney: New South Wales Law Reform Commission, 1993); Yeo (1993); Leader-Elliott (1996) and Bandalli (1995).

7   See Klimchuk (1994) at 464, drawing in part on Bandalli (1995). Horder discusses these issues as well in *Provocation and Responsibility* at 189 discussing *R. v. Duffy* [1949] 1 All ER 932, as do I in *Rethinking the Reasonable Person*, (207-209).

8   Howe (1998), 489; Moran *Rethinking the Reasonable Person*, (213-216).

the sexual harassment debate is also directly focused on the specific equality effects of the reasonable person standard.

The reasonable person assumed this new controversial role when the United States Supreme Court held that sexual harassment was actionable under federal anti-discrimination law if it was severe enough to create a hostile work environment.[9] In order to assess when harassment reached this actionable level, the reasonable person was employed.[10] But while the holding that sexual harassment could amount to employment discrimination was a major victory for feminists, the decision was also greeted by a chorus of concerns about the reasonable person standard.

Critics argued that adopting the reasonable person, given its recent transformation from the reasonable man, seemed to privilege one understanding of social interaction in the workplace (that of men) and simultaneously undermined alternatives to that understanding.[11] Catherine Abrams summarized the worry as follows:

> Judges might view [the reasonable person standard] as authorizing them to decide cases on the basis of their own intuition: the same "common sense" that had marked the administration of the "reasonable person" standard in tort law - and the same "common sense" that had normalized the practices of sexual harassment in the first place.[12]

And in *Ellison* v. *Brady*[13] the Ninth Circuit noted that recourse to the reasonable person test in sexual harassment ran the risk of reinforcing the prevailing level of discrimination.[14] Adoption of a 'reasonable woman' standard accordingly seemed an appropriate response to this danger. Among its other virtues, the Court suggested, a reasonable woman standard would encourage an elaboration of how male and female perspectives in this area differed. But the *Ellison* court gave little sense of how this elaboration might proceed. And although in the wake of the Anita Hill hearings, several courts adopted the reasonable woman standard,[15] the United States Supreme

---

9 *Meritor Savings Bank* v. *Vinson*, 477 U.S. 57 at 67 (1986).

10 *Ibid* at 65. See also *Rabidue* v. *Osceola Refining C.*, 805 F.2d 611 (6th Cir. 1986), *cert. denied* 481 U.S. 1014 (1987).

11 Abrams (1995), 49; Cahn (1992), 1398 at 1404-5 discussing Bordo (1990) and Collins (1977); Ehrenreich (1990), esp. at 1210 ff; Lester (1993), 227. For a challenge to the very idea in play here see Halley (2002). Other critics have suggested that alternative ways to formulate the actionable level of harassment may avoid some of the serious difficulties with the standard in this area: Hadfield (1996).

12 Abrams (1995), 49–50.

13 924 F.2d 872 (9th Cir. 1991).

14 *Ellison*, para. 878. Interestingly, although commentators have suggested that the source of the difficulty that the Court is pointing to is found in the different male and female perspectives on this matter, it seems more likely to me that the core difficulty is instead found in something else that we have already noted – the danger that 'reasonable' may be read as ordinary and may thus simply lack critical power where the behaviour in question is common or ordinary.

15 See for instance *Robinson v. Jacksonville Shipyards, Inc.* 760 F.Supp. 1486 (M.D. Fla. 1991); *Burns v. MacGregor*, 989 F.2d 959 at 965 (8th Cir. 1993). See Ehrenreich (1990), 1217, noting that the reasonable woman construct itself does not constrain judge's discretion

Court declined to do so when it considered the question.[16] Although the details of this debate are not our focus here, the controversy over how to fashion an appropriately egalitarian standard also holds broader lessons for the reasonable person. Let us briefly consider some of these aspects of the sexual harassment debate.

The early critical response to *Vinson's* enshrinement of the reasonable person was a rare moment of feminist solidarity. But there was no similar consensus on the reasonable woman. Feminists began to worry that a separate reasonable woman standard might allow judges to resort to their intuitions about women's difference, reinforcing an essentialist view of women as victims.[17] Some wondered whether the conception of reasonableness could ever be truly egalitarian.[18] But many feminists were reluctant to abandon the hard-won reasonable woman standard which, they suggested, could be seen as an attempt to make the standard responsive to different social realities.[19] So here, as elsewhere, the exclusionary nature of the 'unmodified' reasonable person inquiry provides the impetus for insisting on greater similarity between the ideal and the actual person, particularly when that actual person is very unlikely to find herself well represented in the unmodified reasonable person. But the provocation context and sexual assault contexts illustrate that this resemblance might actually be inimical to egalitarian goals. And many feminists are unwilling to employ this approach to judge male behaviour in cases such as sexual assault.[20]

However, the sexual harassment debate also suggests possibilities other than simply abandoning reasonableness altogether or modifying the standard so that it replicates the implicated individual. For instance, Catharine Abrams argues that judgments about sexual harassment are not a matter of "innate common sense but of informed sensibility."[21] And in developing this sensibility, the reasonable person can play an educative role if it is clear that it refers not to 'the average person, but the person enlightened concerning the barriers to women's equality in the workplace.'[22] So what would such reasonable people know about women, work, and sex that would enable them to assess claims of sexual harassment in a non-oppressive way?[23] By asking this question, Abrams adverts to the distinct role of the reasonable person

---

in making the difficult choices involved in adjudicating sexual harassment claims. See also Abrams (1995), 50, and Cahn (1994), 1415–1420.

16 *Harris* v. *Forklift Systems*, 114 S. Ct. 367 at 371 (1991). In *Harris*, the Court barely addresses the controversy and simply notes, in less than a sentence, that the court should review the plaintiff's claim by reference to the perspective of the reasonable person.

17 Childers (1993), 896; Cahn (1992), 1417; Abrams (1995), 50–51; Ehrenreich (1990), 1218, noting the standard's failure to attend to issues of race and class and arguing that this kind of inattentiveness means that "any unequal social conditions that affect an individual's situation are both perpetuated and condoned by such a standard".

18 Ehrenreich (1990), 1232, footnote 66.

19 Cahn (1992), 1417–1420.

20 Cahn (1992), 1436–1437.

21 Abrams (1995), 52.

22 Abrams (1995), 52.

23 As Abrams intimates, there is a prior issue about how judges can be disabused of their idea that recourse to their common sense will solve everything. This suggests that it will be important to detail how common sense intuitions here have led us astray. Abrams does allow

in the sexual harassment inquiry. She thus points to the potential the reasonable person holds as a tool to educate the judge and other decision-makers so that *they* will effectively be 'reasonable people' in assessing claims of sexual harassment. And this calls our attention to the fact that the reasonable person here could be understood as an image of the ideal *judge*.

Of course, this does not mean that the actual attributes of the claimants are irrelevant. But focusing on what a judge should know makes those attributes relevant as 'correctives' for judges who may underestimate the effects of their own position of privilege. So to effect the necessary transformation and counter the stereotypes that may otherwise prevail, the reasonable person may be used to bring in evidence regarding barriers to women's full participation in the workplace and the role of sexualised treatment in maintaining those barriers.[24] The danger is that without this evidence judges, who still are predominantly privileged and male, may misread the significance of various forms of treatment. So on this view, the reasonable person is best understood as a kind of corrective device which can render the standard of judgment more egalitarian while simultaneously avoiding the essentialist dangers of a more particularised standard.

The sexual harassment debate in this sense usefully encapsulates many of the core difficulties and possibilities of the reasonable person, particularly in a context where equality issues are in play. It thus clarifies how critical it is to disentangle the normative ideal of reasonableness from its too-common companion – the notion of what is ordinary or customary. In addition, it draws our attention to how the reasonable person may function not to assess culpability but rather to provide a viewpoint from which to assess the legal and normative meaning of particular actions. But precisely because the standard in such cases is not explicitly designed to track a particular specified individual's point of view, its exact nature in this instance may be even more perplexing that in its culpability-determining function. Now, with a sharper sense of the various roles the reasonable person can play and with a sense as well of some of the concerns that may thereby be raised, let us turn to consider the Supreme Court of Canada's introduction of the reasonable person into the discrimination analysis under s.15.

The Appearance of the Reasonable Person in S.15's Discrimination Inquiry

The landmark Supreme Court of Canada decision in *Law* marked the first time that the reasonable person played a significant role in a majority s.15 opinion.[25] In *Law* Justice Iacobucci, speaking for the Court, set out a new approach to s.15 focused on whether the relevant difference in treatment demeans the essential human dignity of the claimant. This dignity-driven discrimination inquiry thus became the core of s15. Justice Iacobucci described this inquiry as follows:

---

that a more gender-specific standard may be useful in providing judges with the 'jolt' necessary to force them to question their common sense intuitions (1995, 51).

24 Abrams (1995), 52-53.
25 *Law v. Canada (Minister of Employment and Immigration)*, [1999] 1 S.C.R. 497.

...both subjective and objective: subjective in so far as the right to equal treatment is an individual right, asserted by a specific claimant with particular traits and circumstances; and objective in so far as it is possible to determine whether the individual claimant's equality rights have been infringed only by considering the larger context of the legislation in question, and society's past and present treatment of the claimant and of other persons or groups with similar characteristics or circumstances.[26]

This complex subjective-objective perspective means that the discrimination inquiry is not satisfied merely because a claimant believes that his or her dignity has been adversely affected by a law. It is clear that the law cannot hold the state to a standard that no one feels debased or devalued.[27] So while the particularities of the claimants and their experiences do matter, the assessment of a discrimination claim also demands some objectivity. But how do these subjective and objective elements interact? The reasonable person is the Supreme Court of Canada's response to this quandary.

The reasonable person first made its appearance in the s.15 inquiry in Madam Justice L'Heureux-Dubé's decision in *Egan*.[28] There, she notes that the perspective of the claimant while important cannot be determinative on the question of discrimination. But the reasonable person, she suggests, can be employed to enshrine the relevant point of view:

> Clearly, a measure of objectivity must be incorporated into this determination. This being said, however, it would be ironic and, in large measure, self-defeating to the purposes of s. 15 to assess the absence or presence of discriminatory impact according to the standard of the "reasonable, secular, able-bodied, white male". A more appropriate standard is subjective-objective – the reasonably held view of one who is possessed of similar characteristics, under similar circumstances, and who is dispassionate and fully apprised of the circumstances.[29]

Thus, the discrimination claim ought to be judged from the subjective-objective perspective of an individual who, in all senses relevant to discrimination, resembles the claimant. And while many other questions remain about the role of the reasonable person, it is clear that Justice L'Heureux-Dubé's core concern is to ensure that the invocation of the reasonable person is consistent with the egalitarian purposes of s.15.

This passage from *Egan* is the point of departure for *Law*. Thus, Justice Iacobucci insists that the inquiry into whether a distinction is discriminatory must be understood from the following point of view:

> ...that of the reasonable person, dispassionate and fully apprised of the circumstances, possessed of similar attributes to, and under similar circumstances as, the claimant. Although I stress that the inquiry into whether legislation demeans the claimant's dignity

---

26 *Law*, para. 59.
27 *Egan v. Canada*, [1995] 2 S.C.R. 513 at para. 546 (per Madam Justice L'Heureux-Dubé).
28 *Egan*, *supra* at 553 (per Madam Justice L'Heureux-Dubé).
29 para. 546.

must be undertaken from the perspective of the claimant and from no other perspective, a court must be satisfied that the claimant's assertion that differential treatment imposed by legislation demeans his or her dignity is supported by an objective assessment of the situation. All of that individual's or that group's traits, history, and circumstances must be considered in evaluating whether a reasonable person in circumstances similar to those of the claimant would find that the legislation which imposes differential treatment has the effect of demeaning his or her dignity.[30]

The similarities between this passage and that of Madam Justice L'Heureux-Dubé in *Egan* are noteworthy: both recognise the centrality of the perspective of the claimant in the inquiry into whether an impugned distinction demeans her dignity. And consequently both also insist that the reasonable person must be infused with all of the relevant characteristics of the actual claimant. But the passages also share an important weakness – while the nature of the subjective factors (the claimant's group history, circumstances, traits) is clarified at least to some degree, the same cannot be said of the objective content of the standard. Instead, we simply have references to objective assessments and reasonably held views.

But the history of the reasonable person reminds us that this difficulty is endemic to the standard and especially severe where equality is implicated. Thus in other contexts, courts and commentators have begun to express frustration about how to give any real meaning to the reasonable person.[31] There is no easy response to the vital question of what the reasonable person 'fixes' and what he does not: indeed, one of the few unifying elements across different appearances of the reasonable person is the consistent difficulty articulating its fixed objective content. This vagueness regarding what the standard aims to hold constant is one reason why courts find it so easy to infuse the reasonable person with ideas about what is customary or ordinary – if the reasonable person seems rather obscure, the ordinary person does not. The tendency to read reasonableness as ordinariness is apparent both in negligence cases, in criminal cases involving problems such as provocation, self-defence and sexual assault, and in the sexual harassment context. And across these contexts it is clear that this is part of the reason why the reasonable person is so often inimical to equality.[32] Moreover, the danger posed by the normative 'looseness' of the reasonable person is much more severe when there are significant background patterns of discrimination or inequality. This is why the court in *Ellison* points to the danger that the reasonable person will simply be infused with those common sense beliefs that made sexual harassment prevalent in the first place. Of course, there may well be steps that can be taken to respond to this difficulty, but the very existence of the difficulty suggests the oddity of adopting the reasonable person to assess the most central and controversial of all equality questions – what constitutes discrimination.

In his judgment in *Law* Justice Iacobucci is clearly aware of 'the controversy that exists regarding the biases implicit in some applications of the "reasonable person"

---

30 para. 60.
31 See for instance the House of Lords decision in *R v Smith*, Hubin and Haely (1999), and Moran, *Rethinking the Reasonable Person,* chapter 8.
32 I elaborate this argument in *Rethinking the Reasonable Person.*

standard'.[33] He thus insists that he does not support any use of the reasonable person which would subvert the purpose of s. 15. So the appropriate perspective, he stresses, is not solely that of a 'reasonable person' – a perspective which could, through misapplication, serve as a vehicle for the imposition of community prejudices.[34] In this, he echoes the concerns of courts and commentators and seems to get the core of the egalitarian worry about the reasonable person exactly right. Presumably in part for this reason, he recognises that it is necessary to give more fixed normative content to the standard. So the inquiry, he states, is concerned with the perspective of a person in circumstances similar to those of the claimant, who is informed of and rationally takes into account the various contextual factors that determine whether an impugned law infringes human dignity. Thus, building on the passage of Madam Justice L'Heureux-Dubé in *Egan*, the reasonable person here seems designed in part to draw attention to the relevance of the point of view of the claimant. But his emphasis on the constraint of reasonableness also reminds us that the point of view of the claimant is constructive rather than actual. So what exactly is the relation between the subjective and objective dimensions of the reasonable person?

Reasonable Agents – Subjective and Objective

Part of the genius of the reasonable person is found in the way that he almost seamlessly combines the subjective attributes of the relevant individual along with an objective element. Indeed, this seems to be part of the reason he appeals to the Supreme Court of Canada. However, the nature of the reasonable person varies from context to context and these variations have particular significance for the way that the subjective and objective elements figure in the test. At the 'subjectivised' end of the spectrum we find the culpability-determining functions of the reasonable person in both the criminal and the civil context. At the other relatively objective end of the spectrum, we find a more 'perspectival' or judgment-related use of the reasonable person.

In its culpability-determining function the reasonable person is, unsurprisingly, relatively subjective. Since the test in these cases determines when we can blame the accused, the reasonable person (notionally at least) incorporates the accused's attributes insofar as such incorporation does not undermine the legal standard. Because criminal law has the most demanding fault standard, the reasonable person is most subjectivised in that context. In the law of negligence as well, the reasonable person typically also serves a culpability-related function but since the fault requirement there is more objective, the standard is less sensitive to the individual's actual qualities. Nonetheless, consistent with its basic task of assigning responsibility under a fault standard, the reasonable person in the law of negligence remains significantly responsive to the actual qualities of the defendant, as for instance, in the case of youth.

---

33 *Law, supra* note 16 at 61.
34 *Ibid.*

Alongside these culpability-determining invocations, we can also find a judgment-related use of the reasonable person. In these latter cases, the standard describes the perspective from which to assess the legal and normative significance of some action, provision or the like. An illustration can be found in the American law of sexual harassment where the reasonable person is invoked to determine when harassment is sufficiently severe that it is subject to regulation as sex discrimination. Though this certainly has implications for the culpability of the individual who engages in the alleged harassment, it is designed to give content to norms of non-discrimination in the workplace and thus has implications for the duties of employers, supervisors and the like. This difference between the judgment-related function and the culpability-determining function is perhaps best illustrated by the fact that in the sexual harassment context the 'reasonable person' focuses on what qualities of the alleged *target*, not of the alleged harasser, ought to be incorporated into the standard.

The judgment-related use of the reasonable person does not mean that the 'subjective' qualities of the relevant claimants are irrelevant. However, in addition to problematising whose qualities are relevant, it also raises questions about why those qualities might matter. In the culpability-related role, both questions are structured by the inquiry into fault. Thus, though the analysis may be complex, the questions of whose qualities matter and of why they matter are generally relatively straightforward.[35] The same cannot be said of the judgment-related function of the reasonable person of the kind we see in sexual harassment. The obvious question is why the judge requires the intercession of the reasonable person to shape their point of view. And one response may be that in certain (controversial) contexts, the reasonable person may be an attempt to correct deficiencies in the judicial point of view. This may be why the reasonable person shows up as a way to articulate an idealised judicial point of view in the sexual harassment context and why the complainant's characteristics loom so large in that context. In equality-driven cases characterised by significant power imbalances between the judge and the claimant, the impulse for some kind of corrective to an unproblematised judicial point of view seems both understandable and desirable.

Something like this impulse can also be felt in the s.15 debate. Thus, Madam Justice L'Heureux-Dubé introduces the reasonable person in *Egan* after noting that it would be ironic and even 'self-defeating' to use a 'reasonable, secular, able-bodied, white male' to assess the presence of discrimination. The 'corrective' reading of the reasonable person also helps to explain the emphasis on the subjective experiences of the claimant in her decision in *Egan*. And this also makes it possible to see the egalitarian impulse behind so unlikely a vehicle as the reasonable person. So in the sexual harassment context and in early s.15 cases, it seems plausible to understand the invocation of the reasonable person with its emphasis on the subjective attributes of the individual claiming discrimination as a kind of corrective to the structural inequality that inevitably plagues the adjudication of such claims. So understood,

---

35 The provocation context is the exception but the issue there stems from the difficulties with the rationale for allowing a defence of provocation and its relationship to *mens rea*. See for instance, Moran, *Rethinking the Reasonable Person*, chapter 6; Horder, *Provocation and Responsibility*.

one might think, the 'reasonable claimant' could be a vehicle to encourage judges to be more thoughtful about the limits of their own knowledge and intuitions in such cases.

Judgment, Discrimination and the Reasonable Person

This corrective interpretation suggests that it may be possible to understand the impulse to reach for the reasonable person as consistent with the egalitarian imperatives of s.15. Given the reasonable person's history, however, he is hardly an obvious vehicle for problematising the judicial point of view. After all, for most of his long history, the reasonable person (or, to be precise, man) has performed exactly the opposite function. Far from motivating decision-makers to question their unreflective biases and preconceptions, the reasonable man has actually served as an ideal vehicle for articulating a relatively unchallengeable version of those very beliefs. Indeed, this is the prominent worry articulated by feminist and egalitarian critics of the reasonable person in other contexts. This is also just the equality concern that Justice Iacobucci adverts to in *Law*. The debates on the reasonable person do suggest how to reshape it along more egalitarian lines. Feminist and egalitarian commentators have drawn attention to the nature of the reasonable person 'unmodified'. The gist of the worry is that without modification of his imputed or default characteristics, the reasonable person is presumptively male, white, able-bodied, literate, and the like. It is not that those characteristics could not be displaced – they could. But the broader debates raise profound egalitarian concerns with this as a means of fashioning a standard to assess discrimination claims.

It is worth noting that the default characteristics of the reasonable person are seldom noticed as such until they are identified by a claimant who recognises their significance precisely because they do not share the relevant characteristic. But the implications of this seem problematic from an equality point of view. If the unmodified standard works properly only to the extent that the claimant is privileged, then the risk of any failure to appropriately modify the standard falls most heavily on the least privileged. This is because it is up to the disadvantaged to identify and displace the default characteristics of the reasonable person. The privileged, who find their characteristics already built into the reasonable person, carry no such burden. And even apart from the disproportionate burden on the disadvantaged – especially problematic where the point of the test is to track discrimination – fashioning the standard in this way has additional difficulties.

The debates surrounding provocation and sexual harassment illustrate this. There we see the nature of efforts to reshape the standard along egalitarian lines: those who are most disadvantaged, and hence most divergent from the unmodified reasonable person, are forced to insist on an almost endless specification of their own characteristics. Thus, the illiterate Hispanic woman with a disability must demand attentiveness to all of those characteristics or the standard will not function properly. However, being forced to put the claim in this way makes the claim for simple equal consideration look like a plea for special treatment. Once again, from an equality point of view, this is problematic. And this is augmented by the fact that the deeper and more complex the diversity implicated in any equality inquiry, the more significant this worry will be. In certain contexts, such as self-defence or American sexual harassment law, critics are forced to such modifications because, doctrinally speaking, they are 'stuck' with some form of idealised agent. Until the decision in *Law* however, the Supreme Court of Canada faced no such constraint. In these circumstances, the decision to introduce the reasonable person into the discrimination inquiry seems puzzling at best.

However, it is arguable that the reasonable person, though by no means optimal, could have been used as the kind of corrective that Madam Justice L'Heureux-Dubé seemed to be pointing to in *Egan*. But the career of the reasonable person in more recent s.15 cases points to a troubling shift. As noted above, Madam Justice L'Heureux-Dubé's original passage places the emphasis not on the reasonable person's rather obscure objective content but rather on building attentiveness to the plaintiff's characteristics and situation into that content. This is what makes it plausible to read her as suggesting the corrective function. Justice Iacobucci's passage in *Law* is somewhat more complex in this sense. He too discusses the significance of 'the individual or group's traits, history and circumstances' but in his passage the emphasis is elsewhere – on the question of whether a 'reasonable person in the circumstances similar to the claimant' would find the differential treatment demeaning.[36] Thus, it is possible to see a slight shift from emphasis on the subjective attributes of the claimant to emphasis on the objective content of the test. But the real shift in the Supreme Court of Canada's use of the reasonable person shows up in the cases that follow *Law*.

The corrective function of the reasonable person with its emphasis on the way the claimant's experience may differ from the judge's seems to have given way to a justificatory use of the reasonable person. In this new role, its primary function is as a vehicle to convey the objective content of discrimination. This is well illustrated by two post-*Law* cases where the reasonable person is crucial and the subject of controversy within the judgments. Thus, although the reasonable person may well have been introduced as a corrective to the ordinary judicial point of view, by the time the Supreme Court of Canada majority employed the test in *Gosselin* and *Children's Foundation* the primary role of the reasonable person had gradually shifted from being a way to problematize the judge's point of view to being a way of justifying that point of view.

This is apparent in *Gosselin* where the majority of the Court held there was no violation of s.15 in the case of a provincial 'workfare' scheme which reduced the welfare benefits of young adults to far below the poverty level unless they enrolled in educational or work-related programs. Madam Justice McLachlin, speaking for the majority, stated:

A reasonable welfare recipient under 30 might have concluded that the program was harsh, perhaps even misguided. (As noted, it eventually was repealed.) But she would not reasonably have concluded that it treated younger people as less worthy or less deserving of respect in a way that had the purpose or effect of marginalizing or denigrating younger

---

36 *Law* at 59–60.

people in our society. If anything, she would have concluded that the program treated young people as more able than older people to benefit from training and education, more able to get and retain a job, and more able to adapt to their situations and become fully participating and contributing members of society.[37]

Here, the 'reasonable claimant' focuses not upon the specific characteristics of the claimant but rather on the motivation of the legislature which is presumably the objective content. So the reasonable person here seems designed, not as a way to correct the judge's perspective, but rather as a way to state or justify it.

This is apparent when one contrasts the majority reasoning in *Gosselin* with that of Madam Justice L'Heureux-Dubé's dissent. Although she attributes knowledge of legislative motivation to the reasonable claimant, the emphasis in her passage lies elsewhere:

> The sole remaining question is whether a reasonable person in Ms. Gosselin's position, apprised of all the circumstances, would perceive that her dignity had been threatened.... The reasonable claimant would have made daily life choices in the face of an imminent and severe threat of poverty. The reasonable claimant would likely have suffered malnourishment. She might have turned to prostitution and crime to make ends meet. The reasonable claimant would have perceived that as a result of her deep poverty, she had been excluded from full participation in Canadian society. She would have perceived that her right to dignity was infringed as a sole consequence of being under 30 years of age, a factor over which, at any given moment, she had no control. While individuals may be able to strive to overcome the detriment imposed by merit-based distinctions, Ms. Gosselin was powerless to alter the single personal characteristic that the government's scheme made determinative for her level of benefits...The reasonable claimant would have suffered, as Ms. Gosselin manifestly did suffer, from discrimination as a result of the impugned legislative distinction. I see no other conclusion but that Ms. Gosselin would have reasonably felt that she was being less valued as a member of society than people 30 and over and that she was being treated as less deserving of respect.[38]

Here it is clear that Madam Justice L'Heureux-Dubé is using the reasonable person construct for the kind of corrective purposes suggested by her passage in *Egan*. This is why she emphasizes elements of the claimant's experience that judges, who tend not to be similarly disadvantaged, are all too likely to overlook. There is a telling contrast between her passage, which stresses the experience of the claimant, and the passage of Chief Justice McLachlin where the reasonable person gives voice to the legislative motivation. This motivation is, as Madam Justice McLachlin implies, the 'objective' reason why the claimant's dignity is not actually demeaned and hence her claim of discrimination not made out.

If anything, the use of the reasonable person in *Children's Foundation* is an even more striking example of the shift from a corrective to a justificatory role. In that case the majority speaking again through Chief Justice McLachlin upheld the core of the provisions of the *Criminal Code* which provided parents and teachers with a defence where they were using reasonable force against their children or pupils for

---

37 *Gosselin, v. Quebec (Attorney General)*, [2002] 4 S.C.R. 429, 2002 SCC 84 para 69.
38 Gosselin, paras 131-133.

the purpose of correction. Speaking of the appropriate test, Chief Justice McLachlin stated:

> The test is whether a reasonable person possessing the claimant's attributes and in the claimant's circumstances would conclude that the law marginalizes the claimant or treats her as less worthy on the basis of irrelevant characteristics: *Law, supra*. Applied to a child claimant, this test may well confront us with the fiction of the reasonable, fully apprised preschool-aged child. The best we can do is to adopt the perspective of the reasonable person acting on behalf of a child, who seriously considers and values the child's views and developmental needs. To say this, however, is not to minimize the subjective component; a court assessing an equality claim involving children must do its best to take into account the subjective viewpoint of the child, which will often include a sense of relative disempowerment and vulnerability.[39]

But once again, the conclusion is illuminating. Chief Justice McLachlin reasons as follows:

> I am satisfied that a reasonable person acting on behalf of a child, apprised of the harms of criminalization that s. 43 avoids, the presence of other governmental initiatives to reduce the use of corporal punishment, and the fact that abusive and harmful conduct is still prohibited by the criminal law, would not conclude that the child's dignity has been offended in the manner contemplated by s. 15(1). Children often feel a sense of disempowerment and vulnerability; this reality must be considered when assessing the impact of s. 43 on a child's sense of dignity. Yet, as emphasized, the force permitted is limited and must be set against the reality of a child's mother or father being charged and pulled into the criminal justice system, with its attendant rupture of the family setting, or a teacher being detained pending bail, with the inevitable harm to the child's crucial educative setting. Section 43 is not arbitrarily demeaning. It does not discriminate. Rather, it is firmly grounded in the actual needs and circumstances of children. I conclude that s. 43 does not offend s. 15(1) of the *Charter*.[40]

This passage does not emphasise the subjective experiences of the child but rather the 'objective' purposes and motivations behind the legislation. In this sense then, as in the majority in *Gosselin*, the reasonable person here seems to be a vehicle for stating the judicial point of view, rather than for questioning it. The effect is that the emphasis is shifted from the subjective characteristics and experiences of the complainant to the objective content of the standard.

However, the problems with this are significant. The justificatory power of the reasonable person is weak, particularly in cases where equality concerns are predominant. Even our brief survey of the history of the reasonable person makes clear that he has never been a good tool for either conceptualising or articulating the objective content of the relevant standard. Indeed, it often seems that courts reach for the reasonable person precisely when they are not exactly sure how to articulate the objective content of the relevant norm and yet they have a sense that it is significant. But as the history of the reasonable person in criminal law and in sexual harassment

---

39 *Canadian Foundation for Children, Youth and the Law v. Canada (Attorney General)* [2004] 1 S.C.R. 76, para. 53.

40 *Children's Foundation*, para. 6:68.

illustrates, this kind of unreflective recourse to common sense too often has deeply inegalitarian content. This alone is enough to suggest that the reasonable person is hardly an ideal means of conveying the objective content of discrimination.

The Supreme Court's recent use of the reasonable person as a justificatory device only magnifies these worries. Indeed, the Court's use of the reasonable person to effectively state its own point of view carries the unfortunate message that the unsuccessful equality claimant is unreasonable. *Gosselin* is a case in point: Chief Justice McLachlin implicitly contrasts the actual claimant's understanding of the scheme with what a *reasonable* claimant would have understood. Ms Gosselin is effectively told that a reasonable claimant would not have considered her dignity infringed by the workfare scheme. The message to Ms. Gosselin is that she is not reasonable and that her reaction to the situation was irrational. Particularly in a context of deep diversity where the judiciary is relatively unrepresentative of equality claimants, this very way of answering the discrimination question may actually have anti-egalitarian implications. As such, the reasonable person is very unlikely to provide a convincing justification for the judicial point of view particularly in equality cases. The recent recourse to it as a justification for the finding regarding discrimination under s.15 therefore seems seriously misguided.

This difficulty is exacerbated by another feature of the use of the reasonable person in s.15. Commentators anxious to reform the reasonable person often suggest that the unmodified reasonable person's objective context ought to be modified by reading in norms of equality, usually from the constitutional context. Thus, it may seem plausible to give egalitarian content to the reasonable person by construing him as committed to the principle of equal personhood, which is at the heart of constitutional guarantees of equality. But this seems to plague the s.15 discrimination inquiry with an extremely unhelpful kind of circularity. In order to determine what kind of commitments and attitudes the reasonable person would have towards any given claim of discrimination, this approach requires us to read the commitment to the equality guarantee into the reasonable person. But the most controversial component of this is the assessment of whether the impugned distinction is discriminatory. Oddly then, this suggests that we cannot give content to the normative commitments of the reasonable person for the purpose of holding that constant in the equality analysis until we have already employed the reasonable person to accomplish the very task for which we need him. Thus, modifying the reasonable person to endow him with specifically egalitarian commitments, which is the most common and the most convincing response of egalitarian commentators in other fields, seems unhelpful as a response to the worries about the constitutional context where the reasonable person's very function is to define the core of those commitments.

Conclusion

When the Supreme Court of Canada decided to introduce the reasonable person into the discrimination inquiry in s.15, it showed itself aware of the many controversies concerning that difficult fiction. Virtually all of the other instances of the reasonable person illustrate the extent to which the standard, unmodified, is plagued by equality worries. Indeed, these are acknowledged by Justice Iacobucci in *Law* and have been noted by numerous other courts. Perhaps the most persistent such worry is the extent to which the reasonable person is simply the ordinary man, and as such, serves as a vehicle for the common prejudices and biases that so often characterize him. On occasion however the reasonable person has been employed as part of an effort to delineate an idealised judicial point of view. This may well be the best way to understand the role of the reasonable person in s.15. But while such a corrective is undoubtedly vital, there are also severe equality problems associated with employing the reasonable person in this way.

Even if it were possible to address these problems in the corrective use of the reasonable person, recent cases suggest that the standard is being used in a very different way. Unlikely though it may seem, he has come to be a vehicle for articulating and justifying what judges take to be the central *objective* content of discrimination. As we have seen however, the justificatory power of the reasonable person is weak in the best of circumstances. And given his record on equality-related issues, use of the reasonable person as a justification for difficult conclusions about discrimination is considerably more troubling. This is exacerbated because majorities in the Supreme Court are increasingly stating their holdings on discrimination by contrasting the claimant's point of view with what a 'reasonable claimant' would understand. But in addition to being a rather weak and unpersuasive form of justification, the message that the unsuccessful equality claimant is unreasonable also betrays an unfortunate paternalism that undermines any persuasive power that the opinions might have. In justificatory terms alone, it may be better for the Court to simply try to articulate its own reasons for its holding without the troubling intercession of the reasonable person. It would be preferable for the Court to take responsibility for declaring that it cannot give credence to the claim of discrimination rather than imagining a more reasonable claimant to articulate that view.

This suggests that the Supreme Court of Canada would have done well to heed the lessons of many debates concerning the reasonable person. Though there may be ways to reform the inegalitarian tendencies of the reasonable person, the ultimate question for the Supreme Court of Canada is whether embarking down such a road of reform and controversy is the most productive way to analyse discrimination. No conceptual device will make assessments of claims of discrimination easy. The difficulty with the reasonable person is that he threatens to sidetrack any court that takes equality seriously into a series of efforts to reform him. Perhaps for this reason, the Supreme Court of Canada has backed away from the corrective function associated with the introduction of the reasonable person into the discrimination inquiry. Instead, it has begun to employ him as a means of justifying the conclusion and hence asserting the objective content of the standard. For this role, however, he is singularly unsuited. The Court would do well to consider how to develop a more rigorous and equality-sensitive means of justifying the most difficult of all constitutional equality questions – the question of when a legislative distinction discriminates against a claimant.

References

Abrams, K. (1995), 'The Reasonable Woman: Sense and Sensibility in Sexual Harassment Law', *Dissent* 42, 48–54.

Bandalli, S. (1995), 'Provocation – A Cautionary Note', *Journal of Law & Society* 22, 398–409.

Bordo, S. (1990), 'Feminism, Postmodernism, and Gender-Skepticism', in Nicholson (ed.) (1990), *Feminism/Postmodernism* (New York: Routledge), 133–156.

Cahn, N. R. (1992), 'The Looseness of Legal Language: The Reasonable Woman Standard in Theory and Practice', *Cornell Legal Review* 77, 1398–1446.

Childers, J. (1993), 'Is There a Place for a Reasonable Woman in the Law? A Discussion of Recent Developments in Hostile Environment Sexual Harassment', *Duke Law Journal* 42, 854–904.

Collins, R. K. L. (1977), 'Language, History and Legal Process: A Profile of the 'Reasonable Person', *Rutgers-Camden Law Journal* 8, 311–323.

Department of Justice Canada (1998), 'Reforming Criminal Code Defences'.

Donovan, Dolores and Wildman, Stephanie (1981), 'Is the Reasonable Man Obsolete? A Critical Perspective on Self-Defense and Provocation', 14 *Loyola of Los Angeles Law Review*, 435–468.

Ehrenreich, N. S. (1990), 'Pluralist Myths and Powerless Men: The Ideology of Reasonableness in Sexual Harassment Law', *Yale Law Journal.* 99, 1177–1234.

Estrich, Susan, (1994), 'Don't Be Surprised if OJ Gets Off Easy', *USA Today*, 23 June, 1A.

Hadfield, Gillian (1996), 'Rational Women: A Test for Sex-Based Harassment', 83 California Law Review, 1151.

Halley, Janet, (2002) 'Sexuality Harassment' in W. Brown and J. Halley (eds), *Left Legalism/Left Critique*, Durham, NC: Duke University Press, 80–104.

Horder, J. (1992), *Provocation and Responsibility* Oxford: Clarendon Press.

Howe, A. (1998), '*Green v The Queen* – The Provocation Defence: Finally Provoking Its Own Demise?', *Melbourne University Law Review* 22, 466–490.

Hubin, Donald C. and Haely, Karen (1999), 'Rape and the Reasonable Man', 18 *Law & Philosophy* 193.

Klimchuk, D. (1994), 'Outrage, Self-Control, and Culpability', *University of Toronto Law Journal*, 44, 441–468.

Leader-Elliott, Ian (1996), 'Sex, Race, and Provocation: In Defence of Stingel', *Criminal Law Journal*, 72–96.

Lester, T. (1993), 'The Reasonable Woman Test in Sexual Harassment Law – Will It Really Make a Difference?', *Indiana Law Review*, 26, 227–262.

Moran, Mayo, (2003), *Rethinking the Reasonable Person*, Oxford: Oxford University Press.

Moran, M. (2006), 'Protesting Too Much: Rational Basis Review Under Canada's Equality Guarantee', *Supreme Court Law Review*, 33, 71–93.

New South Wales Law Reform Commission Discussion Paper: Provocation, Diminished Responsibility and Infanticide (1993), Sydney: New South Wales Law Reform Commission.

Yeo, Stanley (1993), 'Resolving Gender Bias in Criminal Defences' 19 *Monash University Law Review*, 104–116.

Chapter 9

Quebec and the Amending Formula: Protection, Promotion and Federalism[1]

Peter C. Oliver

Introduction

No one denies that Quebec is different. Disagreement emerges in determining whether and how this difference should be reflected in the Constitution. This chapter focuses on a central constitutional manifestation of difference and disagreement – the general procedure for amending the Constitution of Canada and the shifting proposals regarding how best to accommodate Quebec.

In the fifty years prior to the enactment of the present amending formula[2] numerous proposals were considered. It will be argued that a matrix of factors is essential to understanding Quebec's position regarding constitutional amendment, and to proposing appropriate changes to the present amending formula. Each side of the matrix has three variables. One side considers *protection, promotion* and *federalism*. By 'protection', I mean Quebec's desire to protect what it has already achieved in three or four hundred years of presence in North America. 'Promotion' is a more complicated idea. It refers to the view that in order to protect what Quebec already has, preservation of the constitutional status quo is insufficient. It may be necessary, for example, to grant special powers to Quebec in order to allow it to fulfil its special role as source, guardian, guiding light, *etc.* of French language and culture in Canada. The final variable, 'federalism', refers to Quebec's ongoing interest in federal institutions. The reference to 'Quebec' here is ambiguous. In recent years, some Quebec governments have shown little interest in developing and improving what goes on at the federal level. But the people of Quebec are naturally affected by what the other part of the division of powers can do so long as Quebec remains part of Confederation. They are naturally interested in federal institutions such as the Supreme Court, the Senate and the House of Commons, and in federal law, constitutional and other, relating to, for example, bilingualism.

The other side of the matrix is represented by Quebec's three main positions on the amending formula: *unanimity, veto* and *opting out*. We will see that these three positions also represent the three key moves in Quebec's negotiating stance

---

1 This chapter is dedicated to the memory of my uncle, Michael Oliver. I was fortunate enough to have the opportunity to discuss with him many of the issues dealt with here, and to benefit from his encouragement and insight.
2 See Part V of the Constitution Act, 1982.

in the fifty-year search for an amending formula prior to 1982. 'Unanimity' refers to an amending formula which requires the consent of all relevant parties: that is, the federal level and all provinces (*including* Quebec, of course). Unanimity, as we shall see, *protects* Quebec's established constitutional position well. However, unanimity has at least two potential disadvantages in the context of this chapter: first, it submerges Quebec's particularity by treating Quebec in the same way as all constitutional parties; and secondly, the rigidity created by requiring unanimous consent makes it more difficult for Quebec to *promote* the sorts of constitutional changes that preservation of its majority language and culture may require.

'Veto' refers to a situation where Quebec can block any important proposal for constitutional amendment (and thereby *protect*), but where the denial of such a veto to *all* provinces introduces a level of flexibility in the amending formula (and therefore greater scope for *promotion* of Quebec's constitutional reform agenda). However, even a more flexible amending formula still requires significant levels of federal/provincial consensus, and this is usually difficult to obtain.

'Opting out' makes consensus involving Quebec optional. It means that if there is the requisite federal/provincial consensus in favour of a constitutional amendment which Quebec does not like, Quebec need not oppose it.[3] Quebec simply opts out of the proposed amendment and collects compensation to implement the change in its own way. Opting out has obvious advantages in terms of *promotion*. However, we shall see that the ineffectiveness of opting out with regard to amendments to the institutions of *federalism* is one of the most important spurs to post-1982 attempts to amend the amending formula.

The 1982 amending formula contained in Part V of the Constitution Act, 1982 specifies unanimity for a narrow range of key constitutional amendments (s. 41). The general amending formula, however, requires the consent of seven out of ten provinces representing at least fifty percent of the population of all the provinces (s. 38(1)). The seven need not include Quebec. The apparent *quid pro quo* for the lack of any veto for Quebec in the general formula is a constitutional permission for any province to opt out of amendments that derogate from the legislative powers of a province (s. 38(3)). However, this permission does not apply to matters of central concern in terms of federalism as set out in sections 41 and 42; and compensation for opting out is in any event only available regarding 'transfers [of] provincial powers relating to education or other cultural matters' (s. 40). Both the absence of a veto in the general amending formula and the lack of compensation in all cases of opting out are ongoing sources of concern for Quebec.

The remainder of this chapter is made up of an account Quebec's position vis-à-vis the amending formula in two periods: pre-1982 and post-1982. This account should amply illustrate the relevance and importance of the variables just identified and briefly discussed: protection, promotion and federalism on the one hand; and unanimity, veto and opting-out on the other. The intersection of these variables leads to certain conclusions regarding future proposals to amend the amending formula. The most important of these conclusions is that a constitutional veto for Quebec

---

3 Opting out is available to any province; however, the focus in this chapter is on Quebec.

appears to be objectively justified. However, this is by no means the end of the story. Whether a constitutional veto for Quebec is re-instated, or whether informal, sub-constitutional reforms work towards a similar objective, will largely depend on whether politicians and voters across the country understand the special role that Canada demands of Quebec, and whether Quebec politicians and voters show a willingness to take on that role and commit themselves to it.

Quebec and the Amending Formula: 1867–1982

Following Confederation, Quebec's position on constitutional amendment was not marked by any set position or justified by any well-developed doctrine, and in that respect Quebec had much in common with the other provinces.[4] It was the Canadian discussions leading up to the Statute of Westminster, 1931, that elicited the most thoughtful responses from the provinces. Ontario Premier Howard Ferguson challenged the federal government's right to act unilaterally in matters of such high constitutional importance, and in doing so he invoked what was known as the 'compact theory' (on this theory, see also Black 1975) – in Ferguson's words, 'the fact that the Confederation of the provinces was brought about by the action of the provinces ... [and] that this agreement should not be altered without the consent of the parties to it' (Gérin-Lajoie 1950, 204). The Quebec government found the compact theory attractive as well. Premier Taschereau seconded Ferguson's position in a letter to then Prime Minister Bennett:

> La Confédération est un contrat, qui a été signé par les différentes provinces canadiennes, après des longues discussions, à des conditions acceptables à toutes les parties contractantes. Je me demandes comment un semblable contrat pourrait être modifié sans l'assentiment de toutes les parties. (Rumilly 1948, 171)[5]

It was as a result of provincial protestations, led by Ontario and Quebec, that the British North America Acts, 1867–1930 were expressly excluded from the application of the Statute of Westminster, 1931.[6]

The weight of historical opinion is now firmly against the compact theory, but it is significant that it remained as the keystone of Quebec's position on constitutional

---

4 Naturally enough, provincial self-interest was a common basis for objections to or interventions in constitutional matters. For example, when Premier Mercier of Quebec perceived that the Canada (Ontario Boundary) Act, 1889 (Imp) might affect Quebec's northern boundary, he quickly voiced his province's objection. He argued that any determination as to Quebec's boundary could not be made without the consent of Quebec. An official protest was made, and the final Act included no change to the Ontario-Quebec boundary. See Gérin-Lajoie 1950, 68.

5 'Confederation is a contract that was signed by each of the Canadian provinces, after long discussions, and according to conditions that were acceptable to all of the contracting parties. I ask myself how such a contract could be amended without the consent of all the parties' (Author's translation).

6 See subsection 7(1) of the 1931 *Statute* which exempted from its operation 'the repeal, amendment or alteration' of the *B.N.A. Acts*.

amendment until at least 1950. The theory dictated unanimous provincial consent for amendment: Quebec would have a veto because all provinces had a veto. When a Committee of Experts in 1935–36 (Hurley 1996, 28–29) raised the possibility of less rigid amendment procedures for certain matters, the idea was condemned by Premier Taschereau. His response emphasised the importance of *protection* and foreshadowed the fact that Quebec was tied to its constitutional veto regardless of whether all provinces had one. Taschereau stated that 'as leader of the government', he was 'not prepared to permit the British North America Act to be changed by the will of a majority of the provinces'. Quebecers had 'built certain things here in this old province' and 'created institutions that are dear to us', and they were not going to see them 'done away with to suit the caprice of even a majority of the provinces'. (Livingston 1956, 53).

If the citizens of Quebec were also concerned about constitutional protection for 'the old province', they found a most forceful spokesman in Maurice Duplessis, successor to Taschereau as Premier of Quebec. Upon coming to power in 1936, Duplessis replaced Ontario's Howard Ferguson as principal proponent of the compact theory, and Duplessis' government began to apply the idea rigorously.[7] Duplessis would continue to do so even when, briefly, he found himself in Opposition.

In 1943, the federal government chose to act unilaterally on an amendment to suspend readjustment of provincial representation in the House of Commons. The federal Liberal government, and especially the Minister of Justice, Louis St Laurent, argued that the provinces had no role in amendments relating to federal institutions. St Laurent explained his view to the House of Commons, beginning by claiming that Confederation was not really a compact between the provinces, and that, to the extent that the people of any province had an interest in changes to their federal institutions, they could express them through their federal representatives. Such a proposition did not conform to the compact theory; furthermore, it would mean that Quebec members of the federal Parliament, necessarily a minority, were the only defenders of Quebec's position on the amendment issue, and always subject to potential defeat by the majority of representatives from other provinces (See Canada, House of Commons, *Debates* 1943, 4305–4306).

Even the Liberal government in Quebec could not swallow the federal refusal to allow the provincial legislatures any say in the composition of the organs of the federal state, especially given that, without the proposed amendment, Quebec stood to benefit from the redistribution of seats in the House of Commons. The legislature of Quebec immediately passed a resolution of protest but was alone amongst the provinces in doing so. Maurice Duplessis, at that time Leader of the Opposition,

---

7 Quebec's point of view was expressed to the Rowell-Sirois Commissioners in Quebec City in 1938 through the chief counsel for the Union Nationale, L. Emery Beaulieu:

[T]he federative pact cannot be amended or modified without the assent of all the parties, that is to say, all of the provinces. It does not belong to the majority of the provinces, even less to the federal government, to change it. ... [A]ny modification [without unanimous consent] ... constitutes an assault on the respect due to contracts. (Quoted in Black 1976, 80)

requested that the federal government transmit the protest to Great Britain, but Prime Minister King refused (Dawson 1975, 125–126; Rémillard 1985, 59–62).

The 1943 amendment to postpone redistribution was followed by a 1946 amendment to carry out the delayed process, but by this time Duplessis had returned to power. Once again, the federal government acted unilaterally, and once again Quebec alone protested (Gérin-Lajoie 1950, 118–119). The offence of unilateral federal action was soon compounded by St Laurent claiming that, strictly speaking, the language provisions of the 1867 Act, section 133, could be amended without the consent of the provincial legislatures. The Duplessis government responded to this broad-based assault on the position of the French language in Canada with an Order-in-Council in which it relied once again on the compact theory, however this time with a new emphasis:

> The federal authorities be warned anew;
> That the Government of the Province of Quebec energetically demands the integral respect of *the Canadian federative pact*;
> That the Province of Quebec reaffirms its irrevocable desire to safeguard integrally the constitutional prerogatives which belong to it and to conserve intact the intangible and inalienable rights of the French language;
> That the government of Canada be further advised that it is the desire of the Province of Quebec that all the provinces, *Quebec in particular*, obtain by procedures in conformity with the spirit and letter of the constitution of Canada a just and reasonable federal representation. (Quebec, *Official Gazette*, 9 July 1946) [emphasis added]

The Quebec government's position seemed to suggest that Quebec should have a say not only as a participant in the original pact, but also, *a fortiori*, as representative of French Canada in Confederation, and as such, it anticipated the 'two-nations' theory which dominated a later period of Quebec and Canadian political and constitutional history. Quebec's new position was capable of sustaining amending formula proposals based either on *unanimity* or on a singular *veto* for Quebec. For the moment, it is also important to note that the Quebec government saw its defensive constitutional role as requiring *protection* of the province's jurisdictional rights *as well as* French Canada's interest in *federal* institutions and *federal* guarantees, linguistic and other.[8]

Although in 1946 the federal government was not deflected from its intention by objections from Quebec or any other province, it did promise a Constitutional Conference, and this took place early in 1950 (Hurley 1996, 31–32). Quebec and six other provinces joined together to call for the repeal of the British North America Act (No. 2), 1949 which had granted a range of amendment powers to the federal government, and this call was duly ignored by Ottawa (Black 1975, 136). When matters turned to the general amending formula, however, some provinces expressed support for a variable or flexible formula, where unanimous consent would not always be the rule. For his part, Duplessis was unwilling to approve any plan that deprived Quebec of its veto (Rémillard 1983, 130; Rémillard 1985, 67). The 1950 Conference

---

8 Writing in the early 1950s, Paul Gérin-Lajoie agreed that Quebec was the natural guardian of language provisions in the constitution, as these guarantees were originally designed to protect that province (Gérin-Lajoie 1950, 173).

was significant in that it signalled clearly that the days of other provinces' strict adherence to the compact theory were over. The theory had fallen into disuse save for the frequent claims by Duplessis in protest against unilateral federal amendments of any sort.

But Quebec was not limited to the compact theory to justify its claim to a constitutional veto. As Duplessis had suggested in 1946 when St Laurent had claimed federal power to amend section 133, Quebec was also guardian of the French language in Canada. If Confederation was in part a pact between English Canadians and French Canadians, the former were predominantly represented by three of the original provinces (now expanded to nine), and the latter predominantly by Quebec. The claim to a distinctive role for the Quebec found its most convincing expression in the *Tremblay Report*, (Quebec 1954; Kwavnik 1973) Quebec's response to the federal-inspired Rowell-Sirois Commission. The *Tremblay Report* stated famously that 'Quebec is not a province like the others' (Kwavnik 1973, 182) for, with regard to 'French-Canadian culture', the province 'assumes alone the responsibilities which the other provinces jointly assume with regard to Anglo-Canadian culture' (Kwavnik 1973, 290). Although in coming decades the *Tremblay Report* would be used as justification for *promoting* special status for Quebec, for the moment it was sufficient to provide a new rationale for the province's traditional claim to a *protective* veto over constitutional amendment.

Ten years after the ill-fated Constitutional Conference of 1950, Ottawa and the provinces met once again to discuss proposals for an amending formula (Hurley 1996, 32–34). Duplessis was now dead, but Quebec's representatives continued to insist on a veto to protect the fundamental aspects of the province's constitutional position. And if Quebec required a veto over fundamental constitutional change, then the other provinces still demanded the same. The 'Fulton Formula', which emerged from the 1960 conference, retained unanimous provincial consent as the general amending procedure. However, even the Fulton proposals were unsatisfactory to Quebec because they perpetuated the unilateral federal amending formula of the British North America Act (No. 2), 1949 (Hurley 1996, 34; Rémillard 1985, 73). By the time a new compromise had been reached, changes in Quebec had out-stepped the slow-moving process of constitutional negotiation.

With a new government in power in Ottawa and a new federal Minister of Justice, Guy Favreau, renewed attempts were made to find the elusive amending formula. Unanimous agreement was reached in October 1964 on a revised proposal, which came to be known as the Fulton-Favreau formula. Significantly for Quebec, it restricted the unilateral federal amendment power to certain matters relating to the executive government of Canada and the Senate and House of Commons (Hurley 1996, 34). The general formula retained the requirement of unanimity that had held the Fulton formula together. By defining in broad terms the class of amendments requiring unanimity, the new formula, according to one distinguished commentator, 'accepted in fact, if not in form, the compact theory of Confederation which the Dominion had so often scouted in the past'. (Dawson 1975, 129). The federal White Paper explaining the new constitutional proposals came close to confirming the compact theory in its explanation of the unanimity provisions:

> This clause specifies certain classes of amendments that may be made by Parliament only with the consent of the legislatures of all the provinces. The subjects included under this provision are those that are believed to be of fundamental concern to all the provinces as well as the federal government. ... [These subjects] could be said to represent essential conditions, on which the original provinces united to form the Canadian Confederation, and on which other provinces subsequently joined the union. (Favreau 1965, 35)

Taschereau, or perhaps even Duplessis, might have embraced such a proposition.

The Quebec government of the time, led by Liberal Jean Lesage, was initially interested in the Fulton-Favreau formula. The new formula contained the attraction of *protecting* through *unanimity* both the jurisdictional rights of the province of Quebec's and the broader interests of French Canadians in the *federation*. However, Lesage and his ministers governed a Quebec society that was profoundly different to that of the Duplessis era. A simple defensive veto was insufficient in the new Quebec.[9]

This point was made forcefully by those participants in the 1965 public debates in Quebec who opposed the Fulton-Favreau formula. Government ministers such as the popular Minister of Natural Resources, René Lévesque, argued that Fulton-Favreau merely recognised the *status quo* and could not, therefore, be seen as either a loss or a gain for Quebec. Anticipating his future role as separatist Prime Minister of Quebec, the Minister reasoned that any change in Quebec's status would eventually involve massive negotiations, and that attempts to effect immediate change would only provoke confrontation and gridlock (Scott 1967, 351). One of the leading spokesmen for Quebec opposition to Fulton-Favreau was Jacques-Yvan Morin, Lévesque's future colleague in the *Parti québécois*. Morin called for what he later referred to as '*au minimum un statut particulier au sein d'une confédération renovée*' in order to promote '*les intérêts canadiens-français*' (Morin 1967, 394).[10] Given such a demand for change, the rigid provisions of the Fulton-Favreau formula could only inhibit Quebec's development (Morin 1967, 395). *Protection* inhibited *promotion*. As public opinion shifted in favour of those who opposed the constitutional proposals, it became clear that the government's position was undermined, and Premier Lesage

---

9 As explained by Gérald-A. Beaudoin: '[A] partir de 1964, en pleine révolution tranquille, alors qu'il commença à être sûr de lui et à faire montrer d'un dynamisme créateur, il convoita de nouveaux pouvoirs, et, il s'aperçu que le veto qui le protégeait pour l'acquis et qu'il était prêt à reconnaître aux autres régions du pays pourrait dorénavant le gêner pour obtenir davantage sur le plan de la décentralisation de compétences législatives; comme il ne pouvait être le seul à disposer du veto, il risquait d'être "gelé" dans le statu quo constitutionnel qu'il commençait déjà à rejeter'(Beaudoin 1981, 94). [After 1964, in the midst of the quiet revolution, just as Quebec began to be more sure of itself and to reveal a creative dynamism, Quebec sought new powers, and it began to see that the veto that protected it and which it was willing to grant to other regions of the country might henceforth get in the way of it making gains regarding the decentralisation of legislative powers; because Quebec could not be the only province to hold a veto, it risked becoming 'frozen' in a constitutional status quo that it was already beginning to reject] (Author's translation). See also Rémillard 1985, 77.

10 'At a minimum special status in a renewed Conferation' in order to promote 'French-Canadian interests' (Author's translation).

announced that further consideration of the Fulton-Favreau formula was indefinitely postponed.[11]

Lesage's government was eventually defeated. The new premier of Quebec, Daniel Johnson, took the position that constitutional reform – redistribution of powers and explicit recognition of two nations as the foundation of the federation – would have to occur first. In his view, to have adopted Fulton-Favreau would have been to place Quebec in a constitutional straitjacket ('*camisole de force*') (quoted in Black 1976, 193). In his opening address to the Confederation of Tomorrow Conference in 1967 (Hurley 1996, 36), Johnson referred to Canada as the home of 'two nations', and to Quebec as 'the heartland and mainstay of French Canada' (Johnson 1968, 16). During the conference, he called for expansion of Quebec's constitutional powers (Johnson 1968, 41), and he added proposals to take into account Canada's bi-national character: a reformed, truly federal Senate; a constitutional tribunal; and a permanent commission on linguistic rights (Johnson 1968, 45). Quebec seemed determined to take the lead in proposing changes to the constitution, including *federal institutions and rights*, speaking on behalf of Quebec and French Canada.

The Quebec government was not unchallenged as leader in constitutional reform and representative of French Canada in the federation. The federal Minister of Justice, Pierre Elliott Trudeau, presented new constitutional proposals in a document entitled *Federalism for the Future* (Trudeau 1968). The federal plan focused on an entrenched charter of rights, reform of the institutions of federalism (notably the Senate and the Supreme Court of Canada), and implementation of the recommendations of the Royal Commission on Bilingualism and Biculturalism (Simeon 1972, 96). Premier Johnson's response to these proposals identified a tension in Quebec-Ottawa relations that would hide beneath the surface of constitutional negotiations for many years to come: was the French-Canadian part of the federal pact adequately protected and promoted by the federal level of government, or was it also necessary to make special accommodation for the province of Quebec as representative of French Canada in the federation? Premier Johnson clearly took the latter view in his reply to the federal proposals: '[T]he equality to be established between our two cultural communities depends not only on extending bilingualism territorially but even more on extending the jurisdiction of Quebec, the homeland of the French Canadians' (Johnson 1968, 41).

Later in 1968, Quebec lost its leading constitutional advocate with the death of Daniel Johnson. This coincided with the election of Pierre Elliott Trudeau as leader of the federal Liberal party and Prime Minister of Canada. The new Prime Minister became an active participant in constitutional reform. However, Trudeau's ideas contemplated neither increased constitutional powers nor special status for Quebec. Trudeau argued, hearkening back to the ideas of Louis St Laurent, that any French Canadian concern for federal institutions and linguistic guarantees could be expressed by the French Canadian representatives in Ottawa (Simeon 1972, 99).

Inevitably Ottawa's renewed interest in constitutional reform turned to the amending formula, 'that old bugbear of constitutional discussion' (Simeon 1972,

---

11 See Letter from Jean Lesage to Lester B. Pearson, reprinted in Appendix III (1967) *McGill L.J.* 12, 596.

100). Quebec's early demands for a type of constitutional change that could reflect her role in a bi-national Canada had been ignored, or, rather, swallowed up by Prime Minister Trudeau's version of representation for French Canada in Ottawa. The next constitutional package, the Victoria Charter, contained in its amending formula a *veto* for Quebec without the great rigidity that condemned the Fulton-Favreau formula to failure. Quebec's veto in the Victoria Charter would have allowed it to block any changes to *federal* institutions or to linguistic guarantees. This would probably have been sufficient in 1965, but by 1971 more was required. Premier Robert Bourassa demanded and obtained increased jurisdiction for the provinces in the area of social policy in order to *promote* Quebec's distinctiveness, but the response to the constitutional package in Quebec was hostile nonetheless. Newspaper editors, trade unions and all three opposition parties objected, claiming that Bourassa had obtained too little for Quebec (Simeon 1972, 120; regarding the Trudeau version of representation for French Canada see Laforest 1995 and Webber 1994, 56 et seq). Bourassa deliberated briefly and finally communicated his province's refusal to Ottawa (Hurley 1996, 36–40).[12]

Despite failure to achieve agreement on the global constitutional reform, the Victoria Charter had very nearly been successful in terms of the amending formula. In its 1972 Report, the Special Joint Committee on the Constitution recommended that the procedure contained in the Victoria Charter be the basis for future discussions.[13] The formula itself appeared to have been satisfactory to Quebec. If the Fulton-Favreau formula *unanimity* requirements could be said to recognise implicitly a 'compact theory' of Confederation, the Victoria Charter amending formula could be seen to acknowledge Quebec's special role in a Canada of two founding nations. Quebec would have possessed a *veto* over constitutional amendment that would have been denied to all other provinces except Ontario. *Promotion* of constitutional reform would have been thereby facilitated. However, the Victoria Charter stopped short of granting significantly increased provincial powers, and this omission proved fatal to the 1971 initiative.

---

12 Jean-Louis Roy has summarised the problems with the Victoria Charter formula as follows: '*Elle ignorait presque complètement ce qui constituait à l'origine l'essentiel de la demande québécoise, soit une nouvelle répartition des compétences ... . Elle n'abordait pas l'importante question du pouvoir de dépenser. Elle ne traitait que partiellement de la réforme "des institutions reliées au fédéralisme'* ['It almost completely ignored that which originally constituted the essence of Quebec's demands, that is a new distribution of powers.... It did not deal with the important issue of the spending power. It only partially dealt with reform of "the institutions associated with federalism"'] Quoted in Rémillard 1985, 90.

13 Canada, Special Joint Committee on the Constitution of Canada, *Final Report* (Chairs: Molgat and MacGuigan) (1972). Of all the amending formulae proposed for Canada, the Victoria Charter formula attracts the greatest and most regular praise. Most recently it has formed the basis for the *Act Respecting Constitutional Amendments, 1996*, though modification was necessary to take into account British Columbia's increased status. The Beaudoin-Edwards report on the amending formula also favoured the Victoria formula. See Canada, Parliament, Special Joint Committee of the Senate and House of Commons, *The Process for Amending the Constitution of Canada* (Chairs: G. Beaudoin and J. Edwards) (20 June 1991) (hereinafter Beaudoin-Edwards). See also Hurley 1996, 37.

The election of the separatist *Parti québécois* government in 1976 signalled the end of another phase of Quebec's position on the amending formula. Since 1964, the province's leaders had insisted on constitutional change *before* agreement on an amending formula. Constitutional change was intended ostensibly to assist Quebec in its role as representative of the French Canadian element in Canada's 'two nations', and this role had been claimed by Quebec leaders at least since the 1940s. In addition to expanded provincial jurisdiction, Daniel Johnson, like his predecessors, had taken a strong interest in federal institutions and linguistic guarantees, as we have seen. The new Quebec government was determined to increase Quebec's jurisdiction even to the point of sovereignty-association. The emphasis was no longer so much on French Canada as on Quebec itself, its government and its National Assembly. Depending on one's perspective, this was either an unprincipled grab for power, or recognition of the fact, alluded to earlier, that for French Canada to survive, Quebec had to have the necessary powers to promote that survival (for more detailed explanation of the *Parti québécois* government's constitutional position see Quebec, Government of Quebec 1979).

Although the Quebec government was committed to future constitutional change outside Confederation it could easily find allies amongst the other provinces in a common cause aimed at increased provincial power. One commentator has labelled this united provincial call for decentralisation a 'ten nations' approach to Confederation (McWhinney 1982, 4). As we shall see, participation in a common front of provinces presented the risk of masking what was by then Quebec's traditional claim to distinctiveness. Unless Quebec could link its constitutional position to its special role in Confederation, the risk was that it would be perceived as merely one grasping province among many. This risk was accentuated by the fact that representation of French-Canadian interests within Confederation had been assumed to such a large extent by Pierre Elliott Trudeau and the federal government.

With the defeat of the pro-sovereignty option in the Quebec referendum of 1980 national constitutional activity recommenced in earnest (Hurley 1996, 52–54).[14] After a summer of abortive negotiations, Prime Minister Trudeau announced his government's intention to proceed with major constitutional change unilaterally by means of a Proposed Resolution for a Joint Address to Her Majesty the Queen Respecting the Constitution of Canada.[15] This proposal included an amending formula that gave Quebec its traditional veto (Scott 1982, 287; McWhinney 1982, 62), but it did not contain the sort of substantive constitutional change that a growing number of Quebecers had demanded at least since 1964. It also proposed an alternative amending formula in the form of a referendum based on the same regional representation as the general formula (s. 42).

---

14 As Hurley notes (1996, 52), '[d]uring the referendum campaign, Prime Minister Trudeau and the majority of the premiers from the other provinces told Quebecers that rejection of the sovereignty-association mandate could and would lead to constitutional renewal'.

15 See Canada, Office of the Prime Minister, *Statement By The Prime Minister*, 2 October 1980, and reprinted in (1985), *McGill LJ*, 646–654 and the Proposed Resolution, also reprinted in (1985), *McGill LJ*, 755–771.

Quebec joined eight provinces (excluding New Brunswick and Ontario) in opposing the federal initiative. Quebec, Manitoba and Newfoundland referred matters to their respective Courts of Appeal in order to determine whether the federal action was constitutional. The Gang of Eight, as the premiers opposed to federal unilateralism came to be known, also signed a constitutional accord on 16 April 1981, which called for patriation of the Constitution by proper means (*i.e.*, *with* provincial participation and approval) as well as adoption of a new amending formula.[16] The April Accord, as it came to be known, contained the text of an amending formula as well as explanatory notes.[17] Both of these represented a radical departure from the traditional Quebec approach to the amending formula. First, the Gang of Eight proposed a general amending procedure which did not grant a *veto* to Quebec. Instead, Quebec or any other province could '*opt out*' of amendments which derogated from 'the legislative powers, the proprietary rights or any other rights or privileges of the legislature or government of a province'.[18] The April Accord also contained the startling statement to the effect that the eight premiers recognised 'the constitutional equality of the provinces'.[19]

By agreeing to the provisions and premises of the April Accord, Premier Lévesque and his advisor on constitutional matters, Claude Morin, departed from Quebec's traditional position with respect to the amending formula. The new general procedure required the consent of either Ontario *or* Quebec, meaning that there was still the threat of English-speaking provinces ganging up to defeat Quebec. Such a threat had been feared and successfully avoided in amending formula negotiations dating back to the time of Taschereau and Duplessis. *Opting out* with compensation enabled Quebec to evolve along a distinct constitutional path, but it left the province with a weaker voice in the ongoing federation. Under the Accord, Quebec retained a veto (*i.e.*, unanimous consent required) over the use of the English and French language and a narrow range of other amendments, but the province could neither opt out of nor halt unwanted changes to fundamental components of the federal system: *e.g.*, the principle of proportionate representation in the House of Commons, the powers of the Senate, and the powers of the Supreme Court of Canada.[20]

The federal constitutional initiative, supported only by New Brunswick and Ontario, was placed before the courts in the form of a constitutional reference. As a result of the Supreme Court of Canada's decision in the *Patriation Reference* the provinces and the federal government were forced back to the bargaining table. To

---

16 See Constitutional Accord: Canadian Patriation Plan, Ottawa, 16 April 1981, reprinted in (1985), *McGill LJ* 30, 678–683 (hereinafter April Accord).

17 See Amending Formula For The Constitution of Canada: Text and Explanatory Notes, reprinted in (1985), *McGill LJ* 30, 659–678.

18 The dissenting province would then be entitled to 'reasonable compensation'. See Amending Formula For The Constitution of Canada: Text and Explanatory Notes, reprinted in (1985), *McGill LJ* 30, 661–662.

19 Amending Formula For The Constitution of Canada: Text and Explanatory Notes, reprinted in (1985), *McGill LJ* 30, 660. The Accord omitted any referendum provisions as being 'inappropriate to the Canadian federal system' (660).

20 See Amending Formula For The Constitution of Canada: Text and Explanatory Notes, reprinted in (1985), *McGill LJ* 30, 665–666.

the surprise of some, the April Accord eventually formed the basis of the November 1981 constitutional compromise, which in turn made up the essentials of Part V of the *Constitution Act, 1982* dealing with amendment. As part of that November 1981 compromise, to which Quebec never agreed, the right to compensation for opting out was removed. It was only partially restored – for 'education or other cultural matters' – prior to proclamation of the Canada Act 1982.[21]

The reaction by the Quebec government to the November 1981 constitutional agreement was swift and indignant. Premier Lévesque claimed that he had only ever relinquished the *veto* power on the assumption that *opting out* and full compensation would be provided in its place.[22] Lévesque attempted to resuscitate Quebec's traditional constitutional position: *'le gouvernement du Québec a toujours maintenu que l'assentiment du Québec était constitutionellement nécessaire à tout accord qui permettait de rapatrier la constitution et d'en fixer le mode d'amendement pour l'avenir'*.[23] As a result of the collapse of the Gang of Eight's united stance, Quebec was now left with no *veto* power in the general amending procedure and limited provision for compensation even where it was entitled to *opt out*. Prime Minister Trudeau stated in his response to Premier Lévesque's objections that Quebec could not criticise Ottawa for the loss of a *veto* power: *'Nous n'avons abandonné ce principe qu'après que vous l'eûtes fait vous-même'*.[24]

Quebec did not limit its protest to an angry exchange of letters with the federal authorities. On 25 November the Quebec government issued an Order in Council which invoked the province's alleged veto to any constitutional change affecting its jurisdiction.[25] The government also expressed its intention to refer to the Court of Appeal the question whether a convention existed requiring Quebec's consent to the proposed resolution.[26]

The Courts had already expressed their views on the law and conventions relating to constitutional amendment. In 1981, the Supreme Court of Canada stated that, as a matter of law, there were no restrictions on the United Kingdom Parliament's powers to enact the unilateral federal resolution. As a matter of constitutional convention, the Court concluded that, where provincial interests were at stake, Canadian political

---

21 This eventually became s. 40 of the *Constitution Act, 1982*.

22 Letter from René Lévesque to P.E. Trudeau, 25 November 1981, reprinted in (1985), *McGill LJ* 30, 701.

23 'the government of Quebec always maintained that the consent of Quebec was constitutionally required before any agreement providing for patriation of the Constitution and a new amending formula' (author's translation). Letter from René Lévesque to P.E. Trudeau, 25 November 1981, reprinted in (1985), *McGill LJ* 30, 701.

24 'We only abandoned this principle after you yourself had done so' (author's translation). Letter from P.E. Trudeau to René Lévesque, 1 December 1981, reprinted in (1985), *McGill LJ* 30, 705. Trudeau also chided Lévesque for having subscribed to the principle of *'l'égalité des provinces'* in the April Accord (704).

25 Quoted in letter from René Lévesque to Margaret Thatcher, 19 December 1981, reprinted in (1985), *McGill LJ* 30, 717.

26 Quoted in letter from René Lévesque to Margaret Thatcher, 19 December 1981, reprinted in (1985), *McGill LJ* 30, 717.

actors had recognised a convention requiring 'at least a substantial measure of provincial consent'.[27]

The new reference case was based on two theoretical approaches both of which had deep roots in Quebec's history: the compact theory, associated with *unanimous provincial consent* to constitutional amendments, and the two-nations theory, associated with Quebec's unique claim to a *veto*. As summarised by the Supreme Court of Canada,[28]

> According to the first submission, there was a convention requiring the unanimous consent of the ten provinces to any constitutional amendment of the type in issue. According to the second submission, because of the principle of duality, Quebec had by convention a power of veto over any constitutional amendment affecting the legislative omnicompetence of the Province or the status or role of its legislature or government within the Canadian federation.

On 6 December 1982, almost eight months after the proclamation of the Canada Act 1982, the Supreme Court of Canada rendered its decision in the *Quebec Veto Reference*. The Court dismissed the submission which alleged a conventional rule of *unanimity* on the basis that the issue had been previously disposed of in the earlier *Patriation Reference*. As to the conventional power of *veto*, the Court found that the convention had not been accepted by Canadian politicians outside Quebec. One might have thought that the refusal to proceed with the Fulton-Favreau and the Victoria constitutional packages might have provided strong support for such a convention. Perhaps the dominant reason for the Court was that the United Kingdom Parliament had legislated and, given the Court's self-imposed refusal to consider the validity of such enactments, the matter was now essentially moot:[29]

> The *Constitution Act, 1982* is now in force. Its legality is neither challenged nor assailable. It contains a new procedure for amending the Constitution of Canada which entirely replaces the old one in its legal as well as in its conventional aspects. Even assuming therefore that there was a conventional requirement for the consent of Quebec under the old system, it would no longer have any object or force.

Responding to the Supreme Court's decision, Premier Lévesque indicated to Prime Minister Trudeau that he could not accept a result which had '*consacré judiciairement cette entente nocturne signée il y a un peu plus d'un an entre les gouvernements anglophones du Canada et le vôtre*'.[30] The Quebec Premier repeated his objection to

---

27 *Reference re Resolution to Amend the Constitution* [1981] 2 SCR 217 (hereinafter *Patriation Reference*, supra).

28 *Reference re Objection to a Resolution to Amend the Constitution* [1982] 2 SCR 793 (hereinafter *Quebec Veto Reference*).

29 *Quebec Veto Reference*, 806.

30 ['judicially confirmed this nocturnal agreement signed just over a year ago by all the anglophone governments of Canada and your government'] Letter from René Lévesque to P.E. Trudeau, 17 December 1982, reprinted in (1985), *McGill LJ* 30, 733. As noted above, Trudeau's argument failed to take into account that, even if it was true to say that the April Accord did not contain a veto for Quebec, signing on with the Gang of Eight did not

Quebec's loss of a *veto*: '*Il sera ... impossible pour tout gouvernement digne de ce nom au Québec ... de se voir imposer une formule d'amendement ne lui accordant aucune protection véritable pour l'avenir*' [emphasis added].³¹ Lévesque relied in his argument on the special role which Quebec played in Confederation, stating that the constitutional *veto* '*n'avait jamais été mise en doute et qu'on a toujours tenu pour l'essentiel à la défense de l'identité du peuple québécois, pierre d'assise des francophones d'Amérique du Nord*'.³² In his reply, Prime Minister Trudeau once again reminded the Quebec leader that his province had abandoned both the *veto* and its claim to distinctiveness as a result of the April Accord:³³

> *Rejetant de revers de la main la formule de Victoria et son droit de* veto *pour le Québec, vous avez alors choisi* 'l'opting out' *en declarant que cette formule 'consacrait l'égalité juridique de toutes les provinces' et qu'elle était à cause de cela 'manifestement préférable, pour tous les Canadiens, à celle que proposait le gouvernement fédéral'.*³⁴

Trudeau's answer acknowledged neither the federal government's pre-referendum promises of constitutional change in Quebec's favour, nor the weak bargaining position that the Quebec government had been placed in as a result of the federal government's own aggressive unilateral action in October 1980. Instead, the Canadian Prime Minister was at pains to explain how the difficult negotiating position in which he had found himself as a result of the Gang of Eight's actions had forced him to abandon the federal government's self-imposed role as protector of Quebec's *veto*. Given that neither side was willing to accept blame for the loss of the *veto*, it was necessary for someone to speak on behalf of those Quebecers who had renounced neither the *veto* nor the sense of Quebec's distinctive role in the federation.

---

necessarily also amount to abandoning its traditional veto over whatever amending formula might eventually appear in the patriation package.

31 ['It would be ... impossible for any Quebec government worthy of that description ... to see imposed on itself an amending formula which provided no true protection for the future.'] Letter from René Lévesque to P.E. Trudeau, 17 December 1982, reprinted in (1985), *McGill LJ* 30, 733.

32 ['had never been placed in doubt, and it was always assumed to be essential for the protection of the identity of the Quebec people, foundation stone of francophones all across North America.'] Letter from René Lévesque to P.E. Trudeau, 17 December 1982, reprinted in (1985), *McGill LJ* 30, 733. Lévesque added: '*Si les représentants du Bas-Canada, en 1865, s'étaient rendu compte que leur adhésion au projet fédéral aboutirait à les priver de toute protection contre les changements constitutionnels imposés par d'autres, cette adhésion, on peut en etre sur, n'aurait jamais été accordée*' (733) ['If the representatives of Lower Canada in 1865 had realised that their support for the federal project would end up depriving them of any and all protection against constitutional changes imposed by others, we can be sure that this support would never have been granted.'] [emphasis added].

33 Letter from P.E. Trudeau to René Lévesque, 30 December 1982, reprinted in (1985), *McGill LJ* 30, 736 [emphasis added].

34 ['having turned your back on the Victoria formula and its veto for Quebec, you then chose "opting out", declaring that this formula "recognised the legal equality of all the provinces" and that accordingly it was "clearly preferable for all Canadians, to that which had been proposed by the federal government"'.]

One such spokesperson was Claude Ryan, Leader of the Quebec Liberal Party. In an article in Montreal's *Le Devoir* newspaper, Ryan explained why the *veto* power was crucial to Quebec's role in the federation, indicating clearly that these reasons went well beyond provincial self-interest:

Ce droit de veto *avait pour le Québec une triple portée:*

1) il protégeait le Québec contre toute violation de ses droits constitutionnels sur son territoire;
2) il assurait au Québec une voix decisive – celle d'un partenaire majeur – dans les modifications constitutionnelles susceptibles d'affecter l'équilibre futur du Canada;
3) en conférant au Québec un rôle-clé dans les modifications constitutionnelles, il consacrait dans la pratique constitutionnelle la dualité fondamentale du Canada. (Le Devoir, 30 December 1982) [emphasis added][35]

Ryan criticised Lévesque for signing the April Accord which denied Quebec's '*caractère distinctif*' and which sacrificed the traditional *veto* power for a simple right to *opt out* with compensation. As Ryan noted, such a formula might please a separatist government, but it could not satisfy the needs of Quebec leaders who might wish to remain in Confederation: '*[Cette formule] ne pouvait toutefois satisfaire les fédéralistes sincères qui militent depuis des années pour* le renouvellement du fédéralisme canadien' (*Le Devoir*, 30 December 1982) [emphasis added].[36]

The sequel to this moment of constitutional creation and division is well known. All the seeds for subsequent difficulty were present. There was enduring tension in the Quebec position between those who still wanted substantive change, even separation, and those who wanted at a minimum adequate protection for the constitutional *status quo*. In terms of Quebec-Ottawa relations there was the tendency, pronounced since Trudeau's time, for the federal government to assume primary responsibility for protecting and promoting the interests of French Canadians. Only some of these interests have been entrenched in the *Constitution Act, 1982*. This left other French Canadian and Quebec interests vulnerable to a potentially unsympathetic majority at the federal level, and it also ran counter to the belief, prominent amongst nationalists and federalists alike, that support from Ottawa was insufficient to keep the French language and culture alive and flourishing in Canada (Oliver 1993; Laforest 1995, 12-13, chapter 4). English language and culture could thrive on its own; the French equivalent required a strong Quebec.[37]

---

35 ['This right to a veto had a triple meaning for Quebec:

1. It protected Quebec against all attacks on its constitutional rights on its territory;

2. It insured that Quebec would have a decisive voice – that of a major partner – in constitutional amendments potentially affecting the future balance of Canada;

3. In conferring on Quebec a key role in constitutional amendment, it recognised the fundamental duality of Canada in constitutional practice'.]

36 ['(This formula) could not however satisfy genuine federalists who have been working for years to achieve the modernisation of Canadian federalism.']

37 Whatever the truth (here assumed) of such claims in broad demographic terms, they often overlooked the situation of local linguistic communities, Franco-Manitobans, English Quebecers and aboriginal Canadians, for example, whose communities are threatened in more insidious ways,

Quebec and the Amending Formula after 1982

As noted in the preceding section, the proposals for changes to the amending formula have largely centred around the province of Quebec. The 5 November 1981 first ministers' agreement[38] which served as the basis for the Constitution Act, 1982 had been arrived at without the consent of the government of Quebec. The Supreme Court of Canada had decided in the *Patriation Reference* that there was a constitutional convention requiring the consent of only a *substantial* number of provinces, and that, in any event, constitutional law required only that the amendment be enacted by the Westminster Parliament whose powers with respect to the Canadian Constitution were untrammelled. This was confirmed in the *Quebec Veto Reference*.

Whatever the legal state of affairs, the Quebec government felt that the new constitution, which it referred to disdainfully as '*le "Canada Bill"*', lacked any legitimacy in Quebec. The government of that province announced that it would not participate in any constitutional conferences until its grievances had been dealt with. With respect to the amending formula, the government of Quebec had two major objections. These had been initially expressed in a Resolution of the National Assembly on 17 December 1981[39] and later appeared in the policy papers of both the nationalist *Parti québécois* government, which had been in power since 1976, and the more federalist Liberal Party, which took over in 1985.[40] First, Quebec called for *a say in modifications to federal institutions*. This was done by reasserting the power of *veto* which had been the cornerstone of its constitutional amendment policy until the 1981 April Accord. Secondly, Quebec demanded that the right to *reasonable compensation* in cases where *opting out* was possible be extended to all matters, not merely those involving education and culture.

As we have seen, the Liberal Government of Pierre Elliott Trudeau had not been particularly sympathetic to Quebec's demands, to say the least. In its view, the *Parti québécois* government would not have accepted *any* agreement in 1981 and was legally bound by the new Constitution, as the Supreme Court of Canada had confirmed in the *Quebec Veto Reference*. Trudeau retired in 1984 and in that same year the Liberal party under its new leader, John Turner, was defeated by the Progressive Conservative Party under Brian Mulroney. Mulroney immediately showed himself to be more sympathetic (or opportunistically attuned) to Quebec's feelings of insult and exclusion, and he undertook to negotiate a new constitutional accord which would allow Quebec to accept the new Constitution 'with honour and enthusiasm'.[41] The *Parti québécois* government in Quebec City was soon replaced by Robert Bourassa's Liberals, and by 1986, federal-provincial discussions were

---

principally by the steady deterioration of community fabric: movement of families, closing of key institutions (hospitals, schools, social services, community centres), *etc*.

38 See *First Ministers' Agreement on the Constitution*, 5 November 1981, reprinted in (1984-85) *McGill LJ* 30, 684–689.

39 Reprinted in (1984-85) *McGill LJ* 30, 720.

40 See Quebec, *Draft Agreement on the Constitution: Proposals by the Government of Quebec* (Quebec, 1985).

41 See Letter from Prime Minister Brian Mulroney to Premier René Lévesque, reprinted in (1984-85) *McGill L.J.* 30, 750–751.

under way. In August of 1986 the other provincial premiers agreed at an Edmonton meeting that the next round of constitutional negotiations should be a 'Quebec Round', that is, motivated principally by a desire to deal, in so far as possible, with the grievances of Quebec. In the end, Quebec's requirements merged with those of other provinces, but an agreement was arrived at by 30 April 1987, and it became known as the Meech Lake Accord.[42]

The Meech Lake Accord

The Accord was quite elaborate and need not, for our purposes, be examined in all of its detail. If we consider, first, Quebec's two demands regarding the amending formula, we can see that Quebec's wishes were satisfied by giving the same protection or compensation to all provinces. This was essentially the *unanimity* approach that had been first put forward in the 1930s. Section 9 of the proposed *Constitution Amendment, 1987* would have given *all* provinces a veto over the matters of federal concern set out in section 42. This would have been accomplished by simply adding subsections 42(a) to (f) to section 41, thereby subjecting them to the *unanimous consent procedure*. Section 9 of the Meech Lake amendment package would have guaranteed reasonable compensation to a province in *all* cases of *opting out* under subsection 38(3). Other amendments to Part V were merely housekeeping matters.

There is still much debate in Canada as to what combination of factors combined to defeat the Meech Lake package of amendments (Simeon 1990; Fournier 1990). Some provinces objected to the parts of the package that would have formally recognised that 'Quebec constitutes within Canada a distinct society'.[43] Others disagreed with the decentralising elements of the agreement.

Despite all the objections, the Accord came very close to being adopted. Just over one year following the initiation of the Meech Lake amendment resolution by the legislative assembly of Quebec, it had been ratified by the House of Commons (twice, thereby circumventing the Senate[44]) and by eight of the ten provincial legislative assemblies representing over ninety three percent of the population of all the provinces.[45] Had the package been divided up into smaller parts, some of it could have been proclaimed under the 7/50 general procedure.[46] Instead, the package was negotiated, initiated and ratified as a whole. The amendments to the amending formula that were proposed were not in the end as controversial as other parts of the package, but their inclusion ensured that unanimous provincial consent was required (paragraph 41 (e)). And, rightly or wrongly, it was assumed that the unanimous consent procedure was governed by a three-year time limit. As the last days of that

---

42 The Meech Lake Accord can be found in a federal document, Canada, *Strengthening the Canadian Federation: The Constitution Amendment, 1987* (Ottawa, 1987) (hereinafter Meech Lake Accord).

43 See Meech Lake Accord, s. 1.

44 See s. 47 *Constitution Act, 1982*.

45 See Canada, Federal-Provincial Relations Office, *Amending the Constitution of Canada: A Discussion Paper* (Ottawa, 1990), 9.

46 Seven provinces representing fifty percent of the population of all the provinces.

three-year period elapsed and as two small provinces succeeded in blocking the way forward for the others, the amending formula came to be seen as more than just a procedure, but in fact part of the problem.

From Meech to Charlottetown

As a result, following the failure of the Meech Lake Accord in June of 1990, the federal government set up a Special Joint Committee of the Senate and the House of Commons on the Process for Amending the Constitution of Canada.[47] The Committee was asked:[48]

> to consult broadly with Canadians and inquire into and report upon the process for amending the Constitution of Canada, including, where appropriate, proposals for amending one or more of the amending formulae with particular reference to:
> (i) the role of the Canadian public in the process;
> (ii) the effectiveness of the existing process and formulae for securing constitutional amendments; and
> (iii) alternatives to the current process and formulae ... .

The first reference point was an acknowledgement that the public had perhaps not had an adequate opportunity to respond to the Meech Lake Accord. In its final report, the Beaudoin-Edwards Committee noted that many expert witnesses had expressed the view that the amending formula itself was not really to blame but that the political process surrounding the formal legal rules of the formula had been inadequate.[49] Accordingly, the Beaudoin-Edwards Committee recommended,[50] for example, that Parliament amend its procedural rules:

> to make mandatory the holding of public hearings on any proposed constitutional amendment initiated by the Government of Canada, or to which the Government of Canada has given agreement in principle, such hearings to be held early enough to allow for changes to the proposal.

It recommended that the provincial legislatures do likewise.[51] This was in direct response to the Meech process whereby a deal which had been negotiated in private by first ministers and their advisers was then presented to the Canadian public as a *fait accompli*. Only Quebec had held public hearings before the private agreement took on its legal form. In the wake of the failure of the Meech Lake Accord, the government was at great pains to make way for public input.[52]

---

47 See Canada, Parliament, Special Joint Committee of the Senate and House of Commons, *The Process for Amending the Constitution of Canada* (Chairs: G. Beaudoin and J. Edwards) (20 June 1991) (hereinafter Beaudoin-Edwards).
48 See Orders of Reference, Beaudoin-Edwards, vii.
49 Beaudoin-Edwards, 14.
50 Beaudoin-Edwards, 55.
51 Beaudoin-Edwards, 55.
52 Following the demise of Meech, the federal government had set up the Joint Committee on the Amending Formula, the Citizen's Forum on Canada's Future and the Joint

The second point of reference gave the Beaudoin-Edwards Committee the opportunity to hear testimony and come to some conclusions on the existing amending formulae which had allegedly been an important factor in the failure of Meech. The Beaudoin-Edwards Committee noted that the central tension in the search for an appropriate amending formula was the need to grant special protection for Quebec and the unwillingness to abandon a doctrine of provincial equality.[53] It was this tension which had been resolved in the Meech Accord by giving *all* provinces vetoes, but that in turn had produced what many saw as excessive rigidity in the proposed constitutional amendment procedure. As we have seen earlier in this chapter, *unanimity* provides excellent *protection* but it makes *promotion* of constitutional change difficult. The Committee proposed that an earlier proposed formula of regional *vetoes* be revived. It would have replaced the general procedure found in sections 38 and 42 and the unanimous procedure in section 41 with a regional formula, according to which a constitutional amendment would require the approval of the Senate and House of Commons and each of four regions, one of those regions being Quebec – effectively a *veto* for Quebec. It was recommended that the unanimous consent procedure be retained respecting the use of the English and the French language, the proprietary rights of the provinces, the offices of the Queen, Governor General and Lieutenant Governor and any changes to those matters.[54]

The third and final point of reference for the Beaudoin-Edwards Committee concerned alternatives to the then-current processes and formulae. The federal government was aware at the time it set up the Beaudoin-Edwards Committee that the failure of Meech had produced a constitutional crisis which might necessitate extraordinary solutions. Not only had the Canadian public expressed in numerous ways a desire to become more involved in the process, but Quebec had announced that it would no longer participate in constitutional discussions until the rest of Canada produced a proposal that was at least as good as Meech;[55] and the rest of the Canadian provinces had made clear that Quebec's round was over and that Canada's round (meaning a full slate of new provincial demands) had now begun. Clearly, new and greater strains were being placed on the process of constitutional amendment.

By way of attempted response, the Committee examined the possibility of using referendums and constituent assemblies. In the end, the Beaudoin-Edwards Committee stopped short of recommending that either be formally included in the

---

Committee on a Renewed Canada which toured the country and heard what the members of the Canadian public had to say on the amending formula, their vision for the future and the full range of possible constitutional changes. See Beaudoin-Edwards, above; Canada, Citizens' Forum on Canada's Future, *Report to the People and Government of Canada* (Chair: Keith Spicer) (27 June 1991); and Canada, Parliament, *Report of the Special Joint Committee on the Constitution of Canada* (Chairs: G. Beaudoin and D. Dobbie) (28 February 1992) (hereinafter Special Joint Committee).

53 Beaudoin-Edwards, 19.

54 This would seem to have left the unanimous procedure vulnerable to indirect amendment using the easier four-region procedure seeing as amendments to the amending formula would have apparently been governed by the easier procedure.

55 Quebec was not to return to the constitutional discussions until August 1992, as discussed below.

amendment procedure. It proposed instead 'that a federal law be enacted which would enable the federal government, at its discretion, to hold a consultative referendum on a constitutional proposal' either to confirm the existence of a national consensus or to facilitate the adoption of the required amending resolutions.[56] In either case the referendum was to require a national majority as well as a majority in each of the four regions. It stopped short of recommending a full-blown constituent assembly made up of specially selected representatives of all sectors of Canadian society. Instead, it opted for a parliamentary solution, proposing the creation of yet another Joint Committee that would consider new federal proposals for large-scale constitutional reform.[57]

A new set of federal proposals appeared in September 1991 in a document entitled *Shaping Canada's Future Together*.[58] This document confirmed that the constitutional agenda now extended well beyond the demands of Quebec, embracing not only entrenchment of the Supreme Court of Canada but also reform of the Senate, aboriginal self-government, legislative and administrative delegation, and more. The proposals were surprisingly vague regarding amendments to the amending formula, although oddly firm in rejecting the Beaudoin-Edwards Committee's regional *veto* proposal only three months after it had been recommended.[59] Federal authorities were clearly of the view that it was a political non-starter as far as other provinces were concerned. The proposals expressed the federal government's general preference for a slightly modified version of the Meech Lake Accord amending formula. Clearly, any hard work regarding changes to the amending formula was being left to the Special Joint Committee on a Renewed Canada which had already been established in response to the Beaudoin-Edwards Committee recommendations.

The Special Joint Committee had been set up in June 1991, immediately upon the publication of the Beaudoin-Edwards Committee's report, referred to above. The federal proposals were made public on 24 September 1991 and on the next day, 25 September 1991, the Special Joint Committee held its first public meeting. It was to hold seventy-eight meetings totalling 227 hours of hearings. It heard from over 700 individuals and received nearly 3 000 submissions before submitting its report in February 1992.[60]

The report was wide-ranging, consistent with the newly-expanded constitutional agenda. Again, the focus here will be on the amending formula, keeping in mind that the prospects for changes to the amending formula were now tied to the progress of a wide array of other constitutional proposals.

The Special Joint Committee dealt with the same, expanded list of amending formula issues that had emerged with Meech and its fall-out, but various changes of emphasis could be sensed. Certain important new proposals now appeared uncontroversial. For example, the Special Joint Committee included the idea of

---

56 Beaudoin-Edwards, 42.
57 Beaudoin-Edwards, 50.
58 Canada, Parliament, *Shaping Our Future Together: Proposals* (Ottawa, 1991).
59 Canada, Parliament, *Shaping Our Future Together: Proposals* (Ottawa, 1991), 23.
60 Special Joint Committee, 3.

reasonable compensation in relation to *any* matter in all of its various proposals.[61] In earlier proposals this idea had seemed more controversial and uncertain. The Special Joint Committee placed special emphasis on the familiar issue of the place of Quebec in the amending formula.

On this key issue the Special Joint Committee made it very clear that in its view resolution of this issue was essential 'if we are to emerge from the current constitutional crisis'.[62] It has already been noted that full compensation in cases of *opting out* was firmly recommended by the Committee. However, *opting out* is useful to Quebec and other provinces in the event of amendments transferring legislative powers; it is of no use when amendments to *federal* institutions are intended. Accordingly, the Committee proposed five approaches to amending the amending formula which might solve this problem:[63]

1) One option is the *unanimity* procedure set out in section 41 of the *Constitution Act, 1982*. It could be expanded to include all the items set out in section 42 which are now subject to the general procedure (with the exception of the establishment of new provinces and the extension of existing provinces which we discuss in detail below). This would mean that the agreement of all provinces would be needed to make changes to representation in the House of Commons, the powers and method of selection of the Senate, the minimum number of members of a province in the Senate and the Supreme Court of Canada....

2) A second option would be to require the consent of two Atlantic provinces, Ontario, Quebec, and two western provinces representing 50 per cent of the population of that region for any amendment to the principle of representation in the House of Commons, the powers and composition of the Senate and the Supreme Court of Canada... This recommendation is similar to other 'regional *veto*' proposals...

3) A third option would be to amend section 42 to require that, with the exception of the creation of new provinces or the extension of existing provinces into the territories, *Quebec must be among the provinces consenting* to any future amendment relating to the matters listed in that section (House of Commons, Senate, Supreme Court of Canada)...

4) A fourth option would be to leave the general procedure for amending the Constitution as it is, but upon the request of any province or combination of provinces representing the regions of Canada, a *referendum* would be required for an amendment under that section to enter into force. Implicit in this suggestion is that Quebec constitutes one of the regions of Canada.

5) A fifth option would be to amend the general procedure for amendment, to *require that Quebec be among the two-thirds of the provinces for all amendments* under that procedure ...

Each of these proposals would indeed have provided a *veto* for Quebec over changes to the federal institutions, although in doing so each would have provided

---

61 Special Joint Committee, 93–94.
62 Special Joint Committee, 92.
63 Special Joint Committee, 93–94 [emphasis added].

a different degree of scope and flexibility. The fourth option was clearly the most radical in that it gave a potential *veto* not to the legislative assembly of Quebec or any other province or region but to the people of that province or region by way of a referendum. And only the first option could be said to respect the idea of the constitutional equality of the provinces, an idea which some provinces had come to insist upon with the same fervour that Quebec had shown in demanding its *veto*. It was not surprising then to see that the proposed accord of July 1992 which was negotiated by the federal government and all provinces except Quebec included a proposal to change the amending formula along the lines described in option one of the Special Joint Committee report.[64]

The July 1992 package was agreed to by the federal government, aboriginal leaders and all provinces except Quebec (which awaited an appropriate offer from the rest of Canada). Whereas the Meech Lake Accord would have made a number of changes that were principally designed to satisfy Quebec's demands, the July 1992 package had a much grander design. It included provisions regarding social and economic union, regional development, a reformed Senate, a constitutionally entrenched Supreme Court of Canada, a re-allocation of federal and provincial powers and aboriginal self-government. The size of the package reflected the attempt to satisfy or at least appease all major constitutional actors in Canada. This of course raised the constitutional stakes, and this even before Quebec had expressed a firm intention to negotiate on the basis of this package.

It has already been noted that the July 1992 package proposed amendments to the amending formula to ensure that any changes to the Senate or Supreme Court of Canada that had been governed by the general procedure should henceforth be governed by the *unanimous consent procedure*. Not surprisingly, the July 1992 package suggested that reasonable compensation should be available in all instances of *opting out*. This package then awaited reaction from Quebec and from a disaffected Canadian public.

Even if the Canadian public remained unenthusiastic, reaction from the government of Quebec was sufficiently positive to organise a series of meetings in August 1992 with the parties to the July 1992 package (federal, aboriginal and nine-province provincial representatives) and a Quebec delegation. Those meetings culminated on 28 August 1992 with unanimous agreement on what came to be known as the Charlottetown Accord.[65]

Amidst much fanfare, Prime Minister Brian Mulroney announced to Parliament, on 8 September 1992, that in accordance with the post-Meech Lake pledge to consult the people over constitutional change, there would be a plebiscite (hence, non-binding), to be held on 26 October 1992, in which Canadians would be asked

---

64 See the 'Summary of proposed constitutional package' in *The Globe and Mail*, 11 July 1992, A6 (hereinafter July 1992 package).

65 See Canada, Consensus Report on the Constitution, *Final Text* (28 August 1992) (hereinafter Charlottetown Accord). This agreement was eventually put into legal form in Canada, Consensus Report on the Constitution, *Draft Legal Text* (9 October 1992) (hereinafter October 1992 Draft Legal Text).

to endorse the Charlottetown Accord.⁶⁶ In the event of a positive response to the plebiscite, the formal, legal ratification process would begin, facilitated, politically-speaking, by a nation-wide popular mandate. The proposed changes to Part V recommended in the Charlottetown Accord resembled closely the July 1992 package discussed above. The Accord, and particularly the October 1992 Draft Legal Text provided a much higher degree of precision.

In the end, the Charlottetown Accord and the detailed October 1992 Draft Legal Text came to nothing. The people of Canada voted overwhelmingly against the constitutional proposals in the 26 October 1992 referendum. Only forty-four percent of Canadians supported the Accord, and, by region, only three provinces and one territory voted in favour.⁶⁷ The Accord had failed to obtain the support of the Canadian people despite what Prime Minister Mulroney had referred to as 'the most far-ranging and thorough process of consultation and discussion ever held by a Canadian Government and, perhaps, by any government in a modern industrialised State'.⁶⁸

The Quebec Referendum and the Act Respecting Constitutional Amendments, 1996

Three years after the failure of the Charlottetown Accord the country was once again in the midst of a constitutional crisis, as the province of Quebec prepared to vote on yet another referendum on sovereignty. On 24 October 1995, towards the end of the Quebec referendum campaign, Prime Minister Chrétien promised that his government would not proceed with any constitutional change without the consent of Quebec. With the narrow defeat of the sovereignty option, Chrétien was eager to make his promise more concrete. This could have been done by means of formal constitutional amendment under the unanimous consent procedure of section 41, but given that this level of consent was unachievable, he opted to honour his promise by enacting federal legislation to limit a federal minister's ability to introduce a constitutional amendment resolution to Parliament.

The federal bill was introduced on 29 November 1995 and adopted by February, 1996. Essentially, the *Act Respecting Constitutional Amendments, 1996* ⁶⁹ provides that no minister shall present a constitutional resolution to Parliament unless the amendment has first been consented to by a majority of provinces, including Ontario, Quebec, British Columbia, two Western Provinces and two Atlantic provinces.⁷⁰

---

66 See Canada, Office of the Prime Minister, *Notes for an Address by Prime Minister Brian Mulroney* (8 September 1992). The plebiscite question was to be: 'Do you agree that the constitution of Canada should be renewed on the basis of the agreement reached on August 28, 1992?'

67 *Maclean's [Magazine]*, 2 November 1992, 18 and 13.

68 See *Notes for an Address by Prime Minister Brian Mulroney* (8 September 1992), p. 1.

69 SC 1996, chapter 1.

70 Pelletier criticises the 1996 *Act* for rendering the Canadian amendment process significantly more rigid, effectively turning the 7/50 general procedure into what he calculates as a 7/93 procedure – or virtual unanimity (Pelletier 1996, 335–336). Both the addition of British Columbia as a region and the requirement of two Atlantic provinces produce the added rigidity.

There is no indication in the Act as to how such consent is to be manifested. Three categories of amendment are expressly exempted from the Act: section 41 (in which all provinces already had a veto); section 43 (where any province to which an amendment applied would already have a veto; and subsection 38(3) (where the right to opt out provides sufficient protection). Sections 44 and 45 are also excluded, the latter because it does not concern the federal Parliament, and the former because it deals with federal legislation rather than resolutions.[71] As Benoît Pelletier has pointed out, although the 1996 Act can be repealed at any moment, it is difficult to imagine the political circumstances that would permit such a repeal (Pelletier 1996, 326). Consequently, the 1996 Act is likely to be part of the constitutional amendment machinery for some time to come. However, due to its unentrenched status as federal legislation, it is not the sort of constitutional protection that is likely to satisfy those in Quebec who demand a *constitutional veto*.

The 'regional veto statute' was accompanied by a resolution of the House of Commons which recognised Quebec as a 'distinct society' and that recorded the House's intention to be 'guided by that reality'. While the statute may show sympathy to Quebec in *protective* terms, by making the amendment process more rigid, it makes affirmative changes to the Constitution (by way of *promotion*) more difficult. This can be seen to militate *against* 'distinct society' recognition.

The Secession Reference and the Clarity Act

It is arguable that for a Quebec frustrated by failed constitutional negotiations, the assertion of an automatic right to secession has replaced the *veto* in terms of both *protection* and *promotion* of Quebec's interests. For those who deny that there was any justice in Quebec's post-1982 sense of grievance, the failure of reforming efforts was a good thing, and the *Secession Reference*[72] a bad thing, in that the latter failed to put Quebec in its deemed proper place. However, for those who feel that there is much more to discuss, despite the apparent difficulty in finding acceptable solutions, the Supreme Court of Canada's rejection of the extremes in the *Secession Reference* (i.e., outright denial of the possibility of Quebec's independence, on the one hand, and assertions of a unilateral right to secession on the other) is helpful. It points

---

71 Pelletier summarises the application of the Act as follows: (1) most of the provisions of the Charter (*i.e.*, excluding only those which are governed by ss. 41 or 43); (2) reform of central institutions; (3) creation of new provinces; (4) adoption of a 'Canada Clause'; (5) constitutional recognition of Quebec's particularity; (6) adoption of certain measures recognising Canada's linguistic duality; (7) limitation of the federal spending power; (8) entrenchment of certain administrative agreements; (9) constitutionalisation of measures destined to encourage the social and economic union of Canada; (10) adoption of constitutional measures favourable to native people; (11) adoption of constitutional measures aimed at making obligatory federal-provincial or interprovincial conferences; (12) adoption of constitutional provisions allowing delegation of powers or other legislative asymmetries (Pelletier 1996, 329–331). It will be observed that many of these items were included in the failed Meech and Charlottetown proposed amendments.

72 *Reference re Secession of Quebec* [1998] 1 SCR 753.

the parties back to the ongoing processes of consultation, negotiation, initiation and amendment.

The federal response to the *Secession Reference* was the so-called Clarity Act.[73] Section 1 of the Act sets out requirements for 'clear' questions regarding independence, and does so in terms that would have disqualified both of the Quebec sovereignty referendum questions. Section 2 deals with the issue of whether the result in an independence referendum is clear, specifying criteria such as the size of the majority and the percentage of eligible voters, but stopping short of detailing specific requirements. Section 3 recognises that there is no right to unilateral secession and specifies a range of issues that would have to be addressed in negotiations before an independence-directed constitutional amendment could be proposed.

Recent Reactions from Quebec

The *Parti québécois* government in Quebec also enacted its interpretation of the *Secession Reference*: An Act respecting the exercise of the fundamental rights and prerogatives of the Quebec people and the Quebec State.[74] Section 3 contradicts the federal legislation by asserting that Quebec does in fact have a right 'to determine alone' its legal and constitutional status. It also contradicts section 2 of the Clarity Act by specifying that a 'clear' vote is 'fifty percent plus one'.

The *Parti québécois* has now ceded power once again to the provincial Liberal Party. In 2001, while still in Opposition, the Liberal Party published *A Project for Quebec: Affirmation, Autonomy and Leadership*.[75] The Pelletier Report is interesting in the way that it wrestles with some of the issues that have been raised in this chapter, and accordingly it will be discussed in some detail.

In a section entitled 'A Quebec That is Both Singular and Plural', the Pelletier Report situates 'the French Fact in Quebec' alongside and interacting with 'the Anglophone community and the cultural communities'. Regarding the French Fact the report is clear that:[76]

> The affirmation of the French Fact [is] a priority because Quebeckers are still extremely concerned about the development of the Quebec language and culture. The French Fact is the basis of Quebec's particularity; it explains why Quebeckers have a different relationship with Canada, and is the reason Quebec must assume a collective responsibility without equal in North America.

The report is full of references to Quebec's role as 'a focal point of the French language and culture'.[77] Quebec is 'the principal bearer of the torch of French civilization in

---

73 An Act to give effect to the requirement for clarity as set out in the opinion of the Supreme Court of Canada in the Quebec Secession Reference, SC 2000, c. 26.

74 SQ 2000, c. 46.

75 Quebec, Special Committee of the Quebec Liberal Party on the Political and Constitutional Future of Quebec Society, *A Project for Quebec: Affirmation, Autonomy and Leadership: Final Report* (October 2001) (hereinafter the Pelletier Report).

76 Pelletier Report, 17.

77 Pelletier Report, 30.

Canada and North America'.[78] The report recommends specific measure in order to fulfil this role: solidarity networks and new alliances, cooperation agreements and partnerships, financial and institutional support and other specific sectors for action. And while 'there is no doubt that Quebec society has a singular character, ... it is also plural in the sense that it is composed of people of various origins'.[79]

In terms of issues relating to constitutional amendment, we see, for example, a renewed call for recognition of 'Quebec's specificity' as an interpretive provision in the Constitution.[80] There is also an interest in the reform of federal institutions, including the Senate and the Supreme Court of Canada.[81] In terms of the amending formula itself, the report links up with the historical claims by Quebec:[82]

> The 1982 amendment procedure ... is flawed because, among other things, it does not grant Quebec a true constitutional right of *veto* with respect to amendments that concern some of the most fundamental relations in the federation. In other words, such amendments may currently be made without Quebec's consent.

In terms of the reasons for Quebec's claim, the report again builds on arguments made since at least the 1950s:[83]

> It seems to us that a right of *veto* would be most appropriate, since Quebec is the main province shouldering the responsibility of ensuring the survival of the French language in Canada ... Ideally, therefore, Quebec should be given a right of *veto* with respect to constitutional amendments that may significantly affect federal-provincial relations...

In order to achieve *veto* protection, the report reverts to a proposal from the early 1990s, suggesting that all 7/50 amendments should include Quebec. However, here a dose of political realism appears: 'This suggestion is not likely to please the other provinces because, in the end, only Quebec would have a right of *veto* in relation to the amendments in question'.[84] The reality is that 'we can no longer reasonably consider granting only Quebec such a right of *veto*'.[85]

In a rare moment of Ottawa-Quebec convergence the report recommends that 'it might be appropriate to consider replacing, in part, the current "7-50" procedure with a "*regional veto*" similar – but not identical – to that found in An Act Respecting Constitutional Amendments'.[86] The report goes even further than the federal Act in recommending that the '*regional veto*' formula could be extended to cover matters now dealt with under section 41 unanimity rules. Again returning to now-accepted

---

78 Pelletier Report, 32.
79 Pelletier Report, 17.
80 Pelletier Report, 59.
81 Pelletier Report, 60, 63.
82 Pelletier Report, 66 [emphasis added].
83 Pelletier Report, 66 [emphasis added].
84 Pelletier Report, 66 [emphasis added].
85 Pelletier Report, 66 [emphasis added].
86 Pelletier Report, 66 [emphasis added].

proposals, the report recommends that compensation be extended beyond education and culture to all cases of opting out.[87]

The report concludes on amendment by stating that its 'proposals regarding the right of *veto* for Quebec are part of a long-term vision of Canada and stem from our desire to ensure that Quebec plays a role in Canada's evolution'.[88] The first point regarding this being a long-term goal is absolutely right; however the second point is a problem. Many in the rest of Canada have lost faith in Quebec's desire to play an ongoing role in Canada's future and therefore mistrust Quebec's ability to wield its veto responsibly.

Conclusion

This chapter began with a matrix of variables that are relevant to Quebec's ongoing debates with the rest of the country regarding how best to accommodate the province in the constitutional amending formula. The balance of the chapter attempted to provide a historical and current context for those variables. It is now time to summarise and to offer some conclusions.

	Protection	**Promotion**	**Federalism**
Unanimity	Yes	No	Yes
Veto	Yes	Yes	Yes
Opting Out	No	Yes	No

Figure 9.1   Quebec and the Amending Formula

As indicated in Figure 9.1, we have seen that *unanimity* offers *protection* for Quebec's interests, including its interest in *federal institutions*; however it puts the *promotion* of those interests in a straitjacket due to its inherent rigidity. *Opting out* offers no *protection* and no guarantee of a voice in *federalism*, but it clearly provides opportunities for Quebec to *promote* its difference by occasionally going its own way. Only a *veto* provides satisfactory *protection, promotion* and input into the development of the *federation*. This no doubt explains in part why so many proposals regarding the amending formula, both before and after 1982, keep coming back to the same form of the veto as the objectively appropriate solution to Quebec's place in the Constitution.

There may be a role for unanimous provincial consent regarding a very small range of central or sacrosanct constitutional amendments, but using it as a general procedure is far too rigid for all concerned, and notably for Quebec. Necessary constitutional changes in the future, both for Quebec and for the rest of the country, are likely to be frustrated if *unanimity* becomes the general procedure for constitutional amendment. *Opting out* with compensation may add some useful flexibility, but it

---

87 Pelletier Report, 67.
88 Pelletier Report, 67.

cannot help where reform of *federal* matters is concerned and where *opting out* is impossible (most obviously with reform of *federal institutions*). It is therefore not surprising that the more flexible regional *veto* approach (including a *veto* for Quebec) has been preferred by so many commentators since the early 1970s.

So if constitutional logic were all that was relevant, the *veto* approach would be preferred. But politically matters are nowhere near that simple. Quebec can argue for a *veto* on the basis of its population and size, but so long as the idea of the constitutional equality of the provinces is presumed that will be a non-starter. A case needs to be made for Quebec's distinct role in Canadian society. That case was convincingly articulated by André Laurendeau in the *Preliminary Report of the Royal Commission on Bilingualism and Biculturalism* (RCBB 1965, App. III). As explained by Michael Oliver, Research Director for the Commission:

> The crucial insight of the B and B Commission was that a stable base for French-English cooperation cannot be achieved just by increasing French minority rights in Canada as a whole (seen as a single community) but must also involve the exercise of a set of powers, adequate for community development, by a common jurisdiction (Quebec) in which the country-wide minority (Francophones) is a majority. (Oliver 1993, 326)

The Pelletier Report picks up on this sort of thinking to a great extent. However, it is not enough for the Liberal government in Quebec to pick up on the rhetoric, especially if a successor government in Quebec is likely to take a more isolationist attitude. But if Quebec does rediscover its historical role within Canada, and if this role can be articulated not just by leaders in Quebec but by counterparts in Ottawa and the other provinces, then there may eventually be a shift away from rigid adherence to the idea of the constitutional equality of the provinces.

This is essentially a matter of trust. If this does not occur, then Quebec's position becomes more like an independent state within a large political entity where the consent of all is required before any changes are made. That has been the case in the European Union for the past forty years, but even Europe would like to move in a more federal direction. Canada can, of course, choose a more confederal or intergovernmental constitutional model. However, if it wishes to preserve its federation and take proper account of the long-standing cultural particularity of Quebec and French Canada, then it may have to abandon strict equality and reunite with the thinking of Laurendeau and those who have shared his point of view.

For now, the right to secession (whether negotiated or declared),[89] has replaced the *veto*. It is the only solution that keeps Quebec's future securely within its own hands. In terms of *protection* and *promotion* it is a crude weapon, and in terms of federalism it negates any secure future for a Confederation stretching from sea to sea. However, if Quebec takes up its traditional role as leading *protector* and *promoter* of French-Canadian language and culture and stops threatening to use the crude *veto* of secession, and if the rest of the country remembers how indispensable that role is, the time may come when all parties accept that Quebec should have a truly *constitutional veto* (however it is dressed up for modern times). For the moment, we

---

89 Of course only the former would be authorised according to the Supreme Court of Canada in the *Secession Reference*.

are in a period when the federal government and legislature are doing most of the work for the French language and culture across Canada, but if Laurendeau was right then this will never be sufficient. French language and culture across Canada will not survive without being sustained by a strong Quebec.

While Quebec and the rest of Canada are rediscovering a workable level of trust, it is probably a good thing that the federal Parliament has guaranteed Quebec's *veto* by legislative means. If it turns out that the presence of an independence-leaning *Parti québécois* makes bestowal of that trust on the Quebec National Assembly difficult, then perhaps that trust should be bestowed on the *people* of Quebec. The present formula could be altered to require a referendum with regional *vetoes* for all amendments under the general procedure where full compensation is not available. Given that the people of Quebec already have a right to vote for negotiated secession, it would seem advantageous to give them a right to influence the course of change *within* the Canadian Constitution. Doing so by means of a *unanimous consent* formula would make necessary constitutional change excessively difficult; doing so by means of one of the many regional *veto* formulas that have been so thoroughly canvassed over the past forty years would satisfy the demands of *protection, promotion* and *federalism*.

References

Beaudoin, G.-A. et al. (eds) (1981), *Mécanismes pour une nouvelle constitution*, Ottawa: Éditions de l'université d'Ottawa.

Black, C. (1976), *Duplessis*, Toronto: McClelland & Stewart.

Black, E.R. (1975), *Divided Loyalties*, Montreal: McGill-Queen's Press.

Canada (1987), *Strengthening the Canadian Federation: The Constitution Amendment, 1987* (Meech Lake Accord), Ottawa.

Canadian Federal-Provincial Relations Office (1990), *Amending the Constitution of Canada: A Discussion Paper*, Ottawa, 9.

Canadian Parliament, Special Joint Committee of the Senate and House of Commons (1991), *The Process for Amending the Constitution of Canada*, Chairs: G. Beaudoin and J. Edwards, 20 June.

Dawson, R.M. (1975), *The Government of Canada*, 5th Edition, Toronto: University of Toronto Press.

Favreau, Hon. G. (1965), *The Amendment of the Constitution of Canada*, Ottawa: Queen's Printer.

Fournier, P. (1990), 'L'Échec du Lac Meech : un point du vue québécois', in Watts, R.L. and Brown, D.M. (eds), *Canada: The State of the Federation: 1990*, Kingston: IPPR.

Gérin-Lajoie, P. (1950), *Constitutional Amendment in Canada*, Toronto: University of Toronto Press.

Hurley, J.R. (1996), *Amending Canada's Constitution: History, Processes, Problems and Prospects*, Ottawa: Canada Communications Group.

Johnson, Hon. D. (1968), 'Opening Address, Confederation of Tomorrow Conference', Toronto, 27–30 November 1967, in Quebec, *The Government of Quebec and the Constitution*, Quebec City, 16–23.

Kwavnick, D. (ed.) (1973), *The Tremblay Report*, Toronto: McLelland & Stewart.

Laforest, G. (1995), *Trudeau and the End of a Canadian Dream*, translated by P.L. Browne and M. Weinroth, Montreal: McGill-Queen's Press, originally published as Laforest, G. (1992), *Trudeau et la fin d'un rêve canadien*, Québec: Septentrion.

Livingston, W.S. (1956), *Federalism and Constitutional Change*, Oxford: Oxford University Press.

McWhinney, E. (1982), *Canada and the Constitution, 1979–1982*, Toronto: University of Toronto Press.

Morin, J.-Y. (1967), 'Les Dessous de la Formule Fulton-Favreau', *McGill Law Journal*, 12, 394.

Oliver, M. (1993), 'The Impact of the Royal Commission on Bilingualism and Biculturalism on Constitutional Thought and Practice in Canada', *International Journal of Canadian Studies*, 7–8, 315–332.

Oliver, P. (2005), *The Constitution of Independence: The Development of Constitutional Theory in Australia, Canada and New Zealand*, Oxford: Oxford University Press.

— (1999a), 'Canada's Two Solitudes: Constitutional and International Law in *Reference re Secession of Quebec*', *International Journal on Minority and Group Rights*, 6, 63–93, reprinted in S. Tierney, (ed.) (2000), *Accommodating National Identity: New Approaches in International and Domestic Law*, London: Kluwer, 65–88.

— (1999b), 'Canada, Quebec, and Constitutional Amendment', *University of Toronto Law Journal*, 49, 519–610.

— (1994), 'The 1982 Patriation of the Canadian Constitution: Reflections on Continuity and Change', *Revue juridique Thémis*, 2, 875–914, reprinted in Baudouin, J-L. *et al.* (eds), *Mélanges Jean Beetz*, Montreal: Thémis, 799–838.

Pelletier, B. (1996), *La modification constitutionnelle au Canada*, Scarborough: Carswell.

Quebec (1956), *Report of the Royal Commission of Inquiry on Constitutional Problems*, Chair: T. Tremblay, Québec: Éditeur Officiel.

Quebec, Government of (1979), *Quebec-Canada: A New Deal*, Quebec: Éditeur Officiel.

Quebec Special Committee of the Liberal Party on the Political and Constitutional Future of Quebec Society (2001), *A Project for Quebec: Affirmation, Autonomy and Leadership: Final Report* (Pelletier Report), October.

Rémillard, G. (1983), *Le fédéralisme canadien: Tome I: La Loi constitutionnelle de 1867*, Montreal: Québec/Amérique.

— (1985), *Le fédéralisme canadien: Tome II: Le rapatriement de la Constitution*, Montréal: Québec/Amérique.

Royal Commission on Bilingualism and Biculturalism (RCBB) (1965), *A Preliminary Report of the Royal Commission on Bilingualism and Biculturalism*, Ottawa.

Rumilly, R. (1948), *L'autonomie provinciale*, Montreal: Fides.

Scott, S. A. (1967), 'Editor's Diary: The Search for an Amending Process (1960-67)', *McGill L.J.*, 12, 351.
— (1982), 'Pussycat, Pussycat, or Patriation and the New Constitutional Amendment Processes', *University of Western Ontario Law Review*, 20, 283.
Simeon, Richard (1972), *Federal-Provincial Diplomacy*, Toronto, University of Toronto Press.
— (1990), 'Why did the Meech Lake Accord Fail?', in Watts and Brown (eds), *Canada: The State of the Federation: 1990*, Kingston: IPPR.
Trudeau, P.E. (1968), *Federalism for the Future*, Ottawa.
Webber, J. (1994), *Reimagining Canada: Language, Culture, Community and the Canadian Constitution*, Kingston: McGill-Queen's Press.

Chapter 10

Understanding the Rule of Law in Canada

Warren Newman

Advocates tend to read into the principle of the rule of law anything which supports their particular view of what the law should be. (Strayer, J.A., Federal Court of Appeal, *Singh v Canada*, [2000] 3 CF 185)

Introduction

The Constitution of Canada, a 'living tree', in Lord Sankey's oft-quoted phrase, is a hybrid plant with deep, cross-cultural roots, combining the British[1] framework of common law and political convention with a written constitution in the American style: a division of powers between central and local state governments, entrenched guarantees of fundamental rights, and judicial review of the validity of Acts passed by the legislative branch. The rule of law is one of the most evocative of the animating principles of the Constitution of Canada – on a par with federalism and democracy, an independent judiciary, and respect for minorities. Crucial to an understanding of many of those principles are foundational rules and values closely associated with the British tradition: a constitutional monarchy, parliamentary sovereignty, and the conventions of responsible government. Indeed, it is largely through that tradition that Canadians have inherited the rule of law as a basic proposition of their constitution.

The rule of law is the first principle of the Canadian constitutional framework, governing the provisions of the constitutional text and under-girding the relationship between the supreme law and the political conventions of the Constitution. The rule of law is also a fundamental tenet of Canada's legal system, grounding the development and application not only of constitutional law *per se* but also of other great branches of public law. Moreover, the rule of law embodies one of the basic

---

1 In employing the term, 'British', I am conscious of the debate about the precise meaning of the term in various contexts, and that Bagehot, Dicey and others often spoke of the 'English' constitution. For some, these terms are interchangeable; for others, they ignore the emerging constitutional roles of other institutions, notably the Scottish Parliament, under the devolution statutes. In a Canadian context, the *British North America Act* (as it then was) declared that Canada was to have 'a Constitution similar in Principle to that of the United Kingdom', and thus I have tended to use the 'British' term in referring to that constitutional heritage.

values of the Canadian polity and has been integral to the development of Canada's political culture.

The opening words of the *British North America Act* – now styled the *Constitution Act, 1867* – solemnly record the desire of the original Provinces to be 'federally united into One Dominion under the Crown' and to ensure that Canada be endowed with 'a Constitution similar in Principle to that of the United Kingdom'. Contemporaneously with that statement, Bagehot, Cox, Hearn, Freeman, Anson, and Dicey were formulating a description of the British constitution that embodied not only the doctrine of parliamentary sovereignty and the conventions of constitutional practice but also what Dicey, perhaps first amongst them, was to term the rule of law.

The late Professor E.C.S. Wade, in his substantial essay introducing the tenth edition of Dicey's *The Law of the Constitution*, observed:

> The method of depicting the constitution in terms of principles rather than by description of its details is one which naturally attracts the political scientist, but it is for the lawyer to ensure that the existing rules of constitutional law are not lost in the generalisations which necessarily accompany an exposition of principles. ... Like Dicey we must never lose sight of what are the rules of the constitution in any endeavour to bring up to date the application of the sovereignty of Parliament and the rule of law to modern conditions. (Wade 1958, xx).

One ought to remember that admonition when examining the operation of those principles in Canada's current constitutional context, especially since the advent of the *Canadian Charter of Rights and Freedoms* in 1982. The preamble to the Charter expressly recognises the rule of law as one of the founding principles of Canada, and the provisions of the Charter reflect, *inter alia*, principles of fundamental justice and equality in relation to the law, two key aspects of Dicey's understanding of the rule of law. The provisions of the Charter are, in virtue of section 52 of the *Constitution Act, 1982*, part of the 'supreme law' of Canada. The principle of the rule of law, to the extent that it is reflected in provisions such as sections 7 and 15 of the Charter, thus enjoys an entrenched and pre-eminent constitutional force and status hitherto unknown in a parliamentary system based on the Westminster model.

In the United Kingdom, where the constitution remains essentially flexible and largely unconsolidated, the sovereignty of Parliament remains a dominant characteristic of that system. However, that principle has come under increasing scrutiny in recent years by advocates of a more expansive and controlling view of the rule of law. Commentators such as Trevor Allan have rejected Dicey's positivist conception of the rule of law, where 'law' means primarily whatever Parliament has established or altered by statute. Professor Allan, in a potent admixture of moral philosophy, political theory and public law, has argued strenuously for 'a liberal theory of the rule of law' that would limit the sovereign power of Parliament by an appeal to principles of liberal constitutionalism and justice, and 'the common law constitution' of Britain (Allan 1992; 2003). Just as forcefully, Jeffrey Goldsworthy has argued that the doctrine of parliamentary sovereignty has a venerable pedigree, and that throughout its long history British judges have never had the authority to invalidate statutes. Professor Goldsworthy submits that '[j]udicial review of the validity of legislation is not an essential prerequisite for the protection of human rights and democracy in every legal system committed to those ideals.' Any move towards asserting the supremacy of the judiciary over Parliament through judicial review in the United Kingdom, Australia and New Zealand should be accomplished transparently, 'by consensus, rather than judicial fiat.' That, he states, 'is surely a requirement of democracy.' It is also, in his view, 'a requirement of law.' (Goldsworthy 1999, 279).

In Canada, adherents of an expansive view of the rule of law include (albeit with certain reservations) Professors David Dyzenhaus (2000; 2003; 2000; 1999) and, more generally from the perspective of *lex non scripta* as fundamental law, Mark Walters (2001), the latter arguing much along the lines of Allan for the 'common law constitution', but with a critical examination of the premises of the Supreme Court of Canada's rulings in the *New Brunswick Broadcasting* case, the *Provincial Court Judges Reference* and the *Quebec Secession Reference*, which have revised our understanding of the residual but significant role played by unwritten constitutional principles in the Canadian constitutional system.[2] Sceptics, particularly with respect to the Supreme Court's unbridled enthusiasm in those cases for unwritten constitutional principles, include Professors Peter Hogg,[3] Jamie Cameron (2002) and Jean Leclair (2002). Amongst those whom one might be tempted to characterize[4] as ranging between the prudently supportive and the agnostic are Professors Patrick Monahan,[5] Robin Elliott (2001), and Sujit Choudhry (2001). Professor Allan Hutchinson, a consistent critic of judicial activism (who has long seen it as stifling the development of direct democracy), is one legal theorist who has come to appreciate[6] that 'the beauty of the judgment' in the *Quebec Secession Reference* 'is that it treats the rule of law as only one principle in the constitutional compact and avoids the temptation to make it do more work than it reasonably should.' (Hutchinson 1999, 198).[7]

All of this begs a deeper question: does the rule of law, as a normative concept, mean only the rule of just or 'good' law? For more than a century, the watchword of the courts was that it was not their role to pass judgment on the wisdom of Parliament's legislative policy choices, but simply upon their legality. Today, can (or should) the principle of the rule of law be employed by the courts to impose procedural and substantive requirements on Parliament (or remedies of invalidity and the like), even when *no* breach of the *provisions* of the Constitution of Canada respecting

---

2   Other proponents of broader resort to unwritten principles include D. Gibson (1999).

3   Hogg, *Constitutional Law of Canada*, (current).

4   Not unfairly, I hope, since I count myself amongst them: Newman 2001; 2001–2002; 2003.

5   Professor Monahan has waxed and waned on the significance of the rule of law as a constitutional principle, from anti-foundationalist critic (in Hutchinson and Monahan (1987)) to enthusiast of the principle as a supreme norm (Monahan 1995), before reclaiming the somewhat critical middle ground (in Monahan 1999).

6   On this point, see generally, Newman 1999. (I disclose that I was of counsel for the Attorney General of Canada in the *Secession Reference*.)

7   Professor Hutchinson's views have also undergone some transformation over the years, and he now identifies himself as a 'non-foundationalist' rather than an 'anti-foundationalist'.

the division of powers or the Charter of Rights or other entrenched guarantees[8] has been established? Would that be consistent with the developing indigenous culture of Canadian constitutionalism?

The Supreme Court of Canada, Constitutionalism and the Rule of Law

The Supreme Court of Canada has called the rule of law 'a fundamental postulate of our constitutional structure'[9] and a 'highly textured expression, importing many things ... but conveying, for example, a sense of orderliness, of subjection to known legal rules and of executive accountability to legal authority.'[10] In its landmark opinion in the *Quebec Secession Reference*, the Supreme Court stated that the elements of the rule of law are threefold. First, 'the rule of law provides that the law is supreme over the acts of both government and private persons. There is, in short, one rule law for all.' Secondly, 'the rule of law requires the creation and maintenance of an actual order of positive laws which preserves and embodies the more general principle of normative order'. Thirdly, 'the exercise of all public power must find its ultimate source in a legal rule'; in other words, 'the relationship between the state and the individual must be regulated by law.' Together, 'these three considerations make up a principle of profound constitutional and political significance.'[11]

> At its most basic level, the rule of law vouchsafes to the citizens and residents of the country a stable, predictable and ordered society in which to conduct their affairs. It provides a shield for individuals from arbitrary state action.[12]

The Supreme Court also took pains, in the *Quebec Secession Reference*, to articulate a distinct but interrelated principle of constitutionalism. The essence of this principle, the Court stated, is reflected in subsection 52(1) of the *Constitution Act, 1982*, which provides that '[t]he Constitution of Canada is the supreme law of Canada, and any law that is inconsistent with the provisions of the Constitution is, to the extent of the inconsistency, of no force or effect.'

> Simply put, the constitutionalism principle requires that all government action comply with the Constitution. The rule of law principle requires that all government action must comply with the law, including the Constitution. This Court has noted on several occasions that with the adoption of the *Charter*, the Canadian system of government was transformed to a significant extent from a system of Parliamentary supremacy to one of constitutional supremacy. The Constitution binds all governments, both federal and provincial, including the executive branch ... They may not transgress its provisions:

---

8   E.g., s.133 of the *Constitution Act, 1867* or s.35 of the *Constitution Act, 1982*.
9   *Roncarelli* v. *Duplessis*, [1959] S.C.R. 121, para. 142, *per* Rand J.
10 *Reference re Resolution to amend the Constitution*, [1981] 1 S.C.R. 753, 805–6.
11 *Reference re Secession of Quebec*, [1998] 2 S.C.R. 217, *per curiam*, para. 72 (incorporating passages from *Reference re Manitoba Language Rights*, [1985] 1 S.C.R. 721, para. 747-52, and *Reference re Remuneration of Judges of the Provincial Court*, [1997] 3 S.C.R. 3, para. 10).
12 *Ibid.*, para. 70.

indeed, their sole claim to exercise lawful authority rests in the powers allocated to them under the Constitution, and can come from no other source.[13]

This is a ringing declaration on the importance of constitutionalism and the rule of law in Canada, and a powerful affirmation by the Supreme Court of the legal and normative value that must be accorded to those principles by governments and citizens alike. The Court's exposition contains, however, some implicit assumptions about the nature of the rule of law and constitutionalism in Canada. These premises are essential to an understanding of the rule of law in this country, and to the distinction that must be drawn between what the late Justice John Sopinka aptly characterised as *legal* constitutionalism and *political* constitutionalism.[14]

When the Supreme Court stated in the *Quebec Secession Reference* that 'all government action must comply with the law, including the Constitution,' it should be clear that here the Court was referring to what Dicey called the *law* of the Constitution, as opposed to the *conventions* of the Constitution. Conventions are unwritten, customary rules of constitutional behaviour and conduct that are binding on governmental actors in a *political*, rather than a *legal*, sense. This fundamental distinction was recognised by a majority of the Court in the *Patriation Reference*, wherein it was stated that '[i]n contradistinction to the laws of the constitution, they [*i.e.*, conventions] are not enforced by the courts' and 'the legal system from which they are distinct does not contemplate formal sanctions for their breach.'[15]

Rather, the courts are concerned primarily with breaches of the provisions of the Constitution. It is to these that subs. 52(1) of the *Constitution Act, 1982* makes reference when it speaks of the 'supreme *law*' of Canada; any law that is inconsistent with 'the *provisions* of the Constitution' is of no force or effect. 'The Constitution binds all governments', the Court states; '[t]hey may not transgress its *provisions*,' and 'their sole claim to exercise *lawful authority* rests in the powers allocated to them under the Constitution, and can come from no other source.' Those are all statements about the *law* of the Constitution, as embodied in its provisions.

Thus, although, as the Court recognised in the *Patriation Reference*, 'it is perfectly appropriate to say that to violate a convention is to do something which is unconstitutional although it entails no direct legal consequence' and 'constitutional conventions plus constitutional law equal the total constitution of the country,'[16] the rule expressed in subs. 52(1) of the *Constitution Act, 1982*, the supremacy clause, is essentially a rule of *law*. '[T]he words "constitutional" and "unconstitutional" may also be used,' the Court noted, 'in a strict legal sense, for instance with respect to a statute which is found *ultra vires* or unconstitutional.'[17] The role of the courts is to enforce the *law* of the Constitution. A statute that is found by the courts to be *ultra*

---

13 *Ibid.*, para. 72.
14 *Osborne v. Canada*, [1991] 2 S.C.R. 69: 'Underlying this distinction between constitutional law and constitutional conventions is the contrast between legal and political constitutionalism.'
15 *Reference re Resolution to Amend the Constitution, supra*, para. 880.
16 *Ibid.*, para. 883.
17 *Ibid.*

vires is unconstitutional because it has breached the *provisions* (as opposed to the conventions) of the Constitution.

None of this is to gainsay the significance of constitutional conventions, which, as the Court also affirmed, 'form an integral part of the constitution and the constitutional system,' and which, 'while they are not laws ... may be more important than some laws.'[18]

Nevertheless, the fundamental proposition with respect to the role of the courts remains the same: the courts enforce the *law* of the Constitution. The classical position was captured well by the Court in the following passage:

> Those parts of the Constitution of Canada which are composed of statutory rules and common law rules are generically referred to as *the law of the constitution*. In cases of doubt or dispute, *it is the function of the courts to declare what the law is* and since the law is sometimes breached, it is generally the function of the courts to ascertain whether it has in fact been breached in specific instances and, if so, to apply such sanctions as are contemplated by the law, whether they are punitive sanctions or civil sanctions such as a declaration of nullity. Thus, when a federal or a provincial statute is found by the courts to be in excess of the legislative competence of the legislature which has enacted it, it is declared null and void and the courts refuse to give effect to it. *In this sense it can be said that the law of the constitution is administered or enforced by the courts.*[19]

Some Preliminary Observations on the Nature of the Rule of Law in Canada

Much of the preceding analysis might be taken as settled law, were it not for the growing recognition, by the courts in Canada, of the important role played by constitutional *principles*. These organizing principles of the Constitution appear to straddle the divide between constitutional law and constitutional conventions, insofar as they infuse the *provisions* of the constitutional text with constitutional meaning, and yet also provide the *raison d'être* for many of the unwritten political rules of conduct embodied in constitutional conventions (Newman 2004, 118). These fundamental principles, our Supreme Court has declared, are the lifeblood of the Constitution. They are said to be 'not merely descriptive' but rather, 'invested with powerful normative force' and 'binding upon both courts and governments'. Constitutional principles 'emerge from an understanding of the constitutional text itself, the historical context, and previous interpretations of constitutional meaning.'[20]

Both constitutional *conventions* and constitutional *provisions* are '*normative*', in that both impose rules in relation to governance that are held to be binding on the conduct of political actors. However, only constitutional provisions establish *legal* rules enforceable by the courts. The norms embodied by constitutional conventions are not rules of law. What, then, is the status of unwritten constitutional *principles*? Certainly, the fact that these principles (such as federalism and democracy) are at the heart of constitutional conventions is not enough to transform those conventions into

---

18 *Ibid.*
19 Para. 877 [emphasis added].
20 *Reference re Secession of Quebec, supra*, paras. 32 and 54.

rules having the force of law. However, when constitutional principles are employed by the courts in construing the written *provisions* of the Constitution, they act as *legal principles* guiding the scope and application of the constitutional text.

This brings us to the nub of the issue. The '*rule of law*' is a foundational principle of the Constitution of Canada, and as such it is relevant to the underlying contexts of both political constitutionalism and legal constitutionalism in this country. However, I shall argue that a proper understanding of the function performed by the rule of law as a *legal* norm ought to be shaped with reference to the development of that principle in the largely 'unwritten' tradition of the British constitutional system; other principles integral to that system, including the principle of parliamentary sovereignty; the supremacy, in the Canadian constitutional framework, of the provisions of the *Constitution Acts, 1867 to 1982* (including the *Canadian Charter of Rights and Freedoms*); and the appropriate role to be played by the judiciary in Canada in determining the validity of statutes and regulations enacted by or under the constitutional authority conferred upon Parliament and the provincial legislatures, respectively.

Moreover, the principle of the rule of law, pivotal though it is as a basic value of the Canadian constitutional system, should not be assumed to operate in the same manner, or with the same direct legal force, as a *provision* of the Constitution of Canada. Whilst the rule of law can be invoked in furtherance of the interpretation and application of constitutional provisions, and can thereby influence – sometimes profoundly – the response as to whether a given statute or regulation is consistent with the terms of the Constitution, the courts should not, in my view, attempt to use the rule-of-law principle independently to invalidate such legislation. Subsection 52(1) of the *Constitution Act, 1982* mandates the courts to strike down any law that is inconsistent with the *provisions* of the Constitution. The rule of law is a broadly textured constitutional principle, not a specific provision. The expression is a convenient and evocative way of encapsulating a series of propositions and understandings about the place of law in a stable, civil society; what the Americans eloquently term 'a government of laws, not of men,'[21] or what the French aptly call *un État de droit*. The French version of the preamble to the *Canadian Charter of Rights and Freedoms* speaks of '*la primauté du droit*': literally, the primacy of law; often referred to by jurists as *le principe de légalité*. The French version of the *Canadian Bill of Rights* of 1960 captured the meaning nicely in the expression, '*le regne du droit*' – again, literally, *the reign of law*, or governed by law.

Whilst elements of the notion of the rule of law form part of the common law principles relating to natural justice, 'the rule of law' is not, in and of itself, a *rule* of law – at least, not in the substantive sense of a particular requirement of positive constitutional law (although it may be reflected in the law's provisions). Administrative action that is inconsistent with a governing legal rule is unlawful, and can therefore be said to offend the principle of the rule of law. However, it

---

21 The expression is attributed to John Adams, who employed it in Article XXX of the Declaration of Rights in the Constitution of the Commonwealth of Massachusetts, 1780. Adams borrowed it from James Harrington, who had described republican government as 'the empire of laws and not of men' in *The Commonwealth of Oceana*, 1656.

would be unwise to conflate the principle of the rule of law with a supreme legal rule that might be employed to invalidate legislation on the basis that it fails to meet some *a priori* substantive yardstick or procedural requirement (other than manner-and-form requirements). Canadian courts ought to remain wary of arguments that would have them expand the scope of the principle of the rule of law to constrain the sovereignty of Parliament and of the provincial legislatures beyond the substantive and procedural requirements already imposed on legislative processes and outcomes by the provisions of the Constitution respecting the division of powers and entrenched protections such as those embodied in the Charter of Rights. When the principles of the rule of law and parliamentary sovereignty are reconciled – as they must be in a society where political institutions are both law-abiding *and* democratic – it should be clear that by definition, the rule of law must include *rule by law*.

The instrumentality of law is not, in and of itself, always sufficient to ensure wise, fair and just legislative policy objectives. The rule of law is an essential check on arbitrary and capricious government, but it is, at the end of the day, just one of the basic values and principles that contribute to the political culture of a free and democratic society.

The Operation of the Principle of Parliamentary Sovereignty in Canada

The British theory of the sovereignty of Parliament was rapidly adapted to the context of the application of the Canadian Constitution. The *British North America Act*[22] had recognised in 1867 that Canada was to have a Constitution similar in principle to that of the United Kingdom, and the principle of parliamentary sovereignty was the pre-eminent foundational principle of the latter's constitutional framework. However, unlike the British constitution, the 'Constitution of Canada', to the degree it was embodied in the provisions of the *Constitution Act, 1867*, was in several respects a controlling document similar in character to the Constitution of the United States of America. Like the American constitution, the Canadian instrument provided for a federal system, under which legislative and executive powers were distributed between a central parliament on the one hand and provincial legislatures on the other. Indeed, the Parliament of Canada and the legislatures of the provinces were established by the *Constitution Act, 1867* and derived all of their legal authority from that instrument.

The hybrid nature of the Constitution of Canada led Dicey to criticize the 'official mendacity' (Dicey 1959 Edition, 153) expressed in the preamble to the *British North America Act*. The Constitution of Canada was similar in principle to that of the United *States*, not the United *Kingdom*, he asserted, and the courts in both countries were the ultimate arbiters of the constitution (Dicey 1959 Edition, 154–5). Nevertheless, it was that very jurisprudence of the courts which ultimately reconciled the British principle of the sovereignty of Parliament with the Canadian principle of federalism and the supremacy of a written constitutional instrument. The theory that that was articulated by the law lords of the Judicial Committee was that the Parliament of

---

22 30-31 Vict., c. 3 (U.K.); now the *Constitution Act, 1867*.

Canada and the provincial legislatures were each, within the limits prescribed by the *Constitution Act, 1867*, sovereign within their respective spheres.

That theory found expression in the decisions of the Privy Council in *Hodge, Liquidators of the Maritime Bank* and other rulings in the late 19th and early 20th centuries. Lord Watson and his spiritual successor, Viscount Haldane, were amongst its main proponents.[23] In *Hodge* v. *The Queen*, Sir Barnes Peacock, writing for the Judicial Committee, observed that provincial legislatures were 'in no sense delegates of or acting under any mandate from the Imperial Parliament' but rather, exercised:

> authority as plenary and as ample within the limits prescribed by sect. 92 as the Imperial Parliament in the plenitude of its powers possessed and could bestow. Within these limits of subjects and area the local legislature is supreme, and has the same authority as the Imperial Parliament, or the Parliament of the Dominion, would have under like circumstances...[24]

This leitmotif was developed by Lord Watson in *Liquidators of the Maritime Bank*, wherein it was affirmed that the provincial legislature 'possesses powers, not of administration merely, but of legislation, in the strictest sense of that word; and within the limits assigned by sect. 92 of the Act of 1867, these powers are exclusive and supreme.'[25]

In *Attorney-General for Ontario* v. *Attorney-General for Canada*, Earl Loreburn L.C., emphasized that the Judicial Committee was not concerned with the wisdom of policy choices made by the Parliament of Canada, but simply with whether the enactment was *intra vires*, having regard to the legislative powers conferred on Parliament by the *Constitution Act, 1867*.

> *A Court of law has nothing to do with a Canadian Act of Parliament, lawfully passed, except to give it effect according to its tenor*... So far as it is a matter of wisdom or policy, it is for the determination of the Parliament. It is true that from time to time the Courts of this and of other countries, whether under the British flag or not, have to consider and set aside as void, transactions on the ground that they are against public policy. *But no such doctrine can apply to an Act of Parliament. It cannot be too strongly put that with the wisdom or policy of an Act, lawfully passed, no Court has a word to say...* [26]

In *Re the Initiative and Referendum Act*, Viscount Haldane returned to the theme advanced in *Hodge* and *Liquidators of the Maritime Bank*: within 'the limits of area and subjects' imposed by the *British North America Act*, each local legislature 'was to be supreme, and had such powers as the Imperial Parliament possessed in the plenitude of its own freedom before it handed them over to the Dominion and the provinces, in accordance with the scheme of distribution which it enacted in 1867.'[27]

---

23 For analysis of the Privy Council's jurisprudence on the operation of the principle of federalism in Canada, see Newman 2004.
24 [1883-84] 9 A.C. 117, para. 132.
25 [1892] A.C. 437, para. 443.
26 [1912] A.C. 571, para. 582-583 [emphasis added].
27 [1919] A.C. 935, para. 942.

These cases demonstrate that the principle of parliamentary sovereignty was carried into Canada within the framework established by the *Constitution Act, 1867*, and in particular, in relation to the division of powers between the Parliament of Canada and the legislatures of the provinces achieved by that Act. The courts would control the constitutional validity of federal and provincial laws; but insofar as each order of government acted within its respective jurisdiction, its legislation would be upheld.

With respect to the protection of human rights from statutory infringement in Canada, a majority of judges of the Supreme Court were, as often as not, able to rely upon the division of powers itself to invalidate abusive measures such as Alberta's *Accurate News and Information Act* and Quebec's 'Padlock Law', *An Act respecting Communistic Propaganda*. Encroachments upon the freedom of expression were matters of criminal law and thus reserved to Parliament, not the provincial legislatures; the statutes were, accordingly, held to be *ultra vires*. Nonetheless, in a series of *obiter dicta*, a strand of reasoning was developed amongst a minority of concurring judges that suggested that the abrogation of fundamental political expression might be beyond the reach of Parliament itself. This theory, sometimes referred to as that of the 'implied Bill of Rights', suggested that because Canada was to have a Constitution similar in principle to that of the United Kingdom, Canada's constitutional structure was interwoven with the British parliamentary tradition, which necessitated freedom of political thought and expression.[28] It was asserted by various judges in several cases that the abrogation of the freedom of political expression might be beyond the powers of not only the provincial legislatures but of Parliament as well.[29] However, these statements remained *obiter*.

The enactment by the United Kingdom Parliament of the *Canada Act 1982* and with it, the *Constitution Act, 1982* and the *Canadian Charter of Rights and Freedoms*, further attenuated but did not eliminate the operation of the principle of parliamentary sovereignty in Canada. As long as the federal Parliament and the provincial legislatures respected both the division of powers under the *Constitution Act, 1867* and the basic rights and freedoms guaranteed by the Charter, the courts would not to impugn the wisdom or advisability of legislative policy. The late Chief Justice Brian Dickson is often cited for having stated that in 1982 Canada moved from a system of parliamentary supremacy to constitutional supremacy,[30] and certainly, the express declaration in s.52 of the *Constitution Act, 1982* that the Constitution of Canada is the 'supreme law' of Canada suggests that the terms 'parliamentary supremacy' and 'parliamentary sovereignty' ought not to be used interchangeably in Canada. However, no one should conclude that Dickson C.J. believed that the principle of parliamentary sovereignty had been abolished in 1982. Indeed, writing for a unanimous Supreme Court of Canada in the *Auditor General's Case* in 1989, Dickson emphasized: 'The *grundnorm* with which the courts must

---

28 *Reference re Alberta Statutes*, [1938] S.C.R. 100.
29 *Switzman v. Elbling*, [1957] S.C.R. 285, *per* Abbott and Rand JJ.
30 *Vriend v. Alberta*, [1998] 1 S.C.R. 203, cited by Iacobucci J.

work in this context is the sovereignty of Parliament.'[31] Outside of Charter of Rights adjudication,

> in the residual area reserved for the principle of Parliamentary sovereignty in Canadian constitutional law, it is Parliament and the legislatures, not the courts, that have ultimate constitutional authority to draw the boundaries. *It is the prerogative of a sovereign Parliament to make its intention known as to the role the courts are to play* in interpreting, applying and enforcing its statutes. *While the courts must determine the meaning of statutory provisions, they do so in the name of seeking out the intention of the sovereign will of Parliament*, however purposively, contextually or policy-oriented may be the interpretive methods used to attribute such meaning.[32]

The principle of parliamentary sovereignty also figured largely in the opinion of the Supreme Court in *Reference re Canada Assistance Plan*.[33] In 1990 the Government of Canada announced measures to reduce the federal deficit, notably by cutting expenditures and limiting the growth of payments made to wealthier provinces under the *Canada Assistance Plan* (embodied in a federal statute of the same name). The changes to the Plan were to be implemented by *An Act to amend certain statutes to enable restraint of government expenditures*. The Government of British Columbia asked the B.C. Court of Appeal whether the Government of Canada had any authority to limit its obligation under the Plan and the federal-provincial agreement made pursuant to it to share the cost of provincial expenditures on social assistance; and whether the terms of that agreement and the subsequent conduct of the Government of Canada gave rise to a legitimate expectation that it would not introduce any bill into Parliament to limit its obligation under the agreement and the Plan without the consent of British Columbia. The Court of Appeal answered the first question in the negative and the second one in the affirmative. The Supreme Court of Canada allowed the appeal.

Justice Sopinka, writing for the Court, cited subsection 42(1) of the *Interpretation Act*, which provides: 'Every Act shall be so construed as to reserve to Parliament the power of repealing or amending it, and of revoking, restricting or modifying any power, privilege or advantage thereby vested in or granted to any person.' He added:

> In my view *this provision reflects the principle of parliamentary sovereignty*. The same results would flow from that principle even in the absence or non-applicability of this enactment. But since the *Interpretation Act* governs the interpretation of the *Plan* and all federal statutes where no contrary intention appears, the matter will be resolved by reference to it.
>
> It is conceded that the government could not bind Parliament from exercising its powers to legislate amendments to the *Plan*. To assert the contrary would be to negate *the*

---

31 *Canada (Auditor General)* v. *Canada*, [1989] 2 S.C.R. 49, para. 103.
32 *Ibid.*, at 91–2 [emphasis added].
33 *Reference re Canada Assistance Plan*, [1991] 2 S.C.R. 525

sovereignty of Parliament. This basic fact of our constitutional life was, therefore, present to the minds of the parties when the *Plan* and Agreement were enacted and concluded.[34]

In a similar vein, the Court roundly rejected the argument that the doctrine of legitimate expectations in administrative law would apply to the legislative process or prevent the Government of Canada from introducing a Bill to amend the legislation in question without the consent of the province.[35] Sopinka J. observed that there was 'no support in Canadian or English cases for the position that the doctrine of legitimate expectations can create substantive rights.' This doctrine was 'part of the rules of procedural fairness which can govern administrative bodies', and where it applied, it might create a right to make representations or to be consulted, but could not fetter the decision-making itself. More to the point, Sopinka J cited a number of leading cases for the proposition that 'the rules governing procedural fairness do not apply to a body exercising purely legislative functions'.[36] He concluded: 'The formulation and introduction of a bill are part of the legislative process with which the courts will not meddl.[37]

With regard to a submission by certain interveners that the changes to the Plan were *ultra vires* Parliament because 'even a sovereign body can restrict itself in respect of the 'manner and form' of subsequent legislation',[38] Sopinka J. carefully reviewed the key cases in which such manner-and-form requirements had been recognised and enforced by the courts.[39] In rejecting the argument, Sopinka J. noted that in cases where the Court had held that there were manner-and-form requirements to be met, it had been in relation to quasi-constitutional statutes and provisions such as the *Canadian Bill of Rights*[40] and s.110 of the *North-West Territories Act*,[41] and that for a manner-and-form restriction to apply in the context of an ordinary statute, the intention on the part of Parliament to do so would have to be manifest.

> Any "manner in form" requirement in an ordinary statute must overcome the clear words of s.42(1) of the *Interpretation Act* [quoted *supra*]... This provision requires that federal statutes ordinarily be interpreted to accord with the doctrine of Parliamentary sovereignty.[42]

There was, moreover, another problem with the manner-and-form argument in the *CAP Reference*. As Sopinka J. explained,

---

34 *Ibid.*, 549 [emphasis added].
35 *Ibid.*, 557.
36 *Ibid.*, 557-558.
37 *Ibid.*, para. 559.
38 *Ibid.*, 561.
39 Leading decisions include *A.G. for New South Wales* v. *Trethowan*, [1932] A.C. 526 (P.C.), *R.* v. *Drybones*, [1970] S.C.R. 282, and *R.* v. *Mercure*, [1988] 1 S.C.R. 234.
40 S.C. 1960, c. 44 (reprinted in R.S.C. 1985, App. III).
41 R.S.C. 1886, c. 50; re-enacted by S.C. 1891, c. 22, s.18. Section 110 required the territorial legislature to print and publish its ordinances in both English and French, and this manner-and-form requirement was held in *Mercure* to extend to the legislature of Saskatchewan.
42 *Reference re Canada Assistance Plan*, para. 562.

It is clear that parliamentary sovereignty prevents a legislature from binding itself as to the substance of its future legislation. The claim that is made in a "manner and form" argument is that the body has restrained itself, *not in respect of substance*, but in respect of the procedure which must be followed to enact future legislation of some sort, or of the form in which such legislation must take.[43]

In the instant case, the restriction that was being contended for was less in the nature of a manner and form requirement than a 'renunciation *pro tanto* of the lawmaking power'.[44]

The Supreme Court also rejected a submission by the Attorney General of Manitoba to the effect that the 'overriding principle of federalism' required that Parliament be unable to interfere in areas of provincial jurisdiction and to protect the autonomy of the provinces, the Court should supervise the federal government's exercise of its spending power.[45] However, Sopinka J. concluded,

> supervision of the spending power is not a separate head of judicial review. *If a statute is neither ultra vires nor contrary to the Canadian Charter of Rights and Freedoms, the courts have no jurisdiction to supervise the exercise of legislative power.*[46]

The Supreme Court of Canada's decisions in *The Auditor General's Case* and the *CAP Reference* stand as a powerful reaffirmation of the importance of the principle of parliamentary sovereignty within the Canadian constitutional framework. If we continue to bear in mind that Dicey's formulation of the rule of law included the sovereignty of Parliament and the distinction between legal rules and political rules of constitutional morality – the conventions of the Constitution – then there are self-defining limits to the rule of law as a constitutional principle. In other words, the rule of law, whilst guaranteeing stability, orderly processes and law-making according to law, ought to give representative democracy and politics room to breath outside the confines of the law school and the court room. In Canada as in the United Kingdom, Parliament is the foremost of the political institutions that hold the promise of full participation by the citizenry in representative and democratic decision-making.[47] The sovereignty of Parliament is an expression of the democratic principle. In Canada, the sovereignty of Parliament is already limited, not only by the terms of a written constitution delineating the division of legislative powers between the federal and provincial levels of government, but also by a constitutionally entrenched Charter of Rights that guarantees procedural and substantive principles of fundamental justice as well as formal and substantive equality before and under the law and the equal protection and benefit of the law.

---

43 Para. 563–4 [emphasis added].

44 Para. 564; the quoted words are drawn from a longer passage cited with approval (as 'fully applicable here') by Sopinka J.; the decision is *West Lakes Ltd.* v. *South Australia* (1980), 25 S.A.S.R. 389, *per* King C.J., at 397–8, dismissing a manner-and-form argument.

45 *Id.*

46 Para. 567 [emphasis added].

47 If there is a 'democratic deficit' in the way in which Parliament functions, the best means of addressing may be through procedural and structural reforms to the institution itself, not in carving out a still larger role for the courts.

The Practice of the Rule of Law in Canada: The *Manitoba Language Rights Reference*

In the *Manitoba Language Rights Reference*,[48] at stake was the validity of all legislation enacted in English only for almost a century, in violation of s.23 of the *Manitoba Act, 1870*. Section 23, like s.133 of the *Constitution Act, 1867* respecting the Parliament of Canada and the legislature of Quebec, required that the laws of the province be printed and published in both English and French. In 1979 the Supreme Court held in *Blaikie*[49] and *Forest*[50] that this constitutional requirement gave official status to both language versions of the statutes and regulations and that the duty of bilingual promulgation extended to the enactment process itself. In Quebec, the legislature of the province re-enacted more than two years of unilingual French statutes and regulations in both languages by means of an omnibus bill which gave official status to unofficial English translations of the laws printed since 1977. In Manitoba, the situation was much worse; the laws of the province had been enacted and promulgated solely in English since 1890. Challenges[51] were launched to enforce the *Forest* decision. In 1983, a proposed constitutional amendment under the 'bilateral' procedure of s.43 of the *Constitution Act, 1982* was reached between the governments of Canada and Manitoba. The amendment would have abrogated the requirement to translate, re-enact and publish the mountain of unilingual provincial legislation enacted prior to 1980, in return for constitutional guarantees of French-language services from the provincial government. The official opposition in the legislative assembly of Manitoba refused repeatedly to answer the call of the legislative bells, thus stymieing the vote on the resolution approving the constitutional amendment. In the wake of this intransigence, the federal government submitted a reference to the Supreme Court on the validity of Manitoba's unilingual laws.

Various solutions, short of the outright invalidity of the *corpus* of Manitoba legislation, were put forward by a number of parties to the reference: *e.g.*, that only laws enacted unilingually since the *Forest* decision in 1979 were null; or that the impugned statutes were not 'void' but 'voidable'; or that (as advanced by the Attorney General of Manitoba) the word 'shall' in s.23 was not imperative but directory. Professor Stephen Scott argued eloquently, however, that invalidity and inoperativity were by far the most effective sanctions for non-compliance with the constitutional guarantee, leaving the legislature with the choice of legislating bilingually or not at all.

> To shrink from the sanctions of invalidity and inoperativity, beyond merely stripping ss. 23 and 133 of much, or most, of their efficacy in respect of language of legislation, would indirectly weaken all constitutional guarantees, – *all* law-making processes, the entire constitutional system. *For it would suggest to the political authorities that constitutional*

---

48 *Reference re Manitoba Language Rights*, [1985] 1 S.C.R. 728. I disclose that I was of counsel in the Reference.

49 *A.G. Quebec v. Blaikie*, [1979] 2 S.C.R. 1016. See also *Blaikie (No. 2)*, [1981] 1 S.C.R. 312.

50 *A.G. Manitoba v. Forest*, [1979] 2 S.C.R. 1032.

51 *Bilodeau v. A.G. Manitoba*, [1981] 5 W.W.R. 393.

processes can be violated with impunity – provided that the consequences of judicial redress are made sufficiently far-reaching: in other words, that in a large-scale confrontation, the courts must retreat. This rewards, and even encourages, massive violation of constitutional processes – the more massive the better. By contrast, a judicial demonstration that constitutional processes will be enforced regardless of consequences would be a clear and salutary lesson to all political authorities in Canada; would immensely strengthen the rule of law; and would represent a major triumph for the constitutional system. Striking down nearly one hundred years of statutes for violation of a constitutional guarantee would be a monument of constitutionalism. It might never have to be repeated.[52]

The Supreme Court did not shirk its duty. The requirement of bilingual enactment was mandatory. Section 133 of the *Constitution Act, 1867* and s.23 of the *Manitoba Act, 1870* were drafted in imperative terms: they commanded that the Acts of the legislatures "*shall*" be printed and published in English and French. They imposed constitutional requirements respecting the manner and form of the enactment and promulgation of legislation. The Court added:

> If more evidence of Parliament's intent is needed, it is necessary only to have regard to the purpose of both s.23 of the *Manitoba Act, 1870* and s.133 of the *Constitution Act, 1867*, which was to ensure full and equal access to the legislatures, the laws and the courts for francophones and anglophones alike. ... Those guarantees would be meaningless and their entrenchment a futile exercise were they not obligatory.[53]

Section 23 of the *Manitoba Act, 1870*, had imposed a constitutional obligation upon the legislature with respect to the manner and form of the enactment of its laws. 'This duty', affirmed the Court, 'protects the substantive rights of all Manitobans to equal access to the law in either the French or the English language.' It also conferred a 'responsibility upon the judiciary to protect the correlative language rights of all Manitobans, including the Franco-Manitoban minority.'[54] The courts were charged with ensuring that the government complied with the Constitution. In an eloquent passage, the Court observed:

> The Constitution of a country is a statement of the will of the people to be governed in accordance with certain principles held as fundamental and certain prescriptions restrictive of the powers of the legislature and government. It is, as s.52 of the *Constitution Act, 1982* declares, the "supreme law" o0f the nation, unalterable by the normal legislative process, and unsuffering of laws inconsistent with it. The duty of the judiciary is to interpret and to apply the laws of Canada and each of the provinces, and it is our duty to ensure that the constitutional law prevails.[55]

The supremacy of the provisions of the Constitution, embodied both in the manner-and-form requirement of s.23 of the *Manitoba Act, 1870*, and the terms of s.52 of the *Constitution Act, 1982*, required the Court to find the unconstitutional laws of

---

52 S.A. Scott, factum on behalf of Intervener Alliance Quebec [emphasis in original].
53 *Re Manitoba Language Rights*, para. 739 (*per curiam*).
54 *Ibid*., para. 744–5.
55 Para. 745.

Manitoba to be 'invalid and of no force and effect'.[56] However, to do so without more might have actually compromised the rule of law in Manitoba because to invalidate ninety years of statutes and regulations could create a legal vacuum and provoke chaos. 'The task the Court faces is to recognize the unconstitutionality of Manitoba's unilingual laws and the Legislature's duty to comply with the "supreme law" of this country, while avoiding a legal vacuum in Manitoba and ensuring continuity in the rule of law.'[57]

As 'a fundamental principle of our Constitution,' the Court said, the rule of law 'must mean at least two things.'[58]

> First, that the law is supreme over officials of government as well as private individuals, and thereby preclusive of the interest of arbitrary power. Indeed, it is because of the supremacy of law over the government, as established in s.23 of the *Manitoba Act, 1870* and s.52 of the *Constitution Act, 1982*, that this Court must find the unconstitutional laws of Manitoba to be invalid and of no force and effect.
>
> Second, the rule of law requires the creation and maintenance of an actual order of positive laws which preserves and embodies the more general principle of normative order. Law and order are indispensable elements of civilized life ...

It was, the Court stated, 'this second aspect of the rule of law' that was of concern in the circumstances.

> The conclusion that the Acts of the Legislature of Manitoba are invalid and of no force and effect means that the positive legal order which has purportedly regulated the affairs of the citizens of Manitoba since 1890 will be destroyed and the rights, obligations and other effects arising under these laws will be invalid and unenforceable ... Such results would certainly offend the rule of law ... The rule of law simply cannot be fulfilled in a province that has no positive law.[59]

While the rule of law was not set out in a specific provision of the Constitution, it was implied in the preamble to the *Constitution Act, 1867* and was expressed in the preamble to the *Constitution Act, 1982*. The founders of the nation must have intended as a matter of basic principle 'that Canada be a society of legal order and of normative structure: one governed by the rule of law.'[60]

> The only appropriate resolution to this Reference is for the Court to fulfill its duty under s.52 of the *Constitution Act, 1982* and declare all the unilingual Acts of the Legislature of Manitoba to be invalid and of no force and effect and then to take such steps as will ensure the rule of law in Manitoba.[61]

---

56 Para. 747.
57 Para. 753.
58 Para. 748.
59 Para. 748–750.
60 Para. 751.
61 Para. 754.

Because '[t]he Constitution will not suffer a province without laws'[62] and Manitoba could not be left in a lawless state, the Court canvassed various exceptional savings doctrines that might blunt some of the consequences for existing legal rights and interests. It also examined the cases on the emergency doctrine of state necessity. The principal remedy the Court settled upon was to 'deem temporarily valid and effective'[63] the unconstitutional laws for the minimum period of time necessary for the legislature of Manitoba to translate, re-enact and publish the laws in both languages.

The Court applied the principle of the rule of law embodied in s.23 of the *Manitoba Act, 1870*, both to invalidate the unilingual laws and to maintain their operation for the minimum period necessary for the legislature to translate and to re-enact the laws in question. This was done *in furtherance of* the principle of constitutionalism at the very heart of s.52 of the *Constitution Act, 1982*. The judicial declaration of invalidity was maintained: 'All unilingually enacted Acts of the Manitoba Legislature are, and always have been, invalid and of no force and effect.'[64] The temporary remedy was necessary to facilitate and ensure the legislature's compliance with its obligations under s.23 with all deliberate speed. That the Court's own duty under s.52 of the *Constitution Act, 1982* had been met was reaffirmed in the *Quebec Secession Reference*:

> [N]othing of our concern in the *Manitoba Language Rights Reference* about the severe practical consequences of unconstitutionality affected our conclusion that, as a matter of law, all Manitoba legislation at issue in that case was unconstitutional. The Court's declaration of unconstitutionality was clear and unambiguous. The Court's concern with maintenance of the rule of law was directed in its relevant aspect to the appropriate remedy, which in that case was to suspend the declaration of invalidity to permit appropriate rectification to take place.

Constitutional Principles and the *Provincial Court Judges Reference*

The Supreme Court's opinion in the *Manitoba Language Rights Reference* provoked renewed interest amongst Canadian commentators and practitioners in the rule of law as a foundational constitutional principle, but it was the Court's exposition in the *Provincial Court Judges Reference* and in the *Quebec Secession Reference* that sparked a wholesale rush to exploit the potential in this and other unwritten norms. Constitutional *conventions* were not easy to establish on the terms of Jennings' test, and in any event were not enforceable by the courts. Constitutional *principles*, on the other hand, seemed tailor-made for lawyers in need of buttressing their arguments with an appeal to the supremacy of constitutional law, but who had few, if any, specific constitutional *provisions* to invoke.

In the *Provincial Judges Reference*, Lamer C.J., for the majority, took the view that the preamble to the *Constitution Act, 1867* was the source of many of the

---

62 Para. 767.
63 Para. 758.
64 Para. 767.

'unwritten rules' and 'organizing principles' of the Constitution of Canada, that these principles could be employed to construe the provisions of the constitutional text, and that the preamble 'invites the use of those organizing principles to fill out gaps in the express terms of the constitutional scheme.' The preamble 'has no enacting force' and 'strictly speaking, is not a source of positive law'; but it 'does have important legal effects' and 'is the means by which the underlying logic of the Act can be given the force of law.'[65]

This view of the preamble to the *Constitution Act, 1867* as being, in the Chief Justice's lofty phrase, 'the grand entrance hall to the castle of the Constitution,'[66] whilst the actual substantive provisions of the Act 'merely elaborate those organizing principles in the institutional apparatus they create or contemplate',[67] did not pass without controversy. Justice La Forest, in a lone but compelling dissent, took exception to the view that the preamble to the *Constitution Act, 1867* was 'a source of constitutional limitations on the power of legislatures to interfere with judicial independence', the specific question at issue in this Reference. Those limitations flowed from the provisions of the *Constitution Act, 1867* and s.11(*d*) of the Charter of Rights. Nor were those express constitutional provisions simply 'elaborations' on underlying constitutional principles. 'On the contrary,' he submitted, those provisions '*are* the Constitution. To assert otherwise is to subvert the democratic foundation of judicial review.'[68]

Justice La Forest was concerned with three issues of broad judicial and philosophical concern. The first was the true source of the entrenched constitutional protection afforded, in Canada, to the principle of judicial independence; which, on the historical record, was difficult to sustain as flowing from the British tradition. The second was the necessary distinction between British constitutionalism and Canadian constitutionalism. The third was the foundational basis for the legitimacy of constitutional judicial review in Canada. This led La Forest J. to set out his key proposition about the nature and legitimacy of judicial review and its relationship to the written text of the Constitution of Canada.

> The ability to nullify the laws of democratically elected representatives derives its legitimacy from a super-legislative source: the text of the Constitution. This foundational document (in Canada, a series of documents) expresses the desire of the people to limit the power of legislatures in certain specified ways. Because the Constitution is entrenched, those limitations cannot be changed by recourse to the usual democratic process. They are not cast in stone, however, and can be modified in accordance with a further expression of democratic will: constitutional amendment.
>
> Judicial review, therefore, is politically legitimate only insofar as it involves the interpretation of an authoritative constitutional instrument...

---

65 *Reference re Provincial Court Judges*, [1997] 3 S.C.R. 3, paras. 94 and 95.
66 Para. 109.
67 Para. 95.
68 Para. 319 [underscoring in original].

This legitimacy is imperilled, however, when courts attempt to limit the powers of legislatures without recourse to express textual authority...[69]

La Forest J. went on to allude to the *dicta* of various judges of the Supreme Court who had suggested in *obiter* that there might be implied limitations on the legislative power of Parliament and the provincial legislatures to curb political expression because of its essential role in ensuring parliamentary democracy. Without endorsing or rejecting the theory, he saw no warrant therein for an argument that the preamble to the *Constitution Act, 1867* implicitly protected judicial independence; or that guarantees of freedom of political expression flowed from the preamble. True to his concern with linking constitutional interpretation to the positive law of the Constitution, La Forest J. affirmed that '[t]he better view is that if these guarantees exist, they are implicit in s.17 of the *Constitution Act, 1867*, which established the Parliament of Canada.[70] 'This', he argued, 'brings us back to the central point:'

> to the extent that courts in Canada have the power to enforce the principle of judicial independence, this power derives from the structure of *Canadian*, and not British, constitutionalism. Our Constitution expressly contemplates both the power of judicial review (in s.52 of the *Constitution Act, 1982*) and guarantees of judicial independence (in ss.96-100 of the *Constitution Act, 1867* and s.11(d) of the *Charter*.) While these provisions have been interpreted to provide guarantees of independence that are not immediately manifest in their language, this has been accomplished through the usual mechanisms of constitutional interpretation, not through recourse to the preamble. The legitimacy of this interpretative exercise stems from its grounding in an expression of democratic will, not from a dubious theory of an implicit constitutional structure.[71]

In light of these concerns, it should be noted that in strict law the majority opinion in the *Provincial Court Judges Reference* turned on the application of s.11(*d*) of the Charter. As the Chief Justice stated at the outset of his discussion on judicial independence, '[d]espite s.11(*d*)'s limited scope, there is no doubt that the appeals can and should be resolved on the basis of that provision.'[72] And subsequent to the Reference, the majority of the Court in *Mackin* was careful to invoke *both* s.11(*d*) of the Charter and the unwritten principle of judicial independence in invalidating, pursuant to s.52(1) of the *Constitution Act, 1982*, the provincial legislation in question.[73] Moreover, in the Reference, Lamer C.J. added an important 'note of caution':

> As I said in *New Brunswick Broadcasting, supra*, at p. 355, the constitutional history of Canada can be understood, in part, as a process of evolution "which [has] culminated in

---

69 At para. 314–6.
70 Para. 318.
71 Para. 319 [underscoring in original].
72 Lamer C.J., para. 82. (This led La Forest J., at para. 302, to qualify the Chief Justice's extensive analysis of unwritten constitutional principles as 'technically *obiter dicta*'; 'if the Chief Justice's discussion was of a merely marginal character — a side-wind so to speak — I would abstain from commenting on it.')
73 *Mackin v. New Brunswick* [2002] 1 S.C.R. 405.

the supremacy of a definitive written constitution". *There are many important reasons for the preference for a written constitution over an unwritten one, not the least of which is the promotion of legal certainty and through it the legitimacy of constitutional judicial review.* Given these concerns, which go to the heart of the project of constitutionalism, it is of the utmost importance to articulate what the source of those unwritten norms is.[74]

Constitutionalism, The Rule of Law and the *Quebec Secession Reference*

The full Court, in the *Quebec Secession Reference*, repeated Chief Justice Lamer's earlier *proviso*, stating that the recognition of constitutional principles 'could not be taken as an invitation to dispense with the written text of the Constitution.'[75]

> On the contrary, we confirmed that *there are compelling reasons to insist upon the primacy of our written constitution.* A written constitution promotes legal certainty and predictability, and it provides a foundation and a touchstone for the exercise of constitutional judicial review.[76]

The Court also noted that the constitutional texts enumerated in s.52(2) of the *Constitution Act, 1982* (and the schedule thereto), albeit not exhaustive, 'have a primary place in determining constitutional rules'.[77] Although the Court, in the *Secession Reference*, continued to make allusion to the preamble of the *Constitution Act, 1867*[78] it formulated a more balanced appreciation of their role in relation to the provisions of the Constitution:

> *Such principles and rules emerge from an understanding of the constitutional text itself,* the historical context, and previous judicial interpretations of constitutional meaning...
>
> *Our Constitution is primarily a written one*, the product of 131 years of evolution. Behind the written word is an historical lineage stretching back through the ages, which aids in the consideration of the underlying constitutional principles. *These principles inform and sustain the constitutional text*; they are the vital unstated assumptions upon which the text is based.[79]

In the *Quebec Secession Reference* the Court underscored the importance of the principles of federalism, democracy, constitutionalism, the rule of law and the protection of minorities to the resolution of the weighty questions before it in the Reference (For an extensive treatment of these legal issues and the political context in which they arose, see Newman 1999.) The Court noted that its enumeration was 'by no means exhaustive', and that other 'supporting principles and rules' include 'constitutional conventions and the workings of Parliament'. The Court also

---

74 *Reference re Provincial Court Judges*, per Lamer C.J., para. 93 [emphasis added].
75 *Reference re Secession of Quebec*, [1998] 2 S.C.R. 217, para. 53 [emphasis added].
76 *Id.*
77 Para. 32.
78 Para. 93.
79 Paras. 32 and 49 [emphasis added].

emphasized that the relevant principles 'function in symbiosis' and that no principle could 'trump or exclude the operation of any other.'[80]

The Supreme Court summarized the three key elements of the rule of law as follows. First, 'the rule of law provides that the law is supreme over the acts of both government and private persons. There is, in short, one rule law for all.' Secondly, 'the rule of law requires the creation and maintenance of an actual order of positive laws which preserves and embodies the more general principle of normative order'. Thirdly, 'the exercise of all public power must find its ultimate source in a legal rule'; in other words, 'the relationship between the state and the individual must be regulated by law.'[81] Professor Elliott has articulated how the normative aspects of these components of the rule of law are usually understood to apply. They clearly fall short of constituting a power for the courts to invalidate legislation on the basis of the principle alone (Elliott 2001, 115). The related principle of constitutionalism, on the other hand, which requires that 'all government action comply with the Constitution',[82] is embodied in subsection 52(1) of the *Constitution Act, 1982*, which affirms that '[t]he Constitution of Canada is the supreme law of Canada, and any law that is inconsistent with the provisions of the Constitution is, to the extent of the inconsistency, of no force or effect.' Here, of course, administrative *or* legislative action that is inconsistent with the provisions of the constitutional text (i.e., that offends constitutional *law* rather than *conventions*) can be struck down by the courts. This was true both prior to and after the enactment of the *Constitution Act, 1982*.[83]

The Constitution of Canada, as the Court emphasized, 'binds all governments, both federal and provincial'.

> They may not transgress its provisions: indeed, their sole claim to exercise lawful authority rests in the powers allocated to them under the Constitution, and can come from no other source.[84]

That is a powerful statement about the force of legal constitutionalism in Canada, based as it is upon the provisions of a supreme law that is largely, if not exclusively (see Newman 2003), 'entrenched beyond the reach of simple majority rule'.[85]

The Court waxed philosophically about the bonds between constitutionalism and the rule of law.

> The consent of the governed is a value that is basic to our understanding of a free and democratic society. Yet democracy in any real sense of the word cannot exist without the rule of law... Equally, however, a system of government cannot survive through adherence to the law alone. A political system must also possess legitimacy, and in our political culture, that requires an interaction between the rule of law and the democratic

---

80 *Reference re Secession of Quebec, supra*, para. 32.

81 *Quebec Secession Reference*, para. 71.

82 *Reference re Quebec Secession*, para. 72: 'Simply put, the constitutionalism principle requires that all government action comply with the Constitution. The rule of law principle requires that all government action comply with the law, including the Constitution.'

83 See *Reference re Manitoba Language Rights, supra*, para. 746.

84 *Reference re Secession of Quebec*, para. 72.

85 *Re Secession of Quebec*, para. 73.

principle. It would be a grave mistake to equate legitimacy with the "sovereign will" or majority rule alone, to the exclusion of other constitutional values....

Constitutionalism facilitates — indeed, makes possible — a democratic political system by creating an orderly framework within which people may make political decisions. Viewed correctly, constitutionalism and the rule of law are not in conflict with democracy; rather, they are essential to it. [86]

The Court's balanced approach to the scope and application of constitutional principles, its recognition of the primacy of the constitutional text, its analysis of the values of legality and legitimacy, and its understanding of the distinct yet interrelated roles played by constitutionalism, the rule of law, democracy and the protection of minorities, are part of what make the Court's opinion an outstanding piece of judicial craftsmanship. The Court recognised that a constitutional democracy is not limited to simple majoritarian rule but requires continuous debate and the acknowledgment of dissenting voices. This debate takes place within a legal framework that helps to ensure an important degree of stability, order, certainty and fairness in governmental decision-making. The principle of the rule of law that the Court adopted is what is called in some academic quarters a 'thin' version; it is not made to do the work of other constitutional principles (For an encapsulation of 'thin' and 'thick' versions of the rule of law, see Hutchinson and Monahan 1987, 205).[87] However, the Court's initial broad generalizations in the *Quebec Secession Reference* about constitutional principles being 'not merely descriptive' but also 'invested with powerful normative force', being 'binding upon both courts and governments'[88] could not fail to encourage litigants to make new arguments based largely on principles rather than provisions.

The Rule of Law Parliamentary Sovereignty after the *Quebec Secession Reference*: From *Bacon* to *Babcock*

In the aftermath of the *Secession Reference*, several challenges to the validity of legislative provisions were brought on the basis that the impugned provisions offended the rule of law. These arguments were dismissed by the Courts of Appeal of Saskatchewan and British Columbia and by the Supreme Court of Canada. In *Bacon*,[89] the legislature of Saskatchewan had enacted legislation which changed the terms of a government insurance programme benefiting farmers and which extinguished potential claims for breach of contract. Some farmers took action against the

---

86 Paras. 67 and 78.

87 *Vide* Hutchinson and Monahan, "Democracy and the Rule of Law", *loc. cit.*, for an encapsulation of 'thin' and 'thick' versions of the rule of law. In 'The Rule of Law Revisited: Democracy and the Courts', *loc. cit.*, at p. 205, footnote 13, Professor Hutchinson states: 'It should be clear that I strongly approve of the Supreme Court's insistence that such matters as equality, liberty and the like be treated separately from the rule of law. There are enough problems grappling with a thin version of the rule of law, without adding the unnecessary larding of the thick version.'

88 Para. 54 of *Reference re Secession of Quebec*.

89 [1999] 11 W.W.R. 51, Sask. C.A. *per* Wakeling J.A.

provincial government, arguing it had no authority to enact the legislation because governments are subject to the rule of law and the obligations they contract are binding upon them. The trial judge agreed that the government's legislative authority was subject to limits imposed by the rule of law and that it could not cancel its contractual undertakings arbitrarily. However, the judge found that the government had not, in fact, acted arbitrarily and thus the legislative amendment in question was valid and the plaintiffs' claim for damages dismissed. The appellants did not invoke sections 7 or 15 of the Charter of Rights nor the division of powers under the Constitution. The appellants also acknowledged that the case involved property and civil rights, a matter within the jurisdiction of the province.[90] Instead, they argued that the case was about the rule of law in a democratic society, a 'legal concept that pre-dates the notion of a formal written Constitution' and which 'provides the basis for the common law control of the state in its interaction with individuals.'[91]

The Court of Appeal disagreed that the principle of the rule of law could be used to strike down legislation. An examination of the Canadian jurisprudence demonstrated that governments and officials in the administration were, like everyone else, subject to the law 'as it exists'.

> However, the law, including the common law, is subject to change by legislation and when changed it is this changed law which is the 'one law for all'. The law, which is applicable to us all, cannot be taken as static and unchangeable. It is forever evolving and Parliament plays a major role in its development. There is no statement in the *Secession* case which would suggest otherwise.[92]

It was true, Wakeling J.A. noted, that the sovereignty of Parliament and the provincial legislatures had been restricted by ss.91 and 92 of the *Constitution Act, 1867* and further restrained by the advent of the *Constitution Act, 1982*; but there was 'no suggestion' in the *Quebec Secession Reference* that the judicial role 'was being expanded beyond the right to determine constitutional limitations on jurisdiction.'[93] The Supreme Court's affirmation that nobody, including governments, is beyond the law, was

> a reference to the law as it exists from time to time and does not create a restriction on Parliament's right to make laws, but it is only a recognition that when they are made they are then applicable to all, including governments.[94]

The foundation for the trial judge's analysis, Wakeling J.A. surmised, was the former's observation that the legislative branch of government is under the control of the executive branch, and if the executive or administrative branch of government is constrained from arbitrary action by the rule of law, then there was 'no logical reason' why this stricture should not also apply to the legislative branch.[95] This was,

---

90 Cited para. 7 of the reasons for judgment of Wakeling J.A.
91 *Ibid.*
92 Para. 26.
93 Para. 27.
94 Paras. 29 and 30.
95 Cited para 34.

in Wakeling J.A.'s view, 'a new direction not charted except perhaps by the writings of adventurous scholars' and not supportable simply on the basis of the *Quebec Secession Reference*.[96] Moreover, it missed the obvious point about the respective roles of the legislative and judicial branches in light of the principle of democracy, as Wakeling J.A. took pains to point out again:

> To say that since the courts do a good job in providing protection in one are against the arbitrary use of power by officials they must also do it in relation to the passage of arbitrary legislation is to misunderstand the democratic process by downgrading the importance of holding a government responsible to the will of the electors.[97]

The trial judge had 'depart[ed] needlessly from the known path which has served well to give full range to the concept of the rule of law, yet recognised that the law by which we are ruled is to a significant extent that which is legislated by Parliament when acting within its constitutional limits.'[98]

The decision of the Saskatchewan Court of Appeal was followed by the Federal Court of Appeal in *Singh* v. *Canada*,[99] a challenge to the validity of s.39 of the *Canada Evidence Act* on the grounds that it was inconsistent with the constitutional principles of judicial independence, the rule of law and the separation of powers. The case arose out of the hearing of the RCMP Public Complaints Commission into alleged misconduct by members of the Force in connection with demonstrations during the APEC conference in 1997. In response to a request from the Commission's counsel for the disclosure of all government records relevant to the hearing, the Clerk of the Privy Council certified, pursuant to s.39 of the *Canada Evidence Act*, that information contained in certain documents constituted Cabinet confidences and thus the documents would not be disclosed. Subsection 39(1) provides that '[w]here a minister of the Crown or the Clerk of the Privy Council objects to the disclosure of information before a court, person or other body with jurisdiction to compel the production of information by certifying in writing that the information constitutes a confidence of the Queen's Privy Council for Canada, disclosure of the information shall be refused without examination or hearing of the information by the court, person or body.' Complainants before the Commission sought declarations that s.39 was inconsistent with s.2(*b*) and s.7 of the *Charter of Rights* and that s.39 was inconsistent with the 'fundamental and organizing principles of the Constitution'. The Federal Court[100] held that s.39 was *intra vires*, that there was no Charter violation, and that the constitutional principles invoked by the plaintiffs, to the extent they might assist the courts in filling in 'gaps' in the written constitutional text, had no application. Strayer J.A., writing for the Federal Court of Appeal, observed that 'the appellants had made a strong argument against the policy embodied in subsection 39(1) of the *Canada Evidence Act*', but it was 'not for the Court to determine the

---

96 Paras. 34 and 35.
97 Para. 36.
98 Para. 37.
99 *Singh* v. *Canada (Attorney General)*, [2000] 3 F.C. 185 (C.A.) (*sub. nom. Westergard-Thorpe et al.*)
100 [1999] 4 F.C. 583 (T.D.), *per* McKeown J.

wisdom' of that policy 'if it breaches no constitutional requirement.'[101] The argument on unwritten principles was derived principally from the 'general comments' of the Supreme Court in the *Provincial Judges* and *Secession References*. 'I do not interpret them as having put an end to another constitutional principle, namely the supremacy of Parliament and the supremacy of legislatures when acting in their own domain.'[102] The appellants had relied upon the Supreme Court's passing observation in the *Secession Reference* that 'with the adoption of the *Charter*, the Canadian system of government was transformed to a significant extent from a system of Parliamentary supremacy to one of constitutional supremacy.' Strayer J.A. remarked that '[i]t is uncertain what significance should be given to this statement, since the supremacy of the Constitution was established well before 1982 and even before Confederation in 1867'.[103]

> Both before and after 1982 our system was and is one of parliamentary sovereignty exercisable within the limits of a written constitution.[104]

With respect to the argument based on the rule of law, Strayer J.A. emphasized that in the *Secession Reference* the Supreme Court had confirmed that the rule of law means the law is supreme over the acts of both government and private persons ('one law for all'); that an actual order of positive laws must be maintained to preserve 'normative order'; and that 'the exercise of all public power must find its ultimate source in a legal rule'; *i.e.*, that 'the relationship between the state and the individual must be regulated by law.'[105] This was, he said, precisely the state of affairs that existed when s.39 of the *Canada Evidence Act* applied to preserve Cabinet documents from disclosure.

> The situation is clearly regulated by law, namely section 39, being an Act of Parliament operating in what has been held to be its field of legislative authority. *The rule of law is not the equivalent of a guarantee of the paramountcy of the common law* (which itself has mutated on this subject of immunity [of documents from disclosure] in recent decades. *In fact the "actual order of positive laws" in our system makes valid legislation paramount over the common law.* That the government is bound by the law, just as are private citizens, is not in dispute here. This does not mean that the law must produce the same results in respect of every citizen and institution in the country: differently situated persons and public bodies require different treatment and it is part of the art and science of law making, both by legislatures and courts, to fashion a content of laws appropriate to the different persons and bodies they regulate. All of this must now, of course, be done within the confines of section 15 of the Charter which is not before us.[106]

The principle of judicial independence had been invoked by the appellants in conjunction with the separation of powers and the rule of law, the position being

---

101 [2000] 3 F.C. 185 (*supra*), para. 11.
102 *Ibid.*, para. 12.
103 Para. 15 of Strayer J.A.'s reasons, *supra*.
104 Para. 16.
105 Para. 33 (drawing from para. 71 of the *Quebec Secession Reference*).
106 Para. 34 [emphasis added].

that a limitation on the jurisdiction of the courts precluding the review of certain government decisions violates the independence of the judiciary. The trial judge and the Federal Court of Appeal rejected this argument. 'None of this can be seen as putting improper pressure on a judge as to the outcome of a given case; he or she is simply barred by Act of Parliament from making certain determinations.' The section was 'really another form of privative clause with which the judicial system has long been familiar.'[107] This did not mean that there was no role for the courts to entertain proceedings in judicial review of certificates issued under s.39.[108]

Babcock[109] also attacked the constitutionality of s.39 on the basis of the principles invoked by the appellants in *Singh*. McLachlin C.J. held on behalf of the Supreme Court that there was no basis under the preamble of the *Constitution Act, 1867* to find that s.39 was unconstitutional. She wrote:

> The respondents in this case challenge the constitutionality of s.39 and argue that the provision is *ultra vires* Parliament because of the unwritten principles of the Canadian Constitution: the rule of law, the independence of the judiciary and the separation of powers. Although the unwritten constitutional principles are capable of limiting government actions, I find they do not do so in this case.
>
> *The unwritten principles must be balanced against the principle of Parliamentary sovereignty...* [110]

More specifically, the Chief Justice noted that Strayer J.A. had upheld the validity of s.39 in *Singh* '[o]n the basis of a thorough and compelling review of the principle of parliamentary sovereignty in the context of unwritten constitutional principles.' McLachlin C.J. underlined that the Federal Court of Appeal had held that federal Crown privilege is an area of law over which Parliament has valid legislative competence,[111] and concluded:

> I share the view of the Federal Court of Appeal that s.39 does not offend the rule of law or the doctrines of separation of powers and the independence of the judiciary. It is well within the power of the legislature to enact laws, even laws which some would consider draconian, as long as it does not fundamentally alter or interfere with the relationship between the courts and the other branches of government.[112]

Whilst protecting s.39 against the *constitutional* challenge to its validity on the basis of the rule of law and other principles by balancing them with the principle of parliamentary sovereignty, the Court also ensured that the protection afforded by the *administrative law* aspects of the rule of law in reviewing the actions of government officials was maintained. As the Chief Justice put it near the outset of her reasons,

---

107   Paras. 39 and 40.
108   Paras. 43 and 44.
109   *Babcock* v. *Canada (Attorney General)*, [2002] 3 S.C.R. 3, *per* McLachlin, C.J.
110   Paras. 54–5.
111   Para. 56.
112   Para. 57.

Cabinet confidentiality is essential to good government. The right to pursue justice in the courts is also of primary importance in our society, as is the rule of law, accountability to the executive, and the principle that official actions must flow from statutory authority clearly granted and properly exercised.[113]

The Court emphasized that the 'British democratic tradition which informs the Canadian tradition has long affirmed the confidentiality of what is said in the Cabinet room, and documents and papers prepared for Cabinet discussions.'[114] Section 39 of the *Canada Evidence Act* provides a mechanism at the federal level 'for the responsible exercise of the power to claim Cabinet confidentiality in the context of judicial and quasi-judicial proceedings.'[115] The exercise of this statutory power was 'subject to the well-established rule' expressed in *Roncarelli* v. *Duplessis*[116] to the effect that official action must be clearly authorized and properly exercised.[117] Although subsection 39(1) 'leaves little scope for judicial review of a certification of Cabinet confidentiality', even language as 'draconian' as that used in the provision 'cannot oust the principle that official actions must flow from statutory authority clearly granted and properly exercised', and thus the certification of the Clerk of the Privy Council could be challenged where the information for which the immunity was claimed under s.39(1) did not *prima facie* come within the terms of that provision, 'or where it can be showed that the Clerk or the minister has improperly exercised the discretion conferred by s.39(1)', *e.g.* through selective disclosure as a litigation tactic to gain advantage in a given matter.[118]

The Supreme Court's decision in *Babcock* and those of the Federal and Saskatchewan Courts of Appeal in *Singh* and *Bacon* demonstrate that while Canadian courts are prepared to give a broad compass to the rule of law as a gold standard by which to measure the legality of administrative action, they are not prepared to ignore Parliament's and the provincial legislatures' powers to change, from time to time, either statute or common law, as long as those legislative bodies exercise those powers within the limits of their respective constitutional jurisdiction and respect the guarantees of the Charter. In a sense, every time a court applies a provision of the Constitution or of a validly-enacted statute or regulation, it can be said to be ensuring respect for the rule of law, because these provisions *are* law. In other words, courts can be said to have maintained respect for the rule of law when they strike down administrative action as unlawful under a given statute, or when they invalidate a statute as inconsistent with the provisions of the Constitution. This is not, however, tantamount to stating that the legislation has fallen because it failed to respect the rule of law, unless it is understood by that that we mean the legislation is invalid because it offends a provision of the supreme law, the Constitution.

Bacon, *Singh* and *Babcock* are not the only cases in which the rule of law has been invoked since the *Quebec Secession Reference* in an attempt to invalidate

---

113 Para. 15.
114 Para. 18.
115 Para. 21.
116 [1959] S.C.R. 121.
117 Para. 20.
118 Paras. 36, 38, and 39.

legislative action as a matter of constitutional principle. In *JTI-Macdonald* v. *British Columbia*, Holmes J. of the B.C. Supreme Court accepted the reasoning in *Singh*, *Bacon* and *Babcock* 'that in any event the rule of law of itself is not a basis for setting aside legislation as unconstitutional.'[119] And in *Hogan* v. *Newfoundland*, the Newfoundland Court of Appeal rejected a challenge to the validity of a constitutional amendment to the Terms of Union, a challenge that invoked, *inter alia*, the principles of the rule of law and the protection of minorities.[120]

The Rule of Law, 'common law constitutional rights' and *Polewsky*

A decision by the Ontario Divisional Court in *Polewsky*[121] deserves mention. The plaintiff moved for a declaration that the Small Claims Court tariff fees violated ss.7 and 15(1) of the Charter. Gillese J. found that there was no constitutional right of unimpeded access to the civil courts and that the fees did not infringe s.15 of the Charter, as poverty was not an analogous ground under s.15(1). She also found that that the guarantees of s.7 of the Charter are limited to a person's physical and mental integrity and do not protect civil and economic rights. The Divisional Court allowed the appeal.

The impugned fees were made by the Lieutenant Governor in Council pursuant to the province's *Administration of Justice Act*. The regulations set the fees and the *Small Claims Court Rules* compelled the payment of the prescribed fee to set a matter down for trial. The Divisional Court agreed with the motions judge that nothing in the *Administration of Justice Act* nor in the relevant regulations 'make any provision for the waiving of the prescribed fees in any circumstances'.[122] The Court also concurred in the former's finding that there was no Charter violation on the facts of the case, neither under s.15(1) nor under s.7: 'We say the fees do not offend the Charter.' However, the Court found that there was 'a constitutional defect which arises from the fact that there is no provision in the Rules for the waiver or reduction of fees in cases where the litigant has a meritorious case and, but for the waiver or reduction of fees, would not be able to proceed.'[123]

> This is a breach of the Rule of Law and the constitutional values that underlie the common law. We see this as a constitutional defect that must be cured.[124]

The Divisional Court accepted the submission of the Advocates' Society that '*in forma pauperis* proceedings are substantive rather than procedural, and that the absence of provision to proceed *in forma pauperis* breaches the Rule of Law.'[125]

---

119 (2000) 18 D.L.R. (4th) 335, para. 150. This view of the rule of law was maintained by the B.C. Court of Appeal and an appeal before the Supreme Court of Canada has been heard.
120 (2000) 183 D.L.R. (4th) 225.
121 (2004) 66 O.R. (3d) 600, *per curiam*.
122 Para. 3.
123 Para. 45.
124 *Id.*
125 Para. 40,

The Advocates' Society also referred the Court to 'the common law right of access to justice' canvassed by the British High Court of Justice, Queen's Bench Division in the *Witham* case, a challenge to article 3 of the *Supreme Court Fees Amendment Order* as being *ultra vires* s.130 of the *Supreme Court Act, 1981* (U.K.).[126] Amongst passages cited by the Divisional Court was one stating that 'the common law has clearly given special weight to the citizen's right of access to the courts' and '[i]t has been described as a constitutional right ...'[127]

The Divisional Court went on to note that the results in *Witham* were repeated in *R. v. Secretary of State for the Home Department and others, ex parte Saleem,*[128] again emphasising 'the fundamental nature of the right of access to the court'.[129]

> This is the rationale that has led us to conclude that, quite apart from the Charter, there is at common law a constitutional right of access to the courts. The fact that the provision to waive or reduce prescribed fees is omitted, deliberately or otherwise, does not make it correct in law. The result is that for persons with demonstrated inability to pay prescribed fees and with meritorious cases, there must be a statutory provision to which they can resort for relief from the requirement to pay fees.[130]

Finally, citing variously Dickson C.J.'s comments in *British Columbia Government Employees' Union*[131] about the rule of law and access to the courts (albeit in a Charter context), the Ontario Court of Appeal in *Lalonde v. Ontario*[132] and Binnie J. in *Re Eurig Estate*,[133] the Divisional Court concluded its judgment in *Polewsky* in the following terms:

> We agree that the Rule of Law infuses this court's determination of the issues raised in this appeal. We say that the existence of *the Rule of Law combined with* what we find to be *the common law constitutional right of access to justice compels the enactment of statutory provisions* that permit persons to proceed *in forma pauperis* in the Small Claims Court.

> It will be apparent from these reasons that we have concluded that, *apart from the Charter, there is a common law constitutional right of access* to the Small Claims Court. We do not say that this right is unimpeded or unrestricted. It must be subject to the exercise of judicial discretion on issues of merit and financial circumstances that trigger the right to proceed *in forma pauperis*. To the extent that no such provision exists in the *Courts of Justice Act*, the rules of the Small Claims Court, the *Administration of Justice Act* or Ontario Regulation [432/93], we say *there will have to be a statutory amendment to give effect to the findings of this court*. We do not say that each of the aforementioned statutes must be amended. It will be up to the legislature to decide which of the statutes is to be

---

126 *R. v. Lord Chancellor ex parte John Witham*, [1997] 2 All E.R. 779 (Q.B.)
127 Para. 49 of *Polewsky*, citing *Witham*, para. 24.
128 [2000] 4 All E.R. 814 (C.A.)
129 Para. 61 of the Divisional Court's reasons, quoting from *Saleem* at p. 821 All E.R.
130 Para. 62.
131 *B.C.G.E.U. v. B. C. (A. G.)*, [1988] 2 S.C.R. 214 at 228: 'the rule of law is the very foundation of the *Charter*...'
132 (2001) 56 O.R. (3d) 505
133 [1998] 2 S.C.R. 565, p. 594: 'implicit principles can and should be used to expound the Constitution, but they cannot alter the thrust of its explicit text.'

amended to give effect to the disposition of this appeal. *We do not say that an immediate amendment is required but that it should be done within a reasonable period of time and not later than 12 months from the date of the release of these reasons.* ... [134]

Whatever the obvious merits of the decision as respects indigent litigants before the Small Claims Court,[135] the judgment of the Divisional Court and its premises regarding the rule of law, constitutional rights and the common law, beg for clarification. Here are some of the issues that come to mind: the Court based its finding on the existence of a 'common law constitutional right' of access on decisions of the English courts (primarily *Witham, supra*). Does that mean, then, that the 'constitutional right' is of the British kind; that is to say, an important entitlement construed to exist by the courts but subject to abrogation or amendment by the clear and express terms of an Act of Parliament (or in Canada, an Act of the provincial legislature)? In other words, if the 'constitutional' right exists at common law, can the common law be modified by statute, as it normally can, in both Canada and the United Kingdom? Or if the 'common law constitutional right', buttressed by 'the Rule of Law', is somehow constitutionally entrenched, on what basis is that so? By what right or power may the Court 'compel' the legislature of Ontario to enact a statute within a year? Does such a judicial declaration breach the principles of the separation of powers (such as it is) and parliamentary sovereignty? It is one thing to make a declaration of invalidity and then to suspend it for twelve months in the hope the legislature will act, on pain of nullity to its statute if it does not; it is another to claim to be able to order positive compliance by the legislature. Assuming the Court possesses such an extraordinary remedial power, it is clear that it does not flow, in the present case, from s.24 of the Charter (the enforcement provision), because the Court found no breach of the Charter. Is its judicial declaration based, then, on s.52(1) of the *Constitution Act, 1982*? If so, what provision of the Constitution has been breached that would permit it to have recourse to s.52(1)? What if the legislature of Ontario were to neglect to act within the 12-month limit set by the Court? And since when can the common law (apart from the interpretation of constitutional provisions such as those in the Charter) compel the enactment of amendments to statute law? What if the Ontario legislature were to enact an express statutory bar to *in forma pauperis* proceedings in the Small Claims Court? Would the common law constitutional right then have to give way to the rule of law as expressed in the statute?

---

134   Paras 76-77.

135   One wonders whether there was an oversight in the regulations or the rules to authorize waiver where merit and financial circumstances warranted it, and whether this issue would not have been dealt with better by a judicial suggestion that representations for change be made by provincial Bench and Bar committees to the Ministry of the Attorney General. The Divisional Court stressed that 'even if there had been a statutory provision allowing him to proceed *in forma pauperis*, this appellant would not have met the requirements' because of evidentiary deficiencies.

Conclusion: Towards a Fuller Understanding of Constitutionalism, The Rule of Law and the Roles of the Courts and the Legislatures in the Canadian Context

These issues illustrate why it is pivotal to be able to understand the source and variable normative scope of constitutional principles derived from the *British* constitutional system, whether they originate in constitutional conventions, statute or common law rules, and to appreciate that they ought not to be imported holus bolus into the *Canadian* constitutional system without first determining whether they are to act as guiding values, conventions and aspirations, or whether they are to be imbued with the same legal force and effect as the provisions of the *Constitution Acts, 1867 to 1982*. Our Constitution may be similar in principle to that of the United Kingdom, but it is, as Dicey himself remarked, in many respects similar in structure to that of the United States: that is, it is largely a written instrument (or instruments) of supreme law, overseen by a degree of judicial review as to the validity of statutes that has never, to this day, been exercised by the courts of the United Kingdom. There are important consequences flowing from both the similarities and distinctions that exist between British constitutionalism and Canadian constitutionalism, as La Forest J. pointed out in his dissenting opinion in the *Provincial Court Judges Reference*, and between political constitutionalism and legal constitutionalism, as Sopinka J. emphasized in the *Osborne* case.

Moreover, British constitutionalism is, as we have seen, based on the paradigm of a flexible, unconsolidated constitution, where even organic statutes like the *Act of Union with Ireland* have been amended; where changes to 'constitutional rules' can be and are effected by ordinary legislation; where the common law contributes to the constitutional law but can be modified by statute law; where conventional rules unenforceable by the courts are often as important in constitutional practice as the rules set out in the statute book or enunciated by the common law; and where the principle of the rule of law co-exists with the doctrine of parliamentary sovereignty (or supremacy) as the fundamental rule of the British constitutional system.

Canadian constitutionalism in the legal sense begins with the *Canada Act 1982* and the *Constitution Acts, 1867 to 1982*, which vest the executive government in the Queen, establish the Parliament of Canada and the provincial legislatures and distribute legislative powers between them, provide for a Supreme Court, entrench fundamental rights and freedoms in the provisions of a Charter, declare the Constitution of Canada to be the supreme law of Canada and that laws inconsistent with its provisions are of no force and effect, mandate constitutional judicial review, and set out a series of complex procedures for constitutional amendment that in most instances require the combined approval of both the federal houses and at least one or more of the provincial legislative assemblies. The *Constitution Acts* are not exhaustive of everything within the phrase, 'the Constitution of Canada', but they play the primary role in our legal and constitutional framework. It is with reference to that basic framework and those provisions that the phrase, 'a Constitution similar in Principle to that of the United Kingdom' must be understood, and the principles and conventions of responsible government as well as other constitutional principles such as parliamentary sovereignty and the rule of law must be construed, adapted and applied.

Mark Walters, in his elegant essay, 'The Common Law Constitution in Canada: Return of *Lex Non Scripta* as Fundamental Law', has argued that '[t]he objective behind the [Supreme] Court's approach to unwritten constitutional principles is commendable. The notion of a fundamental law superior to positive or written law operating as a sort of moral ballast for the legal system, providing it with normative consistency, coherence, and direction, is a compelling idea found throughout the history of jurisprudential writing.'(Walters 2001, 93). Call me a formalist, but I am far from certain that a prescriptive role for unwritten constitutional principles in the judicial elaboration of a fundamental law superior, perhaps, to the *Constitution Acts* themselves is necessarily a commendable objective. Nevertheless, as Professor Walters points out, if such a paradigm shift in our understanding of constitutional law in Canada were to occur, – to move from Dicey to Dyzenhaus, so to speak – that change would need to be articulated with much more transparency and precision than the jurisprudence has provided in regard to its theoretical and practical bases to date.

> [T]he Court's recent decisions are problematic: it seeks to make legal history one component, if not the most important one, in the doctrinal framework that sustains its theory of fundamental unwritten law, but its historical arguments fail to acknowledge, let alone engage with, the historical common law tradition concerning fundamental law and its place in Canadian constitutional law and theory.
>
> ... If the recent judicial acknowledgement of an unwritten or common law constraint on legislative authority represents a shift in Canada's rule of recognition, then perhaps judges have engineered a revolution; perhaps one legal regime in Canada has been surreptitiously jettisoned through extra-legal manipulation in favour of a new one. If so, the Court's critics, who say that it has engaged in a process of rewriting Canada's constitutional texts without precedent or legitimacy, may be right. (Walters 2001, 93–4).

Professor Walters goes on to argue that such criticism is unwarranted and I would hasten to agree, although perhaps for different reasons: he states that '[a]lthough the Court's doctrinal explanation for the unwritten constitution needs strengthening, and its application in specific instances may be questioned, the unwritten constitution itself is not the product of revolutionary or illegitimate judicial activism.' (Walters 2001, 94). I would contend instead that whilst the unwritten tradition of British constitutionalism has an important effect on the interpretation of the written legal framework of the Constitution of Canada, and that there are unwritten constitutional principles, conventions and common law rules which can be seen to complete our written Constitution, there is no 'unwritten constitution' or 'common law constitution' in Canada within the prevailing sense accorded to those expressions in the United Kingdom. Our Constitution is predominantly a written one, and this explains the role and legitimacy of our courts in engaging in constitutional judicial review. Our courts must continue to link constitutional principles and values to the legal structure and provisions from which they emanate and draw their force. 'Courts can indeed "infuse" and "breathe life" into the Constitution, but in so doing they may not stray far from the physical corpus of constitutional law if both are to thrive.' (Newman 2001, 234–5). Courts, including the Supreme Court of Canada, are generally in the business of settling live controversies and disputes. Outside of the opportunities occasioned by references, where the Court can give fuller sway to a philosophical and historical exegesis of the law, it is unreasonable and impractical to expect busy judges – even judges of the calibre of the Justices of the Supreme Court – to engage in prolix existential explorations into the meaning of law, politics and adjudication.

When the courts do attempt this, they occasionally succeed brilliantly, as in the *Manitoba Language Rights* and *Quebec Secession References*. More often, the results are mixed, as in the *Patriation Reference*, the *New Brunswick Broadcasting* decision and the *Provincial Court Judges Reference*, where concurring opinions and vigorous dissents tend to dilute the whole canvass. In any event, these broad-brush attempts to paint a larger picture almost invariably fail to satisfy both the Court's utopian and dystopian critics. There are occasions, as the Judicial Committee of the Privy Council's jurisprudence attests, when less is more, and the discipline of which the Supreme Court is capable is nowhere more evident than in its relatively succinct but effective treatment of vast issues of legal, constitutional, political, historical and international significance in the space of 155 paragraphs in the *Quebec Secession Reference*.

To return more generally to Professor Walters, he argues cogently that:

> To the extent that the Court asserts *lex non scripta* as *justiciable* supreme law, the historical-legal foundation is weaker...
>
> ... It simply cannot be maintained seriously that the framers of the BNA Act intended the preamble's reference to the UK constitution to mean that judges thereafter were to regard certain unwritten British constitutional norms as justiciable constraints upon Canadian legislative authority... (Walters 2001, 137).

Caution is clearly called for. It is salutary that in *Babcock* the Supreme Court of Canada has re-asserted the importance of the principle of parliamentary sovereignty in assessing the validity of legislation in light of the provisions of the Constitution and unwritten constitutional principles such as the rule of law. It is also salutary that in *BellExpressVu*, [136] Justice Iacobucci took pains to set out the relationship of the courts to the development of the common law and the interpretation and application of statute law, respectively.

> *Statutory enactments embody legislative will. They supplement, modify or supercede the common law.* More pointedly, *when a statute comes into play during judicial proceedings, the courts (absent any challenge on constitutional grounds) are charged with interpreting it and applying it in accordance with the sovereign intent of the legislator.* In this regard, although it is sometimes suggested that "it is appropriate for courts to prefer interpretations that tend to promote those [*Charter*] principles and values over interpretations that do not" (Sullivan, *supra*, at p. 325), it must be stressed that, to the extent this Court has recognised a "*Charter* values" interpretative principle, such principle can only receive application in circumstances of genuine ambiguity, i.e. where a statutory provision is subject to differing, but equally plausible, interpretations.[137]

---

136 [2002] 2 S.C.R. 559, *per* Iacobucci J. for the Court.
137 Para. 62 [emphasis added].

If the Supreme Court has expressed reservations about extending 'Charter values' and principles under the guise of developing the common law, notably because it might undermine the role and intent of the legislature in enacting statute law, then *a fortiori*, the Court would likely be concerned by arguments in favour of a 'common law constitution' that would not only, as in the case of *Polewsky*, compel the legislature to enact legislation in accordance with a 'common law constitutional right' on the basis of the principle of the rule of law, – *even* in the face of a judicial finding of the *absence* of a Charter breach on the part of that legislature – but also, as is encouraged by some commentators, to strike down statutes held to be inconsistent, not with the Charter or the division of powers, or some other constitutionally-entrenched provision, but with the 'common law constitution'.

Professor Walters tentatively presents two potential examples where the 'unwritten constitution' might come in handy: where the s.33 Charter override clause is employed by the legislature, or where a constitutional amendment abolishes fundamental rights (Walters 2001, 140). In both cases, the courts would be asked to nullify legislative action (and in the second instance, the very process of constitutional amendment) *expressly contemplated by the provisions of the Constitution*. With respect to the override clause, s.33(1) of the Charter (itself part of the *Constitution Act, 1982*) provides:

> Parliament or the legislature of a province may expressly declare in an Act of Parliament or of the legislature, as the case may be, that the Act or a provision thereof shall operate notwithstanding a provision included in section 2 of sections 7 to 15 of the Charter.

In the *Ford* case,[138] the Supreme Court found that provisions of Quebec's *Charter of the French Language* prohibiting the use of languages other than French on commercial signage was a violation of freedom of expression guaranteed by s.2 of the Charter, and that this infringement could not be justified under s.1. However, the Court also found that Quebec's *An Act respecting the Constitution Act, 1982*, which inserted a 'notwithstanding' clause into *each and every* provincial statute, was a valid exercise by the legislature of the power of override conferred upon it by s.33 of the Charter.[139] At the time of the hearing in *Ford*, the override clauses enacted by the omnibus legislation had expired in accordance with the time limit of five years imposed by s.33(3). However, subsequent to the *Ford* decision, the legislature of Quebec enacted a new override clause to protect unilingual French exterior signage from the effect of s.2 of the Charter. How egregious might the violation to

---

138 [1988] 2 S.C.R. 712, *per curiam*.

139 *Ibid*., pp. 733–745, and *vide* pp. 740–743: 'Section 33 lays down requirements of form only, and there is no warrant for importing into it grounds for substantive review of the legislative policy in exercising the override authority in a particular case... Given the conclusion that the enactment of the standard override provision in the form indicated above is a valid exercise of the authority conferred by s.33 of the *Canadian Charter of Rights and Freedoms*, this court is of the opinion that the validity of its enactment is not affected by the fact that it was introduced into all Quebec statutes enacted prior to a certain date by a single enactment.'

fundamental human rights have to be for the 'unwritten constitution' to kick in and to override the override?

With respect to the hypothesis of a constitutional amendment being invalidated by unwritten constitutional principles or some fundamental construction of the common law superior to positive or written law, if a constitutional amendment respects the procedures set out in s.38, 41 or 43 of Part V of the *Constitution Act, 1982*, respectively,[140] and is in pith and substance directed to the relevant subject matter contemplated by the procedure, it is a valid amendment, and the courts should not impose unwritten and super-added requirements. In the *Quebec Secession Reference*, the Supreme Court expressly rejected the position put forward by Professor Jacques Frémont and others that in Canada there were certain supra-constitutional norms that could not be altered by constitutional amendment:

> The secession of a province from Canada must be considered, in legal terms, to require an amendment to the Constitution, which perforce requires negotiation. The amendments necessary to achieve a secession could be radical and extensive. Some commentators have suggested that secession could be a change of such a magnitude that it could not be considered to be merely an amendment to the Constitution. We are not persuaded by this contention.... The fact that those changes would be profound, or that they would purport to have a significance with respect to international law, does not negate their nature as amendments to the Constitution of Canada.[141]

Perhaps more tellingly, since the *Quebec Secession Reference*, challenges to the validity of two constitutional amendments were dismissed by the Newfoundland Court of Appeal in the *Hogan* case[142] and the Quebec Court of Appeal in the *Potter* case.[143] Both amendments had been made pursuant to the procedure laid down in s.43 of the *Constitution Act, 1982*. Both amendments abrogated constitutionally-entrenched rights and privileges relating to denominational schooling in Quebec and in Newfoundland. Both amendments were challenged, *inter alia*, on the ground that they violated the unwritten constitutional principles of the rule of law and the protection of minorities. Both amendments were upheld by the trial and appellate courts of each province, and applications for leave to appeal to the Supreme Court of Canada were dismissed in both cases.

The rule of law is the first principle of the Canadian constitutional order. That principle, however, operates within a framework and a context borne of an historical attachment to the British constitutional tradition, and with it, to related understandings about the distinction between law and convention (or legal rules and political rules), statute law and common law, parliamentary sovereignty and judicial review, a largely unwritten constitution amenable to change by ordinary legislative act and a primarily written constitution composed of entrenched 'supreme law'. It is those considerations that should obtain when the courts employ the rule of law as a

---

140 Leaving aside considerations pertaining to amendments effected under ss.44 and 45, which proceed by way of the ordinary legislative process.
141 *Reference re Secession of Quebec, supra,* para. 84.
142 *Hogan v. A.G. Newfoundland,* (2000) 183 D.L.R. (4th) 225.
143 *Potter v. A. G. Quebec,* 12 November 2001

prescriptive norm in relation to administrative action on the one hand, and legislative action on the other.

The principle of the rule of law continues to generate vigorous debate in academia and in the courts. In November 2005, the Supreme Court of Canada determined in the *Imperial Tobacco* case[144] that the rule of law could not be invoked to invalidate a statute of the legislature of British Columbia that facilitated a civil action by the provincial government against tobacco companies for the recovery of health care expenditures in treating tobacco-related illnesses. Mr Justice Major, writing for the Court, held that

> several constitutional principles other than the rule of law that have been recognized by this Court — most notably democracy and constitutionalism — very strongly favour upholding the validity of legislation that conforms to the express terms of the Constitution (and to the requirements, such as judicial independence, that flow by necessary implication from those terms). Put differently, the appellants' arguments fail to recognize that in a constitutional democracy such as ours, protection from legislation that some might view as unjust or unfair properly lies not in the amorphous underlying principles of our Constitution, but in its text and the ballot box ...
>
> The rule of law is not an invitation to trivialize or supplant the Constitution's written terms. Nor is it a tool by which to avoid legislative initiatives of which one is not in favour. On the contrary, it requires that courts give effect to the Constitution's text, and apply, by whatever its terms, legislation that conforms to that text.[145]

Nonetheless, on December 1, 2005, in her speech at the Lord Cooke Lecture in Wellington, New Zealand, the Chief Justice of the Supreme Court of Canada appeared to breathe new life, force and coherence into the role of unwritten constitutional principles. She stated:

> Are there some principles or norms that are so important, so fundamental, to a nation's history and identity that a consensus of reasonable citizens would demand that they be honoured by those who exercise state power? What do we mean by a constitution? Is the idea of unwritten constitutional principles really a new idea, or is it merely a new incarnation of established legal thought?
>
> To these questions I would answer as follows. First, unwritten constitutional principles refer to unwritten norms that are essential to a nation's history, identity, values and legal system. Second, constitutions are best understood as providing the normative framework for governance. Seen in this functional sense, there is thus no reason to believe that they cannot embrace both written and unwritten norms. Third - and this is important because of the tone that this debate often exhibits - the idea of unwritten constitutional principles is not new and should not be seen as a rejection of the constitutional heritage our two countries share.
>
> The contemporary concept of unwritten constitutional principles can be seen as a modern reincarnation of the ancient doctrines of natural law. Like those conceptions of justice,

---

144   *British Columbia* v. *Imperial Tobacco Ltd.*, [2005] 2 S.C.R 473.
145   Paras. 66 and 67.

the identification of these principles seems to presuppose the existence of some kind of natural order. Unlike them, however, it does not fasten on theology as the source of the unwritten principles that transcend the exercise of state power. It is derived from the history, values and culture of the nation, viewed in its constitutional context.[146]

Finally, on December 20, 2005, the Court of Appeal for British Columbia, in the *Christie* case,[147] struck down a statute of the provincial legislature that imposed taxes on legal services in the province. The late Dugald Christie, a lawyer who championed the causes of impoverished litigants, had challenged the validity of the provincial tax insofar as it represented, in his view, a bar to access to justice and thereby violated the principle of the rule of law. Two of the three judges of the Court of Appeal agreed. Madam Justice Southin, in her dissent, wrote:

> the issue is stark. Has this or any court in Canada the power to hold a statute, which falls within the enacting authority's legislative mandate under the *Constitution Acts*, s.91 or 92, as the case may be, does not infringe upon any other section of the *Constitution Act* (e.g. s.96), and is not in breach of the express terms of the *Canadian Charter of Rights and Freedoms*, to be of no force and effect?

> If there were ever any doubt that the answer to that question is, "no, the courts have no such power", that answer was settled by the judgment of the Supreme Court of Canada in *British Columbia* v. *Imperial Tobacco Canada Ltd.* ...[148]

The Supreme Court of Canada has granted leave to appeal the *Christie* decision and the appeal will likely be heard in early 2007. Those who are following the development of the principle of the rule of law and other unwritten constitutional principles in this country will be interested to see how the Court deals with this latest chapter in what has become an unfolding saga.

Speaking more generally, the evolving jurisprudence of the courts of Canada on the principles of the rule of law and parliamentary sovereignty provides important insights into the role of the courts in elucidating the text of the Constitution, and the relationship between the provisions of that text and the underlying constitutional values the text enhances and protects. In a country and a political culture governed by the rule of law, it is not a matter of narrow legalism to suggest that when judges purport to propound the *law* of the Constitution, they ought, if their role is to remain legitimate, to relate the grand principles they invoke to the provisions of the supreme law they enforce.

---

146 "Unwritten Constitutional Principles: What is Going On?" Remarks of the Right Honourable Beverly McLachlin, P.C., at the 2005 Lord Cooke Lecture, Wellington, New Zealand, December 1, 2005.

147 *Christie* v. *British Columbia*, 2005 BCCA 631.

148 Paras. 18 and 19.

References

Allan, T.R.S. (1992), *Law, Liberty and Justice – The Legal Foundations of British Constitutionalism*, Oxford: Oxford University Press.
— (2003), *Constitutional Justice – A Liberal Theory of the Rule of Law*, Oxford: Oxford University Press.
Cameron, J. (2002), 'The Written Word and the Constitution's Vital Unstated Assumptions', in Thibeault, Pelletier and Perret (eds), *Essays in Honour of Gérald-A. Beaudoin*, Cowansville: Éditions Yvon Blais.
Choudry, S. (2001), 'Unwritten Constitutionalism in Canada: Where Do Things Stand?', *Canadian Business Law Journal*, 35, 113–122.
Dyzenhaus, D. (1999), 'Recrafting the Rule of Law', survey in Dyzenhaus (ed.), *Recrafting the Rule of Law*, Oxford: Hart Publishing.
— (2000), 'Form and Substance in the Rule of Law: A Democratic Justification for Judicial Review?', in Forsyth (ed.), *Judicial Review and the Constitution*, Oxford: Hart Publishing.
— (2002), 'Constituting the Rule of Law: Fundamental Values in Administrative Law', *Queen's Law Journal.* 27, 445–509.
— (2003), 'The Justice of the Common Law: Judges, Democracy and the Limits of the Rule of Law', in Saunders and Le Roy (eds.), *The Rule of Law*, Sydney: Federation Press.
Elliott, R. (2001), 'References, Structural Argumentation and the Organizing Principles of Canada's Constitution', *Canadian Bar Review*, 80, 67–142.
Gibson, D. (1999), 'Constitutional Vibes: Reflections on the *Secession Reference* and the Unwritten Constitution', *National Journal of Constitutional Law* 11, 49–64.
Goldsworthy, J. (1999), *The Sovereignty of Parliament – History and Philosophy*, Oxford: Oxford University Press.
Hogg, P. W. (forthcoming), *Constitutional Law of Canada*, Loose-leaf Edition., vol. 1, 15.9(g), 'Unwritten constitutional principles', Toronto: Carswell.
Hutchinson, A., (1999), 'The Rule of Law Revisited: Democracy and Courts' in D. Dyzenhaus, ed., *Recrafting the Rule of Law: the Limits of Legal Order*, Oxford: Hart Publishing, 196.
Hutchinson, A., and Monahan, P. J. (1987), 'Democracy and the Rule of Law', in A. Hutchinson and P.J., Monahan (eds), *The Rule of Law: Ideal or Ideology*, Toronto: Carswell 119–127.
Leclair J. and Morrissette, Y.-M.(1998), 'L'indépendance judiciaire et la Cour suprême: reconstruction historique douteuse et théorie constitutionnelle de complaisance' (1998) *Osgoode Hall Law Journal*, 36, 485.
Leclair, J. (2002), 'Canada's Unfathomable Unwritten Constitutional Principles', *Queen's Law Journal*, 27, 389–443.
Monahan, P. J. (1999), 'The Public Policy Role of the Supreme Court of Canada in the *Secession Reference*', (1999*) National Journal of Constitutional Law*, 11, 65–105.
— (1995), 'Is the Pearson Airport Legislation Unconstitutional?: The Rule of Law as a Limit on Contract Repudiation by Government', *Osgoode Hall Law Journal*. 33, 411–452.

Newman, W. J. (1999), *The Quebec Secession Reference, The Rule of Law and the Position of the Attorney General of Canada*, Toronto: York University Centre for Public Law and Public Policy.

— (2001),'"Grand Entrance Hall," Back Door or Foundation Stone? The Role of Constitutional Principles in Construing and Applying the Constitution of Canada', *Supreme Court Law Rev.* 14 (2d), 197–239.

— (2001–2002), 'Réflexions sur la portée véritable des principes constitutionnels dans l'interprétation et l'application de la Constitution du Canada', *National Journal of Constitutional Law*, 13, 117–164.

— (2003a), 'Quelques réflexions sur la portée du principe constitutionnel de l'indépendance judiciaire au Canada', *National Journal of Constitutional Law* 14, 319.

— (2003b), 'Defining the "Constitution of Canada" Since 1982', *Supreme Court Law Review*, 22 (2d), 423.

— (2004), 'Adjudicating Divisions of Powers Issues: A Canadian Perspective', in Le Sueur (ed.), *Building the UK's New Supreme Court – National and Comparative Perspectives*, Oxford: Oxford University Press.

Wade, E. C. S. (1958), preface to 10th ed. of A.V. Dicey, *An Introduction to the Study of the Law of the Constitution*, London: Macmillan Press; reprinted 1975.

Walters, M. D. (2001), 'The Common Law Constitution in Canada: Return of *Lex Non Scripta* as Fundamental Law', *University of Toronto Law Journal*, 51, 91–141.

Index

Aboriginal peoples (*see also* cultural heritage; self-determination) 2, 5, 18, 19–20, 61, 67–9, 71–2
   child welfare 7, 99–102, 117–18
   identity 6, 79–95
   Van der Peet case 6–7, 81, 84–5, 88, 90
   international law 7, 8, 82, 85, 111–18
   self-determination 7, 20, 68–9, 94, 102–11, 111–18

Barry, Brian 40–41, 43, 50

Canada (*see also* Quebec)
   Charlottetown Accord 184–89
   Charter of Rights and Freedoms 9, 68–9, 108–10, 147–48, 154–57, 158–64, 200, 205–06, 208–11, 232–33
   Constitution Act 1982 11, 13, 20, 72, 167–69, 177–82, 203, 205–06, 218–26, 229
   cultural property 139
   federalism 11
   Gomery Commission 12
   language rights 5, 11
   Meech Lake Accord 183–84
   multiculturalism 5, 18, 59
   Supreme Court of Canada 9–10, 11, 13, 14, 82, 103–05, 105–10, 147–48, 154–57, 158–64, 201, 208–11, 212–18, 218–26, 229, 231–35
   unwritten constitutional principles 13–14, 218–29
citizenship 21, 23
collective rights 5, 72–4
constitutionalism 1, 13, 14, 199–204
cultural diversity 1, 3, 45, 79–81, 85–7
   essentialism 88–90, 93–4
   ethnocentricity 90–2, 94
cultural heritage 8–9, 83–4, 123–40
cultural identity (*see also* Aboriginal peoples) 124–26
   hybrid identities 45–55
cosmopolitanism (*see also* liberalism) 40–3, 48

democracy 2, 26–7, 29–31
dominant group(s) 3, 18, 19–24, 30, 52, 85–7

equality 9, 10, 147–64
ethnicity 22, 32–3

federalism 11, 53
First Nations (*see* Aboriginal peoples)

Gellner, Ernest 36
group rights (*see* collective rights)

identity (see Aboriginal peoples; Cultural identity)
immigrants (*see* migrants)
Indians (*see* Aboriginal peoples)
Indigenous peoples (*see* Aboriginal peoples)

Kymlicka, Will 2–5, 6, 9, 35–55, 59–74, 83

language rights (*see also* Canada; Quebec) 20–1, 39–40, 42–3, 51, 70–1, 212–15
liberalism (*see also* cosmopolitanism) 3, 4, 5, 29–31, 35, 40–1
liberal nationalism 4, 36–55

Metics 22–4
migrants 2, 21–2, 52, 83
minority rights 37, 44, 50, 51, 85–7, 94
multiculturalism 1, 17, 32, 59, 83
   causes of 24–31
   multicultural state 2, 3, 17, 18–33
multinational state 2, 20–1, 24, 45, 47, 53

nation (*see also* Aboriginal peoples; sub-state nations) 4
   nation-state 2
   nation-building 2, 18
   national identity 3, 4
   national pluralism 3

property (*see* cultural heritage)
Quebec (*see also* Canada) 2, 10–14, 28, 167–95
  constitutional history 169–81
  language rights 61–2, 65–7, 232–33
  Referendum 189
  Secession Reference 13, 14, 190–93, 201, 202–04, 218–26, 231, 233

religion
  rights of 64–5
rights 2, 5, 25–6, 30, 115–17

secession (*see also* Quebec, Secession Reference) 7, 12
self-determination (*see also* Aboriginal peoples) 4, 5, 35, 50–5,
  Aboriginal peoples 7, 20, 68–9, 94, 102–11, 111–18
sub-state nations (*see also* nation) 1, 4, 20–21, 123